MW01630216

# Intermediate Accounting

Steven M. Bragg

Copyright © 2021 by AccountingTools, Inc.  All rights reserved.


Published by AccountingTools, Inc., Centennial, Colorado.


No part of this publication may be reproduced, stored in a retrieval system, or transmitted in any form or by any means, except as permitted under Section 107 or 108 of the 1976 United States Copyright Act, without the prior written permission of the Publisher. Requests to the Publisher for permission should be addressed to Steven M. Bragg, 6727 E. Fremont Place, Centennial, CO 80112.


Limit of Liability/Disclaimer of Warranty: While the publisher and author have used their best efforts in preparing this book, they make no representations or warranties with respect to the accuracy or completeness of the contents of this book and specifically disclaim any implied warranties of merchantability or fitness for a particular purpose. No warranty may be created or extended by written sales materials. The advice and strategies contained herein may not be suitable for your situation. You should consult with a professional where appropriate. Neither the publisher nor author shall be liable for any loss of profit or any other commercial damages, including but not limited to special, incidental, consequential, or other damages.


For more information about AccountingTools® products, visit our Web site at www.accountingtools.com.


ISBN-13: 978-1-64221-080-4


Printed in the United States of America

# Table of Contents

# Preface

Few aspiring accountants can survive with only a basic knowledge of accounting. The *Intermediate Accounting* textbook addresses almost every advanced topic that a college student will eventually encounter. For example, the text covers the more advanced forms of financial statement presentation, when to recognize revenue, how to account for stock-based compensation, and the best way to account for a business combination. Also, since accounting courses tend to focus excessively on accounting transactions, we include an in-depth discussion of ethical frameworks, which can be useful when deciding how to deal with ethically questionable events. In addition, the textbook illustrates these topics with numerous examples to improve comprehension. Topics are divided into six major accounting areas, which are as follows:

- Part I – Presentation. Chapters 2 through 7 describe the more advanced elements of financial statement presentation, including comprehensive income, changing prices, earnings per share, interim reporting, and segment reporting.
- Part II – Assets and Liabilities. Chapters 8 and 9 describe the concept of goodwill and how it is recognized, as well as the accounting for asset retirement and environmental obligations.
- Part III – Revenue. Chapter 10 focuses solely on the major topic of revenue recognition, exploring all five steps in the revenue recognition process and many issues that can impact the timing of revenue recognition.
- Part IV – Expenses. Chapters 11 through 13 cover several advanced expense topics. They delve into the accounting for stock-based compensation, retirement benefits, and income taxes.
- Part V – Broad Transactions. Chapters 14 through 20 cover a variety of specialized accounting transactions that accountants will encounter from time to time, including business combinations and the accounting for derivatives, foreign currency, interest, leases, and nonmonetary transactions.
- Part VI – Other. Chapters 21 and 22 address the accounting for software and partnership accounting. We finish with a discussion of ethical frameworks in accounting in Chapter 23, as this is a topic that accountants must deal with on an ongoing basis.

*Intermediate Accounting* is designed to give the student a complete grounding in the more advanced elements of accounting. As such, it may earn a place on your bookshelf as a reference tool for years to come.

Centennial, Colorado
December, 2021

# About the Author

**Steven Bragg, CPA,** has been the chief financial officer or controller of four companies, as well as a consulting manager at Ernst & Young. He received a master's degree in finance from Bentley College, an MBA from Babson College, and a Bachelor's degree in Economics from the University of Maine. He has been a two-time president of the Colorado Mountain Club, and is an avid alpine skier, mountain biker, and certified master diver. Mr. Bragg resides in Centennial, Colorado. He has written more than 250 books and courses, including *New Controller Guidebook*, *GAAP Guidebook*, and *Payroll Management*.

Steven maintains the accountingtools.com web site, which contains continuing professional education courses, the Accounting Best Practices podcast, and thousands of articles on accounting subjects.

### Buy Additional AccountingTools Textbooks

AccountingTools offers more than 1,250 hours of CPE courses, with concentrations in accounting, auditing, finance, taxation, and ethics. Related textbooks that you might like include:

- Accounting Information Systems (Textbook)
- Cost Accounting (Textbook)
- Principles of Accounting (Textbook)

Go to accountingtools.com to view these additional textbooks.

# Chapter 1
# Generally Accepted Accounting Principles

## Introduction

In this chapter, we describe both financial accounting and management accounting, provide an introduction to the nature of GAAP, and identify those portions of it that are expanded upon later in this textbook.

## What is Financial Accounting?

This textbook is entirely concerned with *financial accounting*, which is the practice of recording and aggregating financial transactions into financial statements. The intent of financial accounting is to distribute a standard set of financial information to outside users, such as creditors, lenders, and investors. It is usually compared to management accounting, which focuses on an operational analysis of a business to explore how it can be made more efficient or profitable. Management accounting reports are only intended for internal use.

Several accounting frameworks[1] are available that provide the rules under which financial statements are to be constructed, so that the financials issued by the entities in an industry will be comparable. For a for-profit or nonprofit business, these rules are provided (in the United States) by the Generally Accepted Accounting Principles (GAAP) framework and (elsewhere) by the International Financial Reporting Standards (IFRS) framework. If a company is publicly-held and lists its shares on a stock exchange in the United States, then additional rules are mandated by the Securities and Exchange Commission.

The focus of financial accounting is outward, since its work product is read by persons outside of a business. Since lawsuits can arise from the issuance of incorrect financial statements, a strong focus in financial accounting is on ensuring that the information presented fairly represents the financial position, cash flows, and results of a business.

## What is Management Accounting?

Though we do not cover management accounting in this textbook, it is useful to understand the concept, and how it differs from financial accounting. Management accounting is a branch of accounting that focuses on the revenues and expenses of a business, as well as its asset usage. Someone engaged in management accounting notes unusual spikes and declines in revenues and expenses, and reports these variances to management. The intent of this analysis is to take action to improve the financial performance of a business.

Management accounting does not just result in variance reports. It can also produce reports covering any aspect of a business. Examples of the types of information that may be reported include the following:

- Capital budgeting analyses
- Inventory record accuracy
- Loan covenant compliance
- Overdue accounts receivable
- Project profitability
- Sales order backlog analysis
- Transfer pricing analyses

Management accounting results in reports that are intended for use within a business. Since this information is not viewed by outsiders, it does not have to comply with the reporting requirements of any accounting

---

[1] An accounting framework is a published set of criteria that is used to measure, recognize, present, and disclose the information appearing in an entity's financial statements.

frameworks, such as GAAP. Instead, the accountant can generate reports in any desired format, so that actionable information can be highlighted.

## Generally Accepted Accounting Principles

In the following pages, we will refer many times to Generally Accepted Accounting Principles, or GAAP. It is a cluster of accounting standards and common industry usage that have been developed over many years. It is used by organizations to properly organize their financial information into accounting records, summarize the accounting records into financial statements, and disclose certain supporting information. One of the reasons for using GAAP is so that anyone reading the financial statements of multiple businesses has a reasonable basis of comparison, since all companies using GAAP have created their financial statements using the same set of rules.

GAAP is derived from the pronouncements of a series of government-sponsored accounting entities, of which the Financial Accounting Standards Board is the latest. The Securities and Exchange Commission also issues accounting pronouncements through its Accounting Staff Bulletins and other announcements that are applicable only to publicly-held companies, and which are considered part of GAAP. GAAP is codified into the Accounting Standards Codification®, which is available online and (more legibly) in printed form.

GAAP covers a broad array of topics, which are aggregated into the following major categories:

- *Presentation*. Covers the proper formatting and presentation of the financial statements, and includes the following topic areas:
    - Presentation of financial statements
    - Balance sheet
    - Statement of shareholder equity
    - Comprehensive income
    - Income statement
    - Statement of cash flows
    - Notes to financial statements
    - Accounting changes and error corrections
    - Changing prices
    - Earnings per share
    - Interim reporting
    - Limited liability entities
    - Personal financial statements
    - Risks and uncertainties
    - Segment reporting

- *Assets*. Describes the accounting for the main types of assets, and includes the following topic areas:
    - Cash and cash equivalents
    - Receivables
    - Investments – debt and equity securities
    - Investments – equity method and joint ventures
    - Investments – other
    - Inventory
    - Other assets and deferred costs
    - Intangibles – goodwill and other
    - Property, plant, and equipment

- *Liabilities.* Describes the accounting for the main types of liabilities, and includes the following topic areas:
  - Liabilities
  - Asset retirement and environmental obligations
  - Exit or disposal cost obligations
  - Deferred revenue
  - Commitments
  - Contingencies
  - Guarantees
  - Debt
  - Distinguishing liabilities from equity
- *Equity.* Addresses the accounting issues related to equity in general, stock dividends and splits, equity-based payments to non-employees, spinoffs, and similar matters.
- *Revenue recognition.* Covers the accounting issues related to revenue in general, sales of products and services, multiple-element arrangements, the milestone method, construction-type contracts, gains and losses, agent considerations, customer payments, and similar matters.
- *Expenses.* Describes the accounting for a number of the more complex types of expenses, and includes the following topic areas:
  - Cost of sales and services
  - Compensation – general
  - Compensation – nonretirement postemployment benefits
  - Compensation – retirement benefits
  - Compensation – stock compensation
  - Other expenses
  - Research and development
  - Income taxes
- *Broad transactions.* Describes several transaction types that cannot be classified within one of the preceding areas, and which has broad applicability to many industries. The following topic areas are included:
  - Business combinations
  - Collaborative arrangements
  - Consolidation
  - Derivatives and hedging
  - Fair value assessment
  - Financial instruments
  - Foreign currency matters
  - Interest
  - Leases
  - Nonmonetary transactions
  - Related party disclosures
  - Reorganizations
  - Subsequent events
  - Transfers and servicing
- *Industry.* Includes accounting that is specific to certain industries, ranging from agriculture to software, and with a particular emphasis on the entertainment, financial services, and real estate industries.

## The Structure of This Book

The Financial Accounting Standards Board aggregated all GAAP accounting standards into a single source as of 2009, which it calls the Accounting Standards Codification® (ASC). The Codification organized the standards into groupings and then assigned an identification code to each topic. In the following exhibit, we note the topics covered within this textbook, as well as the Codification grouping and identification code assigned to each one.

**Chapter Links to Accounting Standards Codification®**

| Chapter | ASC Grouping | ASC Code | ASC Topic[2] |
|---|---|---|---|
| 2 | Presentation | 220 | Comprehensive Income |
| 3 | Presentation | 250 | Accounting Changes and Error Corrections |
| 4 | Presentation | 255 | Changing Prices |
| 5 | Presentation | 260 | Earnings per Share |
| 6 | Presentation | 270 | Interim Reporting |
| 7 | Presentation | 280 | Segment Reporting |
| 8 | Assets | 350 | Goodwill |
| 9 | Liabilities | 410 | Asset Retirement and Environmental Obligations |
| 10 | Revenue | 606 | Revenue Recognition |
| 11 | Expenses | 710 | Accounting for Stock-Based Compensation |
| 12 | Expenses | 715 | Accounting for Retirement Benefits |
| 13 | Expenses | 740 | Accounting for Income Taxes |
| 14 | Broad Transactions | 805 | Business Combinations and Consolidations |
| 15 | Broad Transactions | 815 | Accounting for Derivatives and Hedges |
| 16 | Broad Transactions | 820 | Fair Value Accounting |
| 17 | Broad Transactions | 830 | Foreign Currency Accounting |
| 18 | Broad Transactions | 835 | Accounting for Interest |
| 19 | Broad Transactions | 840 | Accounting for Leases |
| 20 | Broad Transactions | 845 | Nonmonetary Transactions |
| 21 | Industry | 985 | Accounting for Software |
| 22 | -- | -- | Partnership Accounting |
| 23 | -- | -- | Ethical Frameworks in Accounting |

The exhibit shows that the order in which the following chapters are presented matches the order in which the topics appear in the ASC. The final two chapters include items *not* found in the ASC, but which are quite useful for anyone engaged in accounting at the intermediate level – which are how to account for a partnership and a discussion of accounting ethics.

We have not included in *Intermediate Accounting* every possible topic listed in the ASC, for three reasons. First, the more basic topics were already addressed in our *Principles of Accounting* textbook, covering such matters as financial statement presentation and the accounting for assets, liabilities, and equity. Second, we have avoided minor topics or ones that have little relevance in most situations, such as guarantees, government assistance, and service concession arrangements. And finally, we have mostly avoided

---

[2] We have adjusted the ASC topic in a few cases to match the chapter title. This was done in order to combine some related ASC topics.

industry-specific topics, which are instead addressed in a separate set of AccountingTools courses that cover a broad range of industries, such as the accounting for casinos, churches, commercial fishing, hedge funds, public utilities, and vineyards. This still leaves a great many intermediate accounting topics, as you will see in the following chapters.

Each of the subsequent chapters ends with a set of questions that test your knowledge of the chapter material. The answers to these questions are located in the Answers to Chapter Questions section near the end of this textbook.

## Summary

The contents of this book are targeted at increasing a student's understanding of the more advanced accounting topics. The basic financial accounting concepts were already covered in the author's *Principles of Accounting* textbook, while all management accounting concepts were addressed in the author's *Cost Accounting* textbook. For an in-depth treatment of how accounting systems are structured, see the author's *Accounting Information Systems* textbook.

# Chapter 2
# Comprehensive Income

## Introduction

In the *Principles of Accounting* textbook (also published by AccountingTools), we covered the nature and presentation of the income statement. What we did *not* discuss was an extension of the concept, called comprehensive income; it covers other items that have experienced gains or losses, but have not yet been realized, and so do not appear in the income statement until some later date. To provide early warning to investors regarding potential gains and losses that may be realized in the future, the comprehensive income concept was appended to the income statement. In this chapter, we define comprehensive income and show how it is disclosed.

**Related Podcast Episodes:** Episodes 152 and 155 of the Accounting Best Practices Podcast discuss changes to other comprehensive income and the reporting of other comprehensive income reclassifications, respectively. They are available at: **www.accounting- tools.com/podcasts** or **iTunes**

## Overview of Comprehensive Income

The intent behind the concept of comprehensive income is to report on all changes in the equity of a business, other than those involving the owners of the business. Not all of these transactions appear in the income statement, so comprehensive income is needed to provide a more comprehensive view. Comprehensive income is comprised of net income and other comprehensive income. Net income is already adequately disclosed in the income statement. This means that *other* comprehensive income is the true focus of the comprehensive income topic. Other comprehensive income is comprised of the following items:

Foreign Currency Items

- Foreign currency translation adjustments
- Gains and losses on intra-company foreign currency transactions where settlement is not planned in the foreseeable future

Hedging Items

- Gains and losses on derivative instruments that are cash flow hedges
- Gains and losses on foreign currency translation adjustments that are net investment hedges in a foreign entity

Investment Items

- Unrealized holding gains and losses on available-for-sale debt securities
- Unrealized holding gains and losses resulting from the transfer of a debt security from the held-to-maturity classification to the available-for-sale classification
- Amounts recognized in other comprehensive income for debt securities classified as available-for-sale and held-to-maturity, if the impairment is not recognized in earnings
- Subsequent changes in the fair value of available-for-sale debt securities that had previously been written down as impaired

<u>Postretirement Benefit Items</u>

- Gains and losses from pension or postretirement benefits that have not been recognized as a component of net periodic benefit cost
- Prior service costs or credits associated with pension or postretirement benefits
- Transition assets or obligations linked to pension or postretirement benefits that have not been recognized as a component of net periodic benefit cost

<u>Other</u>

- Changes in fair value that are attributable to the credit risk of specific liabilities for which the  fair value option has been selected

The following items are specifically excluded from other comprehensive income:

- Investments by owners
- Distributions to owners
- Any items that must be reported as direct adjustments to any non-income equity accounts, such as additional paid-in capital and retained earnings. Examples are:
    - Taxes not payable in cash
    - A reduction in equity related to an employee stock ownership plan
    - A net cash settlement resulting from a change in the value of a contract

If a business has a noncontrolling interest in another entity, it should report amounts for net income and comprehensive income attributable to the parent and the minority interest in the financial statements where comprehensive income is presented.

If the items initially stated in other comprehensive income are later displayed as part of net income (typically because the transactions have been settled), this is essentially a reclassification out of the other comprehensive income classification. Otherwise, the items will be double-counted within comprehensive income. For example, an unrealized gain on an investment is initially recorded within other comprehensive income and is then sold, at which point the gain is realized and shifted from other comprehensive income to net income. In short, there is a continual shifting of items from other comprehensive income to net income over time.

## Comprehensive Income Disclosures

If a company has no items of other comprehensive income in any period presented, it can avoid reporting comprehensive income entirely. If it is necessary to present comprehensive income, it should be displayed with the same prominence as the other financial statements.

There is no specific format that GAAP requires for the reporting of other comprehensive income, though presenting it in a format modeled on that of the income statement is encouraged.

Items of comprehensive income must be reported in a financial statement for the period in which they are recognized. If this information is presented within a single continuous income statement, the presentation shall encompass the following:

- Net income and its components
- Other comprehensive income and its components
- Total comprehensive income

**EXAMPLE**

Armadillo Industries presents the following statement of income and comprehensive income.

Armadillo Industries
Statement of Income and Comprehensive Income
For the Year Ended December 31, 20X2

| | | |
|---|---|---|
| Revenues | | $250,000 |
| Expenses | | -200,000 |
| Other gains and losses | | 10,000 |
| Gain on sale of securities | | 5,000 |
| Income from operations before tax | | 65,000 |
| Income tax expense | | -20,000 |
| Net income | | $45,000 |
| | | |
| Other comprehensive income, net of tax | | |
|   Foreign currency translation adjustments | | 2,000 |
|   Unrealized holding gains arising during period | | 11,000 |
|   Defined benefit pension plans: | | |
|     Prior period service cost arising during period | -$4,000 | |
|     Net loss arising during period | -1,000 | -5,000 |
| Other comprehensive income | | 8,000 |
| | | |
| Comprehensive income, net of tax | | $53,000 |

If comprehensive income is portrayed in two separate statements, they shall be presented consecutively. The presentation of other comprehensive income shall encompass the following:

- Begin with net income (optional)
- State the components of and total for other comprehensive income
- State the total for comprehensive income

**EXAMPLE**

Armadillo Industries presents the following separate statement of comprehensive income.

Armadillo Industries<br>
Statement of Comprehensive Income<br>
For the Year Ended December 31, 20X2

| | | |
|---|---|---:|
| Net income | | <u>$45,000</u> |
| | | |
| Other comprehensive income, net of tax | | |
|   Foreign currency translation adjustments | | 2,000 |
|   Unrealized holding gains arising during period | | 11,000 |
|   Defined benefit pension plans: | | |
|     Prior period service cost arising during period | -$4,000 | |
|     Net loss arising during period | -1,000 | <u>-5,000</u> |
| Other comprehensive income | | <u>8,000</u> |
| | | |
| Comprehensive income, net of tax | | <u>$53,000</u> |

When there are reclassification adjustments from other comprehensive income to net income, these adjustments must be disclosed, either on the statement in which comprehensive income is reported, or in the accompanying notes.

In addition, the total of other comprehensive income for the reporting period must be stated in the balance sheet in a component of equity that is stated separately from retained earnings and additional paid-in capital. A suggested title for this line item is *accumulated other comprehensive income.*

**EXAMPLE**

Armadillo Industries reports accumulated other comprehensive income within the equity section of its balance sheet as follows:

| | |
|---|---:|
| Equity: | |
|   Common stock | $1,000,000 |
|   Paid-in capital | 850,000 |
|   Retained earnings | 4,200,000 |
|   Accumulated other comprehensive income | <u>270,000</u> |
| Total equity | <u>$6,320,000</u> |

Another GAAP requirement is to present all changes in the accumulated balances for each component of other comprehensive income stated as a component of equity, either on the face of the financial statements or in the accompanying disclosures. This shall include a separate presentation for each component of other comprehensive income that reveals current period reclassifications out of accumulated other comprehensive income.

**EXAMPLE**

Armadillo Industries presents the following information about the changes in its accumulated other comprehensive income in the notes accompanying its financial statements:

|  | Foreign Currency Items | Unrealized Gains on Securities | Defined Benefit Pension Plans | Accumulated Other Comprehensive Income |
|---|---|---|---|---|
| Beginning balance | $10,000 | $272,000 | -$20,000 | $262,000 |
| Current period change | 2,000 | 11,000 | -5,000 | 8,000 |
| Ending balance | $12,000 | $283,000 | -$25,000 | $270,000 |

GAAP may require that certain amounts be reclassified out of accumulated other comprehensive income and into net income in their entirety. If so, a business must separately disclose information about these effects on net income for each material transfer from a component of accumulated other comprehensive income and into net income. This disclosure can be provided in one of two ways:

- *On the face of the income statement.* In this format, report the changes parenthetically on each impacted line item. Also parenthetically report the aggregate tax effect of these reclassifications on the tax expense line item.
- *Within the accompanying notes.* In this format, report the significant reclassifications for each component of accumulated other comprehensive income. Both before-tax and net-of-tax presentations are allowed.

There are two allowed methods for incorporating income tax effects into the presentation of other comprehensive income information. Either report items of other comprehensive income net of income tax effects, or show them before tax and then add an aggregate income tax expense or benefit line item that relates to all of the individual items presented.

**EXAMPLE**

Armadillo Industries includes the following disclosure in the notes accompanying its financial statements regarding the tax effects on each component of other comprehensive income:

|  | Before-tax Amount | Tax Expense or Benefit | Net of Tax Amount |
|---|---|---|---|
| Foreign currency translation adjustments | $2,700 | -$700 | $2,000 |
| Unrealized holding gains arising during period | 14,850 | -$3,850 | 11,000 |
| Defined benefit pension plans: | | | |
| Prior period service costs arising during period | -5,400 | 1,400 | -4,000 |
| Net loss arising during period | -1,350 | 350 | -1,000 |
| Other comprehensive income | $10,800 | -$2,800 | $8,000 |

## Examples of Comprehensive Income Presentation

In this section, we provide extracts from the presentation of comprehensive income for several major companies, in order to give some perspective on the different type of presentations being used. Extracts from the statements of comprehensive income for Home Depot, Pulte Group, ExxonMobil, and MetLife are noted in the following exhibits. The formatting used is relatively consistent across the four companies. A few of the businesses with more elaborate financial structures (ExxonMobil and MetLife) initially include the effects of noncontrolling interests and then strip out the portion of comprehensive income attributable to noncontrolling interests at the bottom of the report, resulting in a comprehensive income figure that is solely attributable to the business entity.

### Sample from Recent Home Depot Statement of Comprehensive Income

| (amounts in millions) | |
|---|---|
| Net earnings | $7,957 |
| Other comprehensive income (loss): | |
| Foreign currency translation adjustments | -3 |
| Cash flow hedges, net of tax | 34 |
| Total other comprehensive income (loss) | 31 |
| Comprehensive income | $7,988 |

### Sample from Recent Pulte Group, Inc. Statement of Comprehensive Income

| (amounts in thousands) | |
|---|---|
| Net income | $602,703 |
| Other comprehensive income, net of tax: | |
| Change in value of derivatives | 83 |
| Other comprehensive income | 83 |
| Comprehensive income | $602,786 |

### Sample from ExxonMobil Statement of Comprehensive Income

| (amounts in millions) | |
|---|---|
| Net income including noncontrolling interests | $8,375 |
| Other comprehensive income (net of income taxes) | |
| Foreign exchange translation adjustment | -174 |
| Postretirement benefits reserves adjustment | 493 |
| Amortization and settlement of postretirement benefits reserves adjustment included in net periodic benefit costs | 1,086 |
| Total other comprehensive income | 1,405 |
| Comprehensive income including noncontrolling interests | 9,780 |
| Comprehensive income attributable to noncontrolling interests | 668 |
| Comprehensive income attributable to ExxonMobil | $9,112 |

**Sample from MetLife Statement of Comprehensive Income**

| (amounts in millions) | |
|---|---:|
| Net income | $804 |
| Other comprehensive income (loss): | |
| Unrealized investment gains (losses), net of related offsets | 760 |
| Unrealized gains (losses) on derivatives | 573 |
| Foreign currency translation adjustments | -363 |
| Defined benefit plans adjustment | <u>131</u> |
| Other comprehensive income (loss), before income tax | 1,101 |
| Income tax (expense) related to items of other comprehensive income | <u>-437</u> |
| Other comprehensive income, net of income tax | 664 |
| Comprehensive income | 1,468 |
| Less: Comprehensive income attributable to noncontrolling interest, net of income tax | <u>92</u> |
| Comprehensive income attributable to MetLife, Inc. | <u>$1,376</u> |

## Summary

It is entirely possible that a smaller business will have no need to present other comprehensive income information, since these organizations do not usually deal with any of the items that are included in other comprehensive income. Thus, interest in this chapter is likely to be confined to the accounting departments of larger corporations that regularly deal with hedging, foreign currency transactions, complex investments, and pensions.

## Review Questions

1. Accumulated other comprehensive income is listed in the:
    a. Income statement
    b. Balance sheet
    c. Statement of cash flows
    d. Statement of retained earnings

2. The following is specifically excluded from other comprehensive income:
    a. Distributions to owners
    b. Prior service costs associated with pension benefits
    c. Gains and losses on derivatives that are cash flow hedges
    d. Unrealized holding losses on available-for-sale securities

3. To avoid double counting of items recorded in other comprehensive income:
    a. Verify all journal entries prior to entry
    b. Never shift items from other comprehensive income to net income
    c. Shift items from other comprehensive income to net income
    d. The accumulated other comprehensive income account should never be used

# Chapter 3
# Accounting Changes and Error Corrections

## Introduction

From time to time, a company will find that it must alter its accounting to reflect a change in accounting principle or estimate, or it may locate an accounting error that must be corrected. These changes can have a substantial impact on the reported results of a business from period to period, which can make financial statements much less comparable over time. Examples of these changes are:

- An organization switches from reporting its sale transactions as gross sales to net sales, reflecting the finding that the business is really operating as an agent for another party. The effect is a drastic decline in the amount of reported sales.
- An entity switches its inventory costing method from the first in, first out method to the weighted average method, which results in a one-time increase in the value of ending inventory, which in turn boosts net income.
- A firm evaluates its accounts receivable and concludes that a sudden decline in general economic conditions will drastically increase the amount of bad debts it will experience. This calls for a doubling of the balance in the allowance for doubtful accounts, which reduces profits.

In this chapter, we address the rules pertaining to accounting changes and error corrections.

## Changes in Accounting Principle

Accounting principles are the rules and guidelines that an entity must follow when reporting financial information. There is an assumption in GAAP that, once an accounting principle has been adopted by a business, the principle shall be consistently applied in recording transactions and events from that point forward. Consistent application is a cornerstone of accounting, since it allows the readers of financial statements to compare the results of multiple accounting periods. Given how important it is to maintain consistency in the application of accounting principles, a business should only change a principle in one of the two following situations:

- The change is required by an update to GAAP. In recent years, a number of GAAP updates have required changes in accounting principle, such as new standards on revenue recognition, fair value measurement, and business combinations. There are any number of industry-specific standards that are also changed; common targets for these changes are the real estate, financial services, and health care industries.
- The use of an alternative principle is preferable. There are a small number of situations in which there are two or more alternative applications of GAAP that can be used, depending on a number of indicators. If the circumstances of a business change, the indicators could point toward the use of an alternative principle. For example, a business has previously recognized its sales at gross, but its increasing control by a manufacturer indicates that sales should instead be recognized at net, as would be used by an agent.

> **Best Practice:** Thoroughly document the reason for any change in accounting principle, since it will likely be reviewed and possibly contested by the company's auditors. There should be a clearly defensible reason for the change.

Whenever there is a change in accounting principle, retrospective application of the new principle to prior accounting periods is required, unless it is impracticable to do so. Retrospective application means that a principle must be used as the basis for creating financial statements as though the principle had always been used for all periods presented. If it is impracticable to retroactively apply changes to prior interim periods of the current fiscal year, then the change in accounting principle can only be made as of the start of a subsequent fiscal year.

---

**Best Practice:** Where possible, companies are encouraged to adopt changes in accounting principle as of the first interim period of a fiscal year, so that the change covers the entire fiscal year. This makes interim periods more comparable throughout a fiscal year.

---

The activities required for retrospective application are as follows:

1. Alter the carrying amounts of assets and liabilities for the cumulative effect of the change in principle as of the beginning of the first accounting period presented.
2. Adjust the beginning balance of retained earnings to offset the change noted in the first step.
3. Adjust the financial statements for each prior period presented to reflect the impact of the new accounting principle.

If it is impracticable to make these changes, then do so as of the earliest reported periods for which it is practicable to do so. It is considered impracticable to make a retrospective change when any of the following conditions apply:

- *Assumptions.* Making a retrospective application calls for assumptions about what management intended to do in prior periods, and those assumptions cannot be independently substantiated.
- *Efforts made.* The company has made every reasonable effort to enact a retrospective change.
- *Estimates.* Estimates are required, which are impossible to provide due to the lack of information available when the prior-period financial statements were issued and evidence of the circumstances that existed at that time.

---

**EXAMPLE**

The Billabong Machining Company maintains a large number of old-style engine parts that it maintains for the automotive after-market. The company has been using the first in, first out (FIFO) method, but management has decided to switch to the last in, first out (LIFO) method. In order to incorporate this change in accounting principle into the financial statements for prior years, the accounting staff would have to derive assumptions regarding the periods in which different LIFO cost layers occurred, which cannot be independently substantiated. Consequently, the change is made on a go-forward basis.

---

The preceding retrospective application is required, except in situations where there are explicit transition requirements related to the introduction of a new accounting standard.

When making prior period adjustments due to a change in accounting principle, do so only for the direct effects of the change, net of tax. A direct effect is a recognized change in an asset or liability that is *required* in order to switch to the use of a different accounting principle. An indirect effect is one that *results from* a change in accounting principle that is applied retrospectively.

**EXAMPLE**

Armadillo Industries changes from the last in, first out method of inventory accounting to the first in, first out method. Doing so calls for an increase in the ending inventory in the preceding period, which in turn increases net profits for that period. Altering the inventory balance is a direct effect of the change in principle.

An indirect effect of the change in principle would be a change in the corporate accrual for profit sharing in the prior period, since the change will impact profits. Since it is an indirect effect, Armadillo does not record the change.

## Disadvantages of Retrospective Application

The requirement to retrospectively apply changes in accounting principle can present several difficult issues for the accountant and the readers of an organization's financial statements. These issues include:

- *Confusion.* There can be confusion among the recipients of an entity's financial statements when the newest version of a financial statement varies from one that was previously released. This issue can be mitigated by sending an accompanying note to recipients, asking them to destroy the previous version of the financials.
- *Contractual effects.* A business may have agreed to certain loan covenants that require it to meet liquidity or other targets. If a retrospective change is made, a business might find that it has been out of compliance with a loan agreement for a considerable period of time, which could lead to some interesting discussions with the lender.
- *Work load.* The task of making retrospective changes can be complex, since prior periods must be re-opened in the accounting software and altered.

## Changes in Accounting Estimate

A change in accounting estimate occurs when there is an adjustment to the carrying amount of an asset or liability, or the subsequent accounting for it. Examples of changes in accounting estimate are changes in:

- The allowance for doubtful accounts
- The reserve for obsolete inventory
- The useful life of depreciable assets
- The salvage values of depreciable assets
- The amount of expected warranty obligations
- Actuarial assumptions related to pensions
- The quantities of mineral reserves yet to be depleted

Changes in accounting estimate occur relatively frequently, and so would require a major amount of effort to make an ongoing series of retroactive changes to prior financial statements. Instead, GAAP only requires that changes in accounting estimate be accounted for in the period of change and thereafter (which is *prospective* application). Thus, no retrospective change is required or allowed. Also, do not issue pro forma financial statements for prior periods that show what the effects of a change in accounting estimate would have been.

**EXAMPLE**

The controller of Grunge Motor Sports notes that a downward trend in general economic conditions has increased the probability that Grunge's customers will not pay. This leads her to alter the original estimation that 1.2% of all accounts receivable will eventually be charged off as bad debts. Her new estimate is 1.4% of all receivables, which results in the following entry.

|  | Debit | Credit |
|---|---|---|
| Bad debt expense | 28,000 | |
|     Allowance for doubtful accounts | | 28,000 |

This is a change in accounting estimate, so it is accounted for in the period of change.

---

There may be cases in which a change in accounting estimate is indistinguishable from a change in accounting principle. When this situation arises, it should be accounted for as a change in accounting estimate. For example, a business may have previously deferred certain costs and recognized them in later periods, but now elects to charge them to expense, on the grounds that their future benefit is no longer clear. In this case, a new method of accounting is being used to accelerate expense recognition, but the reason for it is that the underlying estimation method can no longer be trusted.

**EXAMPLE**

The controller of Inscrutable Corporation is evaluating the company's fixed assets, and concludes that the pattern of consumption of these assets argues in favor of switching to an accelerated depreciation method from the current straight-line method. Though a different calculation method will now be used for depreciation, the reason for it is based on a change in accounting estimate that is derived from new information. This change should be accounted for on a prospective basis, with no retrospective application.

---

## Disadvantages of Prospective Application

When there are changes in accounting estimates, the financial statements to which these changes have been prospectively applied (i.e., on a go-forward basis) are no longer comparable to those financial statements that were already issued prior to the prospective application. This is usually not considered to be a major issue, since changes in accounting estimate tend to have immaterial effects on the financial statements.

## Changes in Reporting Entity

There are situations where a change in the entities included in consolidated financial statements effectively means that there is a change in the reporting entity. For example:

- Consolidated results are presented instead of the financial statements of an individual entity.
- There is a change in the specific subsidiaries that comprise a group of businesses for which consolidated financial statements are being presented.

In these situations, apply the change in reporting entity retrospectively to all of the periods being reported. The result should be the consistent presentation of financial information for the same reporting entity for all periods, including interim periods. This presentation allows for historical trend analysis across all of the reporting periods.

There are a number of situations that are not considered a change in reporting entity. For example:

- A change in the legal structure of an existing entity is not considered a change in reporting entity. For example, a change from a C corporation to an S corporation does not require the application of the accounting for changes in reporting entity.
- A business combination accounted for using the acquisition method is not a change in reporting entity; there is no retroactive consolidation with the financial statements of the acquiree for any periods presented that are prior to the acquisition date.

## Correction of an Error in Previously Issued Financial Statements

From time to time, financial statements will be inadvertently issued that contain one or more errors. The following are considered to be errors:

- A mathematical miscalculation
- A mistake in the application of GAAP
- The misuse of facts existing when the financial statements were prepared

A change from an unacceptable accounting principle to a generally accepted accounting principle is considered to be the correction of an error. For example, switching from the cash basis of accounting to the accrual basis of accounting (which is recognized under GAAP) is considered to be the correction of an error.

When an error is discovered, the prior period financial statements to which the error applies must be restated. A restatement involves the revision of previously-issued financial statements. Restatement requires the following steps:

1. Alter the carrying amounts of assets and liabilities for the cumulative effect of the error as of the beginning of the first accounting period presented.
2. Adjust the beginning balance of retained earnings to offset the change noted in the first step.
3. Adjust the financial statements for each prior period presented to reflect the impact of the error.

**EXAMPLE**

The controller of Kelvin Corporation is reviewing depreciation records, and finds that the depreciation for certain manufacturing equipment has been incorrectly calculated for the past five years, resulting in a depreciation expense that is cumulatively too low by $82,000. She creates the following adjustment to correct the error:

| | Debit | Credit |
|---|---|---|
| Retained earnings | 82,000 | |
|     Accumulated depreciation | | 82,000 |

**EXAMPLE**

A customer of International Automation pays the company $60,000, which is intended to pay for an automation consulting project that spans the end of 20X3 and the beginning of 20X4, with two-thirds of the work to be completed in 20X4. The accounting staff inadvertently recognizes the entire payment as revenue in 20X3. The correcting entry is:

| | Debit | Credit |
|---|---|---|
| Retained earnings | 40,000 | |
|     Deferred revenue (liability) | | 40,000 |

The correction of an error is not the same as an accounting change. An accounting change, as noted earlier, involves either a change in estimate or a change in accounting principle.

## Corrections Related to Prior Interim Periods

An interim period is a financial reporting period that is shorter than a full fiscal year, such as a three-month reporting period. GAAP specifies several situations in which the financial statements of prior interim periods of the current fiscal year should be adjusted. These adjustments are for the following:

- Adjustment or settlement of litigation
- Income taxes
- Renegotiation proceedings
- Utility revenue under rate-making processes

Adjustments for these items are only necessary if all of the following criteria apply:

- The effect of the change is material to income from continuing operations, or its trend
- The adjustments are directly related to the prior interim periods
- The adjustment amount could not be reasonably estimated prior to the current interim period, but can now be estimated

If an adjustment occurs in any interim period other than the first period, use the following steps to account for it:

1. Include any portion of the adjustment that relates to current business activities in the current interim period.
2. Restate prior interim periods of the current fiscal year to include that portion of the item that relates to the business activities in those periods.
3. Restate the first interim period of the current fiscal year to include that portion of the item that relates to the business activities in prior fiscal years.

## The Materiality of an Error

When an accounting error is discovered, determine whether it is material enough to report. To do so, compare its effect to the full-year estimated income or the full-year earnings trend. If it is not material, there is no need to disclose it. However, if the error is material in relation to the estimated income or earnings trend for an interim period, disclose the error in the financial statements for that interim period.

---

**EXAMPLE**

Armadillo Industries has profits of $1,000,000 in its first quarter, and expects to generate $4,000,000 of profits for the entire fiscal year. The company has historically considered materiality to be 5% of its profits. In the first quarter, the accounting department uncovers a $100,000 error. Though this amount is 10% of first-quarter profits, it is only 2.5% of full-year expected profits. Given the minimal impact on full-year profits, Armadillo does not have to segregate this information for reporting purposes in its first quarter interim reporting, though it must still disclose the information.

---

### The Materiality Principle

The preceding directive in this section to report a material error does not describe the parameters of materiality. This is a concept that is difficult to pin down, since GAAP does not provide a clear definition of what is material or immaterial. One way to view materiality is through the materiality principle, which is based on general usage. Under this principle, an item is considered to be material if it is probable that users of the financial statements would have altered their actions if certain information had not been in error. If users would not have altered their actions, then the error is said to be immaterial.

**The SEC's View of Materiality**

The Securities and Exchange Commission has a conservative view of how to deal with the materiality concept, which it has stated in its staff accounting bulletins (SABs). An SAB is a summarization of the views of the SEC staff regarding how GAAP is to be applied. The views stated in an SAB are followed by the staffs of the Office of the Chief Accountant and the Division of Corporate Finance when reviewing the filings of publicly-held companies. For this reason, SABs are closely adhered to by entities registering their securities within the United States. If a publicly-held company does not incorporate the concepts in these bulletins into their financial statements and disclosures, it may receive a comment letter from the SEC.

The following two issues related to materiality have been addressed by the SEC in an SAB. The text is a slightly compressed version of the full SEC discussion. In essence, the SEC's views on materiality might lead an accountant to engage in a relatively detailed analysis of most issues, with a higher resulting probability that issues must be recognized in the financial statements.

<u>Situation</u>: During the course of preparing or auditing year-end financial statements, financial management or the company's independent auditor becomes aware of misstatements in the company's financial statements. When combined, the misstatements result in a 4% overstatement of net income and a $.02 (4%) overstatement of earnings per share. Because no item in the company's consolidated financial statements is misstated by more than 5%, management and the independent auditor conclude that the deviation from GAAP is immaterial and that the accounting is permissible.

*In the staff's view, may a company or the auditor of its financial statements assume the immateriality of items that fall below a percentage threshold set by management or the auditor to determine whether amounts and items are material to the financial statements?* No. The SEC is aware that certain companies, over time, have developed quantitative thresholds as "rules of thumb" to assist in the preparation of their financial statements, and that auditors also have used these thresholds in their evaluation of whether items might be considered material to users of a company's financial statements. One rule of thumb in particular suggests that the misstatement or omission of an item that falls under a 5% threshold is not material in the absence of particularly egregious circumstances, such as self-dealing or misappropriation by senior management. The SEC reminds companies and the auditors of their financial statements that exclusive reliance on this or any percentage or numerical threshold has no basis in the accounting literature or the law.

The use of a percentage as a numerical threshold, such as 5%, may provide the basis for a preliminary assumption that a deviation of less than the specified percentage with respect to a particular item on the company's financial statements is unlikely to be material. The SEC has no objection to such a "rule of thumb" as an initial step in assessing materiality. But quantifying, in percentage terms, the magnitude of a misstatement is only the beginning of an analysis of materiality; it cannot appropriately be used as a substitute for a full analysis of all relevant considerations. Materiality concerns the significance of an item to users of a company's financial statements. A matter is "material" if there is a substantial likelihood that a reasonable person would consider it important.

As a result of the interaction of quantitative and qualitative considerations in materiality judgments, misstatements of relatively small amounts that come to the auditor's attention could have a material effect on the financial statements. Among the considerations that may well render material a quantitatively small misstatement of a financial statement item are the following:

- Whether the misstatement arises from an item capable of precise measurement or whether it arises from an estimate and, if so, the degree of imprecision inherent in the estimate
- Whether the misstatement masks a change in earnings or other trends
- Whether the misstatement hides a failure to meet analysts' consensus expectations for the enterprise
- Whether the misstatement changes a loss into income or vice versa

- Whether the misstatement concerns a segment or other portion of the company's business that has been identified as playing a significant role in the company's operations or profitability
- Whether the misstatement affects the company's compliance with regulatory requirements
- Whether the misstatement affects the company's compliance with loan covenants or other contractual requirements
- Whether the misstatement has the effect of increasing management's compensation; for example, by satisfying requirements for the award of bonuses or other forms of incentive compensation
- Whether the misstatement involves concealment of an unlawful transaction

For the reasons noted above, a company and the auditors of its financial statements should not assume that even small intentional misstatements in financial statements, for example those pursuant to actions to "manage" earnings, are immaterial.

The materiality of a misstatement may turn on where it appears in the financial statements. For example, a misstatement may involve a segment of the company's operations. In that instance, in assessing materiality of a misstatement to the financial statements taken as a whole, companies and their auditors should consider not only the size of the misstatement but also the significance of the segment information to the financial statements taken as a whole.

In determining whether multiple misstatements cause the financial statements to be materially misstated, companies and the auditors of their financial statements should consider each misstatement separately and the aggregate effect of all misstatements. If the misstatement of an individual amount causes the financial statements as a whole to be materially misstated, that effect cannot be eliminated by other misstatements whose effect may be to diminish the impact of the misstatement on other financial statement items. To take an obvious example, if a company's revenues are a material financial statement item and if they are materially overstated, the financial statements taken as a whole will be materially misleading even if the effect on earnings is completely offset by an equivalent overstatement of expenses.

Even though a misstatement of an individual amount may not cause the financial statements taken as a whole to be materially misstated, it may nonetheless, when aggregated with other misstatements, render the financial statements taken as a whole to be materially misleading. Companies and the auditors of their financial statements accordingly should consider the effect of the misstatement on subtotals or totals. The auditor should aggregate all misstatements that affect each subtotal or total and consider whether the misstatements in the aggregate affect the subtotal or total in a way that causes the company's financial statements taken as a whole to be materially misleading.

Companies and auditors also should consider the effect of misstatements from prior periods on the current financial statements. This may be particularly the case where immaterial misstatements recur in several years and the cumulative effect becomes material in the current year.

<u>Situation</u>: During the course of preparing annual financial statements, a company is evaluating the materiality of an improper expense accrual (e.g., overstated liability) in the amount of $100, which has built up over 5 years, at $20 per year. The company previously evaluated the misstatement as being immaterial to each of the prior year financial statements (i.e., years 1-4). For the purpose of evaluating materiality in the current year (i.e., year 5), the company quantifies the error as a $20 overstatement of expenses.

*Has the company appropriately quantified the amount of this error for the purpose of evaluating materiality for the current year?* No. In this example, the company has only quantified the effects of the identified unadjusted error that arose in the current year income statement. Prior year misstatements should be considered in quantifying misstatements in current year financial statements.

The techniques most commonly used in practice to accumulate and quantify misstatements are generally referred to as the "rollover" and "iron curtain" approaches. The rollover approach, which is the approach used in the example, quantifies a misstatement based on the amount of the error originating in the current year income statement. This approach ignores the effects of correcting the portion of the current year balance sheet misstatement that originated in prior years (i.e., it ignores the "carryover effects" of prior year misstatements). The iron curtain approach quantifies a misstatement based on the effects of correcting the misstatement existing in the balance sheet at the end of the current year, irrespective of the misstatement's year(s) of origination. Had the company in this fact pattern applied the iron curtain approach, the misstatement would have been quantified as a $100 misstatement based on the end of year balance sheet misstatement. Thus, the adjustment needed to correct the financial statements for the end of year error would be to reduce the liability by $100 with a corresponding decrease in current year expense.

As demonstrated in this example, the primary weakness of the rollover approach is that it can result in the accumulation of significant misstatements on the balance sheet that are deemed immaterial in part because the amount that originates in each year is quantitatively small.

In contrast, the primary weakness of the iron curtain approach is that it does not consider the correction of prior year misstatements in the current year (i.e., the reversal of the carryover effects) to be errors. Therefore, in this example, if the misstatement was corrected during the current year such that no error existed in the balance sheet at the end of the current year, the reversal of the $80 prior year misstatement would not be considered an error in the current year financial statements under the iron curtain approach. Implicitly, the iron curtain approach assumes that because the prior year financial statements were not materially misstated, correcting any immaterial errors that existed in those statements in the current year is the "correct" accounting, and is therefore not considered an error in the current year. Thus, utilization of the iron curtain approach can result in a misstatement in the current year income statement not being evaluated as an error at all.

Companies must quantify the impact of correcting all misstatements, including both the carryover and reversing effects of prior year misstatements, on the current year financial statements. This can be accomplished by quantifying an error under both the rollover and iron curtain approaches and by evaluating the error measured under each approach. Thus, a company's financial statements would require adjustment when either approach results in quantifying a misstatement that is material, after considering all relevant quantitative and qualitative factors.

It is possible that correcting an error in the current year could materially misstate the current year's income statement. For example, correcting the $100 misstatement in the current year will:

- Correct the $20 error originating in the current year;
- Correct the $80 balance sheet carryover error that originated in Years 1 through 4; but also
- Misstate the current year income statement by $80.

If the $80 understatement of current year expense is material to the current year, after all of the relevant quantitative and qualitative factors are considered, the prior year financial statements should be corrected, even though such revision previously was and continues to be immaterial to the prior year financial statements.

## Summary

Retrospective changes can require detailed detective work, judgment, and thorough documentation of the changes made. Given the amount of labor involved, it is cost-effective to find justifiable reasons for not making retrospective changes. Two valid methods for doing so are to question the materiality of the necessary changes, or to find reasons to instead treat issues as changes in accounting estimate.

If retrospective application is completely unavoidable, it may make sense to have the company's auditors review proposed retrospective changes in advance. Doing so minimizes the risk that an issue will be discovered by the auditors during the annual audit, which will require additional retrospective changes. When working with the auditors in advance in this manner, fully document the discussion; otherwise, either or both parties may have forgotten essential elements of the retrospective application by the time the annual audit occurs, which could be many months later.

## Review Questions

1. An example of a change in accounting estimate is:
   a. A change in the salvage value of a depreciable asset
   b. A change in expense from period to period
   c. The resetting of a product's price
   d. The revaluation of inventory using a different cost layering method

2. You should adjust the financial statements of prior interim periods of the current fiscal year when:
   a. The adjustment is not related to the prior interim periods
   b. The amount of the adjustment cannot be estimated
   c. The effect of the change is material to income from continuing operations
   d. The effect of the change is immaterial to income from continuing operations

3. The following are all disadvantages of retrospective application, except for:
   a. The application of the change
   b. The comparability of financial statements
   c. The effect on loan covenants
   d. The presence of multiple versions of the financial statements

4. Only change an accounting principle when:
   a. Doing so will impair the comparability of presented reporting periods
   b. The result will yield a larger profit
   c. The change is required by an update to GAAP
   d. The use of an alternative principle is not preferable

5. Retrospective application to prior accounting periods is required:
   a. For a change in accounting procedure
   b. For a change in accounting practice
   c. For a change in accounting principle
   d. In no situations

6. Retrospective application is not considered possible when:
   a. Estimates are required, which are impossible to provide
   b. The company has not made every reasonable effort to make the change
   c. Assumptions about what management intended can be substantiated
   d. There is a change in accounting principle

7. The following are examples of accounting errors, except for:
   a. A mathematical miscalculation
   b. The misuse of facts existing when financial statements were prepared
   c. A mistake in the application of GAAP
   d. Changing from an unacceptable principle to GAAP

8. A disadvantage of only applying a change in estimate on a prospective basis is that:
   a. These changes tend to be material
   b. There is a lack of comparability with prior financial statements
   c. There can be a noticeable impact on prior contractual agreements
   d. The auditors will have to revise their work papers

# Chapter 4
# Changing Prices

## Introduction

The guidance in this chapter addresses the problem of how inflationary environments impact the reported results and financial position of a business. GAAP provides an extensive array of reporting requirements for those companies whose operations are located in areas where there is strong inflationary pressure. If one were to follow the GAAP guidance (which is not mandatory), the result would be supplemental reporting that restates elements of the financial statements to show how the reporting entity would have fared if there had been no inflation. In this chapter, we address the many detailed reporting requirements related to changing prices, and provide a sample report.

The guidance in this chapter applies to all business entities that use GAAP to prepare financial statements that are stated in U.S. dollars, as well as foreign entities that prepare financial statements in the currency of the country where its operations are located, and foreign entities that operate in countries experiencing hyperinflation.

## Overview of Changing Prices

When there is a significant amount of price inflation or deflation, the impact on the financial statements of a company operating in that environment can be so severe that the value of the information in the statements declines to the point of being nearly useless. Consequently, it is acceptable under GAAP to issue price-level adjusted financial statements under the following circumstances:

- The financial statements are denominated in a foreign currency; and
- The financial statements are for businesses operating in countries with highly inflationary economies; and
- The financial statements are intended for readers in the United States.

In the following sub-sections, we address how to measure the various items that are to be disclosed.

### Inventory and Fixed Assets

When deriving the current cost of inventory and fixed assets, use the following measurements:

- *Inventory.* Use the current cost or lower recoverable amount at the measurement date. Current cost is considered the current cost of purchasing the inventory items. If turnover is rapid and no appreciable amounts of depreciation are allocated to inventory, the cost of goods sold as measured with last in, first out (LIFO) costing can be considered a reasonable approximation for current cost (if the effect of LIFO liquidations are excluded).
- *Fixed assets.* Use the current cost or lower recoverable amount at the measurement date, for the remaining service potential of these assets. Current cost is considered the current cost of acquiring the same service potential as the existing fixed assets.
- *Partial contracts.* If there is a partially-completed contract, use the current cost or lower recoverable amount for those resources allocated to the project at the date of their use on the contract or commitment to the contract.

Current costs can be obtained, for example, from price indexes, current invoice prices, vendor price lists, or standard manufacturing costs. Current costs are assumed to be based on the manufacture or purchase of assets in a location that minimizes the total landed cost of inventory and/or fixed assets.

It is also acceptable to use historical costs that are adjusted by a price index, rather than using current costs. This option may be the most cost-effective alternative, since a price index is one of the simplest ways to generate information about changing prices.

If current costs are derived for assets located in foreign locations, and those costs are denominated in a foreign currency, translate the amounts into the company's functional currency at the current exchange rate.

## Specialized Assets

Derive the current cost of mineral resources either at their current market buying prices, or at the current cost required to find and develop the necessary mineral reserves. It is generally easiest to use historical costs that are adjusted by a price index. The same approach is applicable to timberlands, income-producing real estate, and motion picture films.

## Recoverable Amounts

It may be necessary to measure the recoverable amount of an asset. If so, this information can be derived from value in use (i.e., discounted future cash flows) or the current market value of the asset. The value in use option is better if there is no intent to immediately sell the asset. Only use current market value if there is a plan to immediately sell the asset. If there is a choice between measuring assets at their current cost or recoverable amount, and the recoverable amount appears to be materially and permanently lower than the current cost, then measure the assets at their recoverable amount.

If a business is subject to price controls, it may be reasonable to measure recoverable amounts at their historical costs. Recoverable amounts may even be lower than historical costs. However, if there is an expectation that the replacement of the service potential of the assets will be undertaken at some point, then measure the cost of goods sold, depreciation, amortization, and depletion at their current cost-current purchasing power amounts.

## Income from Continuing Operations

The measurement of income from continuing operations on a current cost basis requires the following steps:

- Measure the cost of goods sold as of the date sold, using either its current cost or lower recoverable amount, or when those resources are used on or at least committed to a designated contract.
- Measure depreciation, amortization, and depletion based on either the average current cost of the service potential of the underlying fixed assets or their lower recoverable amount during the usage period.

It is allowable to measure all other revenue and expense items, as well as income taxes, at the amounts stated in the company's income statement.

## Restatement of Current Cost Information

If a business does not have significant foreign operations, or if it uses the U.S. dollar as the functional currency for all of its significant foreign operations, use the consumer price index for all urban consumers (CPIUC) to convert its current costs into units of constant purchasing power.

If operations are measured in a foreign functional currency, measure the effects of inflation on its current cost information either by applying the CPIUC to its results following translation, or by applying a measure of the change in purchasing power for that currency prior to translation. Whichever method is used, apply it consistently for all operations measured in foreign functional currencies.

If a measure of the change in purchasing power for a currency is not available when the financial statements are being constructed, it is allowable for management to estimate the change in the general price level.

## Translation Adjustments

If there is an election to translate results into the U.S. dollar from a foreign currency and then apply the CPIUC, then state the aggregate translation adjustment net of income taxes that were allocated to the translation adjustment in the company's financial statements. Alternatively, if the election is made to translate results by applying a measure of the change in purchasing power for a currency prior to translation, then state the aggregate translation adjustment net of:

- The income taxes that were allocated to the translation adjustment in the company's financial statements; and
- The aggregate parity adjustment. This is the amount required to measure net assets as of the end of the year in either average-for-the-year dollars or end-of-the-year dollars. The choice is based on whether income from continuing operations is based on average-for-the year or end-of-the-year functional currency units.

## Purchasing Power Gains and Losses

The purchasing power gain or loss resulting from net monetary assets is the net gain or loss resulting from the restatement in units of constant purchasing power of the changes in the balances and transactions in monetary assets and liabilities. If the purchasing power gain or loss from net monetary assets is based on translating foreign currency results by first applying a measure of the change in purchasing power for the foreign currency and then translating it into U.S. dollars, then translate the purchasing power gain or loss into its U.S. dollar equivalent using the average exchange rate for the period.

Monetary assets are considered to be cash, time deposits, foreign currencies, trading investments, accounts receivable and notes receivable, the allowance for doubtful accounts, loans to employees, long-term receivables, refundable deposits, the cash surrender value of life insurance, advances to suppliers, deferred tax assets, and deferred life insurance policy acquisition costs.

Monetary liabilities are considered to be accounts payable, notes payable, accrued expenses payable, cash dividends payable, advances from customers, refundable deposits, long-term debt and related premiums and discounts, deferred tax liabilities, life insurance policy reserves, property and casualty insurance loss reserves, deposit liabilities of financial institutions, and capital stock subject to mandatory redemption.

## Restatement Steps

In essence, the restatement steps required to convert historical cost information into current cost-constant purchasing power information are as follows:

1. Review the contents of inventory at the beginning and end of the year, as well as the cost of goods sold, to determine when costs were incurred.
2. Restate both inventory and the cost of goods sold, so that they are presented at current cost.
3. Review fixed assets to determine when they were acquired.
4. Restate fixed assets, depreciation, amortization, and depletion, so that they are presented at current cost.
5. Determine the aggregate amount of net monetary items at the beginning and end of the reporting period, as well as the net change in these items during the period.
6. Calculate the purchasing power gain or loss on the net monetary items.
7. Calculate the change in current cost for both inventory and fixed assets, as well as the effect of changes in the general price level.

## Changing Prices Disclosures

The disclosures stated in this section are encouraged by GAAP, but not required.

### Five-Year Summary

Disclose all of the following information for each of the most recent five years, and present it as supplemental information to the annual financial statements. The following information is not needed in interim financial statements, nor is it needed at a business segment level.

| Disclosure Item | Cost Basis |
| --- | --- |
| Net sales | |
| Income from continuing operations | Current cost |
| Purchasing power gain or loss on net monetary items | |
| Change in current cost or lower recoverable amount of inventory and fixed assets, net of inflation | |
| Aggregate foreign currency translation adjustment | Current cost |
| Net assets at year end | Current cost |
| Income per common share from continuing operations | Current cost |
| Cash dividends declared per common share | |
| Market price per common share at year end | |

The information shown in this five-year summary should be stated using one of the following pricing methodologies:

- In annual-average or end-of-year units of constant purchasing power.
- In dollars with the purchasing power equivalent of dollars of the base period of the CPIUC. If this pricing methodology is used, state the level of the CPIUC used for each of the five years. The CPIUC may have to be extrapolated, if it has not been published by the time the annual report is prepared.

If the business has a significant foreign operation that is measured in a currency other than the U.S. dollar, disclose whether inflationary adjustments to its current cost information are based on the CPIUC or on a functional currency general price level index.

If the company is presenting consolidated results, then this five-year summary should also be presented on a consolidated basis.

Finally, accompany the five-year summary with a discussion of the significance of changing prices on the business, along with an explanation of any specific items disclosed in the summary.

**EXAMPLE**

Armadillo Industries presents the following five-year summary of supplemental information related to changing prices as part of the disclosures that accompany its annual financial statements:

Five-year Comparison of Selected Financial Data
Adjusted for Effects of Changing Prices
In Thousands of Average 20X5 Dollars, except for Per Share Amounts

| | 20X5 | 20X4 | 20X3 | 20X2 | 20X1 |
|---|---|---|---|---|---|
| Net sales and other operating revenues | $363,000 | $342,000 | $330,000 | $309,000 | $294,000 |
| Income from continuing operations | 18,000 | 16,000 | 4,000 | 23,000 | 10,000 |
| Gain from decline in purchasing power of net amounts owed | 14,000 | 9,000 | 2,000 | 17,000 | 7,000 |
| Excess of increase in specific prices of inventory and fixed assets over the increase in the general price level | 23,000 | 18,000 | 1,000 | 29,000 | 3,000 |
| Foreign currency translation adjustment | -2,900 | 3,400 | -5,800 | -3,200 | -1,500 |
| Net assets at year-end | 111,000 | 101,000 | 90,000 | 83,500 | 72,000 |
| Per share information: | | | | | |
| Income from continuing operations | $4.00 | $3.56 | $0.89 | $5.11 | $2.22 |
| Cash dividends declared | 2.00 | 1.75 | -- | 1.50 | 1.25 |
| Market price at year-end | 36 | 32 | 8 | 46 | 20 |

## Summary

Though the guidance for changing prices is well-intentioned, it can also be quite difficult to compile and present the recommended information. Accordingly, consider the cost of these reporting suggestions and the resulting improvement in the value of the information provided to the readers of the company's financial statements. In many cases, the cost-benefit tradeoff will lean heavily in favor of not reporting the effects of changing prices. The reporting is most likely to be of use when a significant proportion of company operations are located in a country experiencing high levels of price inflation.

## Review Questions

1. It is allowable to issue price-level adjusted financial statements:
    a. Whenever the Consumer Price Index for a period exceeds 10%
    b. When the statements are for businesses operating in countries with highly inflationary economies
    c. Only for financial statements whose readers are intended to be foreign
    d. Only for financial statements denominated in U.S. dollars

2. The current cost of inventory is based on:
    a. The retail method of inventory valuation
    b. The weighted-average method of inventory valuation
    c. First in, first out cost layering
    d. Either the current cost of purchasing the items or the lower recoverable amount

3. The current cost of a fixed asset can be derived from:
    a. Its carrying amount
    b. Its gross purchase amount
    c. Its lower recoverable amount
    d. Its short-notice sale price

4. The current cost of timberlands is derived from:
    a. The price of the land or underlying lease
    b. Its current market buying price
    c. The amount for which it could be exchanged in a land swap
    d. The historical cost to develop the resource

5. Monetary assets include:
    a. Inventory
    b. Accrued income taxes
    c. Advances from customers
    d. The cash surrender value of life insurance

# Chapter 5
# Earnings per Share

## Introduction

If a company is publicly-held, it is required to report earnings per share information. A publicly-held entity is an organization whose debt or equity securities are traded on an exchange or the over-the-counter market, or which is required to file reports with the Securities and Exchange Commission (SEC). The investment community and financial press closely follow earnings per share information, considering it to be a key view of corporate profitability.

Two types of earnings per share information are to be reported within the financial statements, which are basic and diluted earnings per share. In this chapter, we describe how to calculate both basic and diluted earnings per share, as well as how to present this information within the financial statements.

A privately-held organization does not have to report earnings per share information. The earnings per share requirements also do not apply if a company has taken itself private; that is, its securities no longer trade on an exchange or in the over-the-counter market. These requirements also do not apply to the financial statements of wholly-owned subsidiaries.

## Basic Earnings per Share

Basic earnings per share is the amount of a company's profit or loss for a reporting period that is available to the shares of its common stock that are outstanding during a reporting period. It is intended to measure the performance of the reporting organization over a specific reporting period. If a business only has common stock in its capital structure, it presents only its basic earnings per share for income from continuing operations and net income. The formula for basic earnings per share is:

$$\frac{\text{Profit or loss attributable to common equity holders of the parent business}}{\text{Weighted average number of common shares outstanding during the period}}$$

In addition, subdivide this calculation for presentation purposes into:

- The profit or loss from continuing operations attributable to the parent company
- The total profit or loss attributable to the parent company

When compiling earnings per share information for the consolidated financial statements of a parent company and its subsidiaries, one may find that certain subsidiaries are less than wholly-owned, which means that there is a noncontrolling interest in these subsidiaries. If so, the income from continuing operations and net income information used to compile the basic earnings per share information should exclude all income from continuing operations and net income that are attributable to the noncontrolling interest.

When calculating basic earnings per share, incorporate into the numerator an adjustment for dividends. Deduct from the profit or loss the after-tax amount of any dividends declared on non-cumulative preferred stock (even if not yet paid), as well as the after-tax amount of any preferred stock dividends, even if the dividends are not declared; this does not include any dividends paid or declared during the current period that relate to previous periods.

Also, incorporate the following adjustments into the denominator of the basic earnings per share calculation:

- *Contingent stock*. If there is contingently issuable stock, treat it as though it were outstanding as of the date when there are no circumstances under which the shares would *not* be issued. This means it should not be possible for basic earnings per share to be restated due to changing circumstances. For example, if an earnout provision is included in a business combination, the contingent issuance of stock to the owners of the acquiree will not be included in basic earnings per share until it is certain that they will receive more shares.
- *Shares issuable for minimal consideration*. If shares can be issued for little consideration (or none at all), consider them to be outstanding common shares that are added to the denominator of the earnings per share calculation. These shares should be added as of the date when any associated conditions of issuance have been satisfied.
- *Weighted-average shares*. Use the weighted-average number of shares during the period in the denominator. This is done by adjusting the number of shares outstanding at the beginning of the reporting period for common shares repurchased or issued in the period. This adjustment is based on the proportion of the days in the reporting period that the shares are outstanding.

There may be cases in which a business issues a stock dividend, which is when a dividend is paid with stock, rather than cash or other assets. When such a dividend is issued for preferred stock, deduct this dividend from net income when computing the amount of income available to the holders of common stock. Or, if there has been a loss, add it back to the net loss.

---

**EXAMPLE**

Lowry Locomotion earns a profit of $1,000,000 net of taxes in Year 1. In addition, Lowry owes $200,000 in dividends to the holders of its cumulative preferred stock. Lowry calculates the numerator of its basic earnings per share as follows:

$$\$1,000,000 \text{ Profit} - \$200,000 \text{ Dividends} = \underline{\$800,000}$$

Lowry had 4,000,000 common shares outstanding at the beginning of Year 1. In addition, it sold 200,000 shares on April 1 and 400,000 shares on October 1. It also issued 500,000 shares on July 1 to the owners of a newly-acquired subsidiary. Finally, it bought back 60,000 shares on December 1. Lowry calculates the weighted-average number of common shares outstanding as follows:

| Date | Shares | Weighting (Months) | Weighted Average |
|---|---|---|---|
| January 1 | 4,000,000 | 12/12 | 4,000,000 |
| April 1 | 200,000 | 9/12 | 150,000 |
| July 1 | 500,000 | 6/12 | 250,000 |
| October 1 | 400,000 | 3/12 | 100,000 |
| December 1 | -60,000 | 1/12 | -5,000 |
| | | | 4,495,000 |

Lowry's basic earnings per share calculation is:

$$\$800,000 \text{ adjusted profits} \div 4,495,000 \text{ weighted-average shares} = \underline{\$0.18} \text{ per share}$$

---

## Diluted Earnings per Share

Diluted earnings per share is the profit for a reporting period per share of common stock outstanding during that period; it includes the number of shares that would have been outstanding during the period if the company had issued common shares for all potential dilutive securities outstanding during the period. Several types of dilutive securities are:

- *Convertible bonds.* Can be traded in for common stock, which eliminates the related amount of interest expense but increases the number of common shares outstanding.
- *Convertible preferred stock.* Can be traded in for common stock, which eliminates the related preferred stock dividends, but increases the number of common shares outstanding.
- *Stock options.* Gives the holder (an employee) the right to buy a certain number of common shares from the company in exchange for the payment of an exercise price. This increases the cash reserves of the company, but also increases the number of common shares outstanding.
- *Warrants.* Gives the holder (a third party) the right to buy a certain number of common shares from the company in exchange for the payment of an exercise price. This increases the cash reserves of the company, but also increases the number of common shares outstanding.

As was the case for basic earnings per share, diluted earnings per share is intended to measure the performance of the reporting organization over a specific reporting period; however, the objective is more expansive, since it also incorporates all dilutive potential common shares that were outstanding during the reporting period.

If a company has more types of stock than common stock in its capital structure, it must present both basic earnings per share and diluted earnings per share information; this presentation must be for both income from continuing operations and net income. This information is reported on the company's income statement.

To calculate diluted earnings per share, include the effects of all dilutive potential common shares. This means that the shares outstanding are increased by the weighted average number of additional common shares that would have been outstanding if the company had converted all dilutive potential common stock to common stock. This dilution may affect the profit or loss in the numerator of the dilutive earnings per share calculation. The formula is:

$$\frac{\text{(Profit or loss attributable to common equity holders of parent company} + \text{After-tax interest on convertible debt} + \text{Convertible preferred dividends} \pm \text{Other changes)}}{\text{(Weighted average number of common shares outstanding during the period} + \text{All dilutive potential common stock)}}$$

It may be necessary to make several adjustments to the *numerator* of this calculation. They are:

- *Interest expense.* If there is convertible debt outstanding in the period, it is presumed to be converted into common stock. If so, add back to the numerator any interest charged that would have been associated with the debt in the reporting period[3]. This add-back of interest expense will result in a higher income level, which may in turn trigger additional changes in the numerator, such as increased profit-sharing or royalty expenses that are calculated based on the income level. Further, these changes may require a change in the amount of income tax recognized in the period, which alters the net income figure used in the numerator. These changes are made as of the beginning of the reporting period or at the time of issuance of the debt, if later.

---

[3] However, for convertible debt for which the principal is required to be paid in cash, the interest charges shall not be added back to the numerator.

**EXAMPLE**

Lowry Locomotion earns a net profit of $2 million, and it has 5 million common shares outstanding. In addition, there is a $1 million convertible loan that has an eight percent interest rate. The loan may potentially convert into 500,000 of Lowry's common shares. Lowry's incremental tax rate is 35 percent.

Lowry's basic earnings per share is $2,000,000 ÷ 5,000,000 shares, or $0.40/share. The following calculation shows the compilation of Lowry's diluted earnings per share:

| | |
|---|---:|
| Net profit | $2,000,000 |
| + Interest saved on $1,000,000 loan at 8% | 80,000 |
| - Reduced tax savings on foregone interest expense | -28,000 |
| = Adjusted net earnings | $2,052,000 |
| | |
| Common shares outstanding | 5,000,000 |
| + Potential converted shares | 500,000 |
| = Adjusted shares outstanding | 5,500,000 |
| | |
| Diluted earnings per share ($2,052,000 ÷ 5,500,000 shares) | **$0.37/share** |

- *Dividends*. If there is convertible preferred stock outstanding in the period, these shares are presumed to be converted into common stock. If so, it is also necessary to add back to the numerator the preferred dividends that are no longer being paid out. These changes are made as of the beginning of the reporting period or at the time of issuance of the preferred stock, if later.
- *Other changes*. There may be other changes in the reported income or loss that would result from the conversion of potential common shares into common stock. For example, a profit sharing expense might change if a conversion were to occur.

The preceding changes to the numerator should not be made if the effect would be antidilutive. This situation arises when the dividend declared in the current period for common shares is greater than the basic earnings per share figure. The effect is also antidilutive when the amount of dividends accumulated through the current period is greater than the basic earnings per share figure. The latter situation only arises when an organization has neglected to pay declared dividends for a period of time.

It may be necessary to make additional adjustments to the *denominator* of the diluted earnings per share calculation. They are:

- *Anti-dilutive shares*. If there are any contingent stock issuances that would have an anti-dilutive impact on earnings per share, do not include them in the calculation. This situation arises when a business experiences a loss, because including the dilutive shares in the calculation would reduce the loss per share. It can also occur when there are anti-dilutive contracts, such as a purchased put option that requires an issuer to buy back its shares. An anti-dilutive contract is always excluded from the diluted earnings per share calculation.
- *Dilutive shares*. If there is potentially dilutive common stock, add all of it to the denominator of the diluted earnings per share calculation. Unless there is more specific information available, assume that these shares are issued at the beginning of the reporting period.
- *Dilutive securities termination*. If a conversion option lapses during the reporting period for dilutive convertible securities, or if the related debt is extinguished during the reporting period, the effect

of these securities should still be included in the denominator of the diluted earnings per share calculation for the period during which they were outstanding.

In addition to these adjustments to the denominator, also apply all of the adjustments to the denominator already noted for basic earnings per share.

> **Best Practice:** The rules related to diluted earnings per share appear complex, but they are founded upon one principle – that you are trying to establish the absolute worst-case scenario to arrive at the smallest possible amount of earnings per share. If you are faced with an unusual situation involving the calculation of diluted earnings per share and are not sure what to do, that rule will likely apply.

In addition to the issues just noted, here are a number of additional situations that could impact the calculation of diluted earnings per share:

- *Most advantageous exercise price.* When calculating the number of potential shares that could be issued, do so using the most advantageous conversion rate from the perspective of the person or entity holding the security to be converted.
- *Settlement assumption.* If there is an open contract that could be settled in common stock or cash, assume that it will be settled in common stock, but only if the effect is dilutive. The presumption of settlement in stock can be overcome if there is a reasonable basis for expecting that settlement will be partially or entirely in cash.
- *Option exercise.* The treasury stock method is used to determine the effects of a presumed option or warrant exercise on diluted earnings per share. See the following section for more information.
- *Put options.* If there are purchased put options, only include them in the diluted earnings per share calculation if the exercise price is higher than the average market price during the reporting period.
- *Written put options.* If there is a written put option that requires a business to repurchase its own stock, include it in the computation of diluted earnings per share, but only if the effect is dilutive. If the exercise price of such a put option is above the average market price of the company's stock during the reporting period, this is considered to be "in the money," and the dilutive effect is to be calculated using the reverse treasury method, which is described in the following section.
- *Call options.* If there are purchased call options, only include them in the diluted earnings per share calculation if the exercise price is lower than the market price.
- *Contingent shares in general.* Treat common stock that is contingently issuable as though it was outstanding as of the beginning of the reporting period, but only if the conditions have been met that would require the company to issue the shares. If the conditions were not met by the end of the period, then include in the calculation, as of the beginning of the period, any shares that would be issuable if the end of the reporting period were the end of the contingency period, and the result would be dilutive.
- *Contingent shares dependency.* If there is a contingent share issuance that is dependent upon the future market price of the company's common stock, include the shares in the diluted earnings per share calculation, based on the market price at the end of the reporting period; however, only include the issuance if the effect is dilutive. If the shares have a contingency feature, do not include them in the calculation until the contingency has been met.
- *Issuances based on future earnings and stock price.* There may be contingent stock issuances that are based on future earnings *and* the future price of a company's stock. If so, the number of shares to include in diluted earnings per share should be based on the earnings to date and the current market price as of the end of each reporting period. If both earnings and share price targets must be reached in order to trigger a stock issuance and both targets are not met, then do not include any related contingently issuable shares in the diluted earnings per share calculation.

- *Issuances based on other conditions.* If stock is to be issued based on some other condition than earnings or market price, the number of contingent shares to include in diluted earnings per share is based on the assumption that the current performance situation will remain unchanged through the end of the contingency period. Examples of these other conditions are issuing a certain number of new products or opening a certain number of new retail stores.

---

**EXAMPLE**

Lethal Sushi has 1,000,000 shares of common stock outstanding at the beginning of the year. Its fiscal year is the same as the calendar year. Lethal Sushi acquires Hunter's Delight, which specializes in the preparation of game meats. Under the terms of the business combination, the former owners of Hunter's Delight will receive an additional 10,000 shares of Lethal common stock for every new restaurant that Hunter's Delight opens in the current year. This is a contingent stock agreement. A new restaurant is opened on February 1 and another on March 1. In the first quarter, the combined entity earned $500,000. The following table illustrates the resulting calculation of basic and diluted earnings per share.

| | First Quarter EPS Calculations |
|---|---|
| **Basic earnings per share computation:** | |
| Numerator | $500,000 |
| Denominator: | |
| Common shares outstanding | 1,000,000 |
| Restaurant opening contingency (1) | 10,000 |
| Total shares | 1,010,000 |
| Basic earnings per share | $0.50 |
| | |
| **Diluted earnings per share computation:** | |
| Numerator | $500,000 |
| Denominator: | |
| Common shares outstanding | 1,000,000 |
| Restaurant opening contingency (2) | 20,000 |
| Total shares | 1,020,000 |
| Diluted earnings per share | $0.49 |

(1) 10,000 shares are issued on February 1 and another 10,000 shares on March 1. The calculation for contingent shares in the basic earnings per share calculation is: (10,000 shares × 2/3) + (10,000 shares × 1/3)

(2) The calculation of diluted earnings per share for contingent shares includes the restaurant-triggered shares as of the *beginning* of the quarter.

---

- *Compensation in shares.* If employees are awarded shares that have not vested or stock options as forms of compensation, then treat these grants as options when calculating diluted earnings per share (but only if the related service condition has been rendered). Consider these grants to be outstanding on the grant date, rather than any later vesting date. The resulting presumed increase in shares should be included in the diluted earnings per share calculation, but only if there is a dilutive effect. This dilutive effect is calculated using the treasury stock method, which is described in the next section. When using the treasury stock method, assume that the proceeds from these compensation arrangements include all of the following:
  - o The exercise price paid by the employee
  - o The amount of compensation cost associated with services to be provided in the future, and not yet recognized
  - o Any excess tax benefits that would be added to additional paid-in capital if the options were to be exercised; this is the deduction caused by any compensation in excess of the compensation expense recognized in the income statement

Always calculate the number of potential dilutive common shares independently for each reporting period presented in the financial statements.

## Treasury Stock and Reverse Treasury Stock Methods

The preceding section addressed the calculation of diluted earnings per share. The dilutive effects of certain types of securities are dealt with using the treasury stock method or the reverse treasury stock method. These calculations are noted in the following sub-sections.

### Treasury Stock Method

When an organization has outstanding call options or warrants, their dilutive effects are calculated using the treasury stock method. This method employs the following sequence of assumptions and calculations:

1. Assume that options and warrants are exercised at the beginning of the reporting period. If they were actually exercised later in the reporting period, use the actual date of exercise.
2. The proceeds garnered by the presumed option or warrant exercise are assumed to be used to purchase common stock at the average market price during the reporting period.
3. The difference between the number of shares assumed to have been issued and the number of shares assumed to have been purchased is then added to the denominator of the computation of diluted earnings per share.

In Step 2 of the process, the average market price during a quarterly reporting period is based on the average market prices during all three months of the reporting period. A simple average of weekly or monthly closing market prices is usually sufficient for this calculation. When prices fluctuate considerably, it might instead be necessary to use an average of the high and low prices for the reporting period.

When the year-to-date average pricing is determined, it is based on the year-to-date weighted average number of incremental shares included in each quarterly earnings per share computation.

The treasury stock method will only have a dilutive effect when the average market price of the common stock in the period is greater than the exercise price of the options or warrants.

The following example illustrates the concept.

---

**EXAMPLE**

Lowry Locomotion earns a net profit of $200,000, and it has 5,000,000 common shares outstanding that sell on the open market for an average of $12 per share. In addition, there are 300,000 options outstanding that can be converted to Lowry's common stock at $10 each.

Lowry's basic earnings per share is $200,000 ÷ 5,000,000 common shares, or $0.0400 per share.

Lowry's controller wants to calculate the amount of diluted earnings per share. To do so, he follows these steps:

1. *Calculate the number of shares that would have been issued at the market price.* Thus, he multiplies the 300,000 options by the average exercise price of $10 to arrive at a total of $3,000,000 paid to exercise the options by their holders.
2. *Divide the amount paid to exercise the options by the market price to determine the number of shares that could be purchased.* Thus, he divides the $3,000,000 paid to exercise the options by the $12 average market price to arrive at 250,000 shares that could have been purchased with the proceeds from the options.
3. *Subtract the number of shares that could have been purchased from the number of options exercised.* Thus, he subtracts the 250,000 shares potentially purchased from the 300,000 options to arrive at a difference of 50,000 shares.
4. *Add the incremental number of shares to the shares already outstanding.* Thus, he adds the 50,000 incremental shares to the existing 5,000,000 to arrive at 5,050,000 diluted shares.

Based on this information, the controller arrives at diluted earnings per share of $0.0396, for which the calculation is:

$200,000 Net profit ÷ 5,050,000 Common shares

---

This method may also be used when a business has issued the following instruments:

- Nonvested stock granted to employees
- Stock purchase contracts
- Partially paid stock subscriptions

**Reverse Treasury Stock Method**

A business may be party to a contract that requires it to buy back its own stock from a shareholder. This type of arrangement is called a put option. If the effect of a put option is dilutive (which occurs when the exercise price is higher than the average market price in a reporting period), it must be included in the diluted earnings per share calculation. The calculation of the effect of a put option is measured using the reverse treasury stock method, which involves the following steps:

1. Assume that enough shares were issued by the company at the beginning of the period at the average market price to raise sufficient funds to satisfy the put option contract.
2. Assume that these proceeds are used to buy back the required number of shares.
3. Include in the denominator of the diluted earnings per share calculation the difference between the numbers of shares issued and purchased in steps 1 and 2.

---

**EXAMPLE**

A third party exercises a written put option that requires Armadillo Industries to repurchase 1,000 shares from the third party at an exercise price of $30. The current market price is $20. Armadillo uses the following steps to compute the impact of the written put option on its diluted earnings per share calculation:

1. Armadillo assumes that it has issued 1,500 shares at $20.
2. The company assumes that the "issuance" of 1,500 shares is used to meet the repurchase obligation of $30,000.
3. The difference between the 1,500 shares issued and the 1,000 shares repurchased is added to the denominator of Armadillo's diluted earnings per share calculation.

---

## Two-Class Method

There may be situations in which an entity issues securities with special features that are designed to attract investors, such as preferred stock that participates in the dividends issued to common stockholders. There may also be several classes of common stock that have different dividend rates. For example, the holders of certain preferred shares might receive a multiple of the dividends paid to common shareholders. There could also be a cap on the amount of these extra dividends. These special securities are called *participating securities*.

The two-class method is used to allocate earnings to participating securities, without requiring that basic or diluted earnings per share be presented for them if the securities are of a type other than common stock. One can report earnings per share for these participating securities that are not common stock, but it is not required.

The calculation methodology for the two-class method covers the following steps:

1. Reduce the amount of income from continuing operations by the dividends declared in the reporting period for each class of stock, and by the contractually-mandated dividends that must be paid for the current period.
2. Allocate the remaining earnings to common stock and the participating securities to the extent that the securities agreement allows for such a distribution.
3. Divide the amount allocated to each security by the number of outstanding shares of the security, to arrive at the earnings per share for the security.
4. Present basic and diluted earnings per share for each class of common stock.

It is possible that losses should also be allocated to a participating security if there is a contractual obligation for the security to share in the losses. This is considered to be the case when the holder is obligated to fund the losses of the issuer, or when the mandatory redemption amount of the security is reduced by the amount of the loss.

All participating securities are to be included in the calculation of basic earnings per share under this two-class method.

**EXAMPLE**

Sawtooth Corporation has the following capital structure:

- 100,000 shares of common stock
- 20,000 shares of Series A preferred stock

The Series A stock is entitled to a $2 annual dividend before any dividends are paid on the common stock. In addition, the Series A stock is to participate in any additional dividends on a 10:90 per-share ratio with common stock, once a $0.10 dividend has been paid on the common stock.

Sawtooth reports $200,000 of net income. In the period, the board of directors authorizes a total of $60,000 in dividends. The breakdown of payments is that Series A stockholders are paid $41,000 and the common stockholders are paid $19,000; these amounts are derived from the following table:

| Share Type | Number of Shares | | Base-Level Dividend | | Base-Level Aggregate Dividend | | Additional Dividend (90:10) | | Total Dividend | Per Share |
|---|---|---|---|---|---|---|---|---|---|---|
| Common | 100,000 | × | $0.10/share | = | $10,000 | + | $9,000 | = | $19,000 | $0.19 |
| Series A | 20,000 | × | $2.00/share | = | 40,000 | + | 1,000 | = | 41,000 | $2.05 |
| Totals | 120,000 | | | | $50,000 | | $10,000 | | $60,000 | |

Sawtooth calculates its undistributed earnings as follows:

| | | |
|---|---|---|
| Net income | | $200,000 |
| Less dividends paid: | | |
| Common | $19,000 | |
| Series A | 41,000 | |
| Undistributed earnings | | $140,000 |

Based on the 10:90 ratio at which the Series A stock participates in any additional undistributed earnings, the basic earnings per share amounts for the two types of stock are as follows:

| | Common Stock | Series A Preferred Stock |
|---|---|---|
| Distributed earnings | $0.19 | $2.05 |
| Undistributed earnings (1)(2) | 1.26 | 0.70 |
| Totals | $1.45 | $2.75 |

(1)  Undistributed earnings for common stock is calculated as: ($140,000 × 90%) ÷ 100,000 shares

(2)  Undistributed earnings for Series A stock is calculated as: ($140,000 × 10%) ÷ 20,000 shares

## Summary

It will have been evident from the discussions of earnings per share that the computation of diluted earnings per share can be quite complex if a business has a correspondingly complex equity structure. In such a situation, it is quite likely that diluted earnings per share will be incorrectly calculated. To improve the accuracy of the calculation, create an electronic spreadsheet that incorporates all of the necessary factors impacting diluted earnings per share. Further, save the calculation for each reporting period on a separate page of the spreadsheet; by doing so, there will be an excellent record of how these calculations were managed in the past.

## Review Questions

1. The profit or loss available to shares of common stock is known as:
   a. Basic earnings per share
   b. Diluted earnings per share
   c. Book value per share
   d. Dividend yield ratio

2. The following method is used to calculate the dilutive effects of a put option:
   a. Two-class method
   b. Treasury stock method
   c. Equity method
   d. Reverse treasury stock method

3. The following item is included in the numerator of the earnings per share calculation that is also included in the numerator for basic earnings per share:
   a. Profit or loss attributable to common equity holders
   b. Other changes
   c. Convertible preferred dividends
   d. After-tax interest on convertible debt

4. The basic earnings per share calculation should be adjusted for:
   a. All dilutive potential common shares
   b. After-tax interest on convertible debt
   c. Convertible preferred dividends
   d. The weighted average number of shares

5. The following is a type of dilutive security:
   a. Convertible bond
   b. Preferred stock
   c. Note payable
   d. Common stock

6. The basic principle underlying the calculation of diluted earnings per share is:
   a. To merge it with the basic earnings per share figure whenever possible
   b. To present an earnings figure that is rounded to the nearest dollar
   c. To properly display the impact of preferred stock on earnings per share
   d. To establish the worst case scenario to arrive at the smallest possible earnings per share

# Chapter 6
# Interim Reporting

## Introduction

If a company is publicly-held, the Securities and Exchange Commission (SEC) requires that the business file a variety of quarterly information on the Form 10-Q. This information is a reduced set of the requirements for the more comprehensive annual Form 10-K. The requirement to issue these additional financial statements may appear to be simple enough, but one must consider whether to report information assuming that quarterly results are stand-alone documents, or part of the full-year results of the business. This chapter discusses the disparities that these different viewpoints can cause in the financial statements, as well as how to report changes in accounting principle and estimate.

## Overview of Interim Reporting

A business will periodically create financial statements for shorter periods than the fiscal year, which are known as *interim periods*. The most common examples of interim periods are monthly or quarterly financial statements, though any period of less than a full fiscal year can be considered an interim period. The concepts related to interim periods are most commonly applicable to the financial statements of publicly-held companies, since they are required to issue quarterly financial statements that must be reviewed by their outside auditors; these financials must account for certain activities in a consistent manner, as well as prevent readers from being misled about the results of the business on an ongoing basis.

### General Interim Reporting Rule

The general rule for interim period reporting is that the same accounting principles and practices be applied to interim reports that are used for the preparation of annual financial statements. The following bullet points illustrate revenues and expenses that follow the general rule, and therefore do not change for interim reporting:

- *Revenue.* Revenue is recognized in the same manner that is used for annual reporting, with no exceptions.
- *Costs associated with revenue.* If a cost is typically assigned to a specific sale (such as cost of goods sold items), expense recognition is the same as is used for annual reporting.
- *Direct expenditures.* If an expense is incurred in a period and relates to that period, it is recorded as an expense in that period. An example is salaries expense.
- *Accruals for estimated expenditures.* If there is an estimated expenditure to be made at a later date but which relates to the current period, it is recorded as an expense in the current period. An example is accrued wages.
- *Depreciation and amortization.* If there is a fixed asset, depreciation (for tangible assets) or amortization (for intangible assets) is ratably charged to all periods in its useful life.

In addition, there are cases where a company is accustomed to only making a year-end adjustment, such as to its reserves for doubtful accounts, obsolete inventory, and/or warranty claims, as well as for year-end bonuses. Where possible, these adjustments should be made in the interim periods, thereby reducing the amount of any residual adjustments still required in the year-end financial statements.

## Variations from the Interim Reporting Rule

There are other cases in which the treatment of certain transactions will vary for interim periods. The following rules should be applied in these cases:

- *Expense allocation.* Non-product expenses should be allocated among interim periods based on time expired, usage, or benefits received. In most cases, this means that expenses will simply be charged to expense in the current period, with no allocation to other interim periods. However, it could result in spreading expense recognition over several months or quarters.
- *Arbitrary assignments.* It is not allowable to make arbitrary assignments of costs to certain interim periods.
- *Gains and losses.* Gains and losses that arise in an interim period shall be recognized at once, and not be deferred to any later interim periods.

---

**EXAMPLE**

Armadillo Industries incurs an annual property tax charge of $60,000. Also, Armadillo has historically earned an annual volume discount of $30,000 per year, based on its full-year purchases from a major supplier.

Since the property tax charge is applicable to all months in the year, the controller accrues a $5,000 monthly charge for this expense. Similarly, the volume discount relates back to volume purchases throughout the year, not just the last month of the year, in which the discount is retroactively awarded. Accordingly, the controller creates a monthly credit of $2,500 to reflect the expected year-end volume discount of $30,000.

---

The concepts of recognizing expenses are more thoroughly discussed in the next two sections, which address the integral view and the discrete view of how to handle interim expense recognition.

There are several specific areas in which the accounting for interim reporting can differ from what is used for annual reporting. In particular:

- *Estimated inventory.* It is acceptable to use the gross profit method or other methods (see the *Principles of Accounting* textbook) to estimate the cost of goods sold during interim periods. This is allowed in order to reduce the amount of time required to derive the cost of goods sold using a formal count of the ending inventory.
- *LIFO layers.* If a company uses the last in, first out (LIFO) method of calculating inventory (see the *Principles of Accounting* textbook), existing inventory cost layers may be liquidated during an interim period. If such a cost layer is expected to be replaced by the end of the fiscal year, the cost of sales for the interim period can include the expected replacement cost of that LIFO cost layer.
- *Lower of cost or market.* If there is a reduction in the market value of inventory, the difference between the market value and its cost should be charged to expense in an interim period (see the lower of cost or market rule in the *Principles of Accounting* textbook). However, it is allowable to offset the full amount of these losses with any market value gains in subsequent periods within the same fiscal year on the same inventory items. Alternatively, it is allowable to avoid recognizing these losses in an interim period if there are seasonal price fluctuations that are expected to result in an offsetting increase in market prices by the end of the year.
- *Purchase price and volume variances.* If a company uses a standard costing system to assign costs to its inventory items, it is acceptable to defer the recognition of any variances from standard cost in interim periods, if it has already been planned that these variances will have been absorbed by the end of the fiscal year. However, if there are unexpected purchase price or volume variances, recognize them in the interim period in which they occur.

---

**EXAMPLE**

Pianoforte International writes down the value of its mahogany wood holdings, due to a crash in world mahogany prices. The amount of the first-quarter write down is $100,000. By year-end, the market price has stabilized at a higher level, allowing Pianoforte to reverse $62,000 of the original write down and report the change in its fiscal year-end results.

---

## Changes in Accounting Principle in Interim Periods

An accounting principle is an acceptable method for recording and reporting an accounting transaction. There is a change in accounting principle when:

- There are several accounting principles that apply to a situation, and the entity switches to a principle that has not been used in the past; or
- When the accounting principle that formerly applied to the situation is no longer generally accepted; or
- There is a change in the method of applying the principle.

Only change an accounting principle when doing so is required by GAAP, or one can justify that it is preferable to use the new principle. If the election is made to proceed with a change in accounting principle, apply it retrospectively to all prior periods, including all interim reporting, unless it is impractical to do so. To complete a retrospective application of a change in accounting principle, follow these steps:

1. Include the cumulative effect of the change on periods prior to those presented in the carrying amount of assets and liabilities as of the beginning of the first period in which financial statements are being presented; and
2. Enter an offsetting amount in the beginning retained earnings balance of the first period in which financial statements are being presented; and
3. Adjust all presented financial statements to reflect the change to the new accounting principle.

From a reporting perspective, a change in accounting principle requires disclosure of the change in principle from those applied in the comparable interim period of the prior annual period, as well as the preceding interim periods in the current fiscal year, and in the annual report for the prior fiscal year.

## Changes in Accounting Estimate in Interim Periods

There is a change in accounting estimate when there is a change that affects the carrying amount of an existing asset or liability, or that alters the subsequent accounting for existing or future assets or liabilities. A change in estimate arises from the appearance of new information that alters the existing situation.

Changes in estimate are a normal part of accounting, and an expected part of the ongoing process of reviewing the current status and future benefits and obligations related to assets and liabilities. All of the following are situations where there is likely to be a change in accounting estimate:

- Allowance for doubtful accounts
- Reserve for obsolete inventory
- Changes in the useful life of depreciable assets
- Changes in the salvage values of depreciable assets
- Changes in the amount of expected warranty obligations
- Changes in the estimated effective annual tax rate

When there is a change in estimate, always account for it in the period of change. There is *no* need to restate earlier financial statements; thus, there is no need to restate any prior-period interim reporting. There should be disclosure in the current and subsequent interim periods of the effect on earnings of the change in estimate, if material in relation to any of the reporting periods presented. This disclosure should continue to be made for as long as necessary, to avoid any misleading comparisons between periods.

> **Best Practice:** Where possible, adopt accounting changes during the first interim period of a fiscal year. Doing so eliminates any comparability problems between the interim periods for the remainder of the fiscal year.

## Error Correction in Interim Periods

When determining the materiality of an error, relate the amount to the estimated profit for the entire fiscal year and the effect on the earnings trend, rather than for the current interim period. Otherwise, a disproportionate number of error corrections will be separately reported within the financial statements.

If an error correction is considered material at the interim period level but not for the full fiscal year, disclose the error in the interim report.

---

**EXAMPLE**

Armadillo Industries has profits of $1,000,000 in its first quarter, and expects to generate $4,000,000 of profits for the entire fiscal year. The company has historically considered materiality to be 5% of its profits. In the first quarter, the accounting department uncovers a $100,000 error. Though this amount is 10% of first-quarter profits, it is only 2.5% of full-year expected profits. Given the minimal impact on full-year profits, Armadillo does not have to segregate this information for reporting purposes in its first quarter interim reporting, though it must still disclose the information.

---

## Adjustments to Prior Interim Periods

If an item impacting a company's profits occurs during an interim period other than the first interim period of the fiscal year, and some portion or all of it is an adjustment relating to a prior interim period of the current fiscal year, report the item as follows:

- Include that portion of the item that relates to the current interim period in the results of the current interim period
- Restate the results of prior interim periods to include that portion of the item relating to each interim period
- If there are any portions of the item relating to activities in prior fiscal years, include the change in a restatement of the first interim period of the current fiscal year

## The Integral View

Under the integral view of producing interim reports, assume that the results reported in interim financial statements are an integral part of the full-year financial results (hence the name of this concept). This viewpoint produces the following accounting issues:

- *Accrue expenses not arising in the period.* If an expense will be paid later in the year that is incurred at least partially in the reporting period, accrue some portion of the expense in the reporting period. Here are several examples:
    - *Advertising.* If advertising is paid for in advance that is scheduled to occur over multiple time periods, recognize the expense over the entire range of time periods. Also, if there are clear benefits from an initial advertising expenditure that extend beyond the interim period in which the expenditure was made, expense recognition can be deferred to later periods (this concept may be difficult to prove to the auditors).

- o *Bonuses*. If there are bonus plans that may result in bonus payments later in the year, accrue the expense in all accounting periods. Only accrue this expense if it is possible to reasonably estimate the amount of the bonus, which may not always be possible during the earlier months covered by a performance contract.
- o *Contingencies*. If there are contingent liabilities that will be resolved later in the year, and which are both probable and reasonably estimated, then accrue the related expense.
- o *Profit sharing*. If employees are paid a percentage of company profits at year-end, and the amount can be reasonably estimated, then accrue the expense throughout the year as a proportion of the profits recognized in each period.
- o *Property taxes*. A local government entity issues an invoice to the company at some point during the year for property taxes. These taxes are intended to cover the entire year, so accrue a portion of the expense in each reporting period.

**EXAMPLE**

The board of directors of Lowry Locomotion approves a senior management bonus plan for the upcoming year that could potentially pay the senior management team a maximum of $240,000. It initially seems probable that the full amount will be paid, but by the third quarter it appears more likely that the maximum amount to be paid will be $180,000. In addition, the company pays $60,000 in advance for a full year of advertising in *Locomotive Times* magazine. Lowry recognizes these expenses as follows:

|  | Quarter 1 | Quarter 2 | Quarter 3 | Quarter 4 | Full Year |
|---|---|---|---|---|---|
| Bonus expense | $60,000 | $60,000 | $30,000 | $30,000 | $180,000 |
| Advertising | 15,000 | 15,000 | 15,000 | 15,000 | 60,000 |

The accounting staff spreads the recognition of the full amount of the projected bonus over the year, but then reduces its recognition of the remaining expense starting in the third quarter, to adjust for the lowered bonus payout expectation.

The accounting staff initially records the $60,000 advertising expense as a prepaid expense, and recognizes it ratably over all four quarters of the year, which matches the time period over which the related advertisements are run by *Locomotive Times*.

One problem with the integral view is that it tends to result in a significant number of expense accruals. Since these accruals are usually based on estimates, it is entirely possible that adjustments should be made to the accruals later in the year, as the company obtains more precise information about the expenses that are being accrued. Some of these adjustments could be substantial, and may materially affect the reported results in later periods.

## The Discrete View

Under the discrete view of producing interim reports, assume that the results reported for a specific interim period are *not* associated with the revenues and expenses arising during other reporting periods. Under this view, record the entire impact of a transaction within the reporting period, rather than ratably over the entire year. The following are examples of the situations that can arise under the discrete method:

- *Reduced accruals*. A substantially smaller number of accruals are likely under the discrete method, since the assumption is that one should not anticipate the recordation of transactions that have not yet arisen.

- *Gains and losses.* Do not spread the recognition of a gain or loss across multiple periods. If this were to be done, it would allow a company to spread a loss over multiple periods, thereby making the loss look smaller on a per-period basis than it really is.

## Comparison of the Integral and Discrete Views

The integral view is clearly the better method from a theoretical perspective, since the causes of some transactions can span an entire year. For example, a manager may be awarded a bonus at the end of December, but he probably had to achieve specific results throughout the year to earn it. Otherwise, if a business were to adopt the discrete view, interim reporting would yield exceedingly varied results, with some periods revealing inordinately high or low profitability.

However, consider adopting the integral view from the perspective of accounting efficiency; that is, it is very time-consuming to maintain a mass of revenue and expense accruals, their ongoing adjustments, and documentation of the reasons for them throughout a year. Instead, use the integral view only for the more material transactions that are anticipated, and use the discrete view for smaller transactions. Thus, the accountant could accrue the expense for property taxes throughout the year if the amount is significant, or simply record it in the month when the invoice is received, if the amount is small.

## Summary

When creating interim financial reports, judiciously apply the integral and discrete views to the statements – that is, the integral method is more accurate, but the discrete view is more efficient; and a key factor in closing the books for an interim period is that there is less time than usual in which to complete all closing activities. In short, restrict the integral view to material transactions, and apply the discrete view to all other transactions.

## Review Questions

1. Expenses not paid for in an interim reporting period should be accrued under the:
    a. Cash basis of accounting
    b. Discrete view of interim reporting
    c. Single entry method
    d. Integral view of interim reporting

2. Under the integral view, the proper treatment of contingencies is:
    a. To accrue them at once
    b. To accrue them only if the amounts are probable and reasonably estimated
    c. To not accrue them
    d. To spread the expense recognition over the remainder of the year

3. Under the integral view, the assumption is that the results reported in an interim period:
    a. Are not related to the full-year financial results
    b. May require different segment reporting
    c. Can be revised later in the year
    d. Are an integral part of the full-year financial results

4. The integral view holds that the accountant should:
    a. Use the income tax relevant to the results of a specific reporting period
    b. Use the expected tax rate for the entire year in every reporting period
    c. Use no tax rate until year-end, and then accrue the tax expense
    d. Apply the historical average tax rate to each reporting period

5. Under the discrete view of interim reporting:
    a. We assume that the results reported for a specific interim period are not associated with other periods
    b. Gains or losses are recognized pro rata across all interim periods in the year
    c. There are an increased number of accruals
    d. The average expected tax rate for the full year is used in each individual interim period

# Chapter 7
# Segment Reporting

## Introduction

If a company is publicly-held, it needs to report segment information, which is part of the disclosures attached to the financial statements. This information is needed to give the readers of the financial statements more insights into the operations and prospects of a business, as well as to allow them to make more informed judgments about a public entity as a whole. In this chapter, we describe how to determine which business segments to report separately, and how to report that information.

## Overview of Segment Reporting

An operating segment is a component of a public entity, and which possesses the following characteristics:

- *Business activities.* It has business activities that can generate revenues and cause expenses to be incurred. This can include revenues and expenses generated by transactions with other operating segments of the same public entity. It can also include activities that do not yet include revenues, such as a start-up business.
- *Results reviewed.* The chief operating decision maker of the public entity regularly reviews its operating results, with the intent of assessing its performance and making decisions about allocating resources to it.
- *Financial results.* Financial results specific to it are available.

Generally, an operating segment has a manager who is accountable to the chief operating decision maker, and who maintains regular contact with that person, though it is also possible that the chief operating decision maker directly manages one or more operating segments.

If a company has a matrix form of organization, where some managers are responsible for geographic regions and others are responsible for products and services, the results of the products and services are considered to be operating segments.

Some parts of a business are not considered to be reportable business segments under the following circumstances:

- *Corporate overhead.* The corporate group does not usually earn outside revenues, and so is not considered a segment.
- *Post-retirement benefit plans.* A benefit plan can earn income from investments, but it has no operating activities, and so is not considered a segment.
- *One-time events.* If an otherwise-insignificant segment has a one-time event that boosts it into the ranks of reportable segments, do not report it, since there is no long-term expectation for it to remain a reportable segment.

The primary issue with segment reporting is determining which business segments to report. The rules for this selection process are quite specific. Report segment information if a business segment passes any one of the following three tests:

1. *Revenue.* The revenue of the segment is at least 10% of the consolidated revenue of the entire business; or
2. *Profit or loss.* The absolute amount of the profit or loss of the segment is at least 10% of the greater of the combined profits of all the operating segments reporting a profit, or of the combined losses

of all operating segments reporting a loss (see the following example for a demonstration of this concept); or

3. *Assets.* The assets of the segment are at least 10% of the combined assets of all the operating segments of the business.

If the preceding tests are run and the accountant arrives at a group of reportable segments whose combined revenues are not at least 75% of the consolidated revenue of the entire business, then add more segments until the 75% threshold is surpassed.

If there is a business segment that used to qualify as a reportable segment and does not currently qualify, but for which there is an expectation of qualification in the future, continue to treat it as a reportable segment.

If there are operating segments that have similar economic characteristics, their results can be aggregated into a single operating segment, but only if they are similar in all of the following areas:

- The nature of their products and services
- The nature of their systems of production
- The nature of their regulatory environments (if applicable)
- Their types of customers
- Their distribution systems

The number of restrictions on this type of reporting makes it unlikely that one would be able to aggregate reportable segments.

After all of the segment testing has been completed, it is possible that there will be a few residual segments that do not qualify for separate reporting. If so, combine the information for these segments into an "other" category and include it in the segment report for the entity. Be sure to describe the sources of revenue included in this "other" category.

Finally, if an operating segment does not meet any of the preceding criteria, it can still be treated as a reportable segment if management decides that information about the segment may be of use to readers of the company's financial statements.

---

**Best Practice:** The variety of methods available for segment testing makes it possible that there will be quite a large number of reportable segments. If so, it can be burdensome to create a report for so many segments, and it may be confusing for the readers of the company's financial statements. Consequently, consider limiting the number of reportable segments to ten; aggregate the information for additional segments for reporting purposes.

---

**EXAMPLE**

Lowry Locomotion has six business segments whose results it reports internally. Lowry's accountant needs to test the various segments to see which ones qualify as being reportable. He collects the following information:

| Segment | (000s) Revenue | (000s) Profit | (000s) Loss | (000s) Assets |
|---|---|---|---|---|
| Diesel locomotives | $120,000 | $10,000 | $-- | $320,000 |
| Electric locomotives | 85,000 | 8,000 | -- | 180,000 |
| Maglev cars | 29,000 | -- | -21,000 | 90,000 |
| Passenger cars | 200,000 | 32,000 | | 500,000 |
| Toy trains | 15,000 | -- | -4,000 | 4,000 |
| Trolley cars | 62,000 | -- | -11,000 | 55,000 |
| | $511,000 | $50,000 | -$36,000 | $1,149,000 |

In the table, the total profit exceeds the total loss, so the controller uses the total profit for the 10% profit test. The controller then lists the same table again, but now with the losses column removed and with test thresholds at the top of the table that are used to determine which segments are reported. An "X" mark below a test threshold indicates that a segment is reportable. In addition, the controller adds a new column on the right side of the table, which is used to calculate the total revenue for the reportable segments.

| Segment | (000s) Revenue | (000s) Profit | (000s) Assets | 75% Revenue Test |
|---|---|---|---|---|
| **Reportable threshold (10%)** | **$51,100** | **$5,000** | **$114,900** | |
| Diesel locomotives | X | X | X | $120,000 |
| Electric locomotives | X | X | X | 85,000 |
| Maglev cars | | | | |
| Passenger cars | X | X | X | 200,000 |
| Toy trains | | | | |
| Trolley cars | X | | | 62,000 |
| | | | Total | $467,000 |

This analysis shows that the diesel locomotive, electric locomotive, passenger car, and trolley car segments are reportable, and that the combined revenue of these reportable segments easily exceeds the 75% reporting threshold. Consequently, the company does not need to separately report information for any additional segments.

## Segment Disclosure

This section contains the disclosures for various aspects of segment reporting that are required under GAAP. At the end of each set of requirements is a sample disclosure containing the more common elements of the requirements.

### Segment Disclosure

The key requirement of segment reporting is that the revenue, profit or loss, and assets of each segment be separately reported for any period for which an income statement is presented. In addition, reconcile this segment information back to the company's consolidated results, which requires the inclusion of any adjusting items. Also disclose the methods by which the determination was made for which segments to report. The essential information to include in a segment report includes:

- The types of products and services sold by each segment
- The basis of organization (such as by geographic region or product line)
- Revenues from external customers
- Revenues from inter-company transactions
- Interest income
- Interest expense
- Depreciation, depletion, and amortization expense
- Material expense items
- Income tax expense or income
- Other material non-cash items
- Profit or loss

If an operating segment only has minimal financial operations, it is not necessary to report any information about interest income or interest expense.

The following two items must also be reported if they are included in the determination of segment assets, or are routinely provided to the chief operating decision maker:

- Equity method interests in other entities.
- The total expenditure for additions to fixed assets. Expenditures for most other long-term assets are excluded from this requirement.

The preceding disclosures should be presented along with the reconciliations that appear in the following exhibit, which should be separately identified and described

**Segment Reconciliations**

| Category | Reconciliation |
|---|---|
| Revenues | Total company revenues to reportable segment revenues |
| Profit or loss | Total consolidated income before income taxes, and discontinued operations to reportable segment profit or loss |
| Assets | Consolidated assets to reportable segment assets |
| Other items | Consolidated amounts to reportable segment amounts for every other significant item of disclosed segment information |

If an operating segment qualifies for the first time as being reportable, also report the usual segment information for it in any prior period segment data that may be presented for comparison purposes, even if the segment was not reportable in the prior period. An exemption is allowed for this prior period reporting if the required information is not available, or if it would be excessively expensive to collect the information.

The operating segment information reported should be the same information reported to the chief operating decision maker for purposes of assessing segment performance and allocating resources. This may result in a difference between the information reported at the segment level and in the public entity's consolidated financial results. If so, disclose the differences between the two figures. This may include a discussion of any policies for the allocation of costs that have been centrally incurred, or the allocation of jointly-used assets.

The following additional items should also be included in the disclosure of operating segment information:

- The basis of accounting for any inter-segment transactions.
- Any changes in the methods used to measure segment profit or loss from the prior period, and the effect of those changes on the reported amount of segment profit or loss.
- A discussion of any asymmetrical allocations, such as the allocation of depreciation expense to a segment without a corresponding allocation of assets.

If a business is reporting condensed financial statements for interim periods, it must disclose the following information for each reportable segment:

- Revenues from external customers for the current quarter and year-to-date, with comparable information for the preceding year
- Revenues from inter-company transactions for the current quarter and year-to-date, with comparable information for the preceding year
- Profit or loss for the current quarter and year-to-date, with comparable information for the preceding year
- Total assets for which there has been a material change from the last annual disclosure
- A description of any differences in the basis of segmentation from the last annual disclosure, or in the method of measuring segment profit or loss
- A reconciliation of the aggregate segment profit or loss to the consolidated income before income taxes, and discontinued operations for the public company

If a public entity alters its internal structure to such an extent that the composition of its operating segments is changed, restate its reported results for earlier periods, as well as interim periods, to match the results and financial position of the new internal structure.

---

**EXAMPLE**

The accountant of Lowry Locomotion produces the following segment report for the segments identified in the preceding example:

| (000s) | Diesel | Electric | Passenger | Trolley | Other | Consolidated |
|---|---|---|---|---|---|---|
| Revenues | $120,000 | $85,000 | $200,000 | $62,000 | $44,000 | $511,000 |
| Interest income | 11,000 | 8,000 | 28,000 | 8,000 | 2,000 | 57,000 |
| Interest expense | -- | -- | -- | 11,000 | 39,000 | 50,000 |
| Depreciation | 32,000 | 18,000 | 50,000 | 6,000 | 10,000 | 116,000 |
| Income taxes | 4,000 | 3,000 | 10,000 | -3,000 | -7,000 | 7,000 |
| Profit | 10,000 | 8,000 | 32,000 | -11,000 | -25,000 | 14,000 |
| Assets | 320,000 | 180,000 | 500,000 | 55,000 | 94,000 | 1,149,000 |

---

## Products, Services, and Customer Disclosure

A publicly-held entity must report the sales garnered from external customers for each product and service or group thereof, unless it is impracticable to compile this information.

The entity must also describe the extent of its reliance on its major customers. In particular, if revenues from a single customer exceed 10% of the entity's revenues, this fact must be disclosed, along with the total revenues garnered from each of these customers and the names of the segments in which these revenues were earned.

It is not necessary to disclose the name of a major customer.

If there is a group of customers under common control (such as different departments of the federal government), the revenues from this group should be reported in aggregate as though the revenues were generated from a single customer.

---

**EXAMPLE**

Armadillo Industries reports the following information about its major customers:

Revenues from one customer of Armadillo's home security segment represented approximately 12% of the company's consolidated revenues in 20X2, and 11% of consolidated revenues in 20X1.

---

## Geographic Area Disclosure

A publicly-held entity must disclose the following geographic information, unless it is impracticable to compile:

- *Revenues*. All revenues generated from external customers, and attributable to the entity's home country, and all revenues attributable to foreign countries. Foreign-country revenues by individual country shall be stated if these country-level sales are material. There must also be disclosure of the basis under which revenues are attributed to individual countries.
- *Assets*. All long-lived assets (for which the definition essentially restricts reporting to fixed assets) that are attributable to the entity's home country, and all such assets attributable to foreign countries. Foreign-country assets by individual country shall be stated if these assets are material.

It is also acceptable to include in this reporting subtotals of geographic information by groups of countries.

Geographic area reporting is waived if providing it is impracticable. If so, the entity must disclose the fact.

---

**EXAMPLE**

Armadillo Industries reports the following geographic information about its operations:

|  | Revenues | Long-Lived Assets |
| --- | --- | --- |
| United States | $27,000,000 | $13,000,000 |
| Mexico | 23,000,000 | 11,000,000 |
| Chile | 14,000,000 | 7,000,000 |
| Other foreign countries | 8,000,000 | 2,000,000 |
| Total | $72,000,000 | $33,000,000 |

---

## Summary

The determination of whether a business has segments is, to a large extent, based upon whether information is tracked internally at the segment level. Thus, if a company's accounting systems are sufficiently primitive, or if management is sufficiently disinterested to not review information about business segments, it is entirely possible that even a publicly-held company will have no reportable business segments.

If there *are* a number of reportable segments, consider using the report writing software in the accounting system to create a standard report that automatically generates the entire segment report for the disclosures. By using this approach, no time will be wasted manually compiling the information, and the accounting staff will avoid running the risk of making a mistake while doing so. However, if the reportable segments change over time, modify the report structure to match the new group of segments.

## Review Questions

1. If there is a segment that no longer qualifies, but which did so in the past and should qualify in the future, the accountant should:
    a. Aggregate its results with those of a reportable segment
    b. Continue to treat it as a reportable segment
    c. Remove it from the segment reporting in prior periods
    d. Ignore it for current period reporting purposes

2. The segment test for revenue states that:
    a. All segments with reportable revenue be listed as a segment
    b. Revenue should be imputed for service centers at the market rate of their services
    c. The revenue of the segment is at least 10% of the consolidated revenue of the entire business
    d. Transfer prices be considered in the determination of revenue

3. If segment tests do not yield a group of segments whose combined revenues are not at least 75% of the business, the accountant should:
    a. Add more segments until the 75% threshold is surpassed
    b. Proceed with no further changes to the group of selected segments
    c. Run the calculations again for the preceding year
    d. Include all segments in segment reporting

# Chapter 8
# Goodwill

## Introduction

A business may record goodwill as part of a business combination, to account for the difference between the fair value of all other assets and liabilities and the purchase price. The initial recognition of goodwill is addressed in the Business Combinations and Consolidations chapter. In this chapter, we deal with the subsequent accounting for goodwill.

> **Related Podcast Episodes:** Episodes 136, 146, and 175 of the Accounting Best Practices Podcast discuss goodwill impairment testing, intangible asset impairment testing, and goodwill amortization, respectively. They are available at: **www.accountingtools.com/podcasts** or **iTunes**

## Goodwill

Goodwill is a common byproduct of a business combination, where the purchase price paid for the acquiree is higher than the fair values of the identifiable assets acquired. After goodwill has initially been recorded as an asset, do not amortize it. Instead, test it for impairment at the reporting unit level. Impairment exists when the carrying amount of the goodwill is greater than its implied fair value.

A reporting unit is defined as an operating segment or one level below an operating segment. At a more practical level, a reporting unit is a separate business for which the parent compiles financial information, and for which management reviews the results. If several components of an operating segment have similar economic characteristics, they can be combined into a reporting unit. In a smaller business, it is entirely possible that one reporting unit could be an entire operating segment, or even the entire entity.

The examination of goodwill for the possible existence of impairment involves a multi-step process, which is:

1. *Assess qualitative factors*. Review the situation to see if it is necessary to conduct further impairment testing, which is considered to be a likelihood of more than 50% that impairment has occurred, based on an assessment of relevant events and circumstances. Examples of relevant events and circumstances that make it more likely that impairment is present are the deterioration of macroeconomic conditions, increased costs, declining cash flows, possible bankruptcy, a change in management, and a sustained decrease in share price. If impairment appears to be likely, continue with the impairment testing process. The accountant can choose to bypass this step and proceed straight to the next step.
2. *Identify potential impairment*. Compare the fair value of the reporting unit to its carrying amount. If the fair value is greater than the carrying amount of the reporting unit, there is no goodwill impairment, and there is no need to proceed to the next step. If the carrying amount exceeds the fair value of the reporting unit, recognize an impairment loss in the amount of the difference, up to a maximum of the entire carrying amount (i.e., the carrying amount of goodwill can only be reduced to zero).

These steps are illustrated in the following flowchart.

## Goodwill Impairment Decision Steps

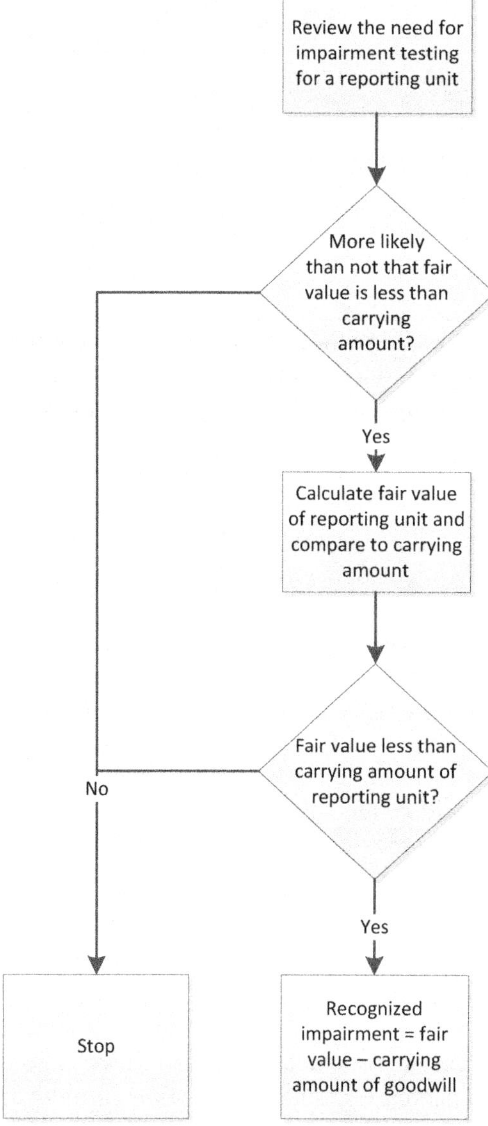


The fair value of the reporting unit is assumed to be the price that the company would receive if it were to sell the unit in an orderly transaction (i.e., not a rushed sale) between market participants. Other alternatives to the quoted market price for a reporting unit may be acceptable, such as a valuation based on multiples of earnings or revenue.

The following additional issues are associated with goodwill impairment testing:

- *Asset and liability assignment.* Assign acquired assets and liabilities to a reporting unit if they relate to the operations of the unit *and* they will be considered in the determination of reporting unit fair value. If these criteria can be met, even corporate-level assets and liabilities can be assigned to a reporting unit. If some assets and liabilities could be assigned to multiple reporting units, assign them in a reasonable manner (such as an allocation based on the relative fair values of the reporting units), consistently applied.

- *Asset recognition.* It is not allowable to recognize an additional intangible asset as part of the process of evaluating goodwill impairment.
- *Impairment estimation.* If it is probable that there is goodwill impairment and the amount can be reasonably estimated, despite the testing process not being complete when financial statements are issued, recognize the estimated amount of the impairment. The estimate should be adjusted to the final impairment amount in the following reporting period.
- *No reversal.* Once impairment of goodwill has been recorded, it cannot be reversed, even if the condition originally causing the impairment is no longer present.
- *Reporting unit disposal.* If a reporting unit is disposed of, include the goodwill associated with that unit in determining any gain or loss on the transaction. If only a portion of a reporting unit is disposed of, associate some of the goodwill linked to the reporting unit to the portion being disposed of, based on the relative fair values of the portions being disposed of and retained. Then test the remaining amount of goodwill assigned to the residual portion of the reporting unit for impairment.

---

**EXAMPLE**

Armadillo Industries is selling off a portion of a reporting unit for $500,000. The remaining portion of the unit, which Armadillo is retaining, has a fair value of $1,500,000. Based on these values, 25% of the goodwill associated with the reporting unit should be included in the carrying amount of the portion being sold.

---

- *Subsidiary goodwill impairment testing.* Any goodwill recognized by a corporate subsidiary should be dealt with in the same manner described elsewhere in this section for the impairment of goodwill. If there is a goodwill impairment loss at the subsidiary level, then also test the reporting unit of which that subsidiary is a part for goodwill impairment, if the triggering event is more likely than not to have also reduced the fair value of that reporting unit below its carrying amount.

> **Best Practice:** From a practical perspective, it is almost always easier to estimate the fair value of the reporting unit based on a multiple of its earnings or revenues, though this should only be done when there are comparable operations whose fair values and related multiples are known, and which can therefore be used as the basis for a fair value estimate of the reporting unit.

Impairment testing is to be conducted at annual intervals. The impairment test may be conducted at any time of the year, provided that the test is conducted thereafter at the same time of the year. If the company is comprised of different reporting units, there is no need to test them all at the same time.

> **Best Practice:** Each reporting unit is probably subject to a certain amount of seasonal activity. If so, select a period when activity levels are at their lowest to conduct impairment testing, so it does not conflict with other activities. Impairment testing should not coincide with the annual audit.

It may be necessary to conduct more frequent impairment testing if there is an event that makes it more likely than not that the fair value of a reporting unit has been reduced below its carrying amount. Examples of triggering events are a lawsuit, regulatory changes, the loss of key employees, and the expectation that a reporting unit will be sold.[4]

The information used for an impairment test can be quite detailed. To improve the efficiency of the testing process, it is permissible to carry forward this information to the next year, as long as the following criteria have been met:

---

[4] A private company or nonprofit entity that elects to do so is not required to monitor for goodwill impairment triggering events during the reporting period. Instead, it can do so at the end of each reporting period.

- There has been no significant change in the assets and liabilities comprising the reporting unit.
- There was a substantial excess of fair value over the carrying amount in the last impairment test.
- The likelihood of the fair value being less than the carrying amount is remote.

As an additional note for publicly-held companies that report segment information, the asset, liability, and goodwill allocations used for goodwill impairment testing do not have to be the same as the amounts stated in segment reports. However, aligning the two sets of information will make it easier to conduct both impairment testing and segment reporting.

## Goodwill Amortization

The effort required to monitor the goodwill asset is considered to be excessive for private companies, while the usefulness of goodwill information is also considered to be limited. Consequently, a private company is allowed to amortize goodwill on a straight-line basis over a ten-year useful life. The entity may amortize goodwill over a shorter period if it can demonstrate that a shorter useful life is more appropriate. If an organization chooses to amortize goodwill, it must still test the goodwill asset for impairment at either the entity or reporting unit level. This test is triggered when there is an event that indicates a possible decline in the entity's or reporting unit's fair value to a point below its carrying amount. If an impairment loss is recognized, then any remaining carrying amount is to be amortized over its remaining useful life.

The amortization of goodwill will eventually reduce the carrying amount of an organization's goodwill asset so much that goodwill impairment will be quite unlikely, thereby reducing the need to spend time on such testing.

## Summary

The testing for goodwill impairment can be both time-consuming and expensive, so take full advantage of the option to avoid testing by reviewing qualitative factors to see if there is a low likelihood of impairment. Also, a private company should make full use of the goodwill amortization option in order to minimize the risk of incurring a goodwill amortization charge at some point in the future.

## Review Questions

1. Goodwill impairment exists when:
   a. The gross amount of the goodwill is greater than its fair value
   b. The acquirer pays more for an acquisition than the fair value of the tangible assets of the ac-
      quiree
   c. The carrying amount of the goodwill is less than its fair value
   d. The carrying amount of the goodwill is greater than its fair value

2. Once goodwill impairment has been recognized:
   a. The impairment can only be reversed if the reversal is for an immaterial amount
   b. The impairment cannot be reversed
   c. The impairment can only be reversed by a publicly-held company
   d. The impairment can be reversed only within the same reporting year

3. When a reporting unit is disposed of:
   a. Recognize any additional intangible assets associated with the reporting unit
   b. Assume all goodwill associated with it has been impaired
   c. Do not allocate goodwill to that unit
   d. Include the goodwill associated with that unit in determining the gain or loss

4. Impairment testing is to be conducted:
   a. On a quarterly basis
   b. On an annual basis
   c. At random intervals
   d. When a company goes public

# Chapter 9
# Asset Retirement and Environmental Obligations

## Introduction

An asset retirement obligation (ARO) is a liability associated with the retirement of a fixed asset, such as a legal requirement to return a site to its previous condition. The concept of an ARO is dealt with in detail within GAAP. An example near the end of the chapter illustrates many of the concepts noted below. In addition, this chapter addresses when to record a liability associated with an environmental obligation, how to determine the amount of the liability and the types of costs that should be included in it.

## Overview of Asset Retirement Obligations

A company usually incurs an ARO due to a legal obligation. It may also incur an ARO if a company promises a third party (even the public at large) that it will engage in ARO activities; the circumstances of this promise will drive the determination of whether there is an actual liability. This liability may exist even if there has been no formal action against the company. When making the determination of liability, base the evaluation on current laws, not on projections of what laws there may be in the future, when the asset retirement occurs.

---

**EXAMPLE**

Glow Atomic operates an atomic power generation facility, and is required by law to bring the property back to its original condition when the plant is eventually decertified. The company has come under some pressure by various environmental organizations to take the remediation one step further and create a public park on the premises. Because of the significant negative publicity generated by these groups, the company issues a press release in which it commits to create the park. There is no legal requirement for the company to incur this additional expense, so the company's legal counsel should evaluate the facts to determine if there is a legal obligation.

---

A business should recognize the fair value of an ARO when it incurs the liability, and if it can make a reasonable estimate of the fair value of the ARO.

---

**EXAMPLE**

Glow Atomic has completed the construction of an atomic power generation facility, but has not yet taken delivery of fuel rods or undergone certification tests. It will incur an ARO for decontamination, but since it has not yet begun operations, it has not begun to contaminate, and therefore should not yet record an ARO liability.

---

If a fair value is not initially obtainable, recognize the ARO at a later date, when the fair value becomes available. If a company acquires a fixed asset to which an ARO is attached, recognize a liability for the ARO as of the fixed asset acquisition date.

If there is not sufficient information available to reasonably estimate the fair value of an ARO, it may be possible to use an expected present value technique that assigns probabilities to cash flows, thereby creating an estimate of the fair value of the ARO. Use an expected present value technique under either of the following scenarios:

- Other parties have specified the settlement date and method of settlement, so that the only uncertainty is whether the obligation will be enforced.

- There is information available from which to estimate the range of possible settlement dates and possible methods of settlement, as well as the probabilities associated with them.

Examples of the sources from which to obtain the information needed for the preceding estimation requirements are past practice within the company, industry practice, the stated intentions of management, or the estimated useful life of the asset (which indicates a likely ARO settlement date at the end of the useful life).

If there is an unambiguous requirement that causes an ARO, but there is a low likelihood of a performance requirement, a liability must still be recognized. When a low probability of performance is incorporated into the expected present value calculation for the ARO liability, this will likely reduce the amount of the ARO to be recognized. Even if there has been a history of non-enforcement of prior AROs for which there was an unambiguous obligation, do not defer the recognition of a liability.

## The Initial Measurement of an Asset Retirement Obligation

In most cases, the only way to determine the fair value of an ARO is to use an expected present value technique. When constructing an expected present value of future cash flows, incorporate the following points into the calculation:

- *Discount rate.* Use a credit-adjusted risk-free rate to discount cash flows to their present value. Thus, the credit standing of a business may impact the discount rate used.
- *Probability distribution.* When calculating the expected present value of an ARO, and there are only two possible outcomes, assign a 50 percent probability to each one until there is additional information that alters the initial probability distribution. Otherwise, spread the probability across the full set of possible scenarios.

---

**EXAMPLE**

Glow Atomic is compiling the cost of a decontamination ARO several years in the future. It is uncertain of the cost, since supplier fees fluctuate considerably. It arrives at an expected weighted average cash flow based on the following probability analysis:

| Cash Flow Estimates | Probability Assessment | Expected Cash Flows |
|---|---|---|
| $12,500,000 | 10% | $1,250,000 |
| 15,000,000 | 15% | 2,250,000 |
| 16,000,000 | 50% | 8,000,000 |
| 22,500,000 | 25% | 5,625,000 |
| | Weighted average cash flows | $17,125,000 |

---

Follow these steps in calculating the expected present value of an ARO:

1. Estimate the timing and amount of the cash flows associated with the retirement activities.
2. Determine the credit-adjusted risk-free rate.
3. Recognize any period-to-period increase in the carrying amount of the ARO liability as *accretion expense.* To do so, multiply the beginning liability by the credit-adjusted risk-free rate derived when the liability was first measured.
4. Recognize upward liability revisions as a new liability layer, and discount them at the current credit-adjusted risk-free rate.
5. Recognize downward liability revisions by reducing the appropriate liability layer, and discount the reduction at the rate used for the initial recognition of the related liability layer.

When an ARO liability is initially recognized, also capitalize the related asset retirement cost by adding it to the carrying amount of the related fixed asset.

## Subsequent Measurement of an Asset Retirement Obligation

It is possible that an ARO liability will not remain static over the life of the related fixed asset. Instead, the liability may change over time. If the liability increases, consider the incremental increase in each period to be an additional layer of liability, in addition to any previous liability layers. The following points will assist in the recognition of these additional layers:

- Initially recognize each layer at its fair value.

---

**EXAMPLE**

Glow Atomic has been operating an atomic power plant for three years. It initially recognized an ARO of $250 million for the eventual dismantling of the plant after its useful life has ended. In the fifth year, Glow detects groundwater contamination, and recognizes an additional layer of ARO liability for $20 million to deal with it. In the seventh year, a leak in the sodium cooling lines causes overheating and a significant release of radioactive steam that impacts 50 square miles of land downwind from the facility. Glow recognizes an additional layer of ARO liability of $150 million to address this issue.

---

- Systematically allocate the ARO liability to expense over the useful life of the underlying asset.
- Measure changes in the liability due to the passage of time, using the credit-adjusted risk-free rate when each layer of liability was first recognized. Recognize this cost as an increase in the liability. When charged to expense, this is classified as accretion expense (which is not the same as interest expense).
- As the time period shortens before an ARO is realized, the assessment of the timing, amount, and probabilities associated with cash flows will improve. It will likely be necessary to alter the ARO liability based on these changes in estimate. If an upward revision is made in the ARO liability, then discount it using the current credit-adjusted risk-free rate. If a downward revision is made in the ARO liability, discount it using the original credit-adjusted risk-free rate when the liability layer was first recognized. If the liability layer to which the downward adjustment relates cannot be identified, use a weighted-average credit-adjusted risk-free rate to discount it.

## Settlement of an Asset Retirement Obligation

An ARO is normally settled only when the underlying fixed asset is retired, though it is possible that some portion of an ARO will be settled prior to asset retirement.

If it becomes apparent that no expenses will be required as part of the retirement of an asset, reverse any remaining unamortized ARO to zero.

If a company cannot fulfill its ARO responsibilities and a third party does so instead, this does not relieve the company from recording an ARO liability, on the grounds that it may now have an obligation to pay the third party instead.

**EXAMPLE**

Glow Atomic operates an atomic power generation facility, and is legally required to decontaminate the facility when it is decommissioned in five years. Glow uses the following assumptions about the ARO:

- The decontamination cost is $90 million.
- The risk-free rate is 5%, to which Glow adds 3% to reflect the effect of its credit standing.
- The assumed rate of inflation over the five-year period is four percent.

With an average inflation rate of 4% per year for the next five years, the current decontamination cost of $90 million increases to approximately $109.5 million by the end of the fifth year. The expected present value of the $109.5 million payout, using the 8% credit-adjusted risk-free rate, is $74,524,000 (calculated as $109.5 million × 0.68058 discount rate).

Glow then calculates the amount of annual accretion using the 8% rate, as shown in the following table:

| Year | Beginning Liability | Accretion | Ending Liability |
|---|---|---|---|
| 1 | $74,524,000 | $5,962,000 | $80,486,000 |
| 2 | 80,486,000 | 6,439,000 | 86,925,000 |
| 3 | 86,925,000 | 6,954,000 | 93,879,000 |
| 4 | 93,879,000 | 7,510,000 | 101,389,000 |
| 5 | 101,389,000 | 8,111,000 | 109,500,000 |

Glow then combines the accretion expense with the straight-line depreciation expense noted in the following table to show how all components of the ARO are charged to expense over the next five years. Note that the accretion expense is carried forward from the preceding table. The depreciation is based on the $74,524,000 present value of the ARO, spread evenly over five years.

| Year | Accretion Expense | Depreciation Expense | Total Expense |
|---|---|---|---|
| 1 | $5,962,000 | $14,904,800 | $20,866,800 |
| 2 | 6,439,000 | 14,904,800 | 21,343,800 |
| 3 | 6,954,000 | 14,904,800 | 21,858,800 |
| 4 | 7,510,000 | 14,904,800 | 22,414,800 |
| 5 | 8,111,000 | 14,904,800 | 23,015,800 |
| | | | $109,500,000 |

After the plant is closed, Glow commences its decontamination activities. The actual cost is $115 million.

Here is a selection of the journal entries that Glow recorded over the term of the ARO:

|  | Debit | Credit |
|---|---|---|
| Facility decontamination asset | 90,000,000 | |
|     Asset retirement obligation liability | | 90,000,000 |
| *To record the initial fair value of the asset retirement obligation* | | |

|  | Debit | Credit |
|---|---|---|
| Depreciation expense | 14,904,800 | |
|     Accumulated depreciation | | 14,904,800 |
| *To record the annual depreciation on the asset retirement obligation* | | |

|  | Debit | Credit |
|---|---|---|
| Accretion expense | As noted in schedule | |
|     Asset retirement obligation liability | | As noted in schedule |
| *To record the annual accretion expense on the asset retirement obligation liability* | | |

|  | Debit | Credit |
|---|---|---|
| Loss on ARO settlement | 5,500,000 | |
|     Remediation expense | | 5,500,000 |
| *To record settlement of the excess asset retirement obligation* | | |

## Overview of Environmental Obligations

There are a number of federal laws that impose an obligation on a business to remediate sites that contain environmentally hazardous conditions, as well as to control or prevent pollution. Remediation can include feasibility studies, cleanup costs, legal fees, government oversight costs, and restoration costs.

In total, these laws can create a serious liability for a business, to the extent of causing the business to go bankrupt. Consider, for example, the extent of liability associated with a Superfund site, where liability can be associated with:

- The current owner or operator of the site
- Previous owners or operators of the site at the time of disposal of hazardous substances
- Parties that arranged for the disposal of hazardous substances found at the site
- Parties that transported hazardous substances to the site

The level of liability imposed by other environmental laws may not be as all-encompassing as the Superfund liability, but the level of liability imposed can still be crushing. Accordingly, the accounting for environmental obligations must be well documented, in order to convey the full scope of the liability.

In general, a liability for an environmental obligation should be accrued if both of the following circumstances are present:

- It is probable that an asset has been impaired or a liability has been incurred. This is based on both of the following criteria:
  - An assertion has been made that the business bears responsibility for a past event; and
  - It is probable that the outcome of the assertion will be unfavorable to the business.
- The amount of the loss or a range of loss can be reasonably estimated.

It is recognized that the liability associated with environmental obligations can change dramatically over time, depending on the number and type of hazardous substances involved, the financial condition of other responsible parties, and other factors. Accordingly, the recorded liability associated with environmental obligations can change. Further, it may not be possible to initially estimate some components of the liability, which does not prevent other components of the liability from being recognized as soon as possible.

---

**EXAMPLE**

Glow Atomics has been notified by the government that it must conduct a remedial investigation and feasibility study for a Superfund site to which it sent uranium waste products in the past. There is sufficient information to estimate the cost of the study, for which Glow records an accrued liability. However, there is no way to initially determine the extent of any additional liabilities associated with the site until the study has at least commenced. Accordingly, Glow continually reviews the preliminary findings of the study, and updates the liability for its environmental obligation based on changes in that information.

---

Once there is information available regarding the extent of an environmental obligation, a business should record its best estimate of the liability. If it is not possible to create a best estimate, then at least a minimum estimate of the liability should be recorded. The estimate is refined as better information becomes available.

In some cases, it is possible to derive a reasonable estimate of liability quite early in the remediation process, because it is similar to the remediation that a business has encountered at other sites. In these instances, the full amount of the liability should be recognized at once.

The costs associated with the treatment of environmental contamination costs should be charged to expense in nearly all cases. The sole exceptions are:

- The costs incurred will increase the capacity of the property, or extend its life, or improve its safety or efficiency
- The costs incurred are needed to prepare a property for sale that is currently classified as held for sale
- The costs improve the property, as well as mitigate or prevent environmental contamination that has yet to occur and that might otherwise arise from future operations

---

**EXAMPLE**

Armadillo Industries spends $250,000 to construct a concrete pad that is designed to prevent fluid leaks from causing groundwater contamination. Making this investment improves the safety of the property, while also preventing future environmental contamination. Consequently, Armadillo can capitalize the $250,000 cost of the concrete pad, and should depreciate it over the remaining useful life of the property.

---

## Measurement of Environmental Obligations

In order to determine the extent of the liability associated with an environmental obligation, follow these steps:

1. Identify those parties likely to be considered responsible for the site requiring remediation. These potentially responsible parties may include the following:

   - Participating parties
   - Recalcitrant parties
   - Unproven parties
   - Unknown parties
   - Orphan share parties

2. Determine the likelihood that those parties will pay their share of the liability associated with site remediation, based primarily on their financial condition. There is a presumption that costs will only be allocated among the participating responsible parties, since the other parties are less likely to pay their shares of the liability.

3. Based on the preceding steps, calculate the percentage of the total liability that the company should record. The sources for this information can include the liability percentages that the responsible parties have agreed to, or which have been assigned by a consultant, or which have been assigned by the Environmental Protection Agency (EPA). If the company chooses to record the liability in a different amount, it should be based on objective, verifiable information, examples of which are:

   - Existing data about the types and amounts of waste at the site
   - Prior experience with liability allocations in comparable situations
   - Reports issued by environmental specialists
   - Internal data that refutes EPA allegations

**EXAMPLE**

Armadillo Industries has been notified by the EPA that it is a potentially responsible party in a groundwater contamination case. The EPA has identified three companies as being potentially responsible. The three parties employ an arbitrator to allocate the responsibility for costs among the companies. The arbitrator derives the following allocations:

|  | Allocation Percentage |
|---|---|
| Armadillo Industries | 40% |
| Boxcar Munitions | 20% |
| Chelsea Chemicals | 20% |
|  | 80% |
| Recalcitrant share (nonparticipating parties) | 15% |
| Orphan share (no party can be identified) | 5% |
| Total | 100% |

The total estimated remediation cost is estimated to be $5 million. Armadillo's direct share of this amount is $2 million (calculated as $5 million total remediation × 40% share). Also, Armadillo should record a liability for its share of those amounts allocated to other parties who are not expected to pay their shares, which is $500,000 (calculated as half of the total allocation for responsible parties × the cost allocated to the recalcitrant and orphan shares).

The costs that should be included in a company's liability for environmental obligations include the following:

- Direct remediation activity costs, such as investigations, risk assessments, remedial actions, activities related to government oversight, and post-remediation monitoring.
- The compensation and related benefit costs for those employees expected to spend a significant amount of their time on remediation activities.

When measuring these costs, do so for the estimated time periods during which activities will occur, which means that an inflation factor should be included for periods further in the future. It may also be possible to include a productivity factor that is caused by gaining experience with remediation efforts over time, and which may reduce mitigation costs. When it is not possible to estimate the costs of inflation, perhaps due to uncertainties about the timing of expenditures, it is acceptable to initially record costs at their current-cost estimates, and adjust them later, as more precise information becomes available.

Any costs related to routine environmental compliance activities, as well as any litigation costs associated with potential recoveries, are not considered part of the remediation effort, and so are not included in the environmental obligation liability. These costs are to be charged to expense as incurred.

Changes in the environmental liability are especially likely when there are multiple parties involved, since additional parties may be added over time, or the apportionment of liability between parties may change. Also, estimates of the exact amount of cost incurred will change continually. For these reasons, the amount of liability recorded for environmental obligations will almost certainly not be the exact amount that is eventually incurred, and so will have to be updated at regular intervals. If so, each update is treated as a change in estimate, which means that there is no retroactive change in the liability reported by a business; instead, the change is recorded only on a go-forward basis.

## Recoveries Related to Environmental Obligations

It is possible that a business may contact other entities concerning the recovery of funds expended on environmental remediation, on the grounds that the other entities are liable for the remediation (or are liable because they are insurers).

The recognition of an asset related to the recovery of an environmental obligation should not be made unless recovery of the claimed amount is considered probable and the amount can be reasonably estimated. If a claim is currently the subject of litigation, it is reasonable to assume that recovery of the claim is not probable, and so should not be recognized.

A recovery can be recorded at its undiscounted amount if the liability is not discounted, and the timing of the recovery is dependent on the timing of the liability payment. This will be the case in most situations, so the recovery will generally be recorded at its undiscounted amount.

## Summary

The accounting for an asset retirement obligation can be complex, especially if there are multiple liability layers and changes to those layers occur with some frequency. Because of the additional accounting effort required to track AROs, it makes sense to use every effort to avoid the recognition of an ARO within the boundaries set by GAAP. In many cases, the amount of an ARO will likely be so minimal as to not require recognition. However, in such industries as mining, chemicals, and power generation, the concept of the ARO is of great concern, and forms a significant proportion of a company's total liabilities.

Environmental obligations can strike any company, large or small, and can result in a massive liability. The accounting for this liability is not especially difficult. However, given its considerable impact on a company's financial results, it is necessary to thoroughly document the calculation of all recorded environmental liabilities, as well as the justification for *not* recording any additional liabilities.

## Review Questions

1. An asset retirement obligation certainly should be recorded based on:
    a. A projection of future laws
    b. A company press release
    c. A current legal obligation
    d. A statement by a company officer

2. If there is a subsequent increase in an asset retirement obligation:
    a. Charge any changes in the liability caused by the passage of time to interest expense
    b. Recognize a new liability layer at its fair value
    c. Charge the new liability to expense at once
    d. Do not subsequently change the estimate of the liability

3. Recognition of an asset retirement obligation should be deferred when:
    a. There is a low likelihood of a performance requirement
    b. There has been a history of non-enforcement
    c. A fair value cannot be obtained for it
    d. An expected present value can be calculated for it

4. When there are only two possible outcomes for the expected present value of an asset retirement obligation and there is no probability distribution, the accountant should:
    a. Assign a 50% probability to each one
    b. Wait until a third outcome can be derived
    c. Do not proceed until the probability distribution is clarified
    d. Assign a 100% probability to one of the outcomes

## Introduction

The overall intent of revenue recognition is to do so in a manner that reasonably depicts the transfer of goods or services to customers, for which consideration is paid that reflects the amount to which the seller expects to be entitled. The following sections describe the five-step process of revenue recognition, as well as a number of ancillary topics.

**Related Podcast Episodes:** Episodes 179 and 205 of the Accounting Best Practices Podcast discuss revenue recognition. They are available at: **accountingtools.com/podcasts** or **iTunes**

## The Nature of a Customer

Revenue recognition only occurs if the third party involved is a customer. A customer is an entity that has contracted to obtain goods or services from the seller's ordinary activities in exchange for payment.

In some situations, it may require a complete examination of the facts and circumstances to determine whether the other party can be classified as a customer. For example, it can be difficult to discern whether there is a customer in collaborative research and development activities between pharmaceutical entities. Another difficult area is payments between oil and gas partners to settle differences between their entitlements to the output from a producing field.

### EXAMPLE

The Red Herring Fish Company contracts with Lethal Sushi to co-develop a fish farm off the coast of Iceland, where the two entities share equally in any future profits. Lethal Sushi is primarily in the restaurant business, so developing a fish farm is not one of its ordinary activities. Also, there is no clear consideration being paid to Lethal. Based on the circumstances, Red Herring is not a customer of Lethal Sushi.

## Steps in Revenue Recognition

Topic 606 establishes a series of actions that an entity takes to determine the amount and timing of revenue to be recognized. The main steps are:

1. Link the contract with a specific customer.
2. Note the performance obligations required by the contract.
3. Determine the price of the underlying transaction.
4. Match this price to the performance obligations through an allocation process.
5. Recognize revenue as the various obligations are fulfilled.

We will expand upon each of these steps in the following sections.

## Step One: Link Contract to Customer

The contract is used as a central aspect of revenue recognition, because revenue recognition is closely associated with it. In many instances, revenue is recognized at multiple points in time over the duration of a contract, so linking contracts with revenue recognition provides a reasonable framework for establishing the timing and amounts of revenue recognition.

A contract only exists if there is an agreement between the parties that establishes enforceable rights and obligations. It is not necessary for an agreement to be in writing for it to be considered a contract. More specifically, a contract only exists if the following conditions are present:

- *Approval*. All parties to the contract have approved the document and substantially committed to its contents (based on all relevant facts and circumstances). The parties can be considered to be committed to a contract despite occasional lapses, such as not enforcing prompt payment or sometimes shipping late. Approval can be in writing or orally.
- *Rights*. The document clearly identifies the rights of the parties.
- *Payment*. The payment terms are clearly stated. It is acceptable to recognize revenue related to unpriced change orders if the seller expects that the price will be approved and the scope of work has been approved.
- *Substance*. The agreement has commercial substance; that is, the cash flows of the seller will change as a result of the contract, either in terms of their amount, timing, or risk of receipt. Otherwise, organizations could swap goods or services to artificially boost their revenue.
- *Probability*. It is probable that the organization will collect substantially all of the amount stated in the contract in exchange for the goods or services that it commits to provide to the other party. In this context, "probable" means "likely to occur." This evaluation is based on the customer's ability and intention to pay when due. The evaluation can incorporate a consideration of the past practice of the customer in question, or of the class of customers to which that customer belongs.

If these criteria are not initially met, the seller can continue to evaluate the situation to see if the criteria are met at a later date. These criteria do not *have* to be re-evaluated at a later date, unless the seller notes a significant change in the relevant facts and circumstances.

---

**EXAMPLE**

Prickly Corporation has entered into an arrangement to sell a large quantity of rose thorns to Ambivalence Corporation, which manufactures a number of potions for the amateur witch brewing market. The contract specifies monthly deliveries over the course of the next year.

Prior to the first shipment, Prickly's collections manager learns through her contacts that Ambivalence has just lost its line of credit and has conducted a large layoff. It appears that the customer's ability to pay has deteriorated significantly, which calls into question the probability of collecting the amount stated in the contract. In this case, there may no longer be a contract for the purposes of revenue recognition.

**EXAMPLE**

Domicilio Corporation, which develops commercial real estate, enters into a contract with Cupertino Beanery to sell a building to Cupertino to be used as a coffee shop. This is Cupertino's first foray into the coffee shop business, having previously only been a distributor of coffee beans to shops within the region. Also, there are a massive number of coffee shops already established in the area.

Domicilio receives a $100,000 deposit from Cupertino when the contract is signed. The contract also states that Cupertino will pay Domicilio an additional $900,000 for the rest of the property over the next three years, with interest. This financing arrangement is nonrecourse, meaning that Domicilio can repossess the building in the event of default, but cannot obtain further cash from Cupertino. Cupertino expects to pay Domicilio from the cash flows to be generated by the coffee shop operation.

Domicilio's management concludes that it is not probable that Cupertino will pay the remaining contractual amount, since its source of funds is a high-risk venture in which Cupertino has no experience. In addition, the loan is nonrecourse, so Cupertino can easily walk away from the arrangement. Accordingly, Domicilio accounts for the initial deposit and future payments as a deposit liability, and continues to recognize the building asset. If it later becomes probable that Cupertino will pay the full contractual amount, Domicilio can then recognize revenue and an offsetting receivable.

---

Whether a contract exists can depend upon standard industry practice, or vary by legal jurisdiction, or even vary by business segment.

There may be instances in which the preceding criteria are not met, and yet the customer is paying consideration to the seller. If so, revenue can be recognized only when one or more of the following events has occurred:

- The contract has been terminated and the consideration received by the seller is not refundable; or
- The seller has no remaining obligations to the customer, substantially all of the consideration has been received, and the payment is not refundable; or
- The seller has transferred control of the goods or services, *and* has stopped transferring goods or services to the customer, *and* has no obligation to transfer additional goods or services, *and* the consideration received cannot be refunded.

These alternatives focus on whether the contract has been concluded in all respects. If so, there is little risk that any revenue recognized will be reversed in a later period, and so is a highly conservative approach to recognizing revenue.

If the seller receives consideration from a customer and the preceding conditions do not exist, then the payment is to be recorded as a liability until such time as the sale criteria have been met.

A contract is not considered to exist when each party to the contract has a unilateral right to terminate a contract that has not been performed, and without compensating the other party. An unperformed contract is one in which no goods or services have been transferred to the customer, nor has the seller received any consideration from the customer in exchange for any promised goods or services.

In certain situations, it can make sense to combine several contracts into one for the purposes of revenue recognition. For example, if there is a portfolio of contracts that have similar characteristics, and the entity expects that treating the portfolio as a single unit will have no appreciable impact on the financial statements, it is acceptable to combine the contracts for accounting purposes. This approach may be particularly valuable in industries where there are a large number of similar contracts, and where applying the model to each individual contract could be impractical.

If the seller enters into two or more contracts with a customer at approximately the same time, these contracts can be accounted for as a single contract if any of the following criteria are met:

- *Basis of negotiation.* The contracts were negotiated as a package, with the goal of attaining a single commercial objective.
- *Interlinking consideration.* The consideration that will be paid under the terms of one contract is dependent upon the price or performance noted in the other contract.
- *Performance obligation.* There is essentially one performance obligation inherent in the two contracts.

---

**EXAMPLE**

Domicilio Corporation enters into three contracts with Milford Sound to construct a concert arena. These contracts involve construction of the concrete building shell, installation of seating, and the construction of a staging system. The three contracts are all needed in order to arrive at a functioning concert arena. Final payment on all three contracts shall be made once the final customer (a local municipality) approves the entire project.

Domicilio should account for these contracts as a single contract, since they are all directed toward the same commercial goal, payment is dependent on all three contracts being completed, and the performance obligation is essentially the same for all of the contracts.

---

## Step Two: Note Performance Obligations

A performance obligation is essentially the unit of account for the goods or services contractually promised to a customer. The performance obligations in the contract must be clearly identified. This is important in recognizing revenue, since revenue is considered to be recognizable when goods or services are transferred to the customer. Examples of goods and services are noted in the following table.

**Examples of Goods and Services**

| Item Sold | Example of the Seller |
|---|---|
| Arranging for another party to transfer goods or services | Travel agent selling airline tickets |
| Asset construction on behalf of a customer | Building construction company |
| Grant of a license | Software company issuing licenses to use its software |
| Grant of options to purchase additional goods or services | Airline granting frequent flier points |
| Manufactured goods | Manufacturer |
| Performance of contractually-mandated tasks | Consultant |
| Readiness to provide goods or services as needed | Snow plow operator, alarm system monitoring |
| Resale of merchandise | Retailer |
| Resale of rights to goods or services | Selling a priority for a new-model car delivery |
| Rights to future goods or services that can be resold | Wholesaler gives additional services to retailer buying a particular product |

There may also be an implicit promise to deliver goods or services that is not stated in a contract, as implied by the customary business practices of the seller. If there is a valid expectation by the customer to receive these implicitly-promised goods or services, they should be considered a performance obligation. Otherwise, the seller might recognize the entire transaction price as revenue when in fact there are still goods or services yet to be provided.

If there is no performance obligation, then there is no revenue to be recognized. For example, a company could continually build up its inventory through ongoing production activities, but just because it has more sellable assets does not mean that it can report an incremental increase in the revenue in its income statement. If such an activity-based revenue recognition model were allowed, organizations could increase their revenues simply by increasing their rate of activity.

If there is more than one good or service to be transferred under the contract terms, only break it out as a separate performance obligation if it is a distinct obligation or there are a series of transfers to the customer of a distinct good or service. In the latter case, a separate performance obligation is assumed if there is a consistent pattern of transfer to the customer.

The "distinct" label can be applied to a good or service only if it meets both of the following criteria:

- *Capable of being distinct.* The customer can benefit from the good or service as delivered, or in combination with other resources that the customer can readily find; and
- *Distinct within the context of the contract.* The promised delivery of the good or service is separately identified within the contract.

Goods or services are more likely to be considered distinct when:

- The seller does not use the goods or services as a component of an integrated bundle of goods or services.
- The items do not significantly modify any other goods or services listed in the contract.
- The items are not highly interrelated with other goods or services listed in the contract.

The intent of these evaluative factors is to place a focus on how to determine whether goods or services are truly distinct within a contract. There is no need to assess the customer's intended use of any goods or services when making this determination.

To reduce the cost of noting performance obligations, it is not necessary to assess whether promised goods or services are performance obligations if they are immaterial in the context of the contract with the customer.

---

**EXAMPLE**

Aphelion Corporation sells a package of goods and services to Nova Corporation. The goods include a deep field telescope, an observatory to house the telescope, and calibration services for the telescope.

The observatory building can be considered distinct from the telescope and calibration services, because Nova could have the telescope installed in an existing facility instead. However, the telescope and calibration services are linked, since the telescope will not function properly unless it has been properly calibrated. Thus, one performance obligation can be considered the observatory, while the telescope and associated calibration can be stated as a separate obligation.

**EXAMPLE**

Norrona Software enters into a contract with a Scandinavian clothing manufacturer to transfer a software license for its clothing design software. The contract also states that Norrona will install the software and provide technical support for a two-year period. The installation process involves adjusting the data entry screens to match the needs of the clothing designers who will use the software. The software can be used without these installation changes. The technical support assistance is intended to provide advice to users regarding advanced features, and is not considered a key requirement for software users.

Since the software is functional without the installation process or the technical support, Norrona concludes that the items are not highly interrelated. Since these goods and services are distinct, the company should identify separate performance obligations for the software license, installation work, and technical support.

---

In the event that a good or service is not classified as distinct, aggregate it with other goods or services promised in the contract, until such time as a cluster of goods or services have been accumulated that can be considered distinct.

An organization can elect to create an accounting policy to account for shipping and handling activities occurring after a customer has gained control of a good, to designate these activities as fulfilling the promise to transfer the good, rather than as an additional promised service. Doing so reduces the complexity of accounting for the overall transaction.

The administrative tasks needed to fulfill a contract are not considered to be performance obligations, since they do not involve the transfer of goods or services to customers. For example, setting up information about a new contract in the seller's contract management software is not considered a performance obligation.

## Step Three: Determine Prices

This step involves the determination of the transaction price built into the contract. The transaction price is the amount of consideration to be paid by the customer in exchange for its receipt of goods or services. The transaction price does not include any amounts collected on behalf of third parties (such as sales taxes).

**EXAMPLE**

The Twister Vacuum Company sells its vacuum cleaners to individuals through its chain of retail stores. In the most recent period, Twister generated $3,800,000 of receipts, of which $200,000 was sales taxes collected on behalf of local governments. Since the $200,000 was collected on behalf of third parties, it cannot be recognized as revenue.

The transaction price may be difficult to determine, since it involves consideration of the effects noted in the following subsections.

### Variable Consideration

The terms of some contracts may result in a price that can vary, depending on the circumstances. For example, there may be discounts, rebates, penalties, or performance bonuses in the contract. Or, the customer may have a reasonable expectation that the seller will offer a price concession, based on the seller's customary business practices, policies, or statements. Another example is when the seller intends to accept lower prices from a new customer in order to develop a strong customer relationship. If so, set the transaction price based on either the most likely amount or the probability-weighted expected value, using whichever method yields that amount of consideration most likely to be paid. In more detail, these methods are:

- *Most likely.* The seller develops a range of possible payment amounts, and selects the amount most likely to be paid. This approach works best when there are only two possible amounts that will be paid.
- *Expected value.* The seller develops a range of possible payment amounts, and assigns a probability to each one. The sum of these probability-weighted amounts is the expected value of the variable consideration. This approach works best when there are a large number of possible payment amounts. However, the outcome may be an expected value that does not exactly align with any amount that could actually be paid.

**EXAMPLE**

Grissom Granaries operates grain storage facilities along the Mississippi River. Its accounting staff is reviewing a contract that has just been signed with a major farming co-operative, and concludes that the contract could have four possible outcomes, which are noted in the following expected value table:

| Price Scenario | Transaction Price | Probability | Probability-Weighted Price |
|---|---|---|---|
| 1 | $1,500,000 | 20% | $300,000 |
| 2 | 1,700,000 | 35% | 595,000 |
| 3 | 2,000,000 | 40% | 800,000 |
| 4 | 2,400,000 | 5% | 120,000 |
| | | Expected Value | $1,815,000 |

The expected value derived from the four possible pricing outcomes is $1,815,000, even though this amount does not match any one of the four pricing outcomes.

Whichever method is chosen, be sure to use it consistently throughout the contract, as well as for similar contracts. However, it is not necessary to use the same measurement method to measure each uncertainty contained within a contract; different methods can be applied to different uncertainties.

Also, review the circumstances of each contract at the end of each reporting period, and update the estimated transaction price to reflect any changes in the circumstances.

**EXAMPLE**

Cantilever Construction has entered into a contract to tear down and replace five bridges along Interstate 70. The state government (which owns and maintains this section of the highway) is extremely concerned about how the work will interfere with traffic on the highway. Accordingly, the government includes in the contract a clause that penalizes Cantilever $10,000 for every hour over the budgeted amount that each bridge demolition and construction project shuts down the interstate, and a $15,000 bonus for every hour saved from the budgeted amount.

Cantilever has extensive experience with this type of work, having torn down and replaced 42 other bridges along the interstate highway system in the past five years. Based on the company's experience with these other projects and an examination of the budgeted hours allowed for shutting down the interstate, the company concludes that the most likely outcome is $120,000 of variable consideration associated with the project. Cantilever accordingly adds this amount to the transaction price.

## Possibility of Reversal

Do not include in the transaction price an estimate of variable consideration if, when the uncertainty associated with the variable amount is settled, it is probable that there will be a significant reversal of cumulative revenue recognized. The assessment of a possible reversal of revenue could include the following factors, all of which might increase the probability of a revenue reversal:

- *Beyond seller's influence*. The amount of consideration paid is strongly influenced by factors outside of the control of the seller. For example, goods sold may be subject to obsolescence (as is common in the technology industry), or weather conditions could impede the availability of goods (as is common in the production of farm products).
- *Historical practice*. The seller has a history of accepting a broad range of price concessions, or of changing the terms of similar contracts.

- *Inherent range of outcomes.* The terms of the contract contain a broad range of possible consideration amounts that might be paid.
- *Limited experience.* The seller does not have much experience with the type of contract in question. Alternatively, the seller's prior experience cannot be translated into a prediction of the amount of consideration paid.
- *Long duration.* A considerable period of time may have to pass before the uncertainty can be resolved.

The probability of a significant reversal of cumulative revenue recognized places a conservative bias on the recognition of revenue, rather than a neutral bias, so there will be a tendency for recognized revenue levels to initially be too low. However, this approach is reasonable when considering that revenue information is more relevant when it is not subject to future reversals.

If management expects that a retroactive discount will be applied to sales transactions, the seller should recognize a refund liability as part of the revenue recognition when each performance obligation is satisfied. For example, if the seller is currently selling goods for $100 but expects that a 20% volume discount will be retroactively applied at the end of the year, the resulting entry should be:

|  | Debit | Credit |
|---|---|---|
| Accounts receivable | 100 | |
| Revenue | | 80 |
| Refund liability | | 20 |

## EXAMPLE

Medusa Medical sells a well-known snake oil therapy through a number of retail store customers. In the most recent month, Medusa sells $100,000 of its potent Copperhead Plus combination healing balm and sunscreen lotion. The therapy is most effective within one month of manufacture and then degrades rapidly, so that Medusa must accept increasingly large price concessions in order to ensure that the goods are sold. Historically, this means that the range of price concessions varies from zero (in the first month) to 80% (after four months). Of this range of outcomes, Medusa estimates that the expected value of the transactions is likely to be revenue of $65,000. However, since the risk of obsolescence is so high, Medusa cannot conclude that it is probable that there will not be a significant reversal in the amount of cumulative revenue recognized. Accordingly, management concludes that the price point at which it is probable that there will not be a significant reversal in the cumulative amount of revenue recognized is actually closer to $45,000 (representing a 55% price concession). Based on this conclusion, the controller initially recognizes $45,000 of revenue when the goods are shipped to retailers, and continues to monitor the situation at the end of each reporting period, to see if the recognized amount should be adjusted.

## EXAMPLE

Iceland Cod enters into a contract with Lethal Sushi to provide Lethal with 10,000 pounds of cod per year, at $15 per pound. If Lethal purchases more than 10,000 pounds within one calendar year, then a 12% retroactive price reduction will be applied to all of Lethal's purchases for the year.

Iceland has dealt with Lethal for a number of years, and knows that Lethal has never attained the 10,000 pound level of purchases. Accordingly, through the first half of the year, Iceland records its sales to Lethal at their full price, which is $30,000 for 2,000 pounds of cod.

In July, Lethal acquires Wimpy Fish Company, along with its large chain of seafood restaurants. With a much larger need for fish to supply the additional restaurants, Lethal now places several large orders that make it quite clear that passing the 10,000 pound threshold will be no problem at all. Accordingly, Iceland's controller records a cumulative revenue reversal of $3,600 to account for Lethal's probable attainment of the volume purchase discount.

**EXAMPLE**

Armadillo Industries is a new company that has developed a unique type of ceramic-based body armor that is extremely light. To encourage sales, the company is offering a 90-day money back guarantee. Since the company is new to the industry and cannot predict the level of returns, there is no way of knowing if a sudden influx of returns might trigger a significant reversal in the amount of cumulative revenue recognized. Accordingly, the company must wait for the money back guarantee to expire before it can recognize any revenue.

## Time Value of Money

If the transaction price is to be paid over a period of time, this implies that the seller is including a financing component in the contract. If this financing component is a significant financing benefit for the customer and provides financing for more than one year, adjust the transaction price for the time value of money. In cases where there is a financing component to a contract, the seller will earn interest income over the term of the contract.

A contract may contain a financing component, even if there is no explicit reference to it in the contract. When adjusting the transaction price for the time value of money, consider the following factors:

- *Standalone price.* The amount of revenue recognized should reflect the price that a customer would have paid if it had paid in cash.
- *Significance.* In order to be recognized, the financing component should be significant. This means evaluating the amount of the difference between the consideration to be paid and the cash selling price. Also note the combined effect of prevailing interest rates and the time difference between when delivery is made and when the customer pays.

If it is necessary to adjust the compensation paid for the time value of money, use as a discount rate the rate that would be employed in a separate financing transaction between the parties as of the beginning date of the contract. The rate used should reflect the credit characteristics of the customer, including the presence of any collateral provided. This discount rate is not to be updated after the commencement of the contract, irrespective of any changes in the credit markets or in the credit standing of the customer.

**EXAMPLE**

Hammer Industries sells a large piece of construction equipment to Eskimo Construction, under generous terms that allow Eskimo to pay Hammer the full amount of the $119,990 receivable in 24 months. The cash selling price of the equipment is $105,000. The contract contains an implicit interest rate of 6.9%, which is the interest rate that discounts the purchase price of $119,990 down to the cash selling price over the two year period. The controller examines this rate and concludes that it approximates the rate that Hammer and Eskimo would use if there had been a separate financing transaction between them as of the contract inception date. Consequently, Hammer recognizes interest income during the two-year period prior to the payment due date, using the following calculation:

| Year | Beginning Balance | Interest (at 6.9% Rate) | Ending Balance |
|---|---|---|---|
| 1 | $105,000 | $7,245 | $112,245 |
| 2 | 112,245 | 7,745 | $119,990 |

As of the shipment date, Hammer records the following entry:

|  | Debit | Credit |
|---|---|---|
| Loan receivable | 105,000 | |
| Revenue | | 105,000 |

At the end of the first year, Hammer recognizes the interest associated with the transaction for the first year, using the following entry:

|  | Debit | Credit |
|---|---|---|
| Loan receivable | 7,245 | |
| Interest income | | 7,245 |

At the end of the second year, Hammer recognizes the interest associated with the transaction for the second year, using the following entry:

|  | Debit | Credit |
|---|---|---|
| Loan receivable | 7,745 | |
| Interest income | | 7,745 |

These entries increase the size of the loan receivable until it reaches the original sale price of $119,990. Eskimo then pays the full amount of the receivable, at which point Hammer records the following final entry:

|  | Debit | Credit |
|---|---|---|
| Cash | 119,990 | |
| Loan receivable | | 119,990 |

---

Also, note that the financing concept can be employed in reverse; that is, if a customer makes a deposit that the seller expects to retain for more than one year, the financing component of this arrangement should be recognized by the seller. Doing so properly reflects the economics of the arrangement, where the seller is using the cash of the customer to fund its purchase of materials and equipment for a project; if the seller had not provided the deposit, the seller would instead have needed to obtain financing.

There is assumed *not* to be a significant financing component to a contract in the presence of any of the following factors:

- *Advance payment.* The customer paid in advance, and the customer can specify when goods and services are to be delivered.
- *Variable component.* A large part of the consideration to be paid is variable, and payment timing will vary based on a future event that is not under the control of either party.
- *Non-financing reason.* The reason for the difference between the contractual consideration and the cash selling price exists for a reason other than financing, and the amount of the difference is proportional to the alternative reason.

**EXAMPLE**

Spinner Maintenance offers global technical support to the owners of rooftop solar power systems in exchange for a $400 fee. The fee pays for service that spans the first five years of the life of the power systems, and is purchased as part of the package of solar panels and initial installation work. This maintenance is intended to provide phone support to homeowners who are researching why their power systems are malfunctioning. The support does not include any replacement of solar panels for hail damage.

The support period is quite extensive, but Spinner concludes that there is no financing component to these sales, for the following reasons:

- The administrative cost of a monthly billing would be prohibitive, since the amount billed on a monthly basis would be paltry.
- Those more technologically proficient customers would be less likely to renew if they could pay on a more frequent basis, leaving Spinner with the highest-maintenance customers who require the most support.
- Customers are more likely to make use of the service if they are reminded of it by the arrival of monthly invoices.

In short, Spinner has several excellent reasons for structuring the payment plan to require an advance payment, all of which are centered on maintaining a reasonable level of profitability. The intent is not to provide financing to customers.

**EXAMPLE**

Glow Atomic sells a nuclear power plant to a French provincial government. The certification process for the plant is extensive, spanning a six-month test period. Accordingly, the local government builds into the contract a provision to withhold 20% of the contract price until completion of the test period. The rest of the payments are made on a milestone schedule, as the construction work progresses. Based on the circumstances and the amount of the withholding, the arrangement is considered to be non-financing, so Glow Atomic does not break out a financing component from the total consideration paid.

## Noncash Consideration

If the customer will be paying with some form of noncash consideration, measure the consideration at its fair value as of the inception date of the contract. If it is not possible to measure the payment at its fair value, instead use the standalone selling price of the goods or services to be delivered to the customer. This approach also applies to payments made with equity instruments. In rare cases, the customer may supply the seller with goods or services that are intended to assist the seller in its fulfillment of the related contract. If the seller gains control of these assets or services, it should consider them to be noncash consideration paid by the customer.

**EXAMPLE**

Industrial Landscaping is hired by Pensive Corporation to mow the lawns and trim shrubbery at Pensive's corporate headquarters on a weekly basis throughout the year. Essentially the same service is provided each week. Pensive is a startup company with little excess cash, so it promises to pay Industrial with 25 shares of Pensive stock at the end of each week.

Industrial considers itself to have satisfied its performance obligation at the end of each week. Industrial should determine the transaction price as being the fair value of the shares at the end of each week, and recognizes this amount as revenue. There is no subsequent change in the amount of revenue recognized, irrespective of any changes in the fair value of the shares.

## Payments to Customers

The contract may require the seller to pay consideration to the customer, perhaps in the form of credits or coupons that the customer can apply against the amounts it owes to the seller. This may also involve payments to third parties that have purchased the seller's goods or services from the original customer. If so, treat this consideration as a reduction of the transaction price. The following special situations may apply:

- *Customer supplies a good or service.* The customer may provide the seller with a distinct good or service; if so, the seller treats the payment as it would a payment to any supplier.
- *Supplier payment exceeds customer delivery.* If the customer provides a good or service to the seller, but the amount paid by the seller to the customer exceeds the fair value of the goods or services it receives in exchange, the excess of the payment is considered a reduction of the transaction price. If the fair value of the goods or services cannot be determined, then consider the entire amount paid by the seller to the customer to be a reduction of the transaction price.

If it is necessary to account for consideration paid to the customer as a reduction of the transaction price, do so when the later of the following two events have occurred:

- When the seller recognizes revenue related to its provision of goods or services to the customer; or
- When the seller either pays or promises to pay the consideration to the customer. The timing of this event could be derived from the customary business practices of the seller.

---

**EXAMPLE**

Dillinger Designs manufactures many types of hunting rifles. Dillinger enters into a one-year contract with Backwoods Survival, which has not previously engaged in rifle sales. Backwoods commits to purchase at least $240,000 of rifles from Dillinger during the contract period. Also, due to the hefty government-mandated safety requirements associated with the sale of rifles, Dillinger commits to pay $60,000 to Backwoods at the inception of the contract; these funds are intended to pay for a locking gun safe to be kept at each Backwoods store, as per firearms laws pertaining to retailers.

Dillinger determines that the $60,000 payment is to be treated as a reduction of the $240,000 sale price. Consequently, whenever Dillinger fulfills a performance obligation by shipping goods under the contract, it reduces the amount of revenue it would otherwise recognize by 25%, which reflects the proportion of the $60,000 payment related to locking gun safes of the $240,000 that Dillinger will be paid by Backwoods.

---

## Refund Liabilities

In some situations, a seller may receive consideration from a customer, with the likelihood that the payment will be refunded. If so, the seller records a refund liability in the amount that the seller expects to refund back to the customer. The seller should review the amount of this liability at the end of each reporting period, to see if the amount should be altered.

## Step Four: Allocate Prices to Obligations

Once the performance obligations and transaction prices associated with a contract have been identified, the next step is to allocate the transaction prices to the obligations. The basic rule is to allocate that price to a performance obligation that best reflects that amount of consideration to which the seller expects to be entitled when it satisfies each performance obligation. To determine this allocation, it is first necessary to estimate the standalone selling price of those distinct goods or services as of the inception date of the contract. If it is not possible to derive a standalone selling price, the seller must estimate it. This estimation should involve all relevant information that is reasonably available, such as:

- Competitive pressure on prices
- Costs incurred to manufacture or provide the item
- Item profit margins
- Pricing of other items in the same contract
- Standalone selling price of the item
- Supply and demand for the items in the market
- The seller's pricing strategy and practices
- The type of customer, distribution channel, or geographic region
- Third-party pricing

The following three approaches are acceptable ways in which to estimate a standalone selling price:

- *Adjusted market assessment.* This involves reviewing the market to estimate the price at which a customer in that market would be willing to pay for the goods and services in question. This can involve an examination of the prices of competitors for similar items and adjusting them to incorporate the seller's costs and margins.
- *Expected cost plus a margin.* This requires the seller to estimate the costs required to fulfill a performance obligation, and then add a margin to it to derive the estimated price.
- *Residual approach.* This involves subtracting all of the observable standalone selling prices from the total transaction price to arrive at the residual price remaining for allocation to any non-observable selling prices. This method can only be used if one of the following situations applies:
  - The seller sells the good or service to other customers for a wide range of prices; or
  - No price has yet been established for that item, and it has not yet been sold on a standalone basis.

The residual approach can be difficult to use when there are several goods or services with uncertain standalone selling prices. If so, it may be necessary to use a combination of methods to derive standalone selling prices, which should be used in the following order:

1. Estimate the aggregate amount of the standalone selling prices for all items having uncertain standalone selling prices, using the residual method.
2. Use another method to develop standalone selling prices for each item in this group, to allocate the aggregate amount of the standalone selling prices.

Once all standalone selling prices have been determined, allocate the transaction price amongst these distinct goods or services based on their relative standalone selling prices.

> **Best Practice:** Appropriate evidence of a standalone selling price is the observable price of a good or service when the seller sells it to a similar customer under similar circumstances.

Once the seller derives an approach for estimating a standalone selling price, it should consistently apply that method to the derivation of the standalone selling prices for other goods or services with similar characteristics.

---

**EXAMPLE**

Luminescence Corporation manufactures a wide range of light bulbs, and mostly sells into the wholesaler market. The company receives an order from the federal government for two million fluorescent bulbs, as well as for 100,000 units of a new bulb that operates outdoors at very low temperatures. Luminescence has not yet sold these new bulbs to anyone. The total price of the order is $7,000,000. Luminescence assigns $6,000,000 of the total price to the fluorescent bulbs, based on its own sales of comparable orders. This leaves $1,000,000 of the total price that is allocable to the low temperature bulbs. Since Luminescence has not yet established a price for these bulbs and has not sold them on a standalone basis, it is acceptable to allocate $1,000,000 to the low temperature bulbs under the residual approach.

---

If there is a subsequent change in the transaction price, allocate that change amongst the distinct goods or services based on the original allocation that was used at the inception of the contract. If this subsequent allocation is to a performance obligation that has already been completed and for which revenue has already been recognized, the result can be an increase or reduction in the amount of revenue recognized. This change in recognition should occur as soon as the subsequent change in the transaction price occurs.

## Allocation of Price Discounts

It is assumed that a customer has received a discount on a bundled purchase of goods or services when the sum of the standalone prices for these items is greater than the consideration to be paid under the terms of a contract. The discount can be allocated to a specific item within the bundled purchase, if there is observable evidence that the discount was intended for that item. In order to do so, all of the following criteria must apply:

1. Each distinct item in the bundle is regularly sold on a standalone basis;
2. A bundle of some of these distinct items is regularly sold at a discount to their standalone selling prices; and
3. The discount noted in the second point is essentially the same as the discount in the contract, and there is observable evidence linking the entire contract discount to that bundle of distinct items.

If this allocation system is used, the seller must employ it before using the residual approach noted earlier in this section. Doing so ensures that the discount is not applied to the other performance obligations in the contract to which prices have not yet been allocated.

In all other cases, the discount is to be allocated amongst all of the items in the bundle. In this latter situation, the allocation is to be made based on the standalone selling prices of all of the performance obligations in the contract.

---

**EXAMPLE**

The Hegemony Toy Company sells board games that re-enact famous battles. Hegemony regularly sells the following three board games:

| Product | Standalone Selling Price |
|---|---|
| Hastings Battle Game | $120 |
| Stalingrad Battle Game | 100 |
| Waterloo Battle Game | 80 |
| Total | $300 |

Hegemony routinely sells the Stalingrad and Waterloo products as a bundle for $120.

Hegemony enters into a contract with the War Games International website to sell War Games the set of three games for $240, which is a 20% discount from the standard price. Deliveries of these games to War Games will be at different times, so the related performance obligations will be settled on different dates.

The $60 discount would normally be apportioned among all three products based on their standalone selling prices. However, because Hegemony routinely sells the Stalingrad/Waterloo bundle for a $60 discount, it is evident that the entire discount should be allocated to these two products.

If Hegemony later delivers the Stalingrad and Waterloo games to War Games on different dates, it should allocate the $60 discount between the two products based on their standalone selling prices. Thus, $33.33 should be allocated to the Stalingrad game and $26.67 to the Waterloo game. The allocation calculation is:

| Game | Allocation |
|---|---|
| Stalingrad | ($100 individual game price ÷ $180 combined price) × $60 discount = $33.33 |
| Waterloo | ($80 individual game price ÷ $180 combined price) × $60 discount = $26.67 |

If the two games are instead delivered at the same time, there is no need to conduct the preceding allocation. Instead, the discount can be assigned to them both as part of a single performance obligation.

---

## Allocation of Variable Consideration

There may be a variable amount of consideration associated with a contract. This consideration may apply to the contract as a whole, or to just a portion of it. For example, a bonus payment may be tied to the completion of a specific performance obligation. It is allowable to allocate variable consideration to a specific performance obligation or a distinct good or service within a contract when the variable payment terms are specifically tied to the seller's efforts to satisfy the performance obligation.

---

### EXAMPLE

Nova Corporation contracts with the Deep Field Scanning Authority to construct two three-meter telescopes that will operate in tandem in the low-humidity Atacama Desert in Chile. The terms of the contract include a provision that can increase the allowable price charged, if the commodity cost of the titanium required to build the telescope frames increases. Based on the prices stated in forward contracts at the contract inception date, it is likely that this variable cost element will increase the transaction price by $250,000. The variable component of the price is allocated to each of the telescopes equally.

---

## Subsequent Price Changes

There are a number of reasons why the transaction price could change after a contract has begun, such as the resolution of uncertain events that were in need of clarification at the contract inception date. When there is a price change, the amount of the change is to be allocated to the performance obligations on the same basis used for the original price allocation at the inception of the contract. This has the following ramifications:

- Do not re-allocate prices based on subsequent changes in the standalone selling prices of goods or services.
- When there is a price change and that price is allocated, the result may be the recognition of additional or reduced revenue that is to be recognized in the period when the transaction price changes.
- When there has been a contract modification prior to a price change, the price allocation is conducted in two steps. First, allocate the price change to those performance obligations identified prior to the modification if the price change is associated with variable consideration promised

before modification. In all other cases, allocate the price change to those performance obligations still remaining to be settled as of the modification date.

The result should be a reported level of cumulative revenue that matches the amount of revenue an organization would have recognized if it had the most recent information at the inception date of the contract.

## Step Five: Recognize Revenue

Revenue is to be recognized as goods or services are transferred to the customer. This transference is considered to occur when the customer gains control over the good or service. Indicators of this date include the following:

- When the seller has the right to receive payment.
- When the customer has legal title to the transferred asset. This can still be the case even when the seller retains title to protect it against the customer's failure to pay.
- When physical possession of the asset has been transferred by the seller. Possession can be inferred even when goods are held elsewhere on consignment, or by the seller under a bill-and-hold arrangement. Under a bill-and-hold arrangement, the seller retains goods on behalf of the customer, but still recognizes revenue.
- When the customer has taken on the significant risks and rewards of ownership related to the asset transferred by the seller. For example, the customer can now sell, pledge, or exchange the asset.
- When the customer accepts the asset.
- When the customer can prevent other entities from using or obtaining benefits from the asset.

It is possible that a performance obligation will be transferred over time, rather than as of a specific point in time. If so, revenue recognition occurs when any one of the following criteria are met:

- *Immediate use.* The customer both receives and consumes the benefit provided by the seller as performance occurs. This situation arises if another entity would not need to re-perform work completed to date if the other entity were to take over the remaining performance obligation. Routine and recurring services typically fall into this classification.

---

**EXAMPLE**

Long-Haul Freight contracts to deliver a load of goods from Los Angeles to Boston. This service should be considered a performance obligation that is transferred over time, despite the fact that the customer only benefits from the goods once they are delivered. The reason for the designation as a transference over time is that, if a different trucking firm were to take over partway through the journey, the replacement firm would not have to re-perform the freight hauling that has already been completed to date.

**EXAMPLE**

Maid Marian is a nationwide home cleaning service run by friars within the Franciscan Order. Its customers both receive and simultaneously consume the cleaning services provided by its staff. Consequently, the services provided by Maid Marian are considered to be performance obligations satisfied over time.

---

- *Immediate enhancement.* The seller creates or enhances an asset controlled by the customer as performance occurs. This asset can be tangible or intangible.
- *No alternative use.* The seller's performance does not create an asset for which there is an alternative use to the seller (such as selling it to a different customer). In addition, the contract gives the seller an enforceable right to payment for the performance that has been completed to date. A lack

of alternative use happens when a contract restricts the seller from directing the asset to another use, or when there are practical limitations on doing so, such as the incurrence of significant economic losses to direct the asset elsewhere. The determination of whether an asset has an alternative use is made at the inception of the contract, and cannot be subsequently altered unless both parties to the contract approve a modification that results in a substantive change in the performance obligation.

Construction contracts are likely to be designated as being performance obligations that are transferred over time. Under this approach, they can use the percentage-of-completion method to recognize revenue, rather than the completed contract method. This means that they can recognize revenue as a construction project progresses, rather than waiting until the end of the project to recognize any revenue.

---

**EXAMPLE**

Oberlin Acoustics is contractually obligated to deliver a highly-customized version of its Rhino brand electric guitar to a diva-grade European rock star. The contract clearly states that this customized version can only be delivered to the designated customer, and it is likely that this individual would pursue legal action if Oberlin were to attempt to sell it elsewhere (such as to the lead guitarist of a rival band). Also, Oberlin might have to incur significant costs to reconfigure the guitar for sale to a different customer. In this situation, there is no alternative use.

However, if Oberlin had instead contracted to deliver one of its standard Rhino brand guitars, the company could easily transfer the asset to a different customer, since the products are essentially interchangeable. In this case, there would be a clear alternative use.

**EXAMPLE**

Tesla Power Company is hired by a local government to construct one of its new, compact fusion power plants in the remote hinterlands of Malawi. There is clearly no alternative use for the power plant, since Tesla would have to incur major costs to dismantle the facility and truck it out of the remote area before it could be sold to a different customer. However, the contract states that 50% of the price will be paid at the end of the contract period, and there is no enforceable right to any payment; this means that Tesla must consider its performance obligation to be satisfied as of a point in time, rather than over time.

**EXAMPLE**

Hassle Corporation is in talks with a potential acquirer. The acquirer insists that Hassle have soil tests conducted in the area around its main production facility, to see if there has been any leakage of pollutants. Hassle engages Wilson Environmental to conduct these tests, which is a three-month process. The contract includes a clause that Wilson will be paid for its costs plus a 20% profit if Hassle cancels the contract. The acquisition talks break off after two months, so Hassle notifies Wilson that it no longer needs the environmental report. Since Wilson cannot possibly sell the information it has collected to a different customer, there is no alternative use. Also, since Wilson has an enforceable right to payment for all work completed to date, the company can recognize revenue over time by measuring its progress toward satisfying the performance obligation.

---

## Measurement of Progress Completion

When a performance obligation is being completed over a period of time, the seller recognizes revenue through the application of a progress completion method. The goal of this method is to determine the progress of the seller in achieving complete satisfaction of its performance obligation. This method is to be consistently applied over time, and shall be re-measured at the end of each reporting period.

Both output methods and input methods are considered acceptable for determining progress completion. The method chosen should incorporate due consideration of the nature of the goods or services being provided to the customer. The following sub-sections address the use of output and input methods.

## Output Methods

An output method recognizes revenue based on a comparison of the value to the customer of goods and services transferred to date to the remaining goods and services not yet transferred. There are numerous ways to measure output, including:

- Surveys of performance to date
- Milestones reached
- The passage of time
- The number of units delivered
- The number of units produced

Another output method that may be acceptable is the amount of consideration that the seller has the right to invoice, such as billable hours. This approach works when the seller has a right to invoice an amount that matches the amount of performance completed to date.

The number of units delivered or produced may not be an appropriate output method in situations where there is a large amount of work-in-process, since the value associated with unfinished goods may be so substantial that revenue could be materially under-reported.

The method picked should closely adhere to the concept of matching the seller's progress toward satisfying the performance obligation. It is not always possible to use an output method, since the cost of collecting the necessary information can be prohibitive, or progress may not be directly observable.

---

**EXAMPLE**

Viking Fitness operates a regional chain of fitness clubs that are oriented toward younger, very athletic people (which may explain why each store is located next to a vitamin supplements shop). Members pay a $1,200 annual fee, which gives them access to all of the clubs in the chain during all operating hours. In effect, Viking's performance obligation is to keep its facilities open for use by members, irrespective of whether they actually use the facilities. Clearly, this situation calls for measurement of progress completion based on the passage of time. Accordingly, Viking recognizes revenue from its annual customer payments at the rate of $100 per member per month.

---

## Input Methods

An input method derives the amount of revenue to be recognized based on the to-date effort required by the seller to satisfy a performance obligation relative to the total estimated amount of effort required. Examples of possible inputs are costs incurred, labor hours expended, and machine hours used. If there are situations where the effort expended does not directly relate to the transfer of goods or services to a customer, do not use that input. The following are situations where the input used could lead to incorrect revenue recognition:

- The costs incurred are higher than expected, due to seller inefficiencies. For example, the seller may have wasted a higher-than-expected amount of raw materials in the performance of its obligations under a contract.
- The costs incurred are not in proportion to the progress of the seller toward satisfying the performance obligation. For example, the seller might purchase a large amount of materials at the inception of a contract, which comprise a significant part of the total price.

**Best Practice:** If the effort expended to satisfy performance obligations occur evenly through the performance period, consider recognizing revenue on the straight-line basis through the performance period.

---

**EXAMPLE**

Eskimo Construction is hired to build a weather observatory in Barrow, Alaska, which is estimated to be a six-month project. Utilities are a major concern, especially since the facility is too far away from town for a power line to be run out to it. Accordingly, a large part of the construction cost is a diesel-powered turbine generator. The total cost that Eskimo intends to incur for the project is:

| | |
|---|---|
| Turbine cost | $1,250,000 |
| All other costs | 2,750,000 |
| Total costs | $4,000,000 |

The turbine is to be delivered and paid for at the beginning of the construction project, but will not be incorporated into the facility until late summer, when the building is scheduled to be nearly complete.

Eskimo intends to use an input method to derive the amount of revenue, using costs incurred. However, this approach runs afoul of the turbine cost, since the immediate expenditure for the turbine gives the appearance of the project being 31.25% complete before work has even begun. Accordingly, Eskimo excludes the cost of the turbine from its input method calculations, only using the other costs as the basis for deriving revenue.

---

The situation described in the preceding example is quite common, since materials are typically procured at the inception of a contract, rather than being purchased in equal quantities over the duration of the contract. Consequently, the accountant should be particularly mindful of this issue and incorporate it into any revenue recognition calculations based on an input method.

A method based on output is preferred, since it most faithfully depicts the performance of the seller under the terms of a contract. However, an input-based method is certainly allowable if using it would be less costly for the seller, while still providing a reasonable proxy for the ongoing measurement of progress.

### Change in Estimate

Whichever method is used, be sure to update it over time to reflect changes in the seller's performance to date. If there is a change in the measurement of progress, treat the change as a change in accounting estimate.

A change in accounting estimate occurs when there is an adjustment to the carrying amount of an asset or liability, or the subsequent accounting for it. Changes in accounting estimate occur relatively frequently, and so would require a considerable effort to make an ongoing series of retroactive changes to prior financial statements. Instead, GAAP only requires that changes in accounting estimate be accounted for in the period of change and thereafter. Thus, no retrospective change is required or allowed.

### Progress Measurement

It is only possible to recognize the revenue associated with progress completion if it is possible for the seller to measure the seller's progress. If the seller lacks reliable progress information, it will not be possible to recognize the revenue associated with a contract over time. There may be cases where the measurement of progress completion is more difficult during the early stages of a contract. If so, it is allowable for the seller to instead recognize just enough revenue to recover its costs in satisfying its performance obligations, thereby deferring the recognition of other revenue until such time as the measurement system yields more accurate results.

### Right of Return

A common right granted to customers is to allow them to return goods to the seller within a certain period of time following the customer's receipt of the goods. This return may take the form of a refund of any amounts paid, a general credit that can be applied against other billings from the seller, or an exchange for a different unit. The proper accounting for this right of return involves three components, which are:

1. Recognize the net amount of revenue to which the seller expects to be entitled after all product returns have been factored into the sale.
2. A refund liability that encompasses the number of units that the seller expects to have returned to it.
3. An asset based on the right to recover products from customers who have demanded refunds. This asset represents a reduction in the cost of goods sold. The amount is initially based on the former carrying amount of the inventory, less recovery costs and expected reductions in the value of the returned products.

This accounting requires the seller to update its assessment of future product returns at the end of each reporting period, both for the refund liability and the recovery asset. This update may result in a change in the amount of revenue recognized.

---

**EXAMPLE**

Ninja Cutlery sells high-end ceramic knife sets through its on-line store and through select retailers. All customers pay up-front in cash. In the most recent month, Ninja sold 5,000 knife sets, which sold for an average price of $250 each ($1,250,000 in total). The unit cost is $150. Based on the history of actual returns over the preceding 12-month period, Ninja can expect that 200 of the sets (4% of the total) will be returned under the company's returns policy. Recovery costs are immaterial, and Ninja expects to be able to repackage and sell all returned products for a profit. Based on this information, Ninja records the following transactions when the knife sets are originally delivered:

|  | Debit | Credit |
|---|---|---|
| Cash | 1,250,000 |  |
|     Revenue |  | 1,200,000 |
|     Refund liability |  | 50,000 |

|  | Debit | Credit |
|---|---|---|
| Cost of goods sold | 720,000 |  |
| Recovery asset | 30,000 |  |
|     Inventory |  | 750,000 |

In these entries, the refund liability is calculated as the 200 units expected to be returned, multiplied by the average price of $250 each. The recovery asset is calculated as the 200 units expected to be returned, multiplied by the unit cost of $150.

---

## Consistency

The preceding five steps must be applied consistently to all customer contracts that have similar characteristics, and under similar circumstances. The intent is to create a system of revenue recognition that can be relied upon to yield consistent results.

## Contract Modifications

A contract modification occurs when there is a scope or price change to the contract, and the change is approved by both signatories to the contract. Other terms may be used for a contract modification, such as a change order. It is possible that a contract modification exists, despite the presence of a dispute between the parties concerning scope or price. All of the relevant facts and circumstances must be considered when determining whether there is an enforceable contract modification that can impact revenue recognition.

## Treatment as Separate Contract

There are circumstances under which a contract modification might be accounted for as a separate contract. For this to be the case, the following two conditions must both be present:

- *Distinct change*. The scope has increased, to encompass new goods or services that are distinct from those offered in the original contract.
- *Price change*. The price has increased enough to encompass the standalone prices of the additional goods and services, adjusted for the circumstances related to that specific contract.

When these circumstances are met, there is an economic difference between a modified contract for the additional goods or services and a situation where an entirely new contract has been created.

---

**EXAMPLE**

Blitz Communications is buying one million cell phone batteries from Creekside Industrial. The parties decide to alter the contract to add the purchase of 200,000 battery chargers for a price increase of $2.8 million. The associated price increase includes a 30% discount, which Creekside was already offering to Blitz under the terms of the original contract. This contract change reflects a distinct change that adds new goods to the contract, and includes an associated price change that has been adjusted for the discount terms of the contract. This contract modification can be accounted for as a separate contract.

---

## Treatment as Continuing Contract

It may not be possible to treat a contract modification as a separate contract. If so, there are likely to be goods or services not yet transferred to the customer as of the modification date. The seller can account for these residual deliveries using one of the following methods:

- *Remainder is distinct*. If the remaining goods or services to be delivered are distinct from those already delivered under the contract, account for the modification as a cancellation of the old contract and creation of a new one. In this case, the consideration that should be allocated to the remaining performance obligations is the sum total of:
  - The original consideration promised by the customer but not yet received; and
  - The new consideration associated with the modification.

---

**EXAMPLE**

Grizzly Golf Carts, maker of sturdy golf carts for overweight golfers, contracts with a local suburban golf course to deliver two golf carts for a total price of $12,000. The carts are different models, but have the same standalone price, so Grizzly allocates $6,000 of the transaction price to each cart. One cart is delivered immediately, so Grizzly recognizes $6,000 of revenue. Before the second cart can be delivered, the golf course customer requests that a third cart be added to the contract; this is a heftier cart that has a built-in barbecue grill. The contract price is increased by $8,000, which is less than the $10,000 standalone price of this model.

Since the second and third carts are distinct from the first cart model, there is a distinct change in the contract, which necessitates treating the change as a new contract. Accordingly, the second and third carts are treated as though they are part of a new contract, with the remaining $14,000 of the transaction price totally allocated to the new contract.

**EXAMPLE**

As noted in an earlier example, Nova Corporation contracted with the Deep Field Scanning Authority to construct two three-meter telescopes. The terms of the contract included a provision that could increase the allowable price charged by $250,000, with this price being apportioned equally between the two telescopes. One month into the contract period, Deep Field completely alters the configuration of the second telescope, from a reflector to a catadioptric model. The change is so significant that this telescope can now be considered a separate contract. However, since the variable price was already apportioned at the inception of the original contract, the $125,000 allocated to each telescope will continue. This is because the variable consideration was promised prior to the contract modification.

---

- *Remainder is not distinct.* If the remaining goods or services to be delivered are not distinct from those already delivered under the contract, account for the modification as part of the existing contract. This results in an adjustment to the recognized amount of revenue (up or down) as of the modification date. Thus, the adjustment involves calculating a change in the amount of revenue recognized on a cumulative catch-up basis.

---

**EXAMPLE**

Domicilio Corporation enters into a contract to construct the world headquarters building of the International Mushroom Farmers' Cooperative. Mushroom requires its architects to be true to the name of the organization, with the result being a design for a squat, dark building with no windows, high humidity, and a unique waste recycling system. Domicilio has not encountered such a design before, and so incorporates a cautious stance into its assumptions regarding the contract terms.

The contract terms state that Domicilio will be paid a total of $12,000,000, broken into a number of milestone payments. There is also a $100,000 on-time completion bonus. At the inception of the contract, Domicilio expects the following financial results:

| | |
|---|---|
| Transaction price | $12,000,000 |
| Expected costs | 9,000,000 |
| Expected profit (25%) | $3,000,000 |

The project manager anticipates trouble with several parts of the construction project, and advises strongly against including any part of the completion bonus in the transaction price.

At the end of seven months, the project manager is surprised to find that Domicilio is on target to complete the work on time. Also, the company has completed 65% of its performance obligation, based on the $5,850,000 of costs incurred to date relative to the total amount of expected costs. Through this point, the company has recognized the following revenues and costs:

| | |
|---|---|
| Revenue | $7,800,000 |
| Costs | 5,850,000 |
| Gross profit | $1,950,000 |

The project manager is still uncomfortable with recognizing any part of the completion bonus.

With one month to go on the project, the project manager finally allows that Domicilio will likely complete the project one week early, though he has completely lost all interest in eating mushrooms. At this point, the company has completed 92.5% of its performance obligation (based on costs incurred), so the controller recognizes an additional $92,500 for that portion of the $100,000 on-time completion bonus that has already been earned.

---

- *Mix of elements.* If the remaining goods or services to be delivered are comprised of a mix of distinct and not-distinct elements, separately identify the different elements and account for them as per the dictates of the preceding two methods.

## Entitlement to Payment

At all points over the duration of a contract, the seller should have the right to payment for the performance completed to date, if the customer were to cancel the contract for reasons other than the seller's failure to perform. The amount of this payment should approximate the selling price of the goods or services transferred to the customer to date; this means that costs are recovered, plus a reasonable profit margin. This reasonable profit margin should be one of the following:

- A reasonable proportion of the expected profit margin, based on the extent of the total performance completed prior to contract termination; or
- A reasonable return on the cost of capital that the seller has experienced on its cost of capital for similar contracts, if the margin on this particular contract is higher than the return the seller typically generates from this type of contract.

An entitlement to payment depends on contractual factors, such as only being paid when certain milestones are reached or when the customer is completely satisfied with a deliverable. There may not be an entitlement to payment if one of these contractual factors is present. Further, there may be legal precedents or legislation that may interfere with or bolster an entitlement to payment. For example:

- There may be a legal precedent that gives the seller the right to payment for all performance to date, even though this right is not clarified within the contract terms.
- Legal precedent may reveal that other sellers having similar rights to payment in their contracts have not succeeded in obtaining payment.
- The seller may not have attempted to enforce its right to payment in the past, which may have rendered its rights legally unenforceable.

Conversely, the terms of a contract may not legally allow a customer to terminate a contract. If so, and the customer still attempts to terminate the contract, the seller may be entitled to continue to provide goods or services to the customer, and require the customer to pay the amounts stated in the contract. In this type of situation, the seller has an enforceable right to payment.

An enforceable right to payment may not match the payment schedule stated in a contract. The payment schedule does not necessarily sync with the seller's right to payment for performance. For example, the customer could have insisted upon delayed payment dates in the payment schedule in order to more closely match its ability to make payments to the seller.

---

**EXAMPLE**

A customer of Hodgson Industrial Design pays a $50,000 nonrefundable upfront payment to Hodgson at the inception of a contract to overhaul the design of the customer's main product. The customer does not like Hodgson's initial set of design prototypes, and cancels the contract. On the cancellation date, Hodgson's billable hours on the project sum to $65,000. Hodgson has an enforceable right to retain the $50,000 it has already been paid. The right to be paid for the remaining $15,000 depends on the contract terms and legal precedents.

---

## Contract-Related Costs

Thus far, the discussion has centered on the recognition of revenue – but what about the costs that an organization incurs to fulfill a contract? In this section, we separately address the accounting for the costs incurred to initially obtain a contract, costs incurred during a contract, and how these costs are to be charged to expense.

### Costs to Obtain a Contract

An organization may incur certain costs to obtain a contract. If so, it is allowable to record these costs as an asset, and amortize them over the life of the contract. The following conditions apply:

- The costs must be incremental; that is, they would not have been incurred if the organization had not obtained the contract.
- If the amortization period will be one year or some lesser period, it is allowable to simply charge these costs to expense as incurred.
- There is an expectation that the costs will be recovered.

An example of a contract-related cost that could be recorded as an asset and amortized is the sales commission associated with a sale, though as a practical expedient it is usually charged to expense as incurred.

---

**EXAMPLE**

A water engineering firm bids on a contract to investigate the level of silt accumulation in the Oswego Canal in New York, and wins the bid. The firm incurs the following costs as part of its bidding process.

| | |
|---|---|
| Staff time to prepare proposal | $18,000 |
| Printing fees | 2,500 |
| Travel costs | 5,000 |
| Commissions paid to sales staff | 15,000 |
| | $40,500 |

The firm must charge the staff time, printing fees, and travel costs to expense as incurred, since it would have incurred these expenses even if the bid had failed. Only the commissions paid to the sales staff can be considered a contract asset, since that cost should be recovered through its future billings for consulting services.

---

### Costs to Fulfill a Contract

In general, any costs required to fulfill a contract should be recognized as assets, as long as they meet all of these criteria:

- The costs are tied to a specific contract;
- The costs will be used to satisfy future performance obligations; and
- There is an expectation that the costs will be recovered.

Costs that are considered to relate directly to a contract include the following:

- *Direct labor*. Includes the wages of those employees directly engaged in providing services to the customer.
- *Direct materials*. Includes the supplies consumed in the provision of services to the customer.
- *Cost allocations*. Includes those costs that relate directly to the contract, such as the cost of managing the contract, project supervision, and depreciation of the equipment used to fulfill the contract.
- *Chargeable costs*. Includes those costs that the contract explicitly states can be charged to the customer.
- *Other costs*. Includes costs that would only be incurred because the seller entered into the contract, such as payments to subcontractors providing services to the customer.

Other costs are to be charged to expense as incurred, rather than being classified as contract assets. These costs include:

- *Administration*. General and administrative costs, unless the contract terms explicitly state that they can be charged to the contract.
- *Indistinguishable*. Costs for which it is not possible to determine whether they relate to unsatisfied or satisfied performance obligations. In this case, the default assumption is that they relate to satisfied performance obligations.
- *Past performance costs*. Any costs incurred that relate to performance obligations that have already been fulfilled.
- *Waste*. The costs of resources wasted in the contract fulfillment process, which were not included in the contract price.

---

**EXAMPLE**

Tele-Service International enters into a contract to take over the phone customer service function of Artisan's Delight, a manufacturer of hand-woven wool shopping bags. Tele-Service incurs a cost of $50,000 to construct an interface between the inventory and customer service systems of Artisan's Delight and its own call database. This cost relates to activities needed to fulfill the requirements of the contract, but does not result in the provision of any services to Artisan's Delight. This cost should be amortized over the term of the contract.

Tele-Service assigns four of its employees on a full-time basis to handle incoming customer calls from Artisan's customers. Though this group is providing services to the customer, it is not generating or enhancing the resources of Tele-Service, and so its cost cannot be recognized as an asset. Instead, the cost of these employees is charged to expense as incurred.

---

## Amortization of Costs

When contract-related costs have been recognized as assets, they should be amortized on a systematic basis that reflects the timing of the transfer of related goods and services to the customer. If there is a change in the anticipated timing of the transfer of goods and services to the customer, update the amortization to reflect this change. This is considered a change in accounting estimate.

## Impairment of Costs

The seller should recognize an impairment loss in the current period when the carrying amount of an asset associated with a contract is greater than the remaining payments to be received from the customer. The calculation is:

$$\text{Remaining consideration to be received}[5] - \text{Costs not yet recognized as expenses}$$

$$= \text{Impairment amount (if result is a negative figure)}$$

It is not allowable to reverse an impairment loss on contract assets that has already been recognized.

## Summary

Revenue recognition is almost entirely principles-based, where the general conceptual aspects of revenue recognition are outlined, rather than imposing massive amounts of rules-based specificity. This principles-based approach is the hallmark of international financial reporting standards, which have been largely constructed on this basis. The approach is quite unusual for GAAP, which is largely rules-based.

---

[5] The remaining consideration to be received includes the residual amount expected to be received in the future and the amount already received but which has not yet been recognized as revenue.

## Review Questions

1. The following conditions are needed for a contract to exist, except for:
    a. The cash flows of the seller will change
    b. Written approval
    c. The rights of the parties are identified
    d. The amount the customer will pay is stated

2. Two contracts with the same customer can be considered a single contract for accounting purposes when:
    a. They are approved by the same authorized representative of the customer
    b. The prices paid are segregated by contract
    c. Multiple commercial objectives are involved
    d. There is one performance obligation inherent in the contracts

3. The assessment of a possible reversal of revenue can include the following factor:
    a. The time that must pass before the uncertainty can be resolved is relatively short
    b. The seller has a history of accepting price concessions
    c. The seller has tight control over the amount paid
    d. There are two possible outcomes for the amounts that may be paid

4. A standalone selling price may be estimated by using all of the following methods, except for:
    a. Residual approach
    b. Adjusted market assessment
    c. Expected cost plus a margin
    d. Transfer pricing

5. The following is an indicator that a customer has gained control over a good or service delivered by the supplier:
    a. The seller retains title to the asset
    b. The goods are segregated on the seller's premises
    c. The customer cannot pledge the asset
    d. The customer has accepted the asset

6. The following is an example of an output method used to measure progress toward the fulfillment of a performance obligation:
    a. Machine hours used
    b. Labor hours expended
    c. Milestones reached
    d. Costs incurred

7. An entity that has contracted to obtain goods or services:
    a. Is a supplier
    b. Is a customer
    c. Cannot also be a subsidiary
    d. Is collaborating on research and development activities

8. Contract criteria must be re-evaluated:
    a. At the end of each reporting period
    b. At the end of the fiscal year
    c. Only when the seller notes a significant change in the relevant facts and circumstances
    d. If the customer does not send back a confirmation as part of the year-end audit

9. A contract does not exist when:
    a. There is no signature on the document
    b. It is being combined with another contract for accounting purposes
    c. Each party has a unilateral right to terminate the agreement and without compensating the other party
    d. There has been no prior legal review of the contract terms

10. A good or service is considered to be distinct when:
    a. The customer separately pays for the item
    b. Delivery of the item is separately identified within the contract
    c. Functionality of the deliverable is not assured unless this item is delivered
    d. There is a standalone price for the item

11. The transaction price includes the following, except for:
    a. Sales tax
    b. Fees for services rendered
    c. Freight charge
    d. Rush charge

12. The expected value method is used when:
    a. There are a large number of possible payment amounts
    b. The result must match one of the prices that could be paid
    c. The amount of consideration to be paid is fixed
    d. All performance obligations have been fulfilled

13. The following factor should be present before including a financing component in a contract:
    a. A short payment interval
    b. There is a significant difference between the contract price and the cash price
    c. The credit rating of the customer
    d. The cash reserves of the seller

# Chapter 11
# Accounting for Stock-Based Compensation

## Introduction

A company may issue shares to its employees or outside parties that are intended to be compensation for past or future services rendered. These payments can take many forms, such as stock grants, stock options, warrants, and discounted employee stock purchase plans. In this chapter, we address how to account for each of these types of stock compensation, as well as similar arrangements.

## Overview of Stock Compensation

A company may issue payments to its employees in the form of shares in the business. When these payments are made, the essential accounting is to recognize the cost of the related services as they are received by the company, at their fair value. The offset to this expense recognition is either an increase in an equity or liability account, depending on the nature of the transaction. Employee services are not recognized by the employer before they are received.

### Stock Compensation Valuation and Cost Recognition Topics

The following issues relate to the measurement and recognition of stock-based compensation:

Essential Concepts

- *Employee designation.* The accounting for stock compensation noted in this chapter only applies to employees, with the exception of the Equity-Based Payments to Non-Employees section. It also applies to the board of directors, as long as they were elected by company shareholders. However, the accounting only applies to stock grants issued in compensation for their services as directors, not for other services provided.
- *Grant date.* The date on which a stock-based award is granted is assumed to be the date when the award is approved under the corporate governance requirements. The grant date can also be considered the date on which an employee initially begins to benefit from or be affected by subsequent changes in the price of a company's stock, as long as subsequent approval of the grant is considered perfunctory.

---

**EXAMPLE**

The board of directors of Coronary Associates approves a stock option award to Dr. Jones, who is an employee of Coronary. The board meeting date on which the award is approved is March 15. This is the grant date.

---

- *Service period.* The service period associated with a stock-based award is considered to be the vesting period, but the facts and circumstances of the arrangement can result in a different service period for the purpose of determining the number of periods over which to accrue compensation expense. This is called the *implicit service period.*

**EXPENSE**

Mrs. Smith is granted 10,000 stock options by the board of directors of Uncanny Corporation, which vest over 24 months. There is no service specified under the arrangement, so the service period is assumed to be the 24-month vesting period. Thus, the fair value of the award should be recognized ratably over the vesting period.

## Costs to be Recognized

- *Expense accrual.* When the service component related to a stock issuance spans several reporting periods, accrue the related service expense based on the probable outcome of the performance condition, with an offsetting credit to equity (usually to the additional paid-in capital account). A performance condition is a condition that affects the determination of the fair value of an award. Thus, always accrue the expense when it is probable that the condition will be achieved. Also, accrue the expense over the initial best estimate of the employee service period, which is usually the service period required in the arrangement related to the stock issuance.

**EXAMPLE**

The board of directors of Armadillo Industries grants stock options to its president that have a fair value of $80,000, which will vest in the earlier of four years or when the company achieves a 20% market share in a new market that the company wants to enter. Since there is not sufficient historical information about the company's ability to succeed in the new market, the controller elects to set the service period at four years, and accordingly accrues $20,000 of compensation expense in each of the next four years, with an offsetting credit to additional paid-in capital.

If both performance conditions had been required before the stock options would be awarded, and there was no way of determining the probability of achieving the 20% market share condition, the controller would only begin to accrue any compensation expense after it became probable that the market share condition could be achieved. In this latter case, compensation expense would be recognized at once for all of the earlier periods during which no compensation expense had been accrued.

- *Service rendered prior to grant date.* If some or all of the requisite service associated with stock-based compensation occurs prior to the grant date, accrue the compensation expense during these earlier reporting periods, based on the fair value of the award at each reporting date. When the grant date is reached, adjust the compensation accrued to date based on the per-unit fair value assigned on the grant date. Thus, the initial recordation is a best guess of what the eventual fair value will be.
- *Service rendered prior to performance target completion.* An employee may complete the required amount of service prior to the date when the associated performance target has been achieved. If so, recognize the compensation expense when it becomes probable that the target will be achieved. This recognition reflects the service already rendered by the employee.
- *Service not rendered.* If an employee does not render the service required for an award, the employer may then reverse any related amount of compensation expense that had previously been recognized.

**EXAMPLE**

Uncanny Corporation grants 5,000 restricted stock units (RSUs) to its vice president of sales, with a three-year cliff vesting provision. The fair value of the RSUs on the grant date is $60,000, so the company accrues $20,000 of compensation expense per year for three years.

One week prior to the cliff vesting date, the vice president of sales unexpectedly resigns. Since the award has not yet vested, the company reverses all of the accrued compensation expense.

- *Employee payments*. If an employee pays the issuer an amount in connection with an award, the fair value attributable to employee service is net of the amount paid. For example, if a stock option has a fair value on the grant date of $100, and the recipient pays $20 for the option, the award amount attributable to employee service is $80.

**EXAMPLE**

Armadillo Industries issues 1,000 shares of common stock to Mr. Jones, the vice president of sales, at a large discount from the market price. On the grant date, the fair value of these shares is $20,000. Mr. Jones pays $1,000 to the company for these shares. Thus, the amount that can be attributed to Mr. Jones' services to the company is $19,000 (calculated as $20,000 fair value - $1,000 payment).

- *Non-compete agreement*. If a share-based award contains a non-compete agreement, the facts and circumstances of the situation may indicate that the non-compete is a significant service condition. If so, accrue the related amount of compensation expense over the period covered by the non-compete agreement.

**EXAMPLE**

Armadillo Industries grants 200,000 restricted stock units (RSUs) to its chief high-pressure module design engineer, which are vested on the grant date. The fair value of the grant is $500,000, which is triple his compensation for the past year. Under the terms of the arrangement, the RSUs will only be transferred to the engineer ratably over the next five years if he complies with the terms of the non-compete agreement.

Since the RSUs are essentially linked to the non-compete agreement, and the amount of the future payouts are quite large, it is evident that the arrangement is really intended to be compensation for future services yet to be rendered to the company. Consequently, the appropriate accounting treatment is not to recognize the expense at once, but rather to recognize it ratably over the remaining term of the non-compete agreement.

- *Clawback arrangements*. There may be an arrangement under which an employee is required to return shares or profits from the sale of shares. This is called a clawback arrangement, and most commonly occurs as a noncompete mechanism, so that employees will not leave to work for a competitor for a certain period of time. This arrangement is not considered in the grant date fair value of an equity award; instead, it is accounted for only when the contingent event actually occurs. If such a return payment is made, it is recognized as a credit in the income statement, and is limited to the lesser of the compensation cost already recognized for the returned payment, or the fair value of the consideration received.
- *Payroll taxes*. Accrue a liability for the payroll taxes associated with stock-based compensation as of the date of the event that triggered measurement of the compensation.
- *Expired stock options*. If stock option grants expire unused, do not reverse the related amount of compensation expense.

- *Subsequent changes.* If the circumstances later indicate that the number of instruments to be granted has changed, recognize the change in compensation cost in the period in which the change in estimate occurs. Also, if the initial estimate of the service period turns out to be incorrect, adjust the expense accrual to match the updated estimate.

---

**EXAMPLE**

The board of directors of Armadillo Industries initially grants 5,000 stock options to the engineering manager, with a vesting period of four years. The shares are worth $100,000 at the grant date, so the controller plans to recognize $25,000 of compensation expense in each of the next four years. After two years, the board is so pleased with the performance of the engineering manager that they accelerate the vesting schedule to the current date. The controller must therefore accelerate the remaining $50,000 of compensation expense that had not yet been recognized to the current date.

---

Valuation Concepts

- *Fair value determination.* Stock-based compensation is measured at the fair value of the instruments issued as of the grant date, even though the stock may not be issued until a much later date. The fair value of a stock option is estimated with a valuation method, such as an option-pricing model. See the following Characteristics used as the Basis for Fair Value Determination sub-section for more information.
- *Fair value of nonvested shares.* The fair value of a nonvested share is based on its value as though it were vested on the grant date.
- *Fair value of restricted shares.* A restricted share cannot be sold for a certain period of time due to contractual or governmental restrictions. The fair value of a restricted share likely to be less than the fair value of an unrestricted share, since the ability to sell a restricted share is sharply reduced. However, if the shares of the issuer are traded in an active market, restrictions are considered to have little effect on the price at which the shares could be exchanged.
- *Reload valuation.* A compensation instrument may have a reload feature, which automatically grants additional options to an employee once that person exercises existing options that use company shares to pay the exercise price. Do not include the value of the reload feature in the fair value of an award. Instead, measure reload options as separate awards when they are granted.

If the offsetting increase to stock-based compensation is equity, it should be to the paid-in capital account, as noted in the following example.

---

**EXAMPLE**

Armadillo Industries issues stock options with 10-year terms to its employees. All of these options vest at the end of four years (known as *cliff vesting*). The company uses a lattice-based valuation model (see the following Fair Value Calculation Alternatives sub-section) to arrive at an option fair value of $15.00. The company grants 100,000 stock options. On the grant date, it assumes that 10% of the options will be forfeited. The exercise price of the options is $25.

Given this information, Armadillo charges $28,125 to expense in each month. The calculation of this compensation expense accrual is:

($15 Option fair value × 100,000 Options × 90% Exercise probability) ÷ 48 Months = $28,125

The monthly journal entry to recognize the compensation expense is:

|  | Debit | Credit |
|---|---|---|
| Compensation expense | 28,125 | |
| Additional paid-in capital | | 28,125 |

Armadillo is subject to a 35% income tax rate, and expects to have sufficient future taxable income to offset the deferred tax benefits of the share-based compensation arrangements. Accordingly, the company records the following monthly entry to recognize the deferred tax benefit:

|  | Debit | Credit |
|---|---|---|
| Deferred tax asset | 9,844 | |
| Deferred tax benefit | | 9,844 |

Thus, the net after-tax effect of the monthly compensation expense recognition is $18,281 (calculated as $28,125 compensation expense - $9,844 deferred tax benefit).

At the end of the vesting period, the actual number of forfeitures matches the originally estimated amount, leaving 90,000 options. All of the 90,000 options are exercised once they have vested, which results in the following entry to record the conversion of options to shares:

|  | Debit | Credit |
|---|---|---|
| Cash (90,000 shares × $25/share) | 2,250,000 | |
| Additional paid-in capital | 1,350,000 | |
| Common stock | | 3,600,000 |

## Stock Volatility

A key component of the value of a company's stock is its volatility, which is the range over which the price varies over time, or is expected to vary. Since an employee holding a stock option can wait for the highest possible stock price before exercising the option, that person will presumably wait for the stock price to peak before exercising the option. Therefore, a stock that has a history or expectation of high volatility is worth more from the perspective of an option holder than one that has little volatility. The result is that a company with high stock price volatility will likely charge more employee compensation to expense for a given number of shares than a company whose stock experiences low volatility.

> **Best Practice:** It is useful for a publicly-held company to engage in a high level of investor relations activity in order to manage stock price expectations and thereby reduce the volatility of the stock price. Doing so reduces the cost of stock-based compensation, which is derived in part from the level of price volatility.

Stock price volatility is partially driven by the amount of leverage that a company employs in its financing. Thus, if a business uses a large amount of debt to fund its operations, its profit will fluctuate in a wider range than a business that uses less debt, since the extra debt can be used to generate more sales, but the associated interest expense will reduce net profits if revenues decline.

## Characteristics used as the Basis for Fair Value Determination

Fair value is relatively easy to determine when the common stock of a publicly-held company is being issued, since there is an established market price for other shares that are essentially identical to the ones being issued. However, there are many other issuances where this is not the case, or where there are special requirements associated with a prospective stock issuance that can alter its fair value. In these situations, fair value must be derived using a valuation technique that takes into account the following information:

- *Exercise price.* The exercise price of the option.
- *Option term.* The expected term of the option, which is the period during which the option is expected to be outstanding; this takes into account the expected exercise of an option by employees. The expected term of an option is generally shorter than its contractual term, and can be based on historical experience, an analysis of employee ages, lengths of service, and so forth. Another choice is to estimate the term based upon expected future price points of the underlying stock; for example, employees may be much more likely to exercise their options once the market price of the underlying shares exceeds 50% of the exercise price. It is also possible to incorporate published academic research into this estimate, or industry averages. An easier alternative is discussed immediately after these bullet points.
- *Share price.* The price of the shares to be issued.
- *Volatility.* The expected volatility of the price of the shares to be issued, spanning the expected option term. A reasonable way to estimate volatility is the historical pattern of changes in the price of a company's stock, adjusted for anticipated future issues that may impact volatility. If a business has a high debt-equity ratio, the extra fixed cost layer imposed by the debt tends to increase the variability of its earnings, which in turn increases the price volatility of its shares.
- *Dividends.* The expected dividends to be paid on the underlying shares during the expected term of the option. Include the historical pattern of changes in dividend payments in the estimation of future dividends.
- *Interest rate.* The risk-free interest rate during the expected term of the option. Use the implied yield on U.S. Treasury zero-coupon issuances over the term of the option.

A nonpublic entity can make a policy election to apply a practical expedient to estimate the expected option term for all awards having performance or service conditions. This election is available as long as the option is granted at the money, there is a limited time to exercise the award if there is a termination of service, and the employee can only exercise the award (as opposed to selling or hedging it). The practical expedient is as follows:

- If the vesting is dependent on a service condition, set the expected term at the midpoint between the required service period and the contractual term of the award.
- If the vesting is dependent upon the completion of a performance condition, and that condition will probably be achieved, then set the expected term at the midpoint between the required service period and the contractual term of the award.
- If the vesting is dependent upon the completion of a performance condition, and that condition will probably *not* be achieved, then set the expected term at either the contractual term of the award or the midpoint between the required service period and the contractual term of the award (if the required service period is stated).

When developing estimates for these inputs to the valuation model, select the amount that is the most likely; if no value appears to be the most likely, use an average of the range of possible outcomes. The derivation of estimates for these inputs usually begins with historical experience, followed by adjustments to reflect how currently available information indicates how the future might reasonably be expected to vary from the past.

**EXAMPLE**

Hassle Corporation operates two subsidiaries, one of which is in a long-term, staid industry in which little changes. The other subsidiary is researching and developing quantum computing solutions, which is a wildly fragmented industry where variable profits and market shares are routine. The revenues from the first subsidiary comprise 90% of the company's total sales.

It would be reasonable for Hassle to base much of its expectations for the determination of stock option fair values on the historical experience of the business, since there is a long history of stock price volatility, option exercise behavior, and dividends that can be used. However, if Hassle's board of directors sells off the first subsidiary, the company is left with an entity whose history is wildly variable. In this latter case, it would make little sense to rely upon historical information as the basis for deriving fair value.

## Fair Value Calculation Alternatives

When a publicly-held company issues stock compensation, it can derive fair value from the current market price of its stock, which is readily available. This information is not available to a privately-held organization, for which there is no ready market for its stock. The alternative is to estimate share value based on the historical volatility of a related industry sector index, which is comprised of companies that are similar to the entity conducting the measurement in terms of size, leverage, industry, and so forth. This latter approach is called the *calculated value method*. If a nonpublic company operates in several markets, it is permissible to model its stock price volatility on a weighted average of several related industry sector indexes that approximately mirror the structure of the company, or simply rely upon that industry sector that is most representative of its operations. Broad-based market indexes are not acceptable, since they are not sufficiently closely-related to a specific industry.

**EXAMPLE**

Abbreviated Corporation is a privately-held company that produces short versions of famous literature. The company grants 60,000 stock options to its editorial staff. The company controller elects to use the calculated value method to derive a valuation for the stock options. She locates an industry stock price index for publicly-held publishing companies, from which she derives historical stock price volatility of 27%. She plugs this information and other factors into the Black-Scholes-Merton formula to derive a fair value of $3.18 per share. When multiplied by the 60,000 options granted, the result is total compensation expense of $190,800. Forfeitures are expected to be 20%, so the net compensation expense is $152,640. Since the vesting period of the options is three years, the controller recognizes the net expense at the rate of $50,880 per year, through the vesting period.

When it is not possible to estimate the fair value of an equity instrument, it is permissible to use an alternative valuation technique, as long as it is applied consistently, reflects the key characteristics of the instrument, and is based on accepted standards of financial economic theory. Models that are commonly used to derive fair value are the Black-Scholes-Merton formula and the lattice model. Key characteristics of these models are:

- *Black-Scholes-Merton formula.* Assumes that options are exercised at the end of the arrangement period, and that price volatility, dividends, and interest rates are constant through the term of the option being measured.
- *Monte Carlo simulation.* Uses multiple trial runs on a computer to approximate the probability of certain outcomes, using random variables. This simulation can be run using the Excel electronic spreadsheet.

- *Lattice model.* Can incorporate ongoing changes in price volatility and dividends over successive time periods in the term of an option. The model assumes that at least two price movements are possible in each measured time period.

---

**EXAMPLE**

Armadillo Industries grants an option on $25 stock that will expire in 12 months. The exercise price of the option matches the $25 stock price. Management believes there is a 40% chance that the stock price will increase by 25% during the upcoming year, a 40% chance that the price will decline by 10%, and a 20% chance that the price will decline by 50%. The risk-free interest rate is 5%. The steps required to develop a fair value for the stock option using the lattice model are:

1. Chart the estimated stock price variations.
2. Convert the price variations into the future value of options.
3. Discount the options to their present values.

The following lattice model shows the range and probability of stock prices for the upcoming year:

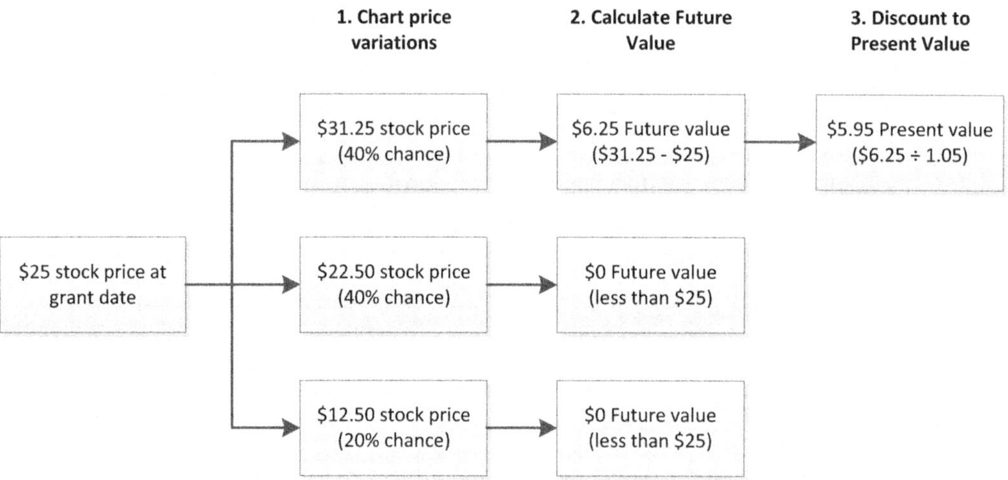


In short, the option will expire unexercised unless the stock price increases. Since there is only a 40% chance of the stock price increasing, the present value of the stock option associated with that scenario can be assigned the following expected present value for purposes of assigning a fair value to the option at the grant date:

$$\$5.95 \text{ Option present value} \times 40\% \text{ Probability} = \$2.38 \text{ Option value at grant date}$$

---

It is acceptable to employ a different valuation model to develop the fair value of different equity instruments. It is also permissible to switch valuation methods if the replacement method can yield a better estimate of fair value. All models must be supportable, in that the assumptions used are fully defensible.

> **Best Practice:** From an accounting efficiency perspective, it is useful to aggregate individual awards into homogeneous groups for valuation purposes.

## Changes in Accounting Estimate

If there is a change in the valuation technique or the method of determining assumptions used in a valuation technique, this is considered a change in accounting estimate. A change in accounting estimate is to be accounted for in the period of change and thereafter. No retrospective change (which is a change to prior-period financial statements) is required or allowed.

## Awards Classified as Equity

In this section, we address a number of variations on how to account for awards that are classified as equity arrangements (that is, the offset to compensation expense is an increase in equity). The bulk of these issues relate to subsequent modifications of existing stock-based awards.

### Award Measurement Problems

When it is not possible to reasonably estimate the fair value of a stock-based award at its grant date, continue to remeasure the award at each successive reporting date until the award has been settled. Once the award has been settled, adjust the compensation-to-date associated with the award to the intrinsic value of the award. Intrinsic value is the excess amount of the fair value of a share over the exercise price of an underlying stock option.

### Award Modifications

An award is considered to have been modified unless *all* of the following conditions apply:

1. The fair value of the modified award is the same as the fair value of the original award.
2. The vesting conditions of the modified award are the same as the conditions that applied to the original award.
3. The classification of the modified award as an equity or liability instrument matches the classification of the original award.

If a stock-based award *is* determined to have been modified, treat the modification as an exchange of the original award for an entirely new award. Thus, the company is assumed to buy back the original award and exchange it for an award of equal or greater value. The accounting for a modified award includes the following points:

- *Fair value basis.* If there is an incremental change in value between the "old" and "new" awards, this is treated as additional compensation expense. The amount of expense is calculated by determining the fair value of the "old" award immediately prior to the terms modification, and subtracting it from the fair value of the modified award.
- *Intrinsic value basis.* If intrinsic value is being used instead of fair value to calculate the associated cost of compensation, measure the incremental change in value by comparing the intrinsic value of the award just prior to modification with the intrinsic value of the modified award.
- *Short-term inducements.* If the company offers short-term inducements to convince employees to accept an alteration of their stock-based compensation plans, only treat these inducements as modifications if they are accepted by employees.
- *Equity restructuring.* If there is an equity restructuring and awards are replaced with new ones that have the same fair values, do not alter the existing accounting. However, if the fair values have changed, treat the effects of the equity restructuring as a modification.
- *Repurchase of award.* If the company repurchases an award, it should charge the amount of the payment to equity, up to the amount of the fair value of the instruments repurchased. If the amount paid exceeds the fair value of the instruments repurchased, charge the difference to compensation expense.
- *Cancellation and replacement.* If the company cancels a stock-based award and concurrently grants a replacement award or other form of payment, treat these two events as the modification of terms of the original award.
- *Award cancellation.* If the company cancels an award outright, without any offer to replace the award, accelerate the recognition of any remaining unrecognized compensation expense to the cancellation date.

**EXAMPLE**

Armadillo Industries issues 10,000 stock options to various employees in 20X1. The designated exercise price of the options is $25, and the vesting period is four years. The total fair value of these options is $20,000, which the company charges to expense ratably over four years, which is $5,000 per year.

One year later, the market price of the stock has declined to $15, so the board of directors decides to modify the options to have an exercise price of $15.

Armadillo incurs additional compensation expense of $30,000 for the amount by which the fair value of the modified options exceeds the fair value of the original options as of the date of the modification. The accounting department adds this additional expense to the remaining $15,000 of compensation expense associated with the original stock options, which is a total unrecognized compensation expense of $45,000. The company recognizes this amount ratably over the remaining three years of vesting, which is $15,000 per year.

## Income Tax Effects

If there is a compensation cost associated with the issuance of equity instruments that would normally result in a tax deduction at a future date, it is considered a deductible temporary difference for income tax purposes. If some portion of this compensation cost is capitalized into the cost of an asset (such as inventory or a fixed asset), the capitalized cost is considered part of the tax basis of the asset.

If there is a compensation cost that does not result in a tax deduction, do not treat it as a deductible temporary difference. If a future event will change the treatment of such an item to a tax deduction, wait until the future event occurs before treating the item as a tax deduction.

## Awards Classified as Liabilities

A key element of stock-based compensation arrangements is whether these arrangements result in an offsetting increase in equity or liabilities. The following situations indicate the presence of a liability, rather than a change in equity:

- *Cash settlement.* An employee can require the issuing company to settle an option by paying in cash or other assets, rather than stock.
- *Indexing.* An award is indexed to some additional factor, such as the market price of a commodity.
- *Puttable shares.* An employee has the right to require the issuing company to repurchase shares at their fair value, where the put feature essentially allows the employee to avoid the risks associated with owning stock.
- *Share classification.* Certain types of share-based payments, such as mandatorily-redeemable shares, are themselves classified as liabilities.

If an award is classified as a liability, the offsetting expense should be remeasured at its fair value as of the end of each reporting period, until the related service has been completed. Any change in value is to be recognized in the measurement period, adjusted for the percentage of required service rendered through the reporting period. Thus, the measurement date for a liability is the settlement date, not the grant date.

If a company is privately-held, management should make a one-time policy decision to either measure the liabilities incurred under share-based payment arrangements at their fair value or their intrinsic value. Further, if the company is unable to estimate the volatility of its share price, the policy decision is to measure the liabilities based on either the calculated value or intrinsic value of the arrangements.

If an award is modified, treat it as the exchange of the "old" award for a "new" award. However, since the accounting for awards classified as liabilities already provides for the ongoing remeasurement of a liability, there is no need for any additional accounting for a modified award.

**EXAMPLE**

Uncanny Corporation grants 20,000 stock appreciation rights (SARs) to its chief executive officer (CEO). Each SAR entitles the CEO to receive a cash payment that equates to the increase in value of one share of company stock above a baseline value of $25. The award cliff vests after two years. The fair value of each SAR is calculated to be $11.50 as of the grant date. The entry to record the associated amount of compensation expense for the first year, along with the company's deferred tax asset at its 35% income tax rate, is:

| | Debit | Credit |
|---|---|---|
| Compensation expense | 115,000 | |
| Share-based compensation liability | | 115,000 |

| | Debit | Credit |
|---|---|---|
| Deferred tax asset | 40,250 | |
| Deferred tax benefit | | 40,250 |

At the end of the first year of vesting, the fair value of each SAR has increased to $12.75, so an additional entry is needed to adjust the vested amount of compensation expense and deferred tax asset for the $12,500 incremental increase in the value of the award over the first year (calculated as $1.25 increase in SAR fair value × 20,000 SARs × 0.5 service period).

At end of the vesting period, the fair value of each SAR has increased again, to $13.00, which increases the total two-year vested compensation expense for the CEO to $260,000. Since $127,500 of compensation expense has already been recognized at the end of the first year, the company must recognize an additional $132,500 of compensation expense, along with the related amount of deferred tax asset. When the cash payment is made to the CEO, the entry is:

| | Debit | Credit |
|---|---|---|
| Share-based compensation liability | 260,000 | |
| Cash | | 260,000 |

## Employee Stock Ownership Plans

An employee stock ownership plan (ESOP) is an employee benefit plan that is designed to invest primarily in the stock of the employer. The essential mechanics of an ESOP are that shares are paid to the ESOP by the employer (there are some variations on the form of payment), which the ESOP retains in a suspense account until it is allowed to allocate them to the accounts of employees. The employees are eventually paid from these accounts as of a later triggering event.

An ESOP is most commonly used to increase employee ownership of a business, but can also be used for the following purposes:

- To fund a 401(k) matching or profit-sharing program
- To replace lost benefits when other retirement plans are terminated
- To give the owners a tax-favorable way to terminate their ownership of the business
- To ward off hostile takeover attempts

The following sub-sections discuss the two types of ESOP, which are leveraged and non-leveraged. Before addressing the specifics of each type of plan, we first make note of two issues that apply to both types of plans, which are:

- *Put options.* If the shares held by an ESOP are not readily tradable, participants in the plan are given put options, which allow them to require the plan to repurchase their shares at fair value. The employer records this buy-back as a purchase of treasury stock.
- *Pension plan reversion.* An ESOP may be created because an employer is terminating a defined benefit pension plan, and wants to avoid the associated excise tax on the plan assets by shifting them into an ESOP. These assets may then be used to either buy employer stock or retire the debt in an existing ESOP. A pension plan reversion usually results in a larger purchase of employer stock than the tax law permits to be allocated to the accounts of employees in a single year, so some of the shares are held in a suspense account until they can be allocated in future years.

## Leveraged ESOP

As the name implies, a leveraged ESOP borrows funds in order to buy shares of the employer's stock. The money can be borrowed from the employer, or from an outside lender. If an outside lender is used, the loan is usually guaranteed by the employer. A loan uses the employer's shares as collateral. The following accounting issues relate to a leveraged ESOP:

- *Direct loan financing.* When the employer sponsors a loan from an outside lender to an ESOP (called a direct loan), the employer reports the ESOP's debt obligation as its own debt. The employer must also accrue interest expense on the debt. Further, the employer must report cash paid to the ESOP that is used by the ESOP to service the debt as reductions of the debt and interest payable.
- *Indirect loan financing.* An indirect loan is a loan made by an employer to an ESOP, which is funded by an outside loan from a lender to the employer. The employer should report the outside loan as debt. The employer does not report its loan to the ESOP as an asset, nor does it record any interest income on this loan. Any employer contributions to the ESOP and concurrent debt servicing payments from the ESOP to the employer are not recognized in the financial statements of the employer.
- *Employer loan financing.* An employer loan is a loan made by an employer directly to an ESOP, which is not funded by an outside loan from a lender to the employer. In this case, the employer does not report the loan to the ESOP as an asset, nor does it record any interest income on this loan.
- *Purchase of shares by ESOP.* When an ESOP buys shares from the employer, the employer reports the issuance when it occurs, along with a charge to unearned employee stock ownership plan shares, which is a contra equity account. If the ESOP is using debt to buy shares and buys shares on the open market rather than from the employer, the employer still charges the contra equity account, with the offsetting credit to either cash or debt.
- *Release of leveraged ESOP shares.* Shares held by an ESOP are designated as committed to be released when they will be released by a future scheduled debt service payment and will be allocated to employees for their services rendered in the current period. When shares are committed to be released, the unearned employee stock ownership plan shares account is credited; depending on the purpose of the release activity, the debit may be to the compensation cost, dividends payable, or compensation liabilities account, depending on the situation.
- *Dividends on plan shares.* The tax code allows employers to use the dividends on ESOP shares that have been allocated to participants for debt service, but only if the allocated shares have a fair value not less than the dividend amounts used for debt service. Dividends on unallocated shares that are used to pay debt service are reported by the employer as a reduction of either debt or accrued interest payable. If dividends on unallocated shares are paid to participants or added to their accounts, this is reported by the employer as compensation cost. Dividends on allocated shares are

charged by the employer to retained earnings; the related dividend payable can be satisfied either by paying into participant accounts, contributing additional shares, or shifting shares from the suspense account into participant accounts.

- *Direct compensation payments.* If an ESOP is not linked to any other employee benefit or compensation promise, all payments made to the ESOP by the employer are considered to be direct compensation of employees. The employer can recognize as compensation cost the fair value of the shares committed to be released. These shares are typically committed to be released ratably over an accounting period as employees perform their service to the employer, so the average fair value of the shares during this period is used to calculate compensation cost.
- *Debt repayment.* Debt is repaid from employer contributions or dividends to the ESOP. As each repayment is made, shares in suspense are allocated to individual accounts as of the end of the ESOP's fiscal year.

The assistance of independent experts may be needed to estimate the fair value of company shares when determining compensation cost.

### Non-Leveraged ESOP

In a non-leveraged ESOP arrangement, the employer contributes either its own shares to the ESOP or cash that is used to purchase company shares. The shares are regularly allocated to the accounts of plan participants based on employee compensation, length of service with the company, or both. The shares are eventually distributed to employees upon their retirement or termination. The following accounting issues relate to a non-leveraged ESOP:

- *Contribution of shares to ESOP.* When the employer makes a contribution to the ESOP, it reports compensation cost in the amount of the contribution.
- *Dividend treatment.* Dividends on shares held by the ESOP are charged to retained earnings.
- *Share allocation.* When the ESOP receives shares from the employer or cash with which to buy shares, the resulting shares are allocated to participant accounts and held by the plan until the shares are distributed to employees at a later date.
- *Compensation cost.* Compensation cost is measured by the employer at the fair value of the shares contributed or committed to the ESOP, or the cash contributed or committed to the ESOP. The assistance of independent experts may be needed to estimate the fair value of company shares when determining compensation cost.

## Employee Share Purchase Plans

A company may offer its employees the opportunity to directly purchase shares in the business through an employee share purchase plan (ESPP). These plans frequently offer sales without any brokerage charge, and possibly also at a price somewhat below the market rate.

From an accounting perspective, the main issue with an ESPP is whether it represents a form of compensation to employees. An ESPP is not considered compensatory if it meets all of the following criteria:

- *Employee qualification.* Essentially all employees meeting a limited set of employment qualifications can participate in the plan.
- *Favorable terms.* The terms offered under the plan are no more favorable than those available to investors at large, or does not offer a purchase discount of greater than five percent (which is considered the per-share cost that would otherwise be required to raise funds through a public offering). It is possible to justify a percentage greater than five percent, but the business must reassess the justification on an annual basis.

- *Option features.* The plan only allows a maximum 31-day notice period to enroll in the plan after the share price has been fixed, the share price is based only on the market price on the purchase date, and employees can cancel their participation before the purchase date.

Under the following circumstances, an ESPP is considered to be compensatory, which means that the company must record the difference between the market price of the stock and the lower price at which employees purchase the shares as compensation expense:

- The purchase discount offered under the plan is greater than five percent.
- The purchase price is the lesser of the market price on the grant date or the market price on the purchase date.

---

**EXAMPLE**

Armadillo Industries has an employee stock purchase plan, under which employees can purchase shares for a 10% discount from the market price of the company's stock. In the most recent quarter, employees authorized the deduction of $90,000 from their pay, which was used to purchase $100,000 of company stock. Since the discount exceeds the 5% threshold, Armadillo must record the $10,000 discount as compensation expense.

---

## Equity-Based Payments to Non-Employees

An equity-based payment is one in which a business pays a provider of goods or services with its equity, such as shares or warrants. This situation is especially common for a start-up business or rapidly growing company that is trying to conserve cash, and is willing to dilute its equity in pursuit of this goal.

The accounting for equity-based payments depends upon the definition of the recipient, since the accounting for a payment to an employee differs from the accounting when payment is made to anyone else. In this section, we deal with the accounting for equity-based payments to non-employees.

The two main rules for equity-based payments to non-employees are that the grantor must:

- Recognize the fair value of the equity instruments issued or the fair value of the consideration received, whichever can be more reliably measured; and
- Recognize the asset or expense related to the provided goods or services at the same time.

The following additional conditions apply to more specific circumstances:

- *Fully vested equity issued.* If fully vested, nonforfeitable equity instruments are issued, the grantor should recognize the equity on the date of issuance. The offset to this recognition may be a prepaid asset, if the grantee has not yet delivered on its obligations.
- *Option expiration.* If the grantor recognizes an asset or expense based on its issuance of stock options to a grantee, and the grantee does not exercise the options, the grantor does not reverse the asset or expense.
- *Sales incentives.* If sales incentives are paid with equity instruments, measure them at the fair value of the equity instruments or the sales incentive, whichever can be more reliably measured.
- *Equity recipient.* If a business is the recipient of an equity instrument in exchange for goods or services, it should recognize revenue in the normal manner.

The grantor usually recognizes an equity-based payment as of a measurement date. The measurement date is the earlier of:

- The date when the grantee's performance is complete; or
- The date when the grantee's commitment to complete is probable, given the presence of large disincentives related to nonperformance. Note that forfeiture of the equity instrument is not considered a sufficient disincentive to trigger this clause.

It is also possible to reach the measurement date when the grantor issues fully vested, nonforfeitable equity instruments to the grantee, since the grantee does not have an obligation to perform in order to receive payment.

If the grantor issues a fully vested, nonforfeitable equity instrument that can be exercised early if a performance target is reached, the grantor measures the fair value of the instrument at the date of grant. If early exercise is granted, then measure and record the incremental change in fair value as of the date of revision to the terms of the instrument. Also, recognize the cost of the transaction in the same period as if the company had paid cash, instead of using the equity instrument as payment.

---

**EXAMPLE**

Armadillo Industries issues fully vested warrants to a grantee. The option agreement contains a provision that the exercise price will be reduced if a project on which the grantee is working is completed to the satisfaction of Armadillo management by a certain date.

In another arrangement, Armadillo issues warrants that vest in five years. The option agreement contains a provision that the vesting period will be reduced to six months if a project on which the grantee is working is accepted by an Armadillo client by a certain date.

In both cases, the company should record the fair value of the instruments when granted, and then adjust the recorded fair values when the remaining provisions of the agreements have been settled.

---

In rare cases, it may be necessary for the grantor to recognize the cost of an equity payment before the measurement date. If so, measure the fair value of the equity instrument at each successive interim period until the measurement date is reached. If some terms of the equity instrument have not yet been settled during these interim periods (as is the case when the amount of equity paid will vary based on market conditions or counterparty performance), measure the instrument at its lowest aggregate fair value during each interim period, until all terms have been settled.

The grantee must also record payments made to it with equity instruments. The grantee should recognize the fair value of the equity instruments paid using the same rules applied to the grantor. If there is a performance condition, the grantee may have to alter the amount of revenue recognized, once the condition has been settled. The grantee measures the fair value of the equity instruments received as of the earlier of:

- The date when the two parties reach an understanding regarding the amount to be paid and the performance commitment (which is a commitment under which performance is probable because of large disincentives for nonperformance); or
- The date when the grantee's performance is complete.

**EXAMPLE**

Gatekeeper Corporation operates a private toll road. It contracts with International Bridge Development (IBD) to build a bridge along the toll way. Gatekeeper agrees to pay IBD $10,000,000 for the work, as well as an additional 1,000,000 warrants if the bridge is completed by a certain date. IBD agrees to forfeit $2,000,000 of its fee if the bridge has not been completed by that date. The forfeiture clause is sufficiently large to classify the arrangement as a performance commitment.

Gatekeeper should measure the 1,000,000 warrants at the performance commitment date, which have a fair value of $500,000. Gatekeeper should then charge the $500,000 to expense over the normal course of the bridge construction project, based on milestone and completion payments.

**EXAMPLE**

Archaic Corporation hires a writer to create a series of books about ancient Greece. The terms of the deal are that Archaic will pay the writer $20,000 and 10,000 warrants per book completed. There is no penalty associated with the writer declining to continue writing books for the series. The writer completes work on the first book in the series on October 31, and then refuses to continue writing books for Archaic.

Archaic should recognize the fair value of the 10,000 warrants associated with the writer's completion of the first book when the writer completes the manuscript on October 31. On that date, the warrants have a fair value of $5,000, so Archaic should recognize a total expense of $25,000, which is comprised of the cash and warrant portions of the payment.

The requirements noted in this section also apply to share-based payment transactions for acquiring goods and services from nonemployees, when the items purchased are to be used in the grantor's own operations. In this situation, the equity instruments issued are measured at their fair value on the grant date, which is the date on which the parties reach a mutual understanding of the key terms and conditions of the award arrangement.

## Additional Stock-Based Compensation Concepts

In the following sub-sections, we note several additional issues that are related to stock-based compensation, but which do not easily fit into any of the preceding topics.

### Capitalized Compensation

The usual assumption when there are stock-based compensation payments is that there will be an immediate charge to compensation expense. This is not necessarily the case. It is also possible that certain stock-based compensation will be included in a factory overhead cost pool, in which case the compensation will be allocated to the number of units produced in the period; this applied overhead cost will eventually be charged to expense when the units are sold or declared obsolete.

A variation on the concept is that stock-based compensation may qualify to be included in the cost of a fixed asset. This situation can arise if the compensation is associated with the design or construction of an asset, or is meant to subsidize the cost of an asset. If so, the compensation cost will be charged to expense over time, as part of the recurring depreciation charge for the asset.

### The Leased Employee

A common employment situation is for a business to lease its employees from a professional employer organization (PEO). The PEO is the legal employer, and provides a range of services to employees (such as human resources counseling), as well as compensation payments and benefits. The lessee business typically makes a periodic bulk payment to the PEO in compensation for these services and expenditures. The preceding discussion of share-based compensation applies to leased employees, but only if all of the following criteria are met:

- The leased person qualifies as a common law employee of the lessee
- The lessor is required to remit payroll taxes to the government on the compensation paid to the leased person for work provided to the lessee
- The lessor and lessee have entered into a written contractual agreement that states the following:
  - The lessee has the exclusive right to grant share-based compensation to the person for services rendered to the lessee
  - The lessee has the right to hire and fire the person, as well as to control his or her activities
  - The lessee has the exclusive right to derive the economic value of the person's services
  - The person can participate in the lessee's benefit plans in the same manner as any other employees of the lessee
  - The lessee agrees to pay the lessor for the compensation and other costs associated with the person

If the preceding criteria cannot be met for an individual and share-based payments are made to that person, then the accounting in the Equity-Based Payments to Non-Employees section applies.

**Tandem Awards**

A tandem award is an award with at least two components, under which the exercise of one award component cancels the other component. For example, an employee could receive either a stock option or a stock appreciation right that is settled in cash. If the employee elects to take the stock appreciation right with its associated cash payment, then the employer will incur a liability for the compensation. If the employer can instead elect to pay out the award as a stock option, then the compensation instead impacts equity, rather than creating a liability. Thus, a tandem award can result in clear differences in being treated as a liability or equity.

Despite the written terms of a tandem award, it is possible that the historical practices of an employer clearly show that payouts are made in cash. If so, and despite the presence of a settlement option that could be in equity, the award is considered to be a substantive liability.

**Dividends Paid on Outstanding Options**

An employer may pay employees the dividends on underlying shares while an option is outstanding; that is, the employee is paid dividends without yet owning the associated shares. If employees are not required to return the dividends received if they forfeit their options or similar awards, then the employer recognizes these payments as compensation expense.

**Share-Based Awards in an Acquisition**

In an acquisition, the acquirer may agree to swap the share-based payment awards granted to employees of the acquiree for payment awards based on the shares of the acquirer. If the acquirer must replace awards made by the acquiree, the fair value of these awards is included in the calculation of the total consideration paid by the acquirer, where the portion attributable to pre-acquisition employee service is considered consideration paid for the acquiree. If the acquirer is not obligated to replace these awards but does so anyways, the cost of the replacement awards is recorded as compensation expense.

## Summary

The measurement of stock-based compensation can be complex, but is not inordinately so, as long as the accountant develops a standard procedure for dealing with these arrangements and follows it consistently.

It is also useful to gain the cooperation of the human resources department in formulating compensation arrangements that consistently include the same terms, so that the pre-existing accounting procedures can be readily applied to them. The worst-case scenario is when stock-based compensation plans are issued with substantially different terms, which forces the accountant to adopt unique and detailed accounting plans to deal with each one. In short, a consistently-applied pay system greatly reduces the effort of accounting for stock-based compensation.

## Review Questions

1.  A stock with a highly volatile price:
    a.  Is worth less to an option holder than a stock with less price volatility
    b.  Is worth more to an option holder than a stock with less price volatility
    c.  Has the same price as a stock with less price volatility
    d.  Typically has fewer shares outstanding, and so is more difficult to buy and sell

2.  A clawback arrangement linked to a stock-based award is designed to:
    a.  Encourage employees to stay with the company
    b.  Extend the required vesting period
    c.  Pay an employee the book value of the underlying shares
    d.  Increase the fixed cost of compensation

3.  The fair value of shares to be paid out as part of a stock-based compensation arrangement must be derived using a valuation technique that takes into account the following item:
    a.  The job classification of the employee being awarded
    b.  The profit margin of the entity
    c.  The number of shares to be issued
    d.  The volatility of the price of the shares to be issued

4.  An employer has set up an employee stock ownership plan (ESOP), and makes a loan to it directly, which is not funded by an outside lender, which is classified as employer loan financing. The correct accounting related to the loan is:
    a.  To record an allowance for uncollectible loans
    b.  To report cash paid to the ESOP that is used by the ESOP to service the debt
    c.  To not report the loan as an asset
    d.  To record interest income on the loan

5.  One of the main rules for equity-based payments to non-employees is that the grantor must:
    a.  Recognize the fair value of the equity instruments issued or the fair value of the consideration received
    b.  Recognize the book value of the equity instruments issued
    c.  Recognize the invoiced amount of the consideration received
    d.  Recognize the fair value of the consideration received, net of any applicable early payment discounts

6.  The implicit service period associated with a stock-based award:
    a.  Is the number of years worked, including gap years
    b.  Is the vesting period stated in a stock-based award agreement
    c.  Covers any years following formal retirement when an employee continues to perform services for the company
    d.  Is the employee service period implied by the facts and circumstances associated with a stock-based award

7. If some of the service associated with stock-based compensation occurs prior to the grant date, accrue the compensation expense during these earlier periods based on the ___ of the award at each reporting date.
    a. Fair value
    b. Expected fair value
    c. Book value
    d. Valuation based on cash flows

8. When a stock option expires unused:
    a. It is available to be awarded to someone else
    b. Reverse the related amount of compensation expense
    c. Do not reverse the related amount of compensation expense
    d. Remeasure the award at its fair value

9. The fair value of a nonvested share is based on:
    a. Its value as though it were vested immediately
    b. An average of the share value during the vesting period
    c. An average of the share value during the service period
    d. Its value as though it were vested on the grant date

10. The lattice model for pricing stock options assumes that:
    a. At least two price movements are possible in each measured time period
    b. Price volatility is constant through the term of the option
    c. Dividends are constant through the term of the option
    d. Interest rates are constant through the term of the option

11. The following are reasons why an employee stock ownership plan is used, except for:
    a. To increase employee ownership of a business
    b. To ensure a smooth management transition to a new generation of the owner's family
    c. To ward off hostile takeover attempts
    d. To replace lost benefits when other retirement plans are terminated

12. An employee share purchase plan is not considered compensatory if:
    a. Few employees qualify for the plan
    b. The terms offered are more favorable than those available to investors at large
    c. It contains a purchase discount of less than five percent
    d. The plan allows a 90-day notice period to enroll in the plan after the share price has been fixed

13. An employer can use share-based accounting for employees when dealing with awards to leased employees, but only if (along with other requirements):
    a. The lessee remits payroll taxes on the compensation paid to the leased employees
    b. The lessor controls the activities of the leased employees
    c. The leased person qualifies as a common law employee of the lessee
    d. The lessor has the exclusive right to derive the economic value of leased persons' services

# Chapter 12
# Accounting for Retirement Benefits

## Introduction

Many organizations offer benefit plans that provide income to retired personnel in exchange for services provided. Of these plans, the bulk of the funds are concentrated in pension plans; a pension plan is a pool of funds to which contributions are made by an employer, which are then made available to employees upon their retirement.

This chapter addresses the accounting for two types of pension plans, called defined benefit plans and defined contribution plans, detailing the accounting required by the employer. Nearly all of the discussion is concentrated on defined benefit plans, which require ongoing estimations of and accounting for future costs that may be incurred, as well as changes to existing benefits.

Some of the complexity of this topic is caused by a rare circumstance in GAAP – where provisions are made to allow a business to defer costs and recognize them in later periods through amortization. This approach contravenes the vastly more common approach of charging all costs to expense as incurred. While this type of modified accounting undoubtedly allows a business to defer expense recognition, it causes ongoing headaches for accountants, and likely increases the profits of the actuarial industry.

## Overview of Retirement Benefits

A retirement benefit is one in which the employer promises to deliver a fixed benefit to its employees at some point in the future. Examples of these benefits are pensions and health benefits to be paid following the retirement of employees. Employees qualify for retirement benefits either through the passage of time, by attaining a certain age, or a combination of both. Retirement benefits paid to employees may begin as soon as they retire, or the benefits may be delayed until a certain age is reached, or even when employees elect to begin accepting benefits.

The underlying principle that drives the accounting for retirement benefits is that the employer only provides these benefits in exchange for the ongoing services of employees, which makes the benefits a form of deferred compensation, where the employer incurs an obligation for the compensation as services are rendered by employees. Consequently, the employer must estimate the amount of future expenditure that will be made and recognize a portion of it in the current period. Expense recognition occurs before the benefits are paid, because employees are earning these future benefits via their services in earlier periods.

It is possible that the service costs associated with retirement benefits will be capitalized into inventory as part of the application of factory overhead to inventory. These costs can also be capitalized into fixed assets, if they relate to employee labor in constructing fixed assets.

## Defined Benefit Plans

In a defined benefit retirement plan, the employer provides a pre-determined periodic payment to employees after they retire. For example, an employer might promise to pay an inflation-adjusted monthly amount of $1,000 to an employee following her retirement, and continuing for the rest of her life. The amount of this future payment depends upon a number of future events, such as estimates of employee lifespan, how long current employees will continue to work for the company, and the pay level of employees just prior to their retirement. As long as the plan continues to operate, the employer is responsible for the payment of the defined benefits; if the amount of money in the pension fund is not sufficient to pay for expected benefits, then the employer must pay in the amount of the expected shortfall. These additional payments may continue through the life of the plan.

In essence, the accounting for defined benefit plans revolves around the estimation of the future payments to be made, and recognizing the related expense in the periods in which employees are rendering the services that qualify them to receive payments in the future under the terms of the plan. Actuaries are used to derive the estimated amounts of future payments based on (for example) mortality rates, expected employee turnover, expected interest income, future salaries, and the early retirement of employees. The accountant then uses these estimates to generate accounting entries.

There are a number of costs associated with defined benefit plans that may at first appear arcane. The following table contains a summary of the relevant costs, which sum to the net periodic pension cost that is recognized in each accounting period.

**Cost Components in a Defined Benefit Plan**

| Cost | Explanation |
|---|---|
| + Service cost | This is the actuarial present value of benefits related to services rendered during the current reporting period. The cost includes an estimate of the future compensation levels of employees from which benefit payments will be derived. |
| + Interest cost | This is the interest on the projected benefit obligation. It accrues each year on the projected benefit obligation, which was originally recorded on a discounted basis. Interest cost is a financial item, rather than a cost related to employee compensation. The actuary assists in the selection of the interest rate to be used to discount the projected benefit obligation.[6] |
| + Actual return on plan assets | This is the difference between the fair values of beginning and ending plan assets, adjusted for contributions and benefit payments. The return on assets is derived from interest and dividends accumulating within the pension plan, as well as from changes in the fair value of the plan's assets. It is a financial item, rather than a cost related to employee compensation. |
| + Amortization of prior service costs | When an employer issues a plan amendment, it may contain increases in benefits that are based on services rendered by employees in prior periods. If so, the cost of these additional benefits is amortized over the future periods in which those employees active on the amendment date are expected to receive benefits. |
| + Gain or loss | This is the gain or loss resulting from a change in the value of a projected benefit obligation from changes in assumptions, or changes in the value of plan assets. |
| = Net periodic pension cost | |

One of the components of a defined benefit plan that was included in the preceding table was the actual return on plan assets. This return is calculated by computing the change in plan assets during the measurement period, and then adding contributions made to the plan during the period and subtracting out any benefits paid. Thus, the calculation is:

$$\textbf{Actual Return} = (\text{Plan assets ending balance} - \text{Plan assets beginning balance}) - (\text{Contributions} + \text{Benefits paid})$$

---

[6] The interest rate used should reflect the rate at which the employer can settle its pension benefits. Thus, an employer should look for rates of return on high-quality fixed income investments that are currently available, and which have cash flows that approximately match the timing and amount of the anticipated benefit payouts.

If the actual return on plan assets is positive, the return is subtracted from the calculation of pension expense. If the actual return is negative, the return is added to the calculation of pension expense.

---

**EXAMPLE**

The controller of Grissom Granaries calculates the actual return on the company's plan assets in the following manner:

| | | |
|---|---:|---:|
| Fair value of plan assets at end of period | | $10,000,000 |
| Less: fair value of plan assets at beginning of period | | 8,400,000 |
| Increase in fair value of plan assets | | 1,600,000 |
| Deduct: Contributions to plan during period | $1,000,000 | |
| Less: Benefits paid during period | 600,000 | - 400,000 |
| Actual return on plan assets | | $1,200,000 |

---

The accounting for the relevant defined benefit plan costs is as follows:

- *Service cost.* The amount of service cost recognized in earnings in each period is the incremental change in the actuarial present value of benefits related to services rendered during the current reporting period.
- *Interest cost.* The interest cost associated with the projected benefit obligation is recognized as incurred. This expense arises because the projected benefit obligation is initially recorded on a discounted basis; the obligation then accrues interest over the life of the employee.
- *Amortization of prior service costs.* These costs are charged to other comprehensive income on the date of the amendment, and then amortized to earnings over time. The amount to be amortized is derived by assigning an equal amount of expense to each future period of service for each employee who is expected to receive benefits. If most of the employees are inactive, the amortization period is instead the remaining life expectancy of the employees. Straight-line amortization of the cost over the average remaining service period is also acceptable. Once established, this amortization schedule is not usually revised, unless there is a plan curtailment or if events indicate that a shorter amortization period is warranted.

---

**EXAMPLE**

Armadillo Industries creates a pension plan amendment that grants $90,000 of prior service costs to the 200 employees in its Mississippi facility. The company expects the employees at this location to retire in accordance with the following schedule:

| Group | Number of Staff | Expected Year of Retirement |
|---|---:|:---:|
| A | 20 | Year 1 |
| B | 40 | Year 2 |
| C | 80 | Year 3 |
| D | 40 | Year 4 |
| E | 20 | Year 5 |
| Total | 200 | |

The company uses the following grid to calculate the service years for each of the employee groups:

| Service Years | | | | | | | |
| Year | Group A | Group B | Group C | Group D | Group E | Total |
| --- | --- | --- | --- | --- | --- | --- |
| 1 | 20 | 40 | 80 | 40 | 20 | 200 |
| 2 | | 40 | 80 | 40 | 20 | 180 |
| 3 | | | 80 | 40 | 20 | 140 |
| 4 | | | | 40 | 20 | 60 |
| 5 | | | | | 20 | 20 |
| Totals | 20 | 80 | 240 | 160 | 100 | 600 |

There are 600 service years listed in the preceding table, over which the $90,000 prior service cost is to be allocated, which is $150 of cost per service year. Armadillo inserts the $150 per year figure into the following table to determine the amount of prior service cost amortization to recognize in each year.

| Year | Total of Service Years | × | Cost per Service Year | = | Amortization per Year |
| --- | --- | --- | --- | --- | --- |
| 1 | 200 | | $150 | | $30,000 |
| 2 | 180 | | 150 | | 27,000 |
| 3 | 140 | | 150 | | 21,000 |
| 4 | 60 | | 150 | | 9,000 |
| 5 | 20 | | 150 | | 3,000 |
| Totals | 600 | | | | $90,000 |

---

- *Prior service credits*. If a plan amendment reduces plan benefits, record it in other comprehensive income on the date of the amendment. This amount is then offset against any prior service cost remaining in accumulated other comprehensive income. Any residual amount of the credit is then amortized using the same methodology just noted for prior service costs.
- *Gains and losses*. Gains and losses can be recognized immediately if the method is applied consistently. If the election is not made to recognize them immediately, it is also possible to account for them as changes in other comprehensive income as they occur. If there is a gain or loss on the difference between the expected and actual amount of return on plan assets, recognize the difference in other comprehensive income in the period in which it occurs, and amortize it to earnings using the following calculation:
    1. Include the gain or loss in net pension cost for a year in which, as of the beginning of that year, the gain or loss is greater than 10% of the greater of the projected benefit obligation or the market-related value of plan assets.
    2. If this test is positive, amortize the excess just noted over the average remaining service period of those active employees who are expected to receive benefits. If most of the plan participants are inactive, amortize the excess over their remaining life expectancy.

A key term that arises in the accounting for defined benefit plans is the *projected benefit obligation*. This is the actuarial present value of future benefits attributed to service already rendered by employees. The "actuarial" part of the definition refers to *expected* payments, since some payments will never be made, due to the turnover of employees before they vest, the death of employees who would otherwise have been entitled to payments, and so forth. The projected benefit obligation also incorporates assumptions regarding the future pay levels and service periods of existing employees, which tends to increase the amount of the benefit obligation in comparison to what the obligation would be based on current employee compensation levels and periods of service.

When a business incurs obligations for future pension payments, it should presumably begin accumulating assets into a pension plan that will be available to pay the pension benefits in the future. If the projected benefit obligation is greater than the fair value of the plan assets on the balance sheet date, the employer should recognize a liability for the difference (known as the *unfunded projected benefit obligation*). In those rare cases where plan assets exceed the projected benefit obligation, the employer recognizes an asset in the amount of the difference. If there are multiple plans, all overfunded plans should be aggregated for reporting purposes, and all underfunded plans should be aggregated for reporting purposes.

It is possible that the unfunded or overfunded projected benefit obligation will result in a temporary difference for income tax purposes. If so, recognize the deferred tax effects of the temporary difference within the year.

If there are adjustments to the funded status of a pension plan, net gains or losses, prior service costs, and so forth, the offset to these entries is other comprehensive income.

When the employer buys annuity contracts to cover the cost of future employee benefits, the cost of the benefits should be the same as the cost of acquiring the annuity contracts.

## Expense Attribution for Delayed Vesting

There are a number of methods available for assigning benefits to employees, usually with the intent of delaying the vesting of benefits. For example, a plan may provide no benefits after nine years of service, and then vests employees in a future benefit payment following the tenth year of service (known as *cliff vesting*). In these situations, do not defer the recognition of a benefit expense until the delayed vesting occurs. Instead, assume that the benefit accumulates over time in proportion to the number of completed periods of service, which means that there should be an ongoing accrual of the related benefit expense over time.

---

**EXAMPLE**

Uncanny Corporation has a defined benefit pension plan, under which it pays a pension benefit of $60 per month for the remainder of each employee's life for each year of service completed, up to a maximum of ten years of service. The actuary employed by Uncanny calculates that the average employee will have 210 months of life expectancy following their retirement from Uncanny, and will have the full 10 years of service completed as of their retirement. The actuarial present value discount is set at 0.35. Based on this information, the actuary calculates the following pension benefits attributable to each of Uncanny's employees:

| | |
|---|---:|
| Years of service period completed | 10 |
| × Pension benefit per month | × $60 |
| = Payment to be made per month to each employee | = $600 |
| × Average life expectancy (in months) | × 210 |
| = Gross pension payment | = $126,000 |
| × Actuarial present value discount rate | × 0.35 |
| = Present value of pension benefit | $44,100 |

---

## Discount Rates

Service costs are based on the actuarial present value of benefits to be paid in the future. A discount rate must be employed to arrive at this actuarial present value. The discount rate should be one that reflects the rate at which benefits can actually be settled. A good source of information for this discount rate is the rate implicit in the current prices of annuity contracts that an employer could purchase to settle a future benefit obligation. Another source of information is the rate of return on high-quality fixed income investments that are expected to be available through the period during which the pension benefits will be paid.

Interest rates vary, depending upon the time period of investments. Thus, the discount rate used for benefits to be paid to a group of 50-year-old employees will likely be different from the discount rate used for benefits to be paid to a group of 30-year-olds.

The discount rate(s) used will likely vary over time, which can have a profound impact on the amount of the employer's obligation, causing ongoing fluctuations in the amount of the reported pension liability.

## Settlements and Curtailments

A benefit plan may be adjusted or terminated at some point. Variations that may be encountered include:

- *Curtailments.* Employee services or the benefit plan itself may be terminated earlier than expected, which reduces or eliminates the accrual of additional benefits.
- *Settlements.* Lump-sum cash payments may be made to plan participants in exchange for their rights to receive pension benefits.

When benefit obligations are settled, curtailed, or terminated, net gains or losses and prior service costs are shifted from accumulated other comprehensive income to earnings. This transfer occurs in the period in which all pension obligations are settled, benefits are no longer accrued, no plan assets remain, employees are terminated, *and* the plan ceases to exist. Also, the plan cannot be replaced by another plan.

If only a portion of the projected benefit obligation is settled, recognize in earnings that portion of the settlement that represents the reduction in the projected benefit obligation.

If the cost of the settlements completed in a year is greater or less than the sum of the service and interest cost components of the net periodic pension cost for that period, record a gain or loss in the amount of the difference. If the cost is lower than the sum of the service and interest cost components, recognition in earnings is permitted, but not required. The manner in which management chooses to deal with a lower-cost situation should be followed consistently.

If an employer purchases an annuity contract in order to settle a benefit plan, and the annuity was purchased from an entity that the employer controls, settlement accounting cannot be used to record the transaction. Similarly, if the employer retains the risks and rewards associated with a benefit obligation, despite purchasing an annuity contract, settlement accounting cannot be used.

If there is a curtailment of a benefit plan, the associated amount of prior service cost already recorded in accumulated other comprehensive income that is related to future years of service should be recognized in earnings as a loss. Also, the projected benefit obligation may be increased or decreased by a curtailment. This is a curtailment gain in the amount by which it exceeds any loss included in accumulated other comprehensive income. This is a curtailment loss in the amount by which it exceeds any net gain included in accumulated other comprehensive income. A curtailment loss should be recognized in earnings when the amount can be reasonably estimated and the curtailment is probable. A curtailment gain should be recognized in earnings when the plan is formally suspended or the impacted employees are terminated.

**EXAMPLE**

Following the devastation of a major earthquake, Armadillo Industries closes down its California facility. The employees located there will no longer earn any benefits. As of the plan curtailment date, the actuarial assumptions associated with the plan are:

- Defined benefit obligation = $300,000
- Plan assets fair value = $275,000
- Net cumulative unrecognized actuarial gains = $15,000

The curtailment event shrinks the present value of the benefit obligation by $20,000, to $280,000. Also, 20% of the net cumulative unrecognized actuarial gains are associated with that portion of the obligation that was eliminated by the curtailment. These alterations are incorporated into the following table:

| | Before Curtailment | Gain on Curtailment | After Curtailment |
|---|---|---|---|
| Present value of obligation | $300,000 | -$20,000 | $280,000 |
| Fair value of plan assets | -275,000 | -- | -275,000 |
| | 25,000 | -20,000 | 5,000 |
| Unrecognized actuarial gains | 15,000 | 3,000 | 18,000 |
| Net liability | $40,000 | -$17,000 | $23,000 |

Based on the preceding "gain on curtailment" information, Armadillo's controller records the following entry to record the gain on curtailment:

| | Debit | Credit |
|---|---|---|
| Accrued pension cost | 17,000 | |
|     Curtailment gain | | 17,000 |

## Termination Benefits

An employer may provide a certain set of benefits to employees that it terminates. Examples of termination benefits are lump-sum cash payments, a series of periodic payments in the future, or a combination of the two. The employer should recognize a liability and expense for the full amount of these benefits as soon as terminated employees accept the termination offer to which the benefits are linked, and the payment amount can be reasonably estimated. This expense should include the amount of any lump-sum payments made, as well as the present value of any future payments to be made. To determine the amount of termination expense to recognize, use the following calculation:

| | |
|---|---|
| + | Actuarial present value of accumulated pension benefits, including termination benefits |
| - | Actuarial present value of accumulated pension benefits, without termination benefits |
| = | Termination benefits to charge to expense |

**Combined Pension Plans**

A company may elect to combine several of its pension plans, which means that the assets of each predecessor plan can now be used to satisfy the obligations of the combined plan. The company should create a single amortization schedule for each of the pension costs that must be amortized. The amortization periods incorporated into these schedules shall be based on a weighted average of the remaining amortization periods used by the individual pension plans before they were combined. However, the prior service cost associated with each individual pension plan shall continue to be amortized under the old amortization schedules formulated prior to the combination of plans.

## Defined Contribution Plans

Under a defined contribution plan, the employer commits to contribute a certain amount to a pension fund in each period, based on a formula that incorporates such factors as the age of each employee, years of service, and employee compensation levels. There is no commitment to pay a specific benefit at a later date – the commitment is only the amount initially paid into the plan. The amount eventually paid to employees is comprised of the original contribution amount, the income generated by the pension fund, and forfeitures of funds by the early termination of employees. This approach massively simplifies the estimation of pension costs.

The accounting for a defined contribution plan is simplicity itself (as opposed to the accounting just described for a defined benefit plan). The employer charges its contributions to expense as incurred. If such a plan calls for additional payments to be made after an employee leaves the company, the estimated cost of these additional payments shall be accrued during the service period of the applicable employee. If the employer does not pay the full amount of its obligation into the pension fund, it reports a liability in this amount on its balance sheet. In those rare cases where the employer pays more than the amount of its obligation into the pension fund, it reports the excess amount as an asset on its balance sheet.

In those cases where an employer terminates a defined benefit plan and shifts the assets in the plan to a defined contribution plan that is a replacement plan, there may be an excess of assets in the replacement plan over the required annual contribution to the plan. If so, the employer should maintain the excess assets in a suspense account until such time as they are needed to fund the replacement account. Until the assets in the suspense account are used to fund the replacement account, the employer continues to retain the risks and rewards of ownership associated with those assets, and so shall account for the assets within its own balance sheet.

## Summary

When a company has a defined benefit plan, the number of variables impacting the amount of future payments makes it extremely difficult to recognize expenses that actually approximate the amounts that are later paid. In many cases, the variance between actual and estimated pension costs can have a profound impact on the financial results reported by a business, to the extent that users of this information may decide that the financial statements cannot be relied upon to reveal the actual results and condition of the business. The result can be additional analysis by investors, who use their own estimates of future pension liabilities to adjust the company's financial statements, and make investment decisions based on their own estimates. The level of confusion engendered by defined benefit plans bolsters the case for not entering into such plans. As an alternative, the accounting for defined contribution plans is neat, simple, and highly predictable, and results in more reliable financial statements. While the complaints of accountants are hardly likely to convince management to avoid using defined benefit plans, these issues can be considered alongside other factors, such as the massive long-term liabilities associated with defined benefit plans, to reduce their use.

## Review Questions

1. The projected benefit obligation does not include the ___ assumption.
   a. Employee turnover
   b. Employee service period
   c. Current pay level
   d. Future pay level

2. The accounting for an element of a defined benefit plan is to recognize the cost as incurred. This element is:
   a. Prior service credits
   b. Amortization of prior service costs
   c. Interest cost
   d. Service cost

3. A curtailment gain should be recognized in earnings when:
   a. The underlying plan is formally suspended
   b. The impacted employees have been notified that their employment will be terminated
   c. There is a large loss in accumulated other comprehensive income
   d. The amount can be reasonably estimated

4. The following are components of net periodic pension cost, except for:
   a. Amortization of future service costs
   b. Service cost
   c. Actual return on plan assets
   d. Amortization of prior service costs

5. The calculation of the actual return on plan assets involves:
   a. Subtracting the ending balance of plan assets
   b. Adding back the beginning balance of plan assets
   c. Adding benefits paid out during the period
   d. Subtracting contributions made during the period

6. The interest rate used to derive the interest on the projected benefit obligation should have the following characteristic:
   a. Be based on the company's own cost of capital
   b. Be derived from investments that roughly match the timing of anticipated benefit payouts
   c. Be based on the risk-free rate
   d. Be based on the rate at which the employer can settle its debt obligations

7. Under a defined contribution plan, the employer:
   a. Charges its contributions to expense as incurred
   b. Charges the actuarial present value of cash flows to expense
   c. Charges the service cost and interest cost to expense
   d. Amortizes prior service costs

# Chapter 13
# Accounting for Income Taxes

## Introduction

If a company generates a profit, it will probably be necessary to record income tax expense that is a percentage of the profit. However, the calculation of income tax is not so simple, since it may be based on a number of adjustments to net income that are allowed by the taxing authorities. The result can be remarkably complex tax measurements. In this chapter, we describe the general concepts of income tax accounting, as well as the calculation of the appropriate tax rate, the evaluation of tax positions, how to treat deferred taxes, the taxation of undistributed earnings, how to record taxes in interim periods, and other related topics.

## Overview of Income Taxes

Before delving into the income taxes topic, we must clarify several concepts that are essential to understanding the related accounting. The concepts are:

- *Temporary differences.* A company may record an asset or liability at one value for financial reporting purposes, while maintaining a separate record of a different value for tax purposes. The difference is caused by the tax recognition policies of taxing authorities, who may require the deferral or acceleration of certain items for tax reporting purposes. These differences are temporary, since the assets will eventually be recovered and the liabilities settled, at which point the differences will be terminated. A difference that results in a taxable amount in a later period is called a *taxable temporary difference*, while a difference that results in a deductible amount in a later period is called a *deductible temporary difference*. Examples of temporary differences are:
    - Revenues or gains that are taxable either prior to or after they are recognized in the financial statements. For example, an allowance for doubtful accounts may not be immediately tax deductible, but instead must be deferred until specific receivables are declared bad debts.
    - Expenses or losses that are tax deductible either prior to or after they are recognized in the financial statements. For example, some fixed assets are tax deductible at once, but can only be recognized through long-term depreciation in the financial statements. As another example, organizational costs are charged to expense as incurred for financial reporting purposes, but are deferred and deducted in a later year for tax purposes.
    - Assets whose tax basis is reduced by investment tax credits.

---

**EXAMPLE**

In its most recent year of operations, Table Furniture earns $250,000. Table also has $30,000 of taxable temporary differences and $80,000 of deductible temporary differences. Based on this information, Table's taxable income in the current year is calculated as:

$250,000 Profit - $30,000 Taxable temporary differences + $80,000 Deductible temporary differences

= $300,000 Taxable profit

---

- *Carrybacks and carryforwards.* A company may find that it has more tax deductions or tax credits (from an operating loss) than it can use in the current year's tax return. If so, it has the option of offsetting these amounts against the taxable income or tax liabilities (respectively) of the tax returns in earlier periods, or in future periods. Carrying these amounts back to the tax returns of prior periods is always more valuable, since the company can apply for a tax refund at once, and recognize a receivable for the amount of the refund. Thus, these excess tax deductions or tax credits are carried back first, with any remaining amounts being reserved for use in future periods. Carryforwards eventually expire, if not used within a certain number of years. A company should recognize a receivable for the amount of taxes paid in prior years that are refundable due to a carryback. A deferred tax asset can be realized for a carryforward, but possibly with an offsetting valuation allowance that is based on the probability that some portion of the carryforward will not be realized.

---

**EXAMPLE**

Spastic Corporation has created $100,000 of deferred tax assets through the diligent generation of losses for the past five years. Based on the company's poor competitive stance, management believes it is more likely than not that there will be inadequate profits (if any) against which the deferred tax assets can be offset. Accordingly, Spastic recognizes a valuation allowance in the amount of $100,000 that fully offsets the deferred tax assets.

---

- *Deferred tax liabilities and assets.* When there are temporary differences, the result can be deferred tax assets and deferred tax liabilities, which represent the change in taxes payable or refundable in future periods.

---

**EXAMPLE**

Armadillo Industries elects to account for a government contract on the percentage of completion method for financial reporting purposes, and on the completed contract method for tax reporting purposes. By doing so, the company recognizes income in its financial statements throughout the term of the contract, but does not do so for tax reporting purposes until the end of the contract.

**EXAMPLE**

Uncanny Corporation has recorded the following carrying amount and tax basis information for certain of its assets and liabilities:

| (000s) | Carrying Amount | Tax Basis | Temporary Difference |
|---|---|---|---|
| Accounts receivable | $12,000 | $12,250 | -$250 |
| Prepaid expenses | 350 | 350 | 0 |
| Inventory | 8,000 | 8,400 | -400 |
| Fixed assets | 17,300 | 14,900 | 2,400 |
| Accounts payable | 3,700 | 3,700 | 0 |
| Totals | $41,350 | $39,600 | $1,750 |

In the table, Uncanny has included a reserve for bad debts in its accounts receivable figure and for obsolete inventory in its inventory number, neither of which are allowed for tax purposes. Also, the company applied an accelerated form of depreciation to its fixed assets for tax purposes and straight-line depreciation for its financial reporting. These three items account for the total temporary difference between the carrying amount and tax basis of the items shown in the table.

---

All of these factors can result in complex calculations to arrive at the appropriate income tax information to recognize and report in the financial statements.

## Accounting for Income Taxes

Despite the complexity inherent in income taxes, the essential accounting in this area is derived from the need to recognize just two items, which are:

- *Current year*. The recognition of a tax liability or tax asset, based on the estimated amount of income taxes payable or refundable for the current year.
- *Future years*. The recognition of a deferred tax liability or tax asset, based on the estimated effects in future years of carryforwards and temporary differences.

Based on the preceding points, the general accounting for income taxes is as follows:

| | |
|---|---|
| +/- | Create a tax liability for estimated taxes payable, and/or create a tax asset for tax refunds, that relate to the current or prior years |
| +/- | Create a deferred tax liability for estimated future taxes payable, and/or create a deferred tax asset for estimated future tax refunds, that can be attributed to temporary differences and carryforwards |
| = | Total income tax expense in the period |

## Tax Positions

A tax position is a stance taken by a company in its tax return that measures tax assets and liabilities, and which results in the permanent reduction or temporary deferral of income taxes. When constructing the proper accounting for a tax position, the accountant follows these steps:

1. Evaluate whether the tax position taken has merit, based on the tax regulations.
2. If the tax position has merit, measure the amount that can be recognized in the financial statements.
3. Determine the probability and amount of settlement with the taxing authorities. Recognition should only be made when it is more likely than not (i.e., more than 50% probability) that the company's tax position will be sustained once it has been examined by the governing tax authorities. This probability is based on the facts, circumstances, and information available at the reporting date.
4. Recognize the tax position, if warranted.

> **Best Practice:** Given the large financial impact of some tax positions, it makes sense to obtain an outside opinion of a proposed position by a tax expert, and document the results of that review thoroughly. This is helpful not only if the position is reviewed by the taxing authorities, but also when it is reviewed by the company's outside auditors.

**EXAMPLE**

Armadillo Industries takes a tax position on an issue and determines that the position qualifies for recognition, and so should be recognized. The following table shows the estimated possible outcomes of the tax position, along with their associated probabilities:

| Possible Outcome | Probability of Occurrence | Cumulative Probability |
|---|---|---|
| $250,000 | 5% | 5% |
| 200,000 | 20% | 25% |
| 150,000 | 40% | 65% |
| 100,000 | 20% | 85% |
| 50,000 | 10% | 95% |
| 0 | 5% | 100% |

Since the benefit amount just beyond the 50% threshold level is $150,000, Armadillo should recognize a tax benefit of $150,000.

---

If a company initially concludes that the probability of a tax position being sustained is less than 50%, it should not initially recognize the tax position. However, it can recognize the position at a later date if the probability increases to be in excess of 50%, or if the tax position is settled through interaction with the taxing authorities, or the statute of limitations keeps the taxing authorities from challenging the tax position. If a company subsequently concludes that it will change a tax position previously taken, it should recognize the effect of the change in the period in which it alters its tax position. A change in tax position should be based on the evaluation of new information, rather than from a new evaluation of information that was available in an earlier reporting period.

---

**EXAMPLE**

Armadillo Industries takes a tax position under which it accelerates the depreciation of certain production equipment well beyond the normally-allowed taxable rate, resulting in a deferred tax liability after three years of $120,000.

After three years, a tax court ruling convinces Armadillo management that its tax position is untenable. Consequently, the company recognizes a tax liability for the $120,000 temporary difference. At the company's current 20% tax rate, this results in increased taxes of $24,000 and the elimination of the temporary difference.

---

A business may conclude that a tax position has been effectively settled following its examination by the relevant taxing authority. The assessment of whether such settlement has occurred depends upon consideration of *all* of the following conditions:

- The taxing authority has finalized its examination procedures, including all administrative reviews and appeals.
- The company does not intend to appeal any part of its tax position or engage in litigation.
- The probability that the taxing authority would examine any aspect of the tax position is remote, based on its policy for reopening closed examinations and the facts and circumstances related to the tax position.

A business should derecognize a tax position that it had previously recognized if the probability of the tax position being sustained drops below 50%, based on the most recent facts and circumstances.

If there is a change in the tax laws or tax rates, a business cannot recognize alterations in its income tax liability in advance of the enactment of these laws and rates. Instead, the company must wait until enactment has been completed, and can then recognize the changes on the enactment date.

## Deferred Tax Expense

Deferred tax expense is the net change in the deferred tax liabilities and assets of a business during a period of time. The amount of deferred taxes should be compiled for each tax-paying component of a business that provides a consolidated tax return. Doing so requires that the business complete the following steps:

1. Identify the existing temporary differences and carryforwards.
2. Determine the deferred tax liability amount for those temporary differences that are taxable, using the applicable tax rate.
3. Determine the deferred tax asset amount for those temporary differences that are deductible, as well as any operating loss carryforwards, using the applicable tax rate.
4. Determine the deferred tax asset amount for any carryforwards involving tax credits.
5. Create a valuation allowance for the deferred tax assets if there is a more than 50% probability that the company will not realize some portion of these assets. Any changes to this allowance are to be recorded within income from continuing operations on the income statement. The need for a valuation allowance is especially likely if a business has a history of letting various carryforwards expire unused, or it expects to incur losses in the next few years. A cumulative loss in recent years is a strong indicator that a valuation allowance is needed. A business should consider its tax planning strategy when determining the amount of a valuation allowance.

A valuation allowance may not be needed when there is positive evidence to support a deferred tax asset. For example:

- The company has a large sales backlog and sufficient production capacity to ensure that it can produce a sufficient amount of taxable income.
- The company has a sufficiently large amount of appreciated asset value to generate taxable income.
- The company has a strong track record of profitability, along with evidence indicating that the loss triggering the deferred tax asset is likely to be an aberration.

## Applicable Tax Rate

In general, when measuring a deferred tax liability or asset, a business should use the tax rate that it expects to apply to the taxable income that results from the realization of deferred tax assets or settlement of deferred tax liabilities. Also consider the following issues:

- *Alternative minimum tax.* The alternative minimum tax may increase the effective tax rate used. It may be necessary to reduce the deferred tax asset for the alternative minimum tax credit carryforward with a valuation allowance, if it is more than 50% probable that the asset will not be realized.
- *Discounting.* Deferred taxes are not to be discounted to their present value when they are recognized.
- *Graduated tax rates.* If the applicable tax law has graduated tax rates, and the graduated rates significantly affect the average tax rate paid, use the average tax rate that applies to the estimated annual taxable income in those periods when deferred tax liabilities are settled or deferred tax assets are realized. If a company earns such a large amount of income that the graduated rate is not significantly different from the top-tier tax rate, use the top-tier rate for the estimation of annual taxable income.
- *New tax laws or rates.* A company should adjust the amount of its deferred tax liabilities and assets for the effect of any changes in tax laws or tax rates, which shall be recorded within income from

continuing operations. Doing so may also call for an adjustment to the related valuation allowance. The effect of these changes should be recognized on the date when they are enacted.

## Interest and Penalties

When there is a requirement in the tax law that interest be paid when income taxes are not fully paid, a company should begin recognizing the amount of this interest expense as soon as the expense would be scheduled to begin accruing under the tax law.

If a company takes a tax position that will incur penalties, it should recognize the related penalty expense as soon as the company takes the position in a tax return. Whether penalties should be recognized may depend on management's judgment of whether a tax position exceeds the minimum statutory threshold required to avoid the payment of a penalty.

If a tax position is eventually sustained, reverse in the current period any related interest and penalties that had been accrued in previous periods under the expectation that the position would not be sustained.

## Change in Tax Status

The tax status of a business may change from taxable to nontaxable, or vice versa. For example, a partnership may convert into a corporation, thereby changing from a nontaxable (pass-through) entity to a taxable entity. When a nontaxable entity becomes taxable, it should recognize a deferred tax liability or asset for any outstanding temporary differences as of the conversion date. The conversion date can be either the date on which the taxing authority approves the change, or the filing date, if approval is not necessary.

When a taxable entity becomes nontaxable, all deferred tax assets and liabilities should be eliminated as of the date of this transition.

## Intraperiod Tax Allocation

Intraperiod tax allocation is the allocation of income taxes to different parts of the results appearing in the income statement of a business, so that some items are stated net of tax. Income taxes are allocated among the following items:

- Continuing operations
- Discontinued operations
- Other comprehensive income
- Items assigned directly to shareholders' equity

The intraperiod tax allocation concept is used to reveal the "true" results of certain transactions net of all effects, rather than disaggregating them from income taxes. For example, a company records a gain of $1 million. Its tax rate is 21%, so the company reports the gain net of taxes, at $790,000.

When allocating income taxes among the various income statement items just noted, allocate the taxes using either of the following methodologies:

- *One allocation target.* First assign income taxes to continuing operations, and then assign all remaining income taxes to the remaining allocation target.
- *Multiple allocation targets.* First assign income taxes to continuing operations, and then assign the remaining income taxes to the other items in proportion to their individual impact on the amount of remaining income taxes.

Note that, though the income tax included in these net calculations is usually an expense, it may also be a credit, so that any of the preceding items presented net of tax would include the tax credit.

Most elements of the income statement are not presented net of the intraperiod tax allocation. For example, revenue, the cost of goods sold, and administrative expenses are not presented net of income taxes.

---

**EXAMPLE**

Uncanny Corporation earns $500,000 of income from continuing operations, and experiences a loss of $150,000 from a discontinued operation. At the beginning of the year, Uncanny had a $600,000 tax loss carryforward. Uncanny applies the tax loss carryforward against the $500,000 income from continuing operations. Since the offset eliminates the $500,000 of income from operations, no income tax is applied to it. The company then applies the remaining $100,000 of tax loss carryforward against the loss from a discontinued operation, leaving $50,000 of taxable loss to be reported for the discontinued operation.

---

## Taxes Related to Undistributed Earnings

There are a few instances where a business is not required to engage in the standard accounting and disclosure of deferred income taxes for temporary differences. These exceptions relate to investments in subsidiaries and corporate joint ventures, and whether they remit earnings to the corporate parent or investors, respectively.

A corporate subsidiary typically remits earnings to the parent entity only after a number of issues have been considered, such as the need for cash by the subsidiary and parent, tax issues, and creditor and government restrictions. Funds may be remitted from a corporate joint venture based on the payout clauses in the original joint venture agreement, or with the agreement of the investing parties. In many situations, no funds are remitted, or only a small portion of the full amount of earnings.

Generally, the accounting for these undistributed earnings is to include them in the earnings of the parent entity, which results in a temporary difference, unless there is a means by which an investment in a domestic subsidiary can be recovered, free of tax. The same accounting approach applies to the pretax income of corporate joint ventures that are unlikely to be remitted to investors, and where the investors account for their investments in the joint ventures with the equity method.

A corporate joint venture may have a limited life span that will likely trigger the release of undistributed earnings to investors at the end of that lifespan. If so, investors should record deferred taxes when the profits or losses of the venture are recorded in its financial statements.

An investor entity should record a deferred tax liability when there is an excess of the reported taxable temporary difference over the tax basis:

- Of an investment in a domestic subsidiary
- In an investee that is ≤ 50% owned

A temporary difference is not considered a taxable temporary difference when there is a method permitted under the tax law for recovering the amount of an investment tax-free, *and* the investing entity expects to use that method. For example, it is possible to do so under certain types of acquisition structures, such as when a subsidiary is merged into the parent company, with noncontrolling shareholders receiving the stock of the parent company in exchange for their shares in the subsidiary.

When there is an excess of tax basis for an investment in a subsidiary or joint venture over the amount recorded in the financial statements, and the temporary difference will reverse in the foreseeable future, the corporate parent or investor should recognize a deferred tax asset in the amount of the difference. For example, the decision to sell a subsidiary would make it likely that a temporary difference will reverse in the near future.

The tax benefit associated with a deferred tax asset should be recognized when it is more than 50% probable that the temporary difference will reverse in the foreseeable future. Similarly, a tax expense should be recognized when it is more than 50% probable that a deferred tax liability will reverse in the foreseeable future.

It may be necessary to create a valuation allowance that will offset a deferred tax asset. The amount of this allowance (if any) shall be based on a periodic assessment of the allowance.

The parent entity should *not* accrue income taxes for unremitted earnings only in those situations where a subsidiary will permanently retain its earnings (which requires a reinvestment plan), or where the remittance will involve a tax-free liquidation. If circumstances change, and it appears that some portion of a subsidiary's undistributed earnings will be remitted, the parent should accrue income taxes related to the amount that will be remitted. If the reverse situation arises, where it no longer appears likely that earnings will be remitted, reduce the amount of income tax expense that had been previously recognized.

## Interim Reporting

If a business reports its financial results during interim reporting periods (such as monthly or quarterly financial statements), it must report income taxes in those interim reports. In general, the proper accounting is to report income taxes using an estimated effective tax rate in all of the interim periods. However, the application of this general principle varies somewhat as noted below:

- *Ordinary income.* Calculate the income tax on ordinary income at the estimated annual effective tax rate.
- *Other items.* Calculate and recognize the income tax on all items other than ordinary income at the rates that are applicable when the items occur. This means that the related tax effect is recognized in the period in which the underlying items occur.

The following factors apply to the determination of the estimated annual effective tax rate:

- The tax benefit associated with any applicable operating loss carryforward
- The tax effect of any valuation allowance used to offset the deferred tax asset
- Anticipated investment tax credits (for the amount expected to be used within the year)
- Foreign tax rates
- Capital gains rates
- The effects of new tax legislation, though only after it has been passed
- Other applicable factors

---

**EXAMPLE**

In the current fiscal year, Armadillo Industries anticipates $1,000,000 of ordinary income, to which will be applied the statutory tax rate of 21%, which will result in an income tax expense of $210,000. Armadillo also expects to take advantage of a $100,000 investment tax credit. Thus, the effective tax rate for the year is expected to be 11%, which is calculated as $110,000 of net taxes, divided by $1,000,000 of ordinary income.

---

Do not include in the determination of the estimated annual effective tax rate the effect of taxes related to unusual or discontinued operations that are expected to be reported separately in the financial statements.

The estimated tax rate is to be reviewed at the end of each interim period and adjusted as necessary, based on the latest estimates of taxable income to be reported for the full year. If it is not possible to derive an estimated tax rate, it may be necessary to instead use the actual effective tax rate for the year to date.

If the estimated tax rate is revised in an interim period from the rate used in a prior period, use the new estimate to derive the year-to-date tax on ordinary income for all interim periods to date.

The tax benefit associated with a loss recorded in an earlier interim period may not be recognized, on the grounds that it is less than 50% probable that the benefit will be realized. If so, do not recognize any income tax for ordinary income reported in subsequent periods until the unrecognized tax benefit associated with the original loss has been offset with income.

**EXAMPLE**

Through its first two quarters, Uncanny Corporation has experienced losses of $400,000 and $600,000. Management concludes that it is more likely than not that the tax benefit associated with these losses will not be realized. The company then earns profits in the third and fourth quarters, resulting in the following application of taxes at the statutory 21% corporate rate:

| (000s) | Ordinary Income | | Income Tax | | |
| --- | --- | --- | --- | --- | --- |
| | Current Period | Cumulative | Cumulative Tax (20%) | Less Previous Amount | Tax Provision |
| Quarter 1 | -$400 | -$400 | -- | --- | -- |
| Quarter 2 | -600 | -1,000 | -- | --- | -- |
| Quarter 3 | 1,100 | 100 | $21 | --- | $21 |
| Quarter 4 | 300 | 400 | 84 | $21 | 63 |
| Totals | $400 | | | | $84 |

If a company records a loss during an interim period, the company should only recognize the tax effects of the loss (i.e., a corresponding reduction in taxes) when there is an expectation that the tax reduction will be realized later in the year, or will be recognized as a deferred tax asset by year-end. This recognition may occur later in the year, if it later becomes more likely than not that the tax effects of the loss can be realized.

**EXAMPLE**

Uncanny Corporation has a history of recording losses in its first and second quarters, after which sales increase during the summer and winter holiday seasons. In the first half of the current year, Uncanny records a $1,000,000 loss, but expects a $2,000,000 profit in the final half of the year. Based on the company's history of seasonal sales, realization of the tax loss appears to be more likely than not, so Uncanny records the tax effect of the loss in the first half of the year.

If a business is subject to a variety of tax rates because of its operations in multiple tax jurisdictions, the estimated tax rate shall be based on a single tax rate for the entire company. When developing the single company-wide tax rate, exclude the effects of ordinary losses within jurisdictions, and develop a separate estimated tax rate for those jurisdictions. Also, if it is impossible to estimate a tax rate or ordinary income in a foreign jurisdiction, exclude that jurisdiction from the computation of the company-wide tax rate.

A company may decide to record a change in accounting principle. If so, the amount of the change included in retained earnings at the beginning of the fiscal year shall include the effect of the applicable amount of tax expense or benefit, employing the tax rate used for the full fiscal year. If the change in principle is made in an interim period other than the first interim period of a fiscal year, retrospectively apply the change to the preceding interim periods in the same year; when doing so, apply the estimated tax rate that originally applied to those periods, modified for the effects of the change in principle.

## Summary

Many accountants consider income tax accounting to be an area best left to a tax specialist, who churns through the information provided and creates a set of tax-related journal entries. While this approach should result in accurate tax accounting, it does not give management a good view of how its actions are affecting the taxes the company is paying – instead, the tax accounting function is treated as a black box whose contents are unknown to all, save the tax specialist who guards it.

A better approach is to engage the management team in tax planning by instructing them on the essential tax issues that can be impacted by strategic and tactical decisions. Even if management does not become conversant at a detailed level in how their actions impact income taxes, they will at least know when to call in a tax expert to advise them. Thus, a certain amount of transparency in the tax area can improve the results of a business.

## Review Questions

1. An excess tax credit can be used as:
   a. A carryback
   b. A deferred tax expense
   c. A tax position
   d. A valuation allowance

2. A business assesses whether a tax position has been effectively settled after having been examined by a taxing authority. In making this determination, the business should consider all of the following, except for:
   a. There is no intent to appeal the current decision
   b. A change in the tax laws or tax rates
   c. There is a remote probability that the taxing authority will examine any part of the tax position
   d. All reviews and appeals have been completed

3. A business takes a stance in its tax return that results in the permanent reduction or temporary deferral of income taxes. This stance is known as a:
   a. Legal brief
   b. Tax dispute
   c. Tax position
   d. Penalty basis

4. The applicable tax rate:
   a. Should incorporate discounting to present value
   b. May be increased by the alternative minimum tax
   c. Should be adjusted for anticipated changes in the tax laws
   d. Should be the minimum tax rate when graduated rates apply

5. Apply the __ tax rate to ordinary income in an interim period.
   a. Applicable graduated
   b. Alternative minimum
   c. Minimum possible
   d. Estimated annual

# Chapter 14
# Business Combinations and Consolidations

## Introduction

A business combination, or acquisition, occurs when one entity gains control over another entity. There are many reasons for engaging in a business combination, including gaining broader geographic coverage, entering into a new product niche, and acquiring technology or expertise.

A considerable amount of detailed accounting is required when a business combination takes place. At its least-complex level, the accounting involves the allocation of the purchase price to the acquiree's assets and liabilities, with any overage assigned to a goodwill asset. However, there are a multitude of additional issues that may apply, such as noncontrolling interests, reverse acquisitions, the production of consolidated financial statements, and more. This chapter deals with the accounting required for all of these issues.

> **Related Podcast Episodes:** Episodes 88 and 198 of the Accounting Best Practices Podcast discuss types of acquisitions and predecessor\successor financial statements, respectively. They are available at: **accountingtools.com/podcasts** or **iTunes**

## Overview of Business Combinations

A business combination has occurred when a group of assets acquired and liabilities assumed constitute a business. A business exists when processes are applied to inputs to create outputs. Examples of inputs are fixed assets, intellectual property, inventory, and employees. An output is considered to have the ability to generate a return to investors.

A business combination is accounted for using the *acquisition method*. This method requires the following steps:

1. *Identify the acquirer.* The entity that gains control of the acquiree is the acquirer. This is typically the entity that pays assets or incurs liabilities as a result of a transaction, or whose owners receive the largest portion of the voting rights in the combined entity. One of the combining entities must be the acquirer.
2. *Determine the acquisition date.* The acquisition date is when the acquirer gains control of the acquiree, which is typically the closing date.
3. *Recognize and measure all assets acquired and liabilities assumed.* These measurements should be at the fair values of the acquired assets and liabilities as of the acquisition date.
4. *Recognize any noncontrolling interest in the acquiree.* The amount recognized should be the fair value of the noncontrolling interest.
5. *Recognize and measure any goodwill or gain from a bargain purchase.* See the Goodwill or Gain from Bargain Purchase section for a discussion of goodwill and bargain purchases.

There are two types of business combinations that can result in some modification of the preceding accounting treatment. These types are:

- *Step acquisition.* A business may already own a minority interest in another entity, and then acquires an additional equity interest at a later date that results in an acquisition event. In this situation, the acquirer measures the fair value of its existing equity interest in the acquiree at the acquisition date, and recognizes a gain or loss in earnings at that time. If some of this gain or loss had previously been recognized in other comprehensive income, reclassify it into earnings.
- *No transfer of consideration.* There are rare cases where no consideration is paid while gaining control of an acquiree, such as when the acquiree repurchases enough of its own shares to raise an

existing investor into a majority ownership position. In this situation, recognize and measure the noncontrolling interest(s) in the acquiree.

There are a number of additional issues that can affect the accounting for a business combination, as outlined below:

- *Contingent consideration.* Some portion of the consideration paid to the owners of the acquiree may be contingent upon future events or circumstances. If an event occurs after the acquisition date that alters the amount of consideration paid, such as meeting a profit or cash flow target, the accounting varies depending on the type of underlying consideration paid, as noted next:
  - o *Asset or liability consideration.* If the consideration paid is with assets or liabilities, re-measure these items at their fair values until such time as the related consideration has been fully resolved, and recognize the related gains or losses in earnings.
  - o *Equity consideration.* If the consideration paid is in equity, do not remeasure the amount of equity paid.

- *Provisional accounting.* If the accounting for a business combination is incomplete at the end of a reporting period, report provisional amounts, and later adjust these amounts to reflect information that existed as of the acquisition date.
- *New information.* If new information becomes available about issues that existed at the acquisition date concerning the acquiree, adjust the recordation of assets and liabilities, as appropriate.

When making a subsequent adjustment to the transaction associated with a business combination, the acquirer should record the related effect on earnings in the current period's financial statements, calculated as though the accounting had been completed at the acquisition date. The acquirer should separately report these changes on the face of the income statement or in the accompanying notes. Thus, these changes are not treated as retrospective adjustments to the financial statements.

---

**EXAMPLE**

Armadillo Industries acquires Cleveland Container on December 31, 20X3. Armadillo hires an independent appraiser to value Cleveland, but does not expect a valuation report for three months. In the meantime, Armadillo issues its December 31 financial statements with a provisional fair value of $4,500,000 for the acquisition. Three months later, the appraiser reports a valuation of $4,750,000 as of the acquisition date, based on an unexpectedly high valuation for a number of fixed assets.

In Armadillo's March 31 financial statements, it adjusts the prior-year information to increase the carrying amount of fixed assets by $250,000, as well as to reduce the amount of goodwill by the same amount.

---

Any changes to the initial accounting for an acquisition must be offset against the recorded amount of goodwill. These changes to the initial provisional amounts should be recorded in the current period, as though all accounting for the acquisition had been finalized at the acquisition date.

The measurement period during which the recordation of an acquisition may be adjusted ends as soon as the acquirer receives all remaining information concerning issues existing as of the acquisition date, not to exceed one year from the acquisition date.

The acquirer will probably incur a number of costs related to an acquisition, such as fees for valuations, legal advice, accounting services, and finder's fees. These costs are to be charged to expense as incurred.

## Identifiable Assets and Liabilities, and Noncontrolling Interests

When the acquirer recognizes an acquisition transaction, it should recognize identifiable assets and liabilities separately from goodwill, and at their fair values as of the acquisition date. It is entirely possible that the acquirer will recognize assets and liabilities that the acquiree had never recorded in its own accounting records. In particular, the acquirer will likely assign value to a variety of intangible assets that the acquiree may have developed internally, and so was constrained by GAAP from recognizing as assets. Examples of intangible assets are noted in the following exhibit.

**Examples of Intangible Assets**

| | | |
|---|---|---|
| Broadcast rights | Internet domain names | Noncompetition agreements |
| Computer software | Lease agreements | Order backlog |
| Customer lists | Licensing agreements | Patented technology |
| Customer relationships | Literary works | Pictures |
| Employment contracts | Motion pictures | Service contracts |
| Franchise agreements | Musical works | Trademarks |

A key intangible asset for which GAAP does not allow separate recognition is the concept of the assembled workforce, which is the collected knowledge and experience of company employees. This intangible must be included in the goodwill asset.

A special option only available to private companies is to not recognize separately from goodwill either of the following two types of intangible assets:

- Customer-related intangible assets, unless they are capable of being sold or licensed independently from other assets
- Noncompetition agreements

If a private company elects to not recognize these types of intangible assets, it must amortize goodwill, as described in the Goodwill Amortization section of Chapter 8.

The accounting treatment for special cases related to the recognition of assets and liabilities is as follows:

- *Contingency fair value not determinable.* It is quite common for a contingent asset or liability to not be measurable on the acquisition date, since these items have not yet been resolved. If so, only recognize them if the amount can be reasonably estimated, and events during the measurement period confirm that an asset or liability existed at the acquisition date.
- *Defined benefit pension plan.* If the acquiree sponsored a defined benefit pension plan, the acquirer should recognize an asset or liability that reflects the funding status of that plan.
- *Indemnification clause.* The seller of the acquiree may agree to an indemnification clause in the acquisition agreement, whereby it will indemnify the acquirer for changes in the value of certain assets or liabilities, such as for unusual bad debt losses from receivables in existence at the acquisition date. In these cases, the seller recognizes an indemnification asset when it recognizes a loss on an item to be indemnified.

> **Best Practice:** Realistically, if you are still attempting to establish a valuation for assets and liabilities more than a few months after an acquisition, they probably had no value at the acquisition date, and so should not be recognized as part of the acquisition.

Acquired assets and liabilities are supposed to be measured at their fair values as of the acquisition date. Fair value measurement can be quite difficult, and may call for different valuation approaches, as noted below:

- *Alternative use assets.* Even if the acquirer does not intend to apply an asset to its best use (or use the asset at all), the fair value of the asset should still be derived as though it were being applied to its best use. This guidance also applies to situations where an asset is acquired simply to prevent it from being used by competitors.
- *Assets where acquiree is the lessor.* If the acquiree owns assets that it leases to a third party (such as a building lease), derive fair values for these assets in the normal manner, irrespective of the existence of the lease.
- *Fair value exceptions.* There are exceptions to the general rule of recognizing acquired assets and liabilities at their fair values. The GAAP related to the recognition of income taxes, employee benefits, indemnification assets, reacquired rights, share-based awards, assets held for sale, and certain contingency situations overrides the use of fair value.
- *Noncontrolling interest.* The best way to measure the fair value of a noncontrolling interest is based on the market price of the acquiree's stock. However, this information is not available for privately-held companies, so alternative valuation methods are allowed. This valuation may differ from the valuation assigned to the acquirer, since the acquirer also benefits from gaining control over the entity, which results in a control premium.
- *Valuation allowances.* Some assets, such as receivables and inventory, are normally paired with a valuation allowance. The valuation allowance is not used when deriving fair values for these assets, since the fair value should already incorporate a valuation allowance.

A few assets and liabilities that are initially measured as part of an acquisition require special accounting during subsequent periods. These items are:

- *Contingencies.* If an asset or liability was originally recognized as part of an acquisition, derive a systematic and consistently-applied approach to measuring it in future periods.
- *Indemnifications.* Reassess all indemnification assets and the loss items with which they are paired in each subsequent reporting period, and adjust the recorded amounts as necessary until the indemnifications are resolved.
- *Reacquired rights.* An acquirer may regain control over a legal right that it had extended to the acquiree prior to the acquisition date. If these reacquired rights were initially recognized as an intangible asset as part of the acquisition accounting, amortize the asset over the remaining period of the contract that the acquiree had with the acquirer.
- *Leasehold improvements.* If the acquirer acquires leasehold improvement assets as part of an acquisition, amortize them over the lesser of the useful life of the assets or the remaining reasonably assured lease periods and renewals.

## Goodwill or Gain from Bargain Purchase

This section addresses the almost inevitable calculation of goodwill that is associated with most acquisitions. It also addresses the considerably less common recognition of a bargain purchase.

### Goodwill Calculation

Goodwill is an intangible asset that represents the future benefits arising from assets acquired in a business combination that are not otherwise identified. Goodwill is a common element in most acquisition transactions, since the owners of acquirees generally do not part with their companies unless they are paid a premium.

The acquirer must recognize goodwill as an asset as of the acquisition date. The goodwill calculation is as follows:

Goodwill = (Consideration paid + Fair value of noncontrolling interest) – (Assets acquired – Liabilities assumed)

If no consideration is transferred in an acquisition transaction, use a valuation method to determine the fair value of the acquirer's interest in the acquiree as a replacement value.

When calculating the total amount of consideration paid as part of the derivation of goodwill, consider the following additional factors:

- *Fair value of assets paid.* When the acquirer transfers its assets to the owners of the acquiree as payment for the acquiree, measure this consideration at its fair value. If there is a difference between the fair value and carrying amount of these assets as of the acquisition date, record a gain or loss in earnings to reflect the difference. However, if these assets are simply being transferred to the acquiree entity (which the acquirer now controls), do not restate these assets to their fair value; this means there is no recognition of a gain or loss.
- *Share-based payment awards.* The acquirer may agree to swap the share-based payment awards granted to employees of the acquiree for payment awards based on the shares of the acquirer. If the acquirer must replace awards made by the acquiree, include the fair value of these awards in the consideration paid by the acquirer, where the portion attributable to pre-acquisition employee service is considered to be consideration paid for the acquiree. If the acquirer is not obligated to replace these awards but does so anyways, record the cost of the replacement awards as compensation expense.

## Bargain Purchase

When an acquirer gains control of an acquiree whose fair value is greater than the consideration paid for it, the acquirer is said to have completed a bargain purchase. A bargain purchase transaction most commonly arises when a business must be sold due to a liquidity crisis, where the short-term nature of the sale tends to result in a less-than-optimum sale price from the perspective of the owners of the acquiree. To account for a bargain purchase, follow these steps:

1. Record all assets and liabilities at their fair values.
2. Reassess whether all assets and liabilities have been recorded.
3. Determine and record the fair value of any contingent consideration to be paid to the owners of the acquiree.
4. Record any remaining difference between these fair values and the consideration paid as a gain in earnings. Record this gain as of the acquisition date.

**EXAMPLE**

The owners of Failsafe Containment have to rush the sale of the business in order to obtain funds for estate taxes, and so agree to a below-market sale to Armadillo Industries for $5,000,000 in cash of a 75% interest in Failsafe. Armadillo hires a valuation firm to analyze the assets and liabilities of Failsafe, and concludes that the fair value of its net assets is $7,000,000 (of which $8,000,000 is assets and $1,000,000 is liabilities), and the fair value of the 25% of Failsafe still retained by its original owners has a fair value of $1,500,000.

Since the fair value of the net assets of Failsafe exceeds the consideration paid and the fair value of the noncontrolling interest in the company, Armadillo must recognize a gain in earnings, which is calculated as follows:

$7,000,000 Net assets - $5,000,000 Consideration - $1,500,000 Noncontrolling interest

= $500,000 Gain on bargain purchase

Armadillo records the transaction with the following entry:

|  | Debit | Credit |
|---|---|---|
| Assets acquired | 8,000,000 | |
| Cash | | 5,000,000 |
| Liabilities assumed | | 1,000,000 |
| Gain on bargain purchase | | 500,000 |
| Equity – noncontrolling interest in Failsafe | | 1,500,000 |

## Reverse Acquisitions

A reverse acquisition occurs when the legal acquirer is actually the acquiree for accounting purposes. The reverse acquisition concept is most commonly used when a privately-held business buys a public shell company for the purposes of rolling itself into the shell and thereby becoming a publicly-held company. This approach is used to avoid the expense of engaging in an initial public offering.

To conduct a reverse acquisition, the legal acquirer issues its shares to the owners of the legal acquiree (which is the accounting acquirer). The fair value of this consideration is derived from the fair value amount of equity the legal acquiree would have had to issue to the legal acquirer to give the owners of the legal acquirer an equivalent percentage ownership in the combined entity.

When a reverse acquisition occurs, the legal acquiree may have owners who do not choose to exchange their shares in the legal acquiree for shares in the legal acquirer. These owners are considered a noncontrolling interest in the consolidated financial statements of the legal acquirer. The carrying amount of this noncontrolling interest is based on the proportionate interest of the noncontrolling shareholders in the net asset carrying amounts of the legal acquiree prior to the business combination.

**EXAMPLE**

The management of High Noon Armaments wants to take their company public through a reverse acquisition transaction with a public shell company, Peaceful Pottery. The transaction is completed on January 1, 20X4. The balance sheets of the two entities on the acquisition date are as follows:

| | Peaceful<br>(Legal Acquirer,<br>Accounting Acquiree) | High Noon<br>(Legal Subsidiary,<br>Accounting Acquirer) |
|---|---|---|
| Total assets | $100 | $8,000 |
| | | |
| Total liabilities | $0 | $4,500 |
| Shareholders' equity | | |
| Retained earnings | 10 | 3,000 |
| Common stock | | |
| 100 shares | 90 | |
| 1,000 shares | | 500 |
| Total shareholders' equity | 100 | 3,500 |
| Total liabilities and shareholders' equity | $100 | $8,000 |

On January 1, Peaceful issues 0.5 shares in exchange for each share of High Noon. All of High Noon's shareholders exchange their holdings in High Noon for the new Peaceful shares. Thus, Peaceful issues 500 shares in exchange for all of the outstanding shares in High Noon.

The quoted market price of Peaceful shares on January 1 is $10, while the fair value of each common share of High Noon shares is $20. The fair values of Peaceful's few assets and liabilities on January 1 are the same as their carrying amounts.

As a result of the stock issuance to High Noon investors, those investors now own 5/6ths of Peaceful shares, or 83.3% of the total number of shares. To arrive at the same ratio, High Noon would have had to issue 200 shares to the shareholders of Peaceful. Thus, the fair value of the consideration transferred is $4,000 (calculated as 200 shares × $20 fair value per share).

Goodwill for the acquisition is the excess of the consideration transferred over the amount of Peaceful's assets and liabilities, which is $3,900 (calculated as $4,000 consideration - $100 of Peaceful net assets).

Based on the preceding information, the consolidated balance sheet of the two companies immediately following the acquisition transaction is:

| | Peaceful | High Noon | Adjustments | Consolidated |
|---|---|---|---|---|
| Total assets | $100 | $8,000 | $3,900 | $12,000 |
| | | | | |
| Total liabilities | $0 | $4,500 | -- | $4,500 |
| Shareholders' equity | | | | |
| Retained earnings | 10 | 3,000 | -10 | 3,000 |
| Common stock | | | | |
| 100 shares | 90 | | -90 | -- |
| 1,000 shares | | 500 | | 500 |
| 600 shares | | | 4,000 | 4,000 |
| Total shareholders' equity | 100 | 3,500 | 3,900 | 7,500 |
| Total liabilities and shareholders' equity | $100 | $8,000 | $3,900 | $12,000 |

## Overview of Consolidations

A financial statement consolidation is intended to present the results and financial position of a parent entity and its subsidiaries, as though they were a single entity. It is also possible to have consolidated financial statements for a portion of a group of companies, such as for a subsidiary and those other entities owned by the subsidiary. Consolidated financial statements are useful for reviewing the financial position and results of an entire group of commonly-owned businesses. Otherwise, reviewing the results of individual businesses within the group does not give an indication of the financial health of the group as a whole.

A consolidation is typically conducted when the parent entity has a controlling financial interest in other entities. A controlling financial interest is considered to be present when there is a direct or indirect majority voting interest of more than 50% of the outstanding voting shares. It is possible that a controlling financial interest is not present despite having more than 50% of the outstanding voting shares, when non-controlling interests interfere with a financial interest.

A power of control may also exist when there is less than 50% ownership of the outstanding voting shares, which (for example) may occur by court order, contract, or an agreement to which other shareholders are parties. If so, the results and financial positions of the entities can be consolidated.

## Recognition of a Consolidation

A consolidation typically occurs when a reporting entity has a majority voting interest in another entity. It is possible to argue against a consolidation when a reporting entity has a majority voting interest in another entity; this is a matter of judgment that depends on the facts and circumstances of each individual case, and is supported when a noncontrolling shareholder is effectively participating in significant decisions of the other entity. Effective participation is occurring when a noncontrolling shareholder can veto the actions of the majority shareholder in certain situations. The following points clarify the issue:

- *Protective rights.* A noncontrolling shareholder may have rights that protect its investment, such as a veto over the liquidation of a business or the sale of major assets. These rights are not considered to interfere with the control of a majority voting interest.
- *Substantive participating rights.* A noncontrolling shareholder may have the right to select, terminate, or set the compensation of management, or to establish operating or capital decisions of the investee. If so, this can be considered to interfere with a majority voting interest.

---

**EXAMPLE**

A noncontrolling shareholder has the right to block the board of directors of Amalgamated Investments from issuing an extraordinary dividend distribution to shareholders. This is a protective right, since it prevents an excessive amount of funds from being removed from Amalgamated. If the blocking right had instead applied to customary dividends, it might be construed as a substantive participating right.

**EXAMPLE**

The same noncontrolling shareholder has the right to block any long-term supplier agreements with a supplier of bauxite to Amalgamated. The total value of this agreement is minor, and there are alternative suppliers that Amalgamated can use. Given the minor impact on the organization of this blocking right, it is not considered a substantive participating right.

---

- *Other factors.* The following additional factors could be considered when deciding whether noncontrolling shareholders are interfering with the control of the majority voting interest:
  - *Percent ownership.* If the majority voting interest is substantially greater than 50%, the rights of other investors are more likely to be protective rights, and so do not keep the majority voting interest from engaging in consolidation accounting.
  - *Voting matters.* The extent to which matters can be put to a shareholder vote should be considered when determining whether a noncontrolling interest has substantive participating rights.
  - *Related parties.* If the noncontrolling interest is related to the controlling interest, this makes it more likely that the majority voting interest has control over the investee.
  - *Minor decisions.* A noncontrolling interest may have rights in regarding to minor operating or capital decisions, such as the name of the investee, the selection of auditors, and the location of the investee's headquarters. These decisions do not interfere with the control of the majority voting interest.
  - *Rare decisions.* A noncontrolling interest may have the right to participate in significant decisions, but ones for which the probability is remote. These decisions do not interfere with the control of the majority voting interest.
  - *Buyout clause.* If the majority voting interest has a right to buy out the interest of a noncontrolling shareholder for fair value or less, and the buyout would be prudent and feasible, this negates the veto rights of the noncontrolling shareholder when deciding whether the majority voting interest has control.

Consolidation accounting is the process of combining the financial results of several subsidiary companies into the combined financial results of the parent company. Consolidated financial statements require considerable effort to construct, since they must exclude the impact of any transactions between the entities being reported on. Thus, if there is a sale of goods between the subsidiaries of a parent company, this intercompany sale must be eliminated from the consolidated financial statements. Another common intercompany elimination is when the parent company pays interest income to the subsidiaries whose cash it is using to make investments; this interest income must be eliminated from the consolidated financial statements. The following steps document the consolidation accounting process flow:

1. *Record intercompany loans.* If the parent company has been consolidating the cash balances of its subsidiaries into an investment account, record intercompany loans from the subsidiaries to the parent company. Also record an interest income allocation for the interest earned on consolidated investments from the parent company down to the subsidiaries.
2. *Charge corporate overhead.* If the parent company allocates its overhead costs to subsidiaries, calculate the amount of the allocation and charge it to the various subsidiaries.

3. *Charge payables.* If the parent company runs a consolidated payables operation, verify that all accounts payable recorded during the period have been appropriately charged to the various subsidiaries.

4. *Charge payroll expenses.* If the parent company has been using a common paymaster system to pay all employees throughout the company, ensure that the proper allocation of payroll expenses has been made to all subsidiaries.

5. *Complete adjusting entries.* At the subsidiary and corporate levels, record any adjusting entries needed to properly record revenue and expense transactions in the correct period.

6. *Investigate asset, liability, and equity account balances.* Verify that the contents of all asset, liability, and equity accounts for both the subsidiaries and the corporate parent are correct, and adjust as necessary.

7. *Review subsidiary financial statements.* Print and review the financial statements for each subsidiary, and investigate any items that appear to be unusual or incorrect. Make adjustments as necessary.

8. *Eliminate intercompany transactions.* If there have been any intercompany transactions, reverse them at the parent company level to eliminate their effects from the consolidated financial statements. Examples of intercompany transactions are:

   - Security holdings
   - Debt
   - Sales (with the reversal of related inventory amounts)
   - Purchases (with the reversal of related inventory amounts)
   - Interest
   - Dividends
   - Gains or losses on asset sales

9. *Eliminate subsidiary retained earnings.* Remove the retained earnings of each subsidiary as of its acquisition date from the consolidated financial statements.

10. *Eliminate LIFO liquidation profits.* If there were inventory transfers between the subsidiaries that caused inventory to be liquidated that was valued using the last-in, first-out (LIFO) method, eliminate the profit related to these transfers.

11. *Eliminate parent shares held by subsidiary.* If a subsidiary holds shares in the parent entity, these are not treated as outstanding shares in the consolidated balance sheet. Instead, they are considered to be treasury stock.

12. *Defer taxes on inter-company profits.* If income taxes have already been paid on inter-company profits, defer them in the consolidated financial statements. An alternative treatment is to reduce the amount of the inter-entity profits to be eliminated by the amount of the taxes.

13. *Review parent financial statements.* Print and review the financial statements for the parent company, and investigate any items that appear to be unusual or incorrect. Make adjustments as necessary.

14. *Close subsidiary books.* Depending upon the accounting software in use, it may be necessary to access the financial records of each subsidiary and flag them as closed. This prevents any additional transactions from being recorded in the accounting period being closed.

15. *Close parent company books.* Flag the parent company accounting period as closed, so that no additional transactions can be reported in the accounting period being closed.

16. *Issue financial statements.* Print and distribute the consolidated financial statements.

If a subsidiary uses a different currency as its operating currency, an additional consolidation accounting step is to convert its financial statements into the operating currency of the parent company.

Given the considerable number of steps, it is useful to convert them into a detailed procedure, which the accounting department should follow religiously as part of its closing process. Otherwise, a key step could be missed, which would throw off the financial statement results.

## Consolidation Examples

This section contains a number of examples that clarify the consolidation outcome for different situations. Each situation is dealt with in a different sub-section.

### Recognition of Noncontrolling Interest

A parent company may find it necessary to sell a share of its ownership interest in a subsidiary to a third party. This event can trigger the recognition of a gain or loss if the amount of the sale differs from the carrying amount of the equity. It will also result in the recognition of a noncontrolling interest, as noted in the following example.

---

**EXAMPLE**

Blitz Communications owns all 100,000 the outstanding shares of Prompt Installers. Blitz manufactures office phone systems, and the subsidiary installs phone systems at client locations. The carrying amount of the equity of Prompt is $1,000,000.

Blitz needs new financing for a production facility, and elects to sell 30,000 of its Prompt shares to a third party for $350,000 in cash. This transaction reduces the ownership of Blitz in Prompt to a 70% interest. This change in ownership is accounted for by recognizing a noncontrolling interest of $300,000, which is calculated as follows:

$$\$1,000,000 \text{ Carrying amount of equity} \times 30\% \text{ Interest} = \$300,000$$

The remaining $50,000 that Blitz received from the third party is recognized as an increase in additional paid-in capital for Blitz.

---

### Sale of Shares by Subsidiary

The managers of a subsidiary may find it necessary to sell shares to third parties. Doing so will reduce the ownership interest of the parent entity. When this happens, multiply the newly-adjusted ownership interest of the parent by the carrying amount of the subsidiary's new equity balance to arrive at the revised investment of the parent in the subsidiary. This situation is addressed in the following example.

---

**EXAMPLE**

Hammer Industries has 50,000 shares of common stock outstanding. Of this amount, 40,000 shares are owned by its parent, Mole Industries, and the remaining shares are owned by unrelated third parties. The carrying amount of the equity of Hammer is $1,000,000. Of the $1,000,000, 80% (or $800,000) is attributed to Mole, and 20% (or $200,000) to the noncontrolling interest in Hammer.

Hammer is in need of additional funding, and elects to sell 10,000 shares to an unrelated third party for $220,000. This transaction reduces Mole's ownership interest in Hammer to 67%, which is calculated as:

$$40,000 \text{ Shares owned by Mole} \div 60,000 \text{ Total shares outstanding} = 66.67\%$$

As a result of the stock sale, Hammer's equity has increased from $1,000,000 to $1,220,000. Mole's share of this increased equity is 66.67%, which is $813,374. This means that Mole recognizes an increase of $13,374 in its Hammer investment, with a corresponding increase in its additional paid-in capital. The noncontrolling interest in Hammer is now $406,626, which is calculated as follows:

$$\$1,220,000 \text{ Carrying amount of equity} \times 33.33\% \text{ Ownership interest} = \$406,626$$

The combined ownership amounts of Mole and the noncontrolling interests equal $1,220,000, which matches the total carrying amount of Hammer's equity.

## Share of Accumulated Other Comprehensive Income

A subsidiary may carry on its books an accumulated other comprehensive income balance. This account is used to accumulate unrealized gains and unrealized losses on those line items in the income statement that are classified within the other comprehensive income category. A transaction is unrealized when it has not yet been settled. Thus, if a subsidiary were to invest in a bond, it would record any gain or loss in its fair value in other comprehensive income until it sells the bond, at which time the gain or loss would be realized, and then shifted out of the accumulated other comprehensive income account.

A noncontrolling interest is assigned a proportional share of the balance in the accumulated other comprehensive income account. If the ownership percentages of the controlling and noncontrolling interests change, then the proportional assignment of the balance in this account must also change. The following example illustrates the concept.

## EXAMPLE

Latham Lumber is a subsidiary of Camelot Construction. Latham has 25,000 shares of common stock outstanding, of which 20,000 shares are owned by Camelot and 5,000 by a third party that has a noncontrolling interest in Latham. The carrying amount of the noncontrolling interest is $40,000, which includes $10,000 of accumulated other comprehensive income.

Camelot pays $20,000 to acquire half of the noncontrolling interest. As a result of this transaction, Camelot has increased its ownership percentage of Latham to 90% from the prior 80% level. The accounting for the transaction is a reduction of the noncontrolling interest to $20,000 (half of the previous amount). Also, Camelot's share of the accumulated other comprehensive income that had been ascribed to the noncontrolling interest is $5,000 (half of the total). This transfer is accomplished with an offsetting decrease in the additional paid-in capital attributable to Camelot.

## Full Consolidation Example

The following example combines a number of issues, including the sale and subsequent partial re-purchase of a noncontrolling interest, and the assignment of accumulated other comprehensive income.

## EXAMPLE

Icelandic Cod has a subsidiary, Canadian Crab. During 20X2, Icelandic owns all of the 50,000 shares outstanding for Canadian, so its ownership interest in Canadian is 100%.

In February of 20X2, Canadian is flush with cash from the king crab season, for which the fishing season ended in January. Accordingly, Canadian purchases $250,000 of securities and classifies them as available for sale. By the end of the year, the carrying amount of these securities has increased to $260,000. For the full year, Canadian earned net profits of $300,000. As of year-end, the detail of Canadian's equity was as follows:

| | |
|---|---|
| Common stock | 50,000 |
| Additional paid-in capital | 100,000 |
| Retained earnings | 350,000 |
| Accumulated other comprehensive income | 10,000 |
| Total equity | $510,000 |

On the first day of the new year, Icelandic elects to sell 10% of its interest in Canadian, so it sells 5,000 shares to a third party for $60,000. In the consolidated financial statements of the entities, the sale of stock is accounted for as follows:

- Recognize a noncontrolling interest of $51,000 (calculated as $510,000 total equity × 10%).
- Recognize an increase in the additional paid-in capital of Icelandic of $9,000, which is the difference between the $60,000 cash received from the third party and the $51,000 carrying amount of the noncontrolling interest.
- Recognize an increase in the additional paid-in capital of Icelandic of $1,000, and a matching reduction of its accumulated other comprehensive income. This change reflects the carrying amount of Canadian's $10,000 of accumulated other comprehensive income related to the available for sale securities, of which 10% is now assigned to the noncontrolling interest.
- These activities result in the following journal entry:

| | Debit | Credit |
|---|---|---|
| Cash | 60,000 | |
| Accumulated other comprehensive income (Icelandic) | 1,000 | |
| Noncontrolling interest | | 51,000 |
| Additional paid-in capital (Icelandic) | | 10,000 |

For the year ended 20X3, Canadian does not enjoy as large a profit, due to overfishing in the king crab fishing areas; its net profit is $100,000. At year-end, the carrying amount of the noncontrolling interest is $64,000, of which $3,000 is accumulated other comprehensive income.

Immediately following year-end, Icelandic thinks better of its earlier decision to sell Canadian shares to a third party, and negotiates to repurchase half of the shares (2,500 shares) for $40,000. This results in an increase in Icelandic's ownership of Canadian to 95%.

Icelandic accounts for this purchase of stock for the consolidated financial statements through the following steps:

- Recognize a reduction of the noncontrolling interest of $25,500 (calculated as $51,000 noncontrolling interest × 50%).
- Recognize a reduction in the additional paid-in capital of Icelandic of $14,500, which is the difference between the $40,000 paid to the third party and the $25,500 reduction in the carrying amount of the noncontrolling interest.
- Recognize a $1,500 reduction in the additional paid-in capital account of Icelandic, which is 50% of the carrying amount of the accumulated other comprehensive income formerly attributed to the third party, which

has been repurchased by Icelandic. The offset to this transaction is an increase of $1,500 in the accumulated other comprehensive income attributable to Icelandic.

- These activities result in the following journal entry:

|  | Debit | Credit |
|---|---|---|
| Noncontrolling interest | 25,500 |  |
| Additional paid-in capital (Icelandic) | 16,000 |  |
|     Accumulated other comprehensive income (Icelandic) |  | 1,500 |
|     Cash |  | 40,000 |

## Termination of a Consolidation

A parent entity should remove from its consolidated financial statements any subsidiary or group of assets as of the date when the parent no longer has a controlling financial interest in it. This means that the following items related to a subsidiary or group of assets are derecognized:

- Assets
- Liabilities
- Equity components, including noncontrolling interests, and amounts recognized in accumulated other comprehensive income

At the time of a deconsolidation, the parent entity recognizes a gain or loss based on the calculation in the following exhibit.

### Parent Entity Gain or Loss on Deconsolidation

| + Fair value of consideration received<br>+ Fair value of any retained noncontrolling investment<br>+ Carrying amount of any noncontrolling interest | - | Carrying amount of the former subsidiary's assets and liabilities, or the carrying amount of the asset group |
|---|---|---|

The control of a parent entity over a subsidiary may decline over time, through multiple transactions. It may be necessary to account for the effect of these transactions as a single event, depending on the terms of these arrangements or their effects. The following are indicators of situations where multiple transactions could be treated as a single transaction:

- The transactions occur at the same time
- One transaction contemplates the occurrence of another transaction at a later date
- They are designed to achieve an aggregated commercial effect
- One transaction is dependent on another transaction
- The outcome of the transactions net to a positive economic outcome, but not individually

The net effect of this analysis might be that a deconsolidation could occur sooner than might be indicated by a single underlying transaction.

## Summary

An accountant may deal with acquisitions on only rare occasions, and so may be unfamiliar with the proper accounting to be used to recognize these transactions. While this chapter provides guidelines for how to structure these transactions, there is still a strong likelihood of incorrectly accounting for an acquisition. If there appears to be a high level of accounting complexity associated with a business combination, it can be useful to engage the services of an acquisition accounting expert, for whom a recommendation may be obtained from the company's certified public accountants.

Part of the text in this chapter was concerned with the control decision – does an organization have control over another entity or not? In most cases the establishment of control is clear, and will rarely change. Nonetheless, it makes sense to schedule a periodic review of the control situation for all business relationships, and to document the outcome of this review. The auditors may want to examine the thought process behind the determination of whether to consolidate, and so will want to examine this documentation.

## Review Questions

1. The acquisition method involves the following step:
    a. Value the acquiree
    b. Sign a letter of intent
    c. Determine the acquisition date
    d. Settle upon the method of payment

2. The calculation of goodwill includes the following components, except for:
    a. Liabilities assumed
    b. Consideration paid
    c. Book value of noncontrolling interest
    d. Assets acquired

3. A step acquisition occurs when:
    a. The acquirer is smaller than the acquiree
    b. The acquirer already owns a minority interest in the acquiree and then buys an additional interest
    c. The acquisition is highly leveraged
    d. Management will be the new owner of the acquired company

4. An example of an intangible asset to which a value can be assigned in an acquisition is:
    a. The potential outcome of a lawsuit
    b. The assembled workforce
    c. Noncompetition agreements
    d. Competitor lists

5. A reverse acquisition is commonly used to:
    a. Convert a "C" corporation into an "S" corporation
    b. Take a company public by acquiring a public shell company
    c. Acquire a tax loss to offset a company's taxable profits
    d. Eliminate a noncontrolling interest

6. A consolidation may not be allowed when there is no clear indication of a controlling financial interest. An example is when:
    a. A subsidiary is engaged in a legal reorganization
    b. A subsidiary is in the process of changing its legal name
    c. A subsidiary is incorporated in a different country
    d. There is a noncontrolling shareholder

7. The presence of ___ can prevent a reporting entity with a majority voting interest from consolidating with another entity.
    a. Protective rights
    b. Shareholder voting rights
    c. A noncontrolling interest
    d. Substantive participating rights

# Chapter 15
# Accounting for Derivatives and Hedges

## Introduction

There are two key concepts in the accounting for derivatives and hedges. The first is that ongoing changes in the fair value of derivatives not used in hedging arrangements are generally recognized in earnings at once. The second is that ongoing changes in the fair value of derivatives and the hedged items with which they are paired may be parked in other comprehensive income for a period of time, thereby removing them from the basic earnings reported by a business. In the following sections, we build upon these concepts by addressing the details of the various types of derivative and hedge accounting, and several related issues.

## What is a Derivative?

A *financial instrument* is a document that has monetary value or which establishes an obligation to pay. Examples of financial instruments are cash, foreign currencies, accounts receivable, loans, bonds, equity securities, and accounts payable. A *derivative* is a financial instrument that has the following characteristics:

- It is a financial instrument or a contract that requires either a small or no initial investment;
- There is at least one *notional amount* (the face value of a financial instrument, which is used to make calculations based on that amount) or payment provision;
- It can be settled *net*, which is a payment that reflects the net difference between the ending positions of the two parties; and
- Its value changes in relation to a change in an *underlying*, which is a variable, such as an interest rate, exchange rate, credit rating, or commodity price, that is used to determine the settlement of a derivative instrument. The value of a derivative can even change in conjunction with the weather.

Examples of derivatives include the following:

- *Call option*. An agreement that gives the holder the right, but not the obligation, to *buy* shares, bonds, commodities, or other assets at a pre-determined price within a pre-defined time period.
- *Put option*. An agreement that gives the holder the right, but not the obligation, to *sell* shares, bonds, commodities, or other assets at a pre-determined price within a pre-defined time period.
- *Forward*. An agreement to buy or sell an asset at a pre-determined price as of a future date. This is a highly customizable derivative, which is not traded on an exchange.
- *Futures*. An agreement to buy or sell an asset at a pre-determined price as of a future date. This is a standardized agreement, so that they can be more easily traded on a futures exchange.
- *Swap*. An agreement to exchange one security for another, with the intent of altering the security terms to which each party individually is subjected.

In essence, a derivative constitutes a bet that something will increase or decrease. A derivative can be used in two ways. Either it is a tool for avoiding risk, or it is used to speculate. In the latter case, an entity accepts risk in order to possibly earn above-average profits. Speculation using derivatives can be extremely risky, since a large adverse movement in an underlying could trigger a massive liability for the holder of a derivative.

When entering into a derivative arrangement, neither party to the arrangement pays the entire value of the instrument up front. Instead, the net difference between the obligations of the two parties is tracked over time, with final settlement being based on the net difference between the final positions of the parties when the instrument is terminated. Also, there is no delivery or receipt of any non-financial item. This arrangement is referred to as *net settlement*.

By minimizing the need for an up-front investment, a business or individual can enter into a derivative arrangement at minimal cost. This makes the use of derivatives much more cost-effective than would be the case if they were paid for up front and in full.

The value of a derivative changes in concert with the variability of the underlying on which it is based. For example, if a derivative is tied to a benchmark interest rate and there is a minimal expectation that the interest rate will change during the life of the derivative, then the seller of the derivative bears little risk of having to pay out, and so will accept a low price for the derivative. Conversely, if there is an expectation of major changes in the underlying, the risk that the seller will have to pay out increases, so the seller will require a much higher price for the derivative.

It is possible for a derivative to not be a financial instrument. In this situation, the terms of the derivative must allow for the option to have a net settlement. Also, it cannot be part of the normal usage requirements of a business.

There may sometimes be uncertainty regarding whether a transaction is not a derivative. If not, the transaction might be a normal purchase or a normal sale. The characteristics of these transactions are:

- There is a probable physical settlement, such as the delivery of goods or services.
- There is documentation of the transaction, such as the basis for a decision that the contract will result in physical delivery.
- There is a clearly and closely related underlying.
- There are normal terms; that is, the terms of the contract are consistent with the terms of an organization's normal purchases and sales.

---

**EXAMPLE**

Winslow Refining enters into a contract to purchase crude oil at a pre-determined price on a future date. The intent is to process all of the acquired crude oil through the company's Houston refinery. Since this transaction is part of the normal usage requirements of the business, it is not a derivative instrument.

**EXAMPLE**

Just down the street from Winslow Refining is the headquarters of Burton Brothers Investments. Burton earns money by speculating on the price of crude oil. Burton enters into a futures contract to purchase 100,000 barrels of crude oil on August 10, and plans to net settle the contract on that date. Thus, Burton does not take delivery of the oil. By the end of June, the price of crude oil has increased by $2 per barrel, so Burton has (so far) earned a profit of $200,000 on the contract. Since this transaction is entirely speculative, the transaction is a derivative.

---

## What is a Hedge?

Hedging is a risk reduction technique, under which an entity uses a derivative or similar instrument to offset future changes in the fair value or cash flows of an asset or liability. The ideal outcome of a hedge is when the distribution of probable outcomes is reduced, so that the size of any potential loss is reduced. The following exhibit shows the effect of hedging on the range of possible outcomes.

**Impact of Hedging on Risk Outcome**

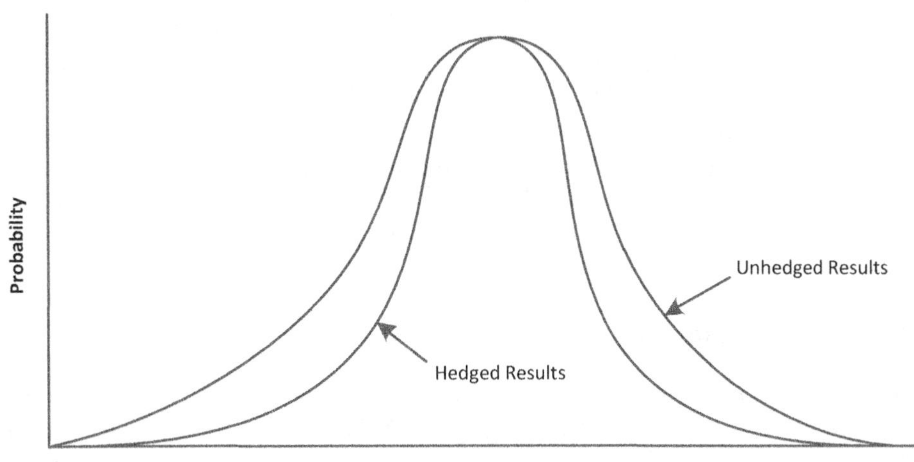


A hedged item can be any of the following individually or in a group with similar risk characteristics:

- A highly probable forecast transaction
- A net investment in a foreign operation
- A recognized asset
- A recognized liability
- An unrecognized firm commitment

It is quite acceptable to hedge a group of similar assets or liabilities, as long as the individual items in such a group share the same risk exposure that is being hedged.

*Hedge effectiveness* is the amount of the changes in the fair value or cash flows of a hedged item that are offset by changes in the fair value or cash flows of a hedging instrument. A highly effective hedging transaction is one in which the net effect of a pairing of a hedged item and a hedging instrument is close to zero.

## Derivative Accounting

The essential accounting for a derivative instrument is outlined in the following bullet points:

- *Initial recognition.* When it is first acquired, recognize a derivative instrument in the balance sheet as an asset or liability at its fair value.
- *Subsequent recognition (hedging relationship).* Recognize all subsequent changes in the fair value of the derivative (known as *marked to market*). If the instrument has been paired with a hedged item, then recognize these fair value changes as noted later in the Presentation of Hedges section.
- *Subsequent recognition (speculation).* Recognize in earnings all subsequent changes in the fair value of the derivative. Speculative activities imply that a derivative has not been paired with a hedged item.

The following additional rules apply to the accounting for derivative instruments when specific types of investments are being hedged:

- *Held-to-maturity investments.* This is a debt instrument for which there is a commitment to hold the investment until its maturity date. When such an investment is being hedged, there may be a change in the fair value of the paired forward contract or purchased option. If so, only recognize a loss in earnings when there is an other-than-temporary decline in the hedging instrument's fair value.

- *Trading securities.* This can be either a debt or equity security, for which there is an intent to sell in the short term for a profit. When this investment is being hedged, recognize any changes in the fair value of the paired forward contract or purchased option in earnings.
- *Available-for-sale securities.* This can be either a debt or equity security that does not fall into the held-to-maturity or trading classifications. When such an investment is being hedged, there may be a change in the fair value of the paired forward contract or purchased option. If so, only recognize a loss in earnings when there is an other-than-temporary decline in the hedging instrument's fair value. If the change is temporary, record it in other comprehensive income.

## Hedge Accounting - General

The accounting for hedges involves matching a derivative instrument to a hedged item, and then recognizing gains and losses from both items in the same period. A derivative is always measured at its fair value. If the instrument is effective for a period of time, this may mean that incremental changes in its fair value are continually being recorded in the accounting records.

The intent behind hedge accounting is to allow a business to record changes in the value of a hedging relationship in other comprehensive income (except for fair value hedges), rather than in earnings. This is done in order to protect the core earnings of a business from periodic variations in the value of its financial instruments before they have been liquidated. Once a financial instrument has been liquidated, any accumulated gains or losses stored in other comprehensive income are shifted into earnings.

When a business uses a derivative as a hedge, it can elect to designate the derivative as belonging to one of the following three hedging classifications:

- *Fair value hedge.* The derivative is used to hedge the risk of changes in the fair value of an asset or liability, or of an unrecognized firm commitment.
- *Cash flow hedge.* The derivative is used to hedge variations in the cash flows associated with an asset or liability, or of a forecasted transaction.
- *Foreign currency hedge.* The derivative is used to hedge variations in the foreign currency exposure associated with a net investment in a foreign operation, a forecasted transaction, an available-for-sale security, or an unrecognized firm commitment.

If a derivative instrument is designated as belonging within one of these classifications, the gains or losses associated with the hedge are matched to any gains or losses incurred by the asset or liability with which the derivative is paired. However, the hedging relationship must first qualify for hedge accounting. To do so, the relationship must meet all of the following criteria:

- *Designation.* The hedging relationship must be designated as such at its inception. The documentation of the relationship must include the following:
  - The hedging relationship
  - The risk management objective and strategy, which includes identification of the hedging instrument and the hedged item, the nature of the risk being hedged, and the method used to determine hedge effectiveness.
  - If there is a fair value hedge of a firm commitment, a method for recognizing in earnings the asset or liability that represents the gain or loss on the hedged commitment.
  - If there is a cash flow hedge of a forecasted transaction, the period when the forecasted transaction will occur, the nature of the asset or liability involved, either the amount of foreign exchange being hedged or the number of items encompassed by the transaction, and the current price of the forecasted transaction.

- *Eligibility (hedged item).* Only certain types of assets and liabilities can qualify for special accounting as a hedging relationship.
- *Eligibility (hedging item).* Designate either all or a portion of the hedging instrument as such. Also, several derivative instruments can be jointly designated as the hedging instrument.
- *Effectiveness.* There is an expectation that the pairing will result in a highly effective hedge that offsets prospective changes in the cash flows or fair value associated with the hedged risk. A highly effective hedge is one in which the change in fair value or cash flows of the hedge falls between 80% and 125% of the opposing change in the fair value or cash flows of the financial instrument that is being hedged. A regression analysis can be used instead of these percentage boundaries to determine hedge effectiveness. Over the life of a hedging relationship, the effectiveness of the pairing must be examined at least quarterly. A prospective analysis should also be made to estimate whether the relationship will be highly effective in future periods, typically using a probability-weighted analysis of changes in fair value or cash flows. If the relationship is no longer highly effective through the date of this assessment, then the pairing no longer qualifies for hedge accounting. It is possible to evaluate a hedging relationship on a qualitative basis if an initial quantitative test was conducted that revealed a highly effective relationship, and there is an expectation of high effectiveness in subsequent periods. If the facts and circumstances supporting a qualitative assessment later change, then conduct a quantitative assessment at that time.

If a hedging relationship is not fully documented or is never documented at all, then all subsequent changes in fair value associated with these instruments must be immediately recorded as gains or losses in earnings.

Even if a hedge is considered to be effective, it is quite possible that some portion of the risk inherent in an underlying transaction will not be covered by a hedge. In this situation, gains and losses on the unhedged portion of a hedged pairing should be recorded in earnings.

---

**EXAMPLE**

Suture Corporation pays $1 million for an investment that is denominated in pounds. Suture's treasurer enters into a hedging transaction that is also denominated in pounds, and which is designed to be a hedge of the investment. One year later, Suture experiences a loss of $12,000 on the investment and a $9,000 gain on the hedging instrument. The full $9,000 gain on the hedging instrument is considered effective, so only the difference between the investment and its hedge - $3,000 – is recorded as a loss in earnings.

---

There may be cases in which a hedging instrument is being employed, where the third party is actually another entity under the umbrella of a parent company. In this case, risk is not being offloaded to a third party. Consequently, such a hedging instrument is not considered to be a hedge for the purposes of hedge accounting.

## Hedge Accounting – Fair Value Hedges

The fair value of an asset or liability could change, which may affect the profits of a business. A fair value hedge is designed to hedge against this exposure to changes in fair value that are caused by a specific risk. It is possible to only hedge the risks associated with a portion of an asset or liability, as long as the effectiveness of the related hedge can be measured.

When a hedging relationship has been established for a fair value hedge, continually re-measure the fair value of the hedge and the item with which it is paired. The accounting for this re-measurement is as follows:

- *Hedging item*. Record a gain or loss in earnings for the change in fair value of the hedging instrument.
- *Hedged item*. Record a gain or loss in earnings for the change in fair value of the hedged item that can be attributed to the risk for which the hedge pairing was established. This also means that the carrying amount of the hedged item must be adjusted to reflect its change in fair value.

If the hedging relationship is fully effective, either the gain on the hedging instrument will exactly offset the loss on the hedged item that is associated with the hedged risk, or vice versa. The net result of a fully effective hedge is no change in earnings. If there is a net gain or loss appearing in earnings, it is because the hedging relationship does not perfectly offset fair value changes in the hedged item.

---

**EXAMPLE**

Prickly Corporation buys ten bonds having an aggregate face value of $10,000. The bonds pay a 6% interest rate, which matches the current market rate. Prickly records the acquisition as an available-for-sale investment.

Prickly's treasurer reviews the investment, and concludes that an increase in the market rate of interest will reduce the value of the bonds. To hedge this risk, the treasurer enters into an interest rate swap whereby Prickly swaps the fixed 6% interest payments it is receiving from the bond issuer for payments from a third party that are based on a floating interest rate. The treasurer documents the interest rate swap as a hedge of the ten bonds.

Over the following months, the applicable market interest rate does indeed increase, which reduces the value of the bonds by an aggregate amount of $800. However, the interest rate swap yields an offsetting $800 gain, since the variable interest rate payments being received have increased to match the change in the market rate of interest. Prickly first records the following entry to document the loss in value of the bonds:

| | Debit | Credit |
|---|---|---|
| Hedging loss | 800 | |
| Available-for-sale investment (asset) | | 800 |

Prickly also records the following entry to document the increased value of the interest rate swap:

| | Debit | Credit |
|---|---|---|
| Swap asset (asset) | 800 | |
| Hedging gain | | 800 |

There is no net gain or loss arising from the increase in the market rate of interest, since the loss on the investment is exactly offset by the gain on the hedging instrument. This means the hedge pairing has been 100% effective.

---

Fair value hedge accounting should be terminated at once if any of the following situations arise:

- The hedging arrangement is no longer effective
- The hedging instrument expires or is sold or terminated
- The organization revokes the hedging designation

As noted in the preceding example, changes in the fair value of the hedged item are being used to adjust its carrying amount over time. Once the item is eventually disposed of, the adjusted carrying amount of the asset is recorded as the cost of the asset sold.

**EXAMPLE**

The treasurer of Prickly Corporation needs cash for operational requirements, and elects to sell the ten bonds that the company had acquired in the preceding example. In that example, the carrying amount of the bonds had been written down by $800 to reflect an increase in the market interest rate. The bonds are then sold for $9,200, resulting in the following entry:

|  | Debit | Credit |
|---|---|---|
| Cash | 9,200 | |
|     Available-for-sale investment (asset) | | 9,200 |

## Hedge Accounting – Cash Flow Hedges

There could be variations in the cash flows associated with an asset or liability or a forecasted transaction, which may affect the profits of a business. A cash flow hedge is designed to hedge against this exposure to changes in cash flows that are caused by a specific risk. It is possible to only hedge the risks associated with a portion of an asset, liability, or forecasted transaction, as long as the effectiveness of the related hedge can be measured. The accounting for a cash flow hedge is as follows:

- *Hedging item.* Include in other comprehensive income the entire change in the fair value of the hedging instrument that was included in the assessment of hedge effectiveness, which are then reclassified to earnings when the hedged item affects earnings.
- *Hedged item.* Initially recognize the effective portion of any gain or loss in other comprehensive income. Reclassify these gains or losses into earnings when the forecasted transaction affects earnings.

There are several additional special situations involving cash flow hedges that require different accounting transactions. The following scenarios reveal the more likely accounting variations:

1. *Exclusions from strategy.* If the documented risk management strategy does not include a certain component of the gains or losses experienced by the hedged item, recognize this excluded amount in earnings. Doing so reduces the aggregate amount of gains or losses in other comprehensive income. Next;
2. *Adjust other comprehensive income.* Reduce the amount of accumulated other comprehensive income related to a hedging relationship to the lesser of:

    - The cumulative gain or loss on the derivative from the date when the hedge began, less any gains or losses already reclassified into earnings; or
    - The cumulative gain or loss on the derivative that will be needed to offset the cumulative change in expected future cash flows on the hedged transaction from the date when the hedge began, less any gains or losses already reclassified into earnings.

3. *Further gain or loss recognition.* Recognize in earnings any remaining gain or loss on the hedging derivative, or to revise the accumulated other comprehensive income amount to match the balance derived in step 2.
4. *Foreign currency adjustments.* If a foreign currency position is being hedged, and hedge effectiveness is based on the total changes in the cash flow of an option, then reclassify from other

comprehensive income to earnings an amount sufficient to adjust earnings for the amortization of the option cost.

A key issue with cash flow hedges is when to recognize gains or losses in earnings when the hedging transaction relates to a forecasted transaction. These gains or losses should be reclassified from other comprehensive income to earnings when the hedged transaction affects earnings.

---

**EXAMPLE**

Suture Corporation has acquired equipment from a company in the United Kingdom, which Suture must pay for in 60 days in the amount of £150,000. Suture's functional currency is the U.S. Dollar. At the time of the purchase, Suture could settle this obligation for $240,000, based on the exchange rate then in effect.

To hedge against the risk of an unfavorable change in exchange rates during the intervening 60 days, Suture enters into a forward contract with its bank to buy £150,000 in 60 days, at the current exchange rate. Suture's controller designates the forward contract as a hedge of its exposure to adverse changes in the dollar to pounds exchange rate.

At the end of the next month, the pound has increased in value against the dollar, so that it would now require $242,000 to settle the obligation. Luckily, the value of the forward contract has also increased by $2,000, which results in the following entry:

|  | Debit | Credit |
|---|---|---|
| Forward asset (asset) | 2,000 | |
|     Other comprehensive income | | 2,000 |

The exchange rate remains the same for the following month, after which the treasurer settles the forward contract and the controller records the following entry:

|  | Debit | Credit |
|---|---|---|
| Cash (asset) | 2,000 | |
|     Forward asset (asset) | | 2,000 |

The payables staff then pays the $242,000 obligation to the United Kingdom supplier, as noted in the following entry. The transaction also includes a $2,000 reduction of the purchase price, which represents the deferred gain on the forward contract.

|  | Debit | Credit |
|---|---|---|
| Fixed assets – Equipment (asset) | 240,000 | |
| Other comprehensive income | 2,000 | |
|     Cash (asset) | | 242,000 |

The net result of this hedging transaction is that Suture has used a hedging instrument to offset the risk of an adverse change in the applicable exchange rate, and so is able to pay for the equipment at the original purchase price.

**EXAMPLE**

Suture Corporation borrows $10 million on January 1, to be repaid with a balloon payment of $10 million on December 31 of the same year. The interest rate on the loan is SIBOR plus 2.0%, and is to be paid semi-annually. SIBOR on January 1 is 4.50%, so the initial interest rate on the loan is 6.50%. The treasurer of Suture is concerned that interest rates will increase during the borrowing period, and so enters into an interest rate swap with 3rd National Bank on the same day. Under the terms of the swap, Suture pays a fixed interest rate of 6.80% semi-annually for one year, while 3rd National takes over the variable interest payments of Suture. The notional amount of the swap arrangement is $10 million. Suture's cost of capital is 7%.

The swap arrangement qualifies as a cash flow hedge.

On June 30, the interest paid for the first six months of the loan is based on the initial 6.50% interest rate, so Suture records the following entry for a half-year of interest at 6.50% for a $10 million loan:

|  | Debit | Credit |
|---|---|---|
| Interest expense | 325,000 | |
| Cash (asset) | | 325,000 |

In addition, Suture also pays the net difference in the swapped interest rates of 0.3% on the notional contract amount of $10 million for the same six-month period. The entry is:

|  | Debit | Credit |
|---|---|---|
| Interest expense | 15,000 | |
| Cash (asset) | | 15,000 |

On June 30, the reference rate adjusts upward to 5.50%, which means that the interest rate on Suture's loan will now be 7.50% for the remaining six months of the loan period. This also means that Suture will be paid the 0.7% difference between the new 7.50% variable interest rate and the 6.80% fixed-rate amount stated in the swap agreement, with this payment being made by 3rd National on the next (and final) payment date, which is December 31. The amount of this payment will be $35,000; when discounted to its present value at Suture's 7% cost of capital for six months, the amount is approximately $33,775. The entry to record this future payment on June 30 is:

|  | Debit | Credit |
|---|---|---|
| Swap contract | 33,775 | |
| Other comprehensive income | | 33,775 |

On the loan termination date of December 31, Suture makes the following interest expense payment to the lender, based on the 7.50% interest rate that applied to the preceding six-month period:

|  | Debit | Credit |
|---|---|---|
| Interest expense | 375,000 | |
| Cash (asset) | | 375,000 |

In addition, Suture reverses its accrual of the present value of the swap contract that it recorded on June 30, and replaces it with a recordation of the cash received from 3$^{rd}$ National in settlement of the swap contract. As calculated earlier, the amount of this payment is $35,000.

|  | Debit | Credit |
|---|---|---|
| Other comprehensive income | 33,775 |  |
|     Swap contract |  | 33,775 |
| Cash (asset) | 35,000 |  |
|     Interest expense |  | 35,000 |

The net undiscounted effect of the interest rate swap is a net decline in Suture's interest expense of $20,000 over the full year covered by the loan, which represents a net decline of 0.2% in the interest rate paid.

---

Cash flow hedge accounting should be terminated at once if any of the following situations arises:

- The hedging arrangement is no longer effective
- The hedging instrument expires or is terminated
- The organization revokes the hedging designation

If it is probable that the hedged forecasted transaction will not occur within the originally-stated time period or within two months after this period, shift the derivative's gain or loss from accumulated other comprehensive income to earnings.

## Hedge Accounting – Net Investment Hedges

A business may have an investment in operations in another country. If so, changes in the exchange rate between the functional currency of the parent entity and the currency of the foreign operations could create gains or losses. In this situation, it is possible to create a net investment hedge that is equal to or less than the carrying amount of the net assets of the foreign operation.

The accounting for such a hedge is to recognize in other comprehensive income the entire change in the fair value of the hedging instrument that was included in the assessment of hedge effectiveness, which is then reclassified to earnings when the hedged item affects earnings. If the parent entity ever disposes of the foreign operations, shift the cumulative net amount of any gains or losses recognized in other comprehensive income as part of the hedging instrument into earnings.

---

**EXAMPLE**

Suture Corporation invests $20 million in a new subsidiary located in England. The functional currency of this subsidiary is the pound. The exchange rate on the investment date is $1 = £0.6463, so the initial investment is priced at £12,926,000. Suture takes out a loan in England in the amount of £9,695,000 (which translates to $15,000,000) and designates it as a hedge of its investment in the subsidiary. The stated strategy is that any change in the fair value of the loan attributed to foreign exchange risk will offset 75% of the translation gains or losses on the Suture investment.

One year later, the exchange rate has changed to $1 = £0.6600, which yields the following loss on the investment for Suture:

$$(£12,926,000 \div 0.6600 = \$19,585,000) - \$20,000,000$$

$$= \$(415,000) \text{ Investment translation loss}$$

Against this loss is set the following gain on the related loan:

$$(£9,695,000 \div 0.6600 = \$14,689,000) - \$15,000,000$$

$$= \$311,000 \text{ Loan translation gain}$$

Suture creates the following entry to record the reduction in value of its investment, as well as the translation gain related to its loan:

|  | Debit | Credit |
|---|---|---|
| Cumulative translation adjustment | 415,000 |  |
|     Investment in subsidiary |  | 415,000 |
| Pound-denominated debt | 311,000 |  |
|     Cumulative translation adjustment |  | 311,000 |

## Embedded Derivatives

An embedded derivative is an element of a financial instrument that has the characteristics of a derivative. Thus, the embedded derivative must require that some portion of the cash flows associated with the overall instrument be adjusted in relation to changes in an underlying, as noted earlier. To be an embedded derivative, it is not possible for this element of a financial instrument to be transferred separately from the rest of the contract.

When there is an embedded derivative within a financial instrument, the entire instrument is considered a hybrid financial instrument.

It is possible to separately account for an embedded derivative, but only when both of the following conditions are present:

- The economic characteristics and risks of the derivative element are not closely related to the economic characteristics and risks of the financial instrument in which it is embedded; and
- A separate instrument with the characteristics and risks of the embedded derivative would have been classified as a derivative instrument.

There are several alternatives available for accounting for an embedded derivative, including the following:

- *No separate measurement possible.* If it is not possible to reliably measure an embedded derivative, then measure the entire hybrid financial instrument at its fair value. Also, when there is a change in this fair value, recognize the change in earnings in the reporting period in which the change occurs.
- *Election to combine.* A one-time and irrevocable election can be made to measure the entire hybrid financial instrument at its fair value, with no breakout of the embedded derivative. When there is a change in this fair value, recognize the change in earnings in the reporting period in which the change occurs.
- *Separate accounting.* If the preceding two conditions are present that allow for the separate accounting for an embedded derivative, then the derivative and the contract in which it is embedded are tracked and accounted for separately, based on their respective fair values. However, the sum of their fair values cannot exceed the overall fair value of the hybrid instrument.

**EXAMPLE**

Hubble Corporation purchases 50 convertible bonds that have been issued by Medusa Medical. Hubble acquires the bonds at face value, so the total amount paid is $50,000. The conversion terms incorporated into the bonds state that each bond contains an option to purchase two shares of Medusa common stock for $14 per share.

The economic characteristics and risks of the option feature are not closely related to the debt features of the bond to which it is attached, and a separate instrument with the option features would have been classified as a derivative instrument. The estimated fair value of the option feature, in aggregate for all 50 bonds, is $600.

Based on this information, Hubble's accountant elects to separately account for the option feature and the bonds. The result is the following initial entry:

|  | Debit | Credit |
|---|---|---|
| Investments (asset) | 49,400 | |
| Derivative asset (asset) | 600 | |
| Cash (asset) | | 50,000 |

## Sample Hedging Procedure

When a business has current or expected holdings or obligations involving foreign currencies, it may be prudent to create a hedging transaction to mitigate the company's potential losses arising from exchange rate fluctuations. A foreign exchange hedging procedure is outlined below:

1. **Calculate hedge requirements.** Based on the company's forecast of foreign currency holdings or obligations, determine the amount and duration of the hedging transaction needed to offset these holdings or obligations.
   *Responsible party:* Treasury staff

2. **Examine preliminary hedge.** Obtain information about the prospective hedge, and address the following issues:
   - Verify the sufficiency of the counterparty's credit rating
   - Determine the level of effectiveness of the hedging strategy
   - Review the proposed contract for legal issues
   - Obtain approval of the hedge

   *Responsible party:* Treasury staff, treasurer, and corporate counsel
   *Control issues:* It may be useful to use a proposed hedge signoff sheet, so that each person involved in a hedge can formally document that their assigned tasks were completed.

3. **Begin hedge.** Enter into the hedging transaction.
   *Responsible party:* Treasury staff
   *Control issues:* Be sure to confirm the details of the hedging transaction with the counterparty. Otherwise, you may find that the terms of the hedge do not meet the company's expectations, and may need to close out the transaction and start over.

4. **Document the hedge.** Create all hedging documentation required under the applicable accounting standards. This includes documentation of:

   - How the company plans to measure the effectiveness of the hedging transaction
   - The relationship between the foreign exchange position and the hedging instrument
   - The risk management objectives of the company
   - The specifics of the hedging strategy

   This information is needed to properly account for the hedge.
   *Responsible party:* Treasury staff
   *Control issues:* Be sure to confirm the details of the hedging transaction with the counterparty. Otherwise, you may find that the terms of the hedge do not meet the company's expectations.

5. **Account for the hedge.** At the end of each reporting period, charge to other comprehensive income any gains or losses resulting from having marked the hedge to market. If any hedge losses are considered to be non-recoverable and they have previously been recorded in other comprehensive income, shift them to earnings.
   *Responsible party:* Accounting staff
   *Control issues:* To ensure that this step is completed, include it in the list of period-end closing activities.

6. **Close out the hedge.** Once the hedging transaction has been completed and settled, move all gains and losses initially recorded in the other comprehensive income account to earnings.
   *Responsible party:* Accounting staff
   *Control issues:* Review the other comprehensive income account to ensure that all transactions related to a closed hedge have been removed from that account.

The following exhibit shows a streamlined view of the foreign exchange hedging procedure.

**Foreign Exchange Hedging Process Flow**

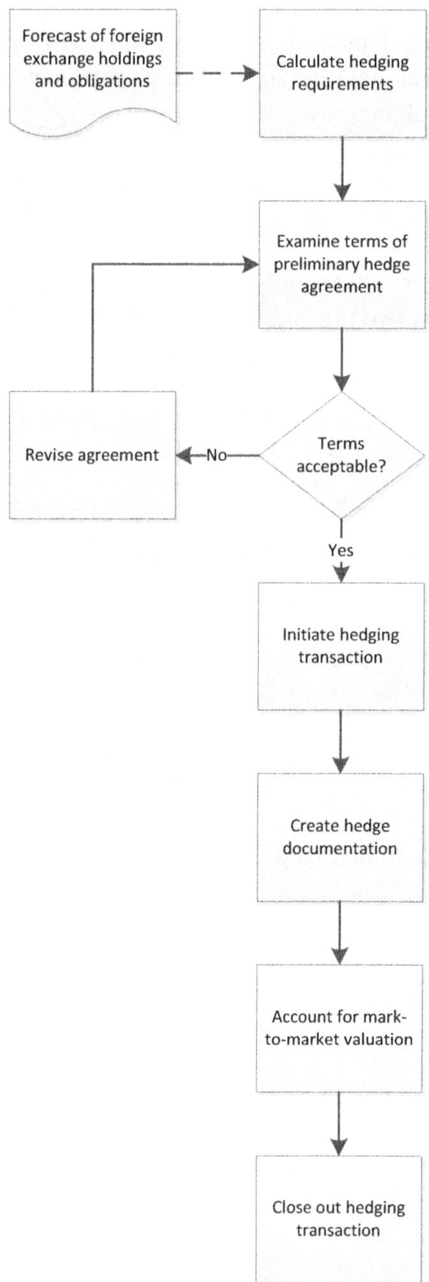


The sample procedure shown in this section could be expanded upon to deal with other types of hedging transactions.

## Unhedged Foreign Exchange Gains and Losses

There may be circumstances when a choice is made not to create a hedge against a foreign exchange position, and the company subsequently incurs a gain or loss on that position. It is also possible that the company does not have an adequate foreign exchange forecasting system, and so does not know that it even has unhedged positions, which will most certainly result in unhedged gains or losses.

In either case, it is extremely useful to keep track of gains or losses arising from unhedged foreign currency positions, in order to estimate when the size of these gains or losses warrants the imposition of a more extensive hedging program. The simplest form of metric is a trend line analysis. This trend line will likely yield results that routinely bounce between gains and losses. The key issue to watch for is an increasing trend in the *size* of the gains or losses over time. When they become large enough to seriously impact the company's reported results from operations, it is time to consider a combination of a better forecasting system and a more active hedging program.

## Summary

The accounting for derivatives and hedges is among the most complex in all of accounting, especially for outlier situations where the circumstances must be closely examined to ensure that the proper accounting rules are followed. In many instances, and especially when the accountant is dealing with a new transaction, it can make sense to consult with the company's auditors regarding the proper accounting to use.

The payoff for this high level of accounting complexity is a delay in the recognition of gains or losses in earnings. If management is not concerned about more immediate recognition, or if the gains or losses are minor, it may make sense to ignore the multitude of compliance issues associated with hedge accounting. Instead, simply create hedges as needed and record gains or losses on foreign exchange holdings and hedges at once, without worrying about the proper documentation of each hedging relationship and having to repeatedly measure hedge effectiveness.

## Review Questions

1. The documentation of a hedge must include the following, except for:
   a. The method used to determine hedge effectiveness
   b. How the transaction was authorized
   c. Identification of the hedging instrument
   d. The nature of the hedging relationship

2. A cash flow hedge should be terminated in all of the following situations, except for:
   a. The hedging instrument is terminated
   b. The hedging transaction is expected to occur one month after the originally-stated time period
   c. The hedging arrangement is no longer effective
   d. The organization revokes the hedging designation

3. An element of a financial instrument that has the characteristics of a derivative is called a(n):
   a. Swap
   b. Forward contract
   c. Futures contract
   d. Embedded derivative

4. The key issue that shifts a transaction from other comprehensive income to earnings is:
   a. The cost principle
   b. When the business entity changes
   c. When costs match revenues under the matching concept
   d. Realization

5. When a party is engaged in speculation, the proper accounting for a derivative is to:
   a. Maintain the original cost unadjusted until the position is closed
   b. Recognize changes in the carrying amount in other comprehensive income
   c. Recognize changes in fair value in earnings
   d. Bill the seller for the gross amount of the change in value of the derivative

6. The investment intent behind an investment classified as a trading security is to:
   a. Sell it in the short term for a profit
   b. Hold it for dividend income for the long term
   c. Hold a minority interest in another entity
   d. Hold it until its maturity date

7. The following are the main types of hedging classifications, except for:
   a. Foreign currency hedge
   b. Fair value hedge
   c. Cash flow hedge
   d. Earnings hedge

8. A highly effective hedge is one in which the change in fair value or cash flows of the hedge falls between ___ and ___ of the opposing change in the fair value or cash flows of the financial instrument that is being hedged.
   a. 90% | 110%
   b. 80% | 100%
   c. 80% | 125%
   d. 98% | 102%

9.  The net result of a fully effective fair value hedge is:
    a.  An increase in earnings
    b.  An increase in other comprehensive income
    c.  An increase in accumulated other comprehensive income
    d.  No change in earnings

# Chapter 16
# Fair Value Accounting

## Introduction

There is a growing emphasis within the generally accepted accounting principles framework to recognize assets and liabilities at their fair values, rather than the costs at which they were originally purchased or assumed (their historical costs). This chapter outlines the concept of fair value, where it is used, how to measure it, and when it is allowable to use the fair value option.

## The Fair Value Concept

The easiest form of accounting is to record a transaction at its original amount, and to never adjust that amount in later reporting periods. This gives the accounting department a highly provable basis for its financial statements, since all assets and liabilities can be traced back to verifiable source documents. The trouble is that the value of these items may change over time. For example, securities held for investment purposes are *supposed* to vary (preferably upward). Consequently, the accounting standards have gradually changed to require that more and more assets and liabilities be valued at their fair values, rather than their historical costs. The following table describes the extent to which the fair value concept has been incorporated into the financial statements.

**Fair Value Usage in Financial Reporting**

| Asset or Liability | Fair Value Usage |
|---|---|
| Financial assets (general) | There is an option available that allows a business to report most types of financial assets at their fair values |
| Trading securities and available-for-sale securities | Investments classified as trading securities or available-for-sale securities are to be reported at their fair values |
| Noncurrent receivables | Longer-term receivables are recorded at their discounted present values, with interest income being recognized over the term of the receivables |
| Financial liabilities (general) | There is an option available that allows a business to report most types of financial liabilities at their fair values |
| Noncurrent liabilities | Longer-term liabilities are recorded at their discounted present values, with interest expense being recognized over the term of the liabilities |
| Asset retirement obligations | AROs are recognized at their fair values |

Fair value is the estimated price at which an asset can be sold or a liability settled in an orderly transaction to a third party under current market conditions. This is a hypothetical transaction – there is no need to actually sell an asset or settle a liability. The definition of fair value includes the following concepts:

- *Current market conditions.* The derivation of fair value should be based on market conditions on the measurement date, rather than a transaction that occurred at some earlier date.
- *Intent.* The intention of the holder of an asset or liability to continue to hold it is irrelevant to the measurement of fair value. Such intent might otherwise alter the measured fair value. For example, if the intent is to immediately sell an asset, this could be inferred to trigger a rushed sale, which may result in a lower sale price.
- *Orderly transaction.* Fair value is to be derived based on an orderly transaction, which infers a transaction where there is no undue pressure to sell. Undue pressure can arise, for example, in a

corporate liquidation. This also implies that the counterparty is also not being forced to acquire an asset or settle a liability.

- *Third party*. Fair value is to be derived based on a presumed sale to an entity that is not a corporate insider or related in any way to the seller. Otherwise, a related-party transaction might skew the price paid. In addition, a third party that may participate in a sale or settlement transaction should have a reasonable knowledge of the asset or liability in question, based on customary levels of due diligence.

## The Active Market Concept

The ideal determination of fair value is based on prices offered in an active market. An active market is one in which there is a sufficiently high volume of transactions to provide ongoing pricing information. Also, the market from which a fair value is derived should be the principal market for the asset or liability, since the greater transaction volume associated with such a market should presumably lead to the best prices for the seller. The market in which a business normally sells the asset type in question or settles liabilities is assumed to be the principal market. Thus, the designation of a principal market is from the perspective of the reporting entity; a different market might be the principal market for a competitor.

If there is no principal market for the assets or liabilities being valued, the alternative is to obtain a fair value from the most advantageous market, which is the market in which the best price can be obtained, net of transaction costs.

## Transaction Costs and Other Conditions

The price in the principal market that is used to measure fair value is not to be adjusted for transaction costs. These costs are not directly connected to the assets or liabilities being valued, but rather to the nature of the transaction, and so could vary depending upon how an organization elects to acquire or settle its assets and liabilities, respectively.

In addition, the determination of fair value should be based on the condition and location of the asset, as well as any restrictions on the use of the asset. For example, shares in a company that are restricted will have a substantially lower fair value than unrestricted shares. Also, machinery that has been used more than the average number of hours will have a lower fair value.

## Transportation Costs

The fair value derived in a principal market should be adjusted for the cost required to transport an asset from its current location to that market.

---

**EXAMPLE**

A fishing operation routinely catches tuna, which it delivers to a nearby dock. The principal market for the tuna is a daily auction at a city located 40 miles away. The cost required to transport the tuna to the auction is a valid adjustment to the fair value that can be derived from sale transactions in that market.

---

## Price Quotes

It is possible to derive a price from a quote issued by a broker. In this case, the resulting price is considered more reliable when it is associated with a binding offer. An issuance of a price by a broker without a commitment to buy or sell is considered less reliable.

## Bid and Ask Pricing

When both a bid price and ask price are available, which one should be used to develop a fair value figure? In this situation, use the price most representative of the fair value of the asset or liability. This may mean using a bid price for an asset valuation and an ask price for a liability.

## Measuring Fair Value when Transaction Volume is Low

A company may rely upon the prices obtained in a particular market to derive its fair value calculations. These prices can require significant adjustment if the volume of activity in the market has declined. In such an environment, individual transaction prices could be well above or below what would be found if there were more willing buyers and sellers in the marketplace. Evidence of such a decline includes:

- A reduced number of recent transactions
- There are large swings in quoted prices, either over time or among market makers
- There is no longer a strong correlation between an index and the fair value of an asset or liability
- A wide bid-ask spread, or a notable increase in the spread
- There has been a decline in the market for new issuances
- There is little publicly-available information for related transactions

If there has been a decline in the volume of activity, transaction prices may still fairly reflect fair value. However, if these transactions no longer represent fair value, it will be necessary to adjust the transactions or quoted prices to arrive at a reasonable fair value measurement.

---

### EXAMPLE

Moribund Corporation is publicly-held, but has stopped filing reports with the Securities and Exchange Commission, and has been delisted from a major stock exchange. Its shares now only trade sporadically in the Over the Counter (OTC) market. Eldritch Times owns 1,000 shares of Moribund's stock. The controller of Eldritch is attempting to determine a fair value for these shares, and finds that recent OTC trades have wildly gyrating prices and involve minimal purchase quantities. The controller can reasonably state that these transactions no longer represent the fair value of the shares.

---

There is no prescribed methodology in GAAP for making this adjustment, though the market approach, cost approach, and income approach (as described later in the Fair Value Measurement Approaches section) can be used. Whatever method is used should include a risk premium that market participants would likely demand in order to compensate them for the uncertain cash flows of the asset or liability. It may be appropriate to use multiple valuation techniques, and settle upon a point within the range of resulting outcomes that is most representative of fair value.

## Identifying Transactions That Are Not Orderly

We noted earlier that fair value is the estimated price at which an asset can be sold or a liability settled in an *orderly* transaction to a third party under current market conditions. How can we tell if a transaction is not orderly? The following points are evidence of such a situation:

- *Inadequate marketing.* A transaction may not have involved a sufficient amount of marketing to attract bidders.
- *Single prospective buyer.* All marketing by the seller was targeted at a single buyer.
- *Distressed.* The seller is in a financially distressed condition, and so is forced to sell on a rushed basis in order to obtain cash.

- *Regulatory requirement.* The seller was forced to sell due to regulatory requirements.
- *Outlier.* The price at which a transaction was settled is well outside of the normal range of prices.

If the conclusion is reached that a transaction was not orderly, place little reliance on that price. If there is not sufficient information to determine whether a transaction was orderly, place a lesser weighting on this transaction than the information gleaned from other transactions that are known to have been orderly.

## Highest and Best Use

An additional consideration when determining fair value is the concept of highest and best use. Under this concept, fair value is determined based on the price at which an asset could theoretically be employed in its highest and best use, rather than the use in which the asset is currently employed. The highest and best use is subject to the following limitations:

- *Physically possible.* The physical characteristics and location of the asset may limit its alternative uses. For example, machinery that is bolted into a concrete platform may be so immovable that any other potential highest and best uses are not possible.
- *Legally permissible.* There may be legal restrictions on how an asset may be used, which bar certain alternative uses. For example, zoning regulations may prevent a plot of land in an industrial area from being used to construct high-rise residential apartments.
- *Financially feasible.* The alternative use must incorporate the costs incurred to convert the asset to that use, while still producing investment returns.

---

**EXAMPLE**

Creekside Industrial buys a patent for $1,000,000 that would allow the company to build a technologically-advanced lithium-ion battery. However, Creekside simply sits on the patent, thereby preventing any competitors from using the technology. The fair value of the patent should be based on licensing the patent to competitors, since doing so would yield substantially higher profits than not using the patent, as is currently the case.

**EXAMPLE**

Creekside Industrial acquires a plot of land that is zoned for industrial use. An adjacent plot has already been developed as a retail shopping area, which produces higher cash flows than any possible industrial applications. The highest and best use of the land should be determined by evaluating the land as an industrial site against changing it to a residential or retail site.

---

The highest and best use concept usually only applies to non-financial assets. There is rarely a use for it when valuing liabilities.

## The Unit of Measure

The fair value of an asset or liability may be in relation to the item as a standalone asset or liability, such as a specific machine or a share of stock. However, it could also refer to a mixed group of assets and liabilities, such as a business that could be sold as a coherent unit. In the latter case, the fair value of the business could be much higher than the sum of its individual assets and liabilities, though it is unlikely to be lower – the business could be broken up and sold as separate assets and liabilities at their individual fair values.

## Entry and Exit Prices

When an entity acquires an asset or assumes a liability, the price required to do so is called the *entry price*. After a period of time during which the asset or liability is held, the entity may then sell the asset or pay a third party to take on the liability. In this latter case, the price paid is called the *exit price*. It is possible that there may be a substantial difference between the entry and exit prices.

The exit price may be at some point in the future, and so can only be estimated. The fair value concept drives the entity holding these assets and liabilities to derive exit prices (not entry prices) based on fair value, even if there is no intent to sell the assets or transfer the liabilities.

**When the Transaction Price May Not Equal Fair Value**

One might assume that the price at which a transaction is initially recognized is its fair value, but this is not necessarily the case. The entity might have paid or accepted in payment a different amount when any of the following factors are present:

- *Related parties.* The transaction is between related parties, which could mean that there is a strong incentive between the parties to transfer the goods or assets at an unusually high or low price.
- *Duress.* The circumstances might force the seller to accept an unusually low price in exchange for selling an asset, or (less likely) an unusually high price to accept a liability. This situation most commonly occurs when a business is approaching bankruptcy, and will enter into unfavorable transactions in order to generate cash. It is also possible that the seller was required to sell in order to meet new regulatory requirements, such as when an acquirer is required by the government to spin off a business unit as part of an acquisition of another entity.
- *Unusual elements.* The seller may be including additional warranties or bundling other products or services with the item being sold, which makes it difficult to compare prices.
- *Different market.* The transaction may have taken place in a different market than the most advantageous market. If so, the demand level may be lower, or participants are not as knowledgeable, resulting in a different pricing outcome. For example, securities may be sold in a local market, where there are fewer bidders than on a national exchange.

In these situations, do not place reliance on the information for deriving fair values, for the results could vary significantly from actual fair market values. Conversely, if these factors are not present, *and* the volume of market transactions is large, *and* the comparison transactions are close to the measurement date, the derived fair values can probably be relied upon.

## Fair Value Measurement Approaches

There are several general approaches that GAAP permits for deriving fair values. The most favored approaches are those that maximize the use of relevant observable inputs and minimize the use of unobservable inputs. Observable inputs are derived from market data that properly reflect the assumptions that third parties would use when setting prices for assets and liabilities. Examples of markets that are considered to provide observable inputs are stock exchanges, dealer markets, and brokered markets. The different types of fair value measurement approaches are outlined below:

- *Market approach.* Uses the prices associated with actual market transactions for similar or identical assets and liabilities to derive a fair value. For example, the prices of securities held can be obtained from a national exchange on which these securities are routinely bought and sold. Another possibility is to derive a valuation based on market multiples that come from a set of comparable transactions.
- *Income approach.* Uses estimated future cash flows or earnings, adjusted by a discount rate that represents the time value of money and the risk of cash flows not being achieved, to derive a discounted present value. An alternative way to incorporate risk into this approach is to develop a probability-weighted-average set of possible future cash flows. Option pricing models can also be used under the income approach.

- *Cost approach*. Uses the estimated cost to replace an asset (or the capabilities of the asset), adjusted for the obsolescence of the existing asset. The obsolescence concept includes the deterioration of an asset, its technological obsolescence, and its economic obsolescence.

None of these measurement approaches is considered to be the preferred method to use. The selection of a method should be based on the availability of information that can be applied to a method and the nature of the item being valued. It can require a detailed knowledge of an asset or liability to determine the best possible method to use.

---

**EXAMPLE**

High Noon Armaments routinely evaluates the fair value of its acquisitions within the firearms industry, and so uses the market approach to conduct an annual review of the revenue and EBITDA (earnings before interest, taxes, depreciation and amortization) multiples associated with the smaller publicly-held companies in the same industry.  Accordingly, the acquisitions staff prepares the following multiples analysis.

| Name | Market Capitalization | One Year Revenues | One Year EBITDA | Revenue Multiple | EBITDA Multiple |
|---|---|---|---|---|---|
| Arbuckle Weapons | $145,000 | $174,000 | $19,300 | 1.2x | 7.5x |
| Billy the Kid Designs | 90,000 | 117,000 | 11,500 | 1.3x | 7.8x |
| Heston Shotguns | 128,000 | 160,000 | 24,200 | 0.8x | 5.3x |
| Patton Siege Guns | 210,000 | 210,000 | 30,000 | 1.0x | 7.0x |
| Plasma Weapons | 52,000 | 24,000 | 3,900 | 2.2x | 13.2x |
| Quigley Artillery | 360,000 | 240,000 | 42,400 | 1.5x | 8.5x |
| Rifled Custom Guns | 76,000 | 19,000 | 3,200 | 4.0x | 24.0x |
| Totals | $1,061,000 | $944,000 | $134,500 | 1.1x | 7.9x |

Thus, the review shows a weighted-average revenue multiple of 1.1x and a weighted-average EBITDA multiple of 7.9x that can be applied to the revenues and EBITDA of its acquirees to estimate their fair values.

**EXAMPLE**

The controller of Morose Press is conducting an annual update of the fair value of its major asset, which is a massive high-speed rotary press. The estimated cash flows from the press are expected to be $800,000 per year for the next ten years. The controller decides to use the income approach to establish a fair value for the machine. Accordingly, she consults a table of present values for an ordinary annuity, using a discount rate of 4%, which results in the following calculation of the present value of cash flows for the press:

$800,000 Annual cash flows × 8.1109 Annuity factor = $6,488,720 Present value

The controller uses this value as the fair value of the rotary press.

**EXAMPLE**

A company recently purchased a machine and heavily customized it to meet the needs of the organization's unique production line. Since the machine has been so heavily customized, there are no comparable market transactions that relate to it. Also, since the machine is part of a production line, there is no way to associate any cash flows specifically to it. These concerns leave the business no alternative other than to use the cost approach to derive fair value. The company determines that it would require a $380,000 expenditure to replace the capabilities of this asset, adjusted for the amount of existing wear and tear on the equipment.

---

When fair value information can be derived from quotes in an active market, it is probably sufficient to use just one of the preceding methods. However, when inputs are of lesser quality, it may be necessary to employ several methods. In the latter case, there will be a range of possible fair values. If so, a fair value should be selected from this range that is the most representative of fair value, under the specific circumstances involving the entity.

No matter which method is chosen, it may be necessary to include a risk adjustment in the formulation of fair value. This risk adjustment may be a premium that a counterparty would require in order to take on any uncertainties in the cash flows associated with an asset or liability.

If there is a change in valuation technique, this may result in a change in the derived fair value of an asset or liability. If so, this change is to be accounted for as a change in accounting estimate. GAAP only requires that changes in accounting estimate be accounted for in the period of change and thereafter. Thus, no retrospective change is required or allowed when there is a change in valuation technique.

## Calibration of the Valuation Technique

There may be a situation in which the price of a transaction can be initially recognized at its fair value, but for which subsequent fair value measurements will require unobservable inputs. If so, there is a risk that the later measurements will yield outcomes that vary substantially from the initial measurement. To mitigate this risk, adjust the valuation technique so that it would have yielded the same transaction price on the transaction date as the fair value on that date. This calibration should improve the comparability of the valuation technique's outputs to the actual fair value over time.

> **Best Practice:** It is helpful to select at the transaction date the valuation technique to be used in later periods, so that calibration between it and the fair value on that date can be performed at once.

## Switching Valuation Techniques

Whichever valuation technique is chosen to measure fair value should continue to be used in a consistent manner. However, it is acceptable to alter the technique under certain circumstances if the result is more representative of fair value. Here are several examples of situations in which switching valuation techniques might be warranted:

- *Information is not available.* The entity loses access to information that it formerly used to derive fair values. For example, a database of asset sale prices is taken private and so can no longer be accessed.
- *New information.* The entity gains access to new transaction information that had not been available to it before. For example, a company is acquired and gains access to the parent company's database of asset trading information.
- *New market conditions.* The circumstances of trade in a market may alter, resulting in alterations in the quality of the resulting fair market information. For example, an exchange may limit trading to a smaller group of pre-qualified participants, which reduces the amount of bidding and therefore weakens the quality of the resulting price information.
- *New market.* A new market develops from which better fair value information can be obtained. For example, the results of securities sales from a small regional exchange can be replaced by the results from a national exchange.
- *Valuation methods improve.* The entity may adopt a more sophisticated valuation model. For example, a company's auditors recommend replacing a primitive valuation system with a more refined version that has been forwarded from another client of the auditors.

Shifting valuation techniques can mean shifting from one method to another. It can also be applied to situations in which multiple valuation techniques are being used, and the weighting applied to each method is altered.

If there is a change in valuation technique, treat it as a change in accounting estimate, which means that any changes are applied on a go-forward basis.

## Hierarchy of Information Sources

The ideal conditions are not always available for obtaining the fair value of an asset or liability. Consequently, GAAP provides a hierarchy of information sources that range from Level 1 (best) to Level 3 (worst). The general intent of these levels of information is to step the accountant through a series of valuation alternatives, where solutions closer to Level 1 are preferred over Level 3. The characteristics of the three levels are as follows:

- *Level 1.* This is a quoted price for an identical item in an active market on the measurement date. This is the most reliable evidence of fair value, and should be used whenever this information is available. It may be necessary to adjust a Level 1 input when a quoted price does not represent fair value, as may be the case when significant events alter the price that parties are willing to pay. When a quoted Level 1 price is adjusted, doing so automatically shifts the result into a lower level. Also, do not alter a Level 1 price just because the company's holdings of a security are quite large in comparison to the normal daily trading volume of the relevant market. Level 1 pricing is commonly available for securities, which may be actively traded in multiple markets, such as the New York Stock Exchange or the NASDAQ.
- *Level 2.* This is directly or indirectly observable inputs other than quoted prices. This definition includes prices for assets or liabilities that are (with key items noted in bold):
  - For **similar** items in active markets; or
  - For identical or similar items in **inactive** markets; or
  - For inputs **other than** quoted prices, such as credit spreads and interest rates; or
  - For inputs **derived from** correlation with observable market data.

  An example of a Level 2 input is a valuation multiple for a business unit that is based on the sale of comparable entities. Another example is the price per square foot for a building, based on prices involving comparable facilities in similar locations.

  It may be necessary to adjust the information derived from Level 2 inputs, since it does not exactly match the assets or liabilities for which fair values are being derived. Adjustments may be needed for such factors as the condition or location of assets and the transaction volume of the markets from which information is derived.
- *Level 3.* This is an unobservable input. It may include the company's own data, adjusted for other reasonably available information. These inputs should reflect the assumptions that would be used by market participants to formulate prices, including assumptions about risk. Examples of a Level 3 input are an internally-generated financial forecast and the prices contained within an offered quote from a distributor.

The information sources in Level 1 are considered to supply the most objective information to the derivation of fair value information, since they are coming from the marketplace. Conversely, the information sources in Level 3 are considered to supply the most subjective information, since they are largely derived internally.

These three levels are known as the *fair value hierarchy*. Please note that these three levels are only used to select inputs to valuation techniques (such as the market approach). The three levels are not used to directly create fair values.

If information in a higher category of the fair value hierarchy is being used and it is adjusted with information from a lower level of the hierarchy, it may be necessary to designate the outcome as being from the lower level of the hierarchy. This happens when the adjustment results in a significantly higher or lower fair value measurement.

---

**EXAMPLE**

Gatekeeper Corporation owns shares in Pensive Corporation. Pensive is privately-held, and the shares are restricted. Gatekeeper finds that shares of similar companies are selling in the range of $3.20 to $5.60. In addition, the company's own experience with restricted stock indicates that this reduces the value of shares by one-half, which reduces the share valuation to the range of $1.60 to $2.80.

The adjustment is an unobservable input that has a significant impact on the fair value estimate of the Pensive shares, so the measurement should be classified within Level 3 of the fair value hierarchy.

---

## Fair Value Measurements for Liabilities

It is much less common to derive a fair value for a liability than for an asset. When it is necessary to do so, it is quite possible that there are few markets available on which similar liabilities are sold. If so, here are several alternatives for deriving fair value:

- *Offsetting asset in active market.* There may be a market in which other parties hold the same item, but as the counterparty. This means they are holding the item as an asset. If so, use the quoted price for sale of the asset.
- *Offsetting asset in inactive market.* A less-reliable source of information is the same as the last bullet point, but in an inactive market for the same asset.
- *Income approach.* In the absence of the first two alternatives, estimate the income that a counterparty can be expected to receive from holding the liability as an asset. Alternatively, estimate the cash flows that a market participant would likely incur to fulfill the requirements of the liability, including a premium for taking on the risk that the liability could be higher than expected. For example, an organization might charge a 20% premium for taking on a liability, if it sees that there is a risk of incurring a greater-than-expected liability payout.

When developing the fair value of a liability based on the value of an asset held by a counterparty, it may be necessary to adjust the fair value. For example, the characteristics of the related asset may vary somewhat from the characteristics of the liability in question, as may be the case with the credit quality of a receivable, or for a bundle of receivables.

The entity should consider the effect of its own credit risk when determining the fair value of a liability. This risk could vary, depending on the terms of the liability and whether the obligation relates to the delivery of cash or of a nonfinancial liability, such as goods or services.

---

**EXAMPLE**

Glow Atomic operates an atomic power generation facility, and is legally required to decontaminate the facility when it is decommissioned in five years. Glow uses the following assumptions about the asset retirement obligation:

- The decontamination cost is $90 million.
- The risk-free rate is 5%, to which Glow adds 3% to reflect the effect of its credit standing.
- The assumed rate of inflation over the five-year period is four percent.

With an average inflation rate of 4% per year for the next five years, the current decontamination cost of $90 million increases to approximately $109.5 million by the end of the fifth year. The expected present value of the $109.5 million payout, using the 8% credit-adjusted risk-free rate, is $74,524,000 (calculated as $109.5 million × 0.68058 discount rate).

---

## Fair Value Measurement Process Flow

When an organization engages in the measurement of asset and liability fair values, it should obtain the following information:

1. The specific identification of the asset or liability for which a fair value measurement is to be obtained. If the asset is nonfinancial, determine the highest and best use that will be applied to its measurement.
2. The market designated as the principal market for the asset or liability.
3. The valuation technique to be used to develop a fair value.

We have already addressed the concepts of highest and best use and the principal market, which were key components of the preceding fair value process flow. We now turn to the types of valuation techniques that can be used.

## Valuation Techniques

The key element of the fair value measurement process flow noted in the preceding section is the valuation technique to be used. There are many possible techniques available, of which we have noted several of the more popular ones in the following sub-sections.

### Price/Earnings Analysis

There are many cases in which an organization wants to derive a fair value for its holdings of shares in other businesses. These shares may not be traded on a stock exchange, so the organization instead takes the following steps to derive a valuation:

1. Determine the industry in which the investee is located. Note those companies within the industry whose shares are traded on a stock exchange and in sufficient volume to ensure that there is an active market for the shares. From this group, select just those businesses whose operations most closely align with those of the investee.
2. Calculate the average ratio of share prices to reported earnings for these companies.
3. Determine the average price-earnings ratio for this group, eliminating any outliers.
4. Multiply the earnings per share of the investee by the average price-earnings ratio for its industry to derive the preliminary fair value of the shares held.
5. Adjust the fair value of the shares held to the extent necessary. For example, the shares of publicly-held businesses tend to trade at a premium to the shares of privately-held entities, because their shares can be more easily bought and sold.

---

**EXAMPLE**

Entwhistle Electric owns 100,000 shares of Billups Batteries, and the controller wants to calculate the fair value of these shares. Billups is privately-held, so the controller decides to obtain price-earnings information for a comparative group of publicly-held battery manufacturers, and apply the resulting valuation information to the Billups shares. She conducts an industry analysis and decides that the following five companies will be the comparison group:

| Company Name | Share Price | Earnings/ Share | P/E |
|---|---|---|---|
| Cadmium Designs | $23.15 | $11.02 | 2.1x |
| Electrolyte Corporation | 17.05 | 11.37 | 1.5x |
| Glass Mat Batteries | 5.40 | 2.84 | 1.9x |
| Lithium Batteries International | 9.80 | 4.26 | 2.3x |
| Primary Cell Corporation | 2.75 | 1.72 | 1.6x |
| | | Average | 1.9x |

The information in the table reveals that the average price/earnings ratio for this group is 1.9x.

In its most recent year of operations, Billups generated earnings per share of $5.00. Using the average P/E of 1.9x, this translates into a fair value for the shares of $9.50 each, or $950,000 in total.

---

There are several variations on this approach, such as the use of a share price to sales ratio or a share price to book value ratio. Earlier in this chapter, we presented an example of another valuation technique for the market approach to fair value measurements, which compared the market capitalizations of a representative set of publicly-held companies to their revenues and EBITDA (earnings before interest, taxes, depreciation, and amortization).

## Present Value Analysis

In many instances, the present value technique is used, since it is based on the discounted cash flows associated with an asset or liability – which can be readily estimated for certain assets and liabilities.

Present value is the current worth of cash to be received or spent in the future, which has been discounted at a market rate of interest. The present value of future cash flows is always less than the same amount of future cash flows, since one can immediately invest cash received now, thereby achieving a greater return than from the prospect of cash receipts in the future. The concept is most commonly employed in an electronic spreadsheet. For example, the present value formula in Excel is:

$$(1/(1+\text{Interest rate})^{\wedge}\text{Number of years})$$

As an example, if the discount rate is 10% and you want to determine the discount for cash flows that will occur three years in the future, the Excel calculation is:

$$(1/(1+0.1)^{\wedge}3) = 0.75131$$

The easiest way to calculate present value is to use the preceding formula in Excel for the monetary amount and time period in question. However, what if an electronic spreadsheet is not available? The present value discount factor can also be derived from a present value table, which is commonly available in textbooks and on the Internet. The following present value table states the discount factors for the present value of 1 due in N periods for a common range of interest rates.

**Present Value Factors for 1 Due in N Periods**

| Number of Years | 6% | 7% | 8% | 9% | 10% | 11% | 12% |
|---|---|---|---|---|---|---|---|
| 1 | 0.9434 | 0.9346 | 0.9259 | 0.9174 | 0.9091 | 0.9009 | 0.8929 |
| 2 | 0.8900 | 0.8734 | 0.8573 | 0.8417 | 0.8265 | 0.8116 | 0.7972 |
| 3 | 0.8396 | 0.8163 | 0.7938 | 0.7722 | 0.7513 | 0.7312 | 0.7118 |
| 4 | 0.7921 | 0.7629 | 0.7350 | 0.7084 | 0.6830 | 0.6587 | 0.6355 |
| 5 | 0.7473 | 0.7130 | 0.6806 | 0.6499 | 0.6209 | 0.5935 | 0.5674 |
| 6 | 0.7050 | 0.6663 | 0.6302 | 0.5963 | 0.5645 | 0.5346 | 0.5066 |
| 7 | 0.6651 | 0.6228 | 0.5835 | 0.5470 | 0.5132 | 0.4817 | 0.4524 |
| 8 | 0.6274 | 0.5820 | 0.5403 | 0.5019 | 0.4665 | 0.4339 | 0.4039 |
| 9 | 0.5919 | 0.5439 | 0.5003 | 0.4604 | 0.4241 | 0.3909 | 0.3606 |
| 10 | 0.5584 | 0.5084 | 0.4632 | 0.4224 | 0.3855 | 0.3522 | 0.3220 |
| 11 | 0.5268 | 0.4751 | 0.4289 | 0.3875 | 0.3505 | 0.3173 | 0.2875 |
| 12 | 0.4970 | 0.4440 | 0.3971 | 0.3555 | 0.3186 | 0.2858 | 0.2567 |
| 13 | 0.4688 | 0.4150 | 0.3677 | 0.3262 | 0.2897 | 0.2575 | 0.2292 |
| 14 | 0.4423 | 0.3878 | 0.3405 | 0.2993 | 0.2633 | 0.2320 | 0.2046 |
| 15 | 0.4173 | 0.3625 | 0.3152 | 0.2745 | 0.2394 | 0.2090 | 0.1827 |

To use the table, move to the column representing the relevant interest rate, and move down to the "number of years" row indicating the discount rate to apply to the applicable year of cash flow. Thus, if an analysis were to indicate $100,000 of cash flow in the fourth year, and the interest rate were 10%, multiply the $100,000 by 0.6830 to arrive at a present value of $68,300 for those cash flows.

The interest rate to be used in the present value calculation is the rate on risk-free investments that have durations coinciding with the cash flows being measured. The yield on U.S. Treasury securities is commonly used for this interest rate. This rate should be adjusted to account for the perceived risk of the underlying cash flows. For example, if cash flows were perceived to be highly problematic, a higher discount rate might be justified, which would result in a smaller present value.

An alternative derivation of the discount rate is to use the observed rates of return for comparable assets or liabilities that are traded in a market. This derivation should only be based on observed rates of return where the nature of the cash flows and other factors are similar to those of the asset or liability being measured. These other factors may include credit scores, the presence of collateral, the duration of cash flows, and the existence of any restrictions on cash flows.

One way to derive fair value with the present value technique is to calculate a probability-weighted average of several possible future cash flows. These are called *expected cash flows*. This approach is most applicable when there are a number of possible cash flow outcomes, and especially when these outcomes are relatively far apart. The following example illustrates the concept, and also employs the use of a risk premium that is applied to the discount rate.

**EXAMPLE**

There are several possible cash flows expected from the use of an asset. Management assigns the following probabilities to each scenario:

| Cash Flow Scenario | Probability | Probability-Weighted Cash Flows |
|---|---|---|
| $800,000 | 10% | $80,000 |
| 1,500,000 | 70% | 1,050,000 |
| 3,000,000 | 20% | 600,000 |
| | 100% | $1,730,000 |

The risk-free interest rate is 3%, and the estimated risk premium for the variability of cash flows is 4%, for a combined discount rate of 7%. The discounted cash flows of these probability-weighted cash flows are therefore $1,730,000 ÷ 1.07, or $1,616,822. This is the fair value of the asset, using the income approach.

## Lattice Model Analysis

A valuation technique that varies substantially from the present value approach is the lattice model, which is also known as the binomial model. Under the lattice model, ongoing changes in price volatility over successive time periods are described; a core assumption is that at least two price movements are possible in each measured time period. The concept is frequently applied to the pricing of stock options. The concept is best demonstrated with an example, which follows.

**EXAMPLE**

Armadillo Industries grants an option on $25 stock that will expire in 12 months. The exercise price of the option matches the $25 stock price. Management believes there is a 40% chance that the stock price will increase by 25% during the upcoming year, a 40% chance that the price will decline by 10%, and a 20% chance that the price will decline by 50%. The risk-free interest rate is 5%. The steps required to develop a fair value for the stock option using the lattice model are:

4. Chart the estimated stock price variations.
5. Convert the price variations into the future value of options.
6. Discount the options to their present values.

The following lattice model shows the range and probability of stock prices for the upcoming year:

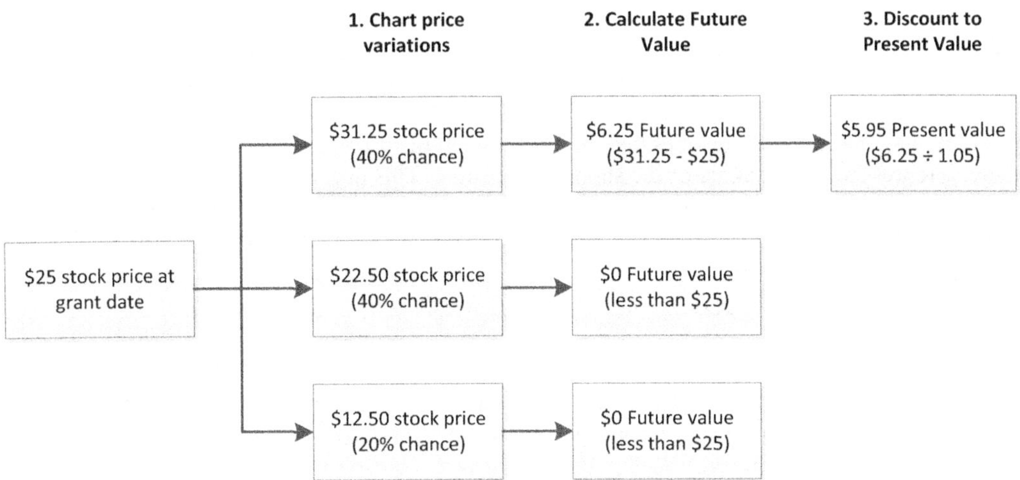


In short, the option will expire unexercised unless the stock price increases. Since there is only a 40% chance of the stock price increasing, the present value of the stock option associated with that scenario can be assigned the following expected present value for purposes of assigning a fair value to the option at the grant date:

$5.95 Option present value × 40% Probability = $2.38 Option value at grant date

The main problem with the lattice model is that even a slightly complex situation can lead to quite a large model, which can be difficult to maintain.

## Use of Multiple Valuation Methods

It is allowable to estimate fair value using a number of valuation methods. This is especially common when deriving the fair value of a substantial asset, such as a reporting unit. The result is likely to be a fairly wide range of valuations. If so, it will be necessary to derive a single value from this information that will then be used as the fair value of the asset. The ideal result is one that best represents the asset's fair value. The designation of this fair value point should be the result of a careful evaluation of the inputs to the valuation methods, the nature of the valuation methods, the amount of subjective judgments made, and possibly a weighting of the various results. If there is still a wide range of valuations, this can indicate that additional analysis is required.

Ideally, the valuation chosen should maximize the use of observable inputs in the analysis process. Observable inputs are derived from market data that properly reflect the assumptions that third parties would use when setting prices for assets and liabilities.

**EXAMPLE**

Creekside Industrial acquires a stamping machine as part of a business combination. The acquiree bought the machine three years ago from the original manufacturer. The original manufacturer made several modifications to the machine that are commonly found among similar machines. The controller of Creekside decides to use both the cost approach and market approach to determining the fair value of the machine. It is not possible to use the income approach, since the machine is to be integrated into an existing production line, and no cash flows can be specifically assigned to the machine.

Cost approach – The controller estimates the amount that would be required to construct a substitute stamping machine that has a similar level of utility, taking into account the current level of usage. There has been no functional obsolescence during the past three years, while there has been an increase in market demand for this type of machine. Based on these considerations, the controller develops a price in the range of $65,000 to $72,000.

Market approach – The controller researches quoted prices for similar machines, adjusting these quotes for the enhancements made to the machine, its level of usage, and location. This results in a price range of $62,000 to $66,000.

Based on these ranges, the controller decides that the lower end of the price range developed from the market approach is most likely to represent the fair value of the stamping machine. This decision is partially based on the ready availability of quoted prices for similar machines that have similar modifications. Further, the range of prices using the market approach is narrower than the price range developed using the cost approach, and also exhibits some overlap with the cost approach price range.

In the preceding example, if extensive and unique customization work had been performed on the stamping machine, it would have been more difficult to obtain quotes for similar machines, which would have made it more likely that the results of the cost approach would have been given a greater weighting.

**EXAMPLE**

Mole Industries acquires a company that has developed a highly-precise GPS location device that Mole intends to attach to its ditch digging products. It is not possible to obtain information for a valuation using the market approach, since there are no comparable transactions in the marketplace. The controller can use the income approach to estimate a stream of cash flows, since the company expects that customers will pay a premium if this device is attached to their digging machines. This results in a valuation estimate of $2,000,000. The controller also oversees an analysis using the cost approach that estimates what it would cost Mole to develop a substitute location device, which indicates a valuation of $1,800,000.

The controller finds that the cost approach valuation of $1,800,000 is questionable, since the acquiree's device used patent-protected technology that would not have been available to someone attempting to reconstruct the device. Consequently, he determines that the fair value of the GPS device is $2,000,000, as derived from the income approach.

## The Fair Value Option

The accounting standards allow a business to adopt a more expanded approach to fair value reporting, where it has the option to record its financial instruments at their fair values. This is a reasonable approach to take when a business has a significant monetary investment in financial instruments that are subject to change during the holding period. GAAP allows this treatment for the following items:

- A financial asset or financial liability
- A firm commitment that only involves financial instruments
- A loan commitment
- An insurance contract where the insurer can pay a third party to provide goods or services in settlement, and where the contract is not a financial instrument (i.e., requires payment in goods or services)
- A warranty in which the warrantor can pay a third party to provide goods or services in settlement, and where the contract is not a financial instrument (i.e., requires payment in goods or services)

The fair value option cannot be applied to the following items:

- An investment in a subsidiary or variable interest entity that will be consolidated
- Deposit liabilities of depository institutions
- Financial assets or financial leases recognized under lease arrangements

- Financial instruments classified as an element of shareholders' equity
- Obligations or assets related to pension plans, postemployment benefits, stock option plans, and other types of deferred compensation

When an election is made to measure an item at its fair value, do so on an instrument-by-instrument basis. Once the election is made to follow the fair value option for an instrument, the change in reporting is irrevocable. The fair value election can be made on either of the following dates:

- The election date, which can be when an item is first recognized, when there is a firm commitment, when qualification for specialized accounting treatment ceases, or there is a change in the accounting treatment for an investment in another entity.
- In accordance with a company policy for certain types of eligible items.

It is acceptable not to apply the fair value option to eligible items when reporting the results of a subsidiary or consolidated variable interest entity, but to apply the fair value option to these items when reporting consolidated financial statements.

> **Best Practice:** It is much easier to apply the fair value option for both subsidiary-level and consolidated financial results, so do not attempt separate treatment, even though it is allowed by GAAP.

In most cases, it is acceptable to choose the fair value option for an eligible item, while not electing to use it for other items that are essentially identical.

If the choice is made to take the fair value option, report unrealized gains and losses on the elected items at each subsequent reporting date.

## Summary

A considerable amount of work can be required to devise the fair values of some assets and liabilities. To lessen the burden, consider avoiding any transactions that will require the company to delve into Level 3 of the fair value hierarchy, where the murky nature of the information requires additional disclosure. Also, try to standardize transactions from period to period, so that the same valuation procedures can be copied forward over time, reducing the amount of original accounting effort that might otherwise be required.

## Review Questions

1. The following is a valid reason why the fair value for an asset or liability may vary from the actual price paid:
    a. The market in which the sale is made is the company's principal market for that item
    b. The absence of unusual elements in a comparison transaction
    c. The buyer and seller may be related
    d. The company sells an asset or settles a liability in the normal course of business

2. Developing fair values based on the prices associated with actual market transactions is called the:
    a. Cost approach
    b. Market approach
    c. Income approach
    d. Level 1 approach

3. The following are valid alternatives for deriving the fair value of a liability, except for:
    a. Find an active market in which other parties hold the same item, but as a counterparty
    b. Estimate the income that a counterparty can be expected to receive from holding the liability as an asset
    c. Poll the employees to determine the amount they would require to take on the liability
    d. Find an inactive market in which other entities hold the same item, but as a counterparty

4. The fair value election can be made on this date:
    a. When there is a firm commitment
    b. When a qualification for specialized accounting treatment begins
    c. At the beginning of the fiscal year
    d. On the date of the board meeting when the board authorizes the election

5. The orderly transaction concept implies that:
    a. The proper legal forms are used
    b. There is no undue pressure to sell
    c. Asset sales are approved by authorized managers
    d. Quotes are obtained

6. For fair value purposes, the principal market is:
    a. The one in which the highest price can be obtained
    b. A market with national distribution
    c. Whichever one company management chooses to use for fair value pricing purposes
    d. The market in which a business normally sells the asset or settles the liability in question

7. Fair value is determined based on:
    a. The use in which an asset is currently employed
    b. The use in which an asset is typically used within the same industry
    c. The highest and best use concept
    d. The expected use of an asset

8. In fair value analysis, an observable input is:
    a. Only used for tangible assets
    b. Based on a paper document
    c. Usually an internally-generated cash forecast
    d. Derived from market data

9. The following are examples of Level 2 inputs, except for:
    a. A quoted price for an identical item in an active market
    b. A price for a similar item in an active market
    c. An identical item in an inactive market
    d. Information derived from a correlation with observable market data

10. The fair value option can be applied to:
    a. A loan commitment
    b. Deposit liabilities of depository institutions
    c. Obligations related to pension plans
    d. Financial assets recognized under lease arrangements

# Chapter 17
# Foreign Currency Accounting

## Introduction

When a business has subsidiaries in foreign countries, they may deal largely in the local currency, and so have chosen to produce financial statements that are denominated in the local currency. If so, the parent entity needs to convert these financial statements into the denomination of its reporting currency before completing a consolidation of all subsidiary financial statements into its own financials, using a single currency. In the following sections, we address the steps required to translate the financial statements of subsidiaries into the currency of the parent entity, and note how this impacts the period-end closing process.

## Financial Statement Translation

A company may have subsidiaries located in other countries, and creates financial statements for those subsidiaries that are denominated in the local currency. If so, the parent company will need to translate the results of these subsidiaries into the currency used by the parent company when it creates consolidated financial statements for the entire entity (called the *reporting currency*). The steps in this process are as follows:

1. Determine the functional currency of the foreign entity.
2. Remeasure the financial statements of the foreign entity into the reporting currency of the parent company.
3. Record gains and losses on the translation of currencies.

The concept of the functional currency is somewhat different when there is a highly inflationary economy. This difference is noted later in the Hyperinflationary Effects subsection.

### Determination of Functional Currency

The financial results and financial position of a company should be measured using its functional currency, which is the currency that the company uses in the majority of its business transactions.

If a foreign business entity operates primarily within one country and is not dependent upon the parent company, its functional currency is the currency of the country in which its operations are located. However, there are other foreign operations that are more closely tied to the operations of the parent company, and whose financing is mostly supplied by the parent or other sources that use the dollar. In this latter case, the functional currency of the foreign operation is probably the dollar. These two examples anchor the ends of a continuum on which foreign operations will be found. Unless an operation is clearly associated with one of the two examples provided, it is likely that it will be necessary to make a determination of functional currency based on the unique circumstances pertaining to each entity. For example, the functional currency may be difficult to determine if a business conducts an equal amount of business in two different countries. An examination of the factors noted in the following exhibit can assist in determining a functional currency.

## Determination of Functional Currency

| Indicators | Indicates Use of Foreign Currency as Functional Currency | Indicates use of Reporting Currency as Functional Currency |
| --- | --- | --- |
| Cash flow | The cash flows relating to an entity's assets and liabilities are primarily in the foreign currency, and have no direct impact on the cash flows of the parent | The cash flows relating to an entity's assets and liabilities directly affect the cash flows of the parent and are available for remittance to it |
| Expenses | The labor, material, and other costs of the entity are primarily obtained locally, even though some items may be obtained via imports | The labor, material, and other costs of the entity are primarily obtained from the parent's country |
| Financing | Any financing obtained is primarily denominated in a foreign currency, and locally-generated funds should be able to service the entity's existing and expected debts | Financing is obtained from the parent or is in dollar-denominated obligations, or locally-generated funds are not sufficient for the servicing of existing and expected debts without a cash infusion from the parent |
| Intra-entity transactions | There are few intra-entity transactions, and operations are not tightly integrated with those of the parent, though there may be reliance on the competitive advantages of the parent | There are many intra-entity transactions, and operations are more likely to be tightly integrated with those of the parent; this also applies when the foreign entity is a shell corporation that holds the assets of the parent |
| Sales market | There is an active local market for the products of the entity, even though the entity may have significant export activity, as well | The primary market for the entity's products is the country of the parent, or sales are denominated in the currency of the parent's country |
| Sales price | Sales prices are mostly based on local competition and government regulations, rather than on exchange rate changes | Sales prices are mostly based on exchange rate changes, which can be driven by international price competition |

Several additional factors to consider when determining the functional currency are as follows:

- *Entity with several operations.* It is possible that a foreign entity has several distinct and separable operations, each of which has different operating characteristics. Thus, one operation might be classified as using the local currency, while another operation might be designated as using the reporting currency. If so, each operation could be considered a separate entity with a different functional currency.
- *Multiple entities.* A parent entity may have a large number of divisions or branches. If so, it will be necessary to treat each one as a separate entity for the purpose of determining functional currencies.
- *Equity method investees.* When a business accounts for an investment in another entity using the equity method, this implies that the business exercises significant influence over the investee. This implied level of control could indicate that the functional currency is the reporting currency.
- *Use of multiple currencies.* There may be situations in which an operation uses multiple currencies, in which case the functional currency is not clearly identifiable. If so, management must examine the economic facts and circumstances to establish a functional currency in which the greatest degree of relevance and reliability can be achieved. When a decision is reached, document the reasons for it, in case the auditors make an inquiry.

> **Best Practice:** If a company is rolling out a number of essentially identical subsidiaries (such as retail stores) in a country, the operating characteristics of each entity in the group should essentially match those of the other entities. This means that it should be possible to determine the functional currency just once, and apply the same designation to every similar entity in the country.

The functional currency in which a business reports its financial results should rarely change. A shift to a different functional currency should be used only when there is a significant change in the economic facts and circumstances. If there is a change in functional currency, do not restate previously-issued financial statements into the new currency.

---

**EXAMPLE**

Armadillo Industries has a subsidiary in Australia, to which it ships its body armor products for sale to local police forces. The Australian subsidiary sells these products and then remits payments back to corporate headquarters. Armadillo should consider U.S. dollars to be the functional currency of this subsidiary.

Armadillo also owns a subsidiary in Russia, which manufactures its own body armor for local consumption, accumulates cash reserves, and borrows funds locally. This subsidiary rarely remits funds back to the parent company. In this case, the functional currency should be the Russian ruble.

---

**Translation into Functional Currency**

When the determination is made regarding what the functional currency of an entity should be, it may be found that the entity is not actually recording transactions in that currency. If so, its transactions must be remeasured into the functional currency; this must take place *before* the financial statements of the entity are translated into the reporting currency. The intent of this translation is to create the same financial statements that would have been produced if the accounting records of the entity had originally been kept in the functional currency. To create such financial statements, it will be necessary to do the following:

- Use historical exchange rates between the functional currency and the currency in which the transactions were actually recorded for the following accounts:
    - Marketable securities recorded at cost (includes equity securities and debt securities not being held to maturity)
    - Inventories recorded at cost
    - Prepaid expenses
    - Fixed assets and the associated accumulated depreciation
    - Intangible assets (such as patents, trademarks, and licenses)
    - Goodwill
    - Deferred charges
    - Deferred income
    - Common stock
    - Preferred stock
    - Revenues and expenses associated with nonmonetary items (such as the cost of goods sold, depreciation, and amortization)
- Use the current exchange rate between the functional currency and the currency in which the transactions were actually recorded for all other accounts.
- Recognize in income all exchange gains and losses caused by the remeasurement of monetary assets and liabilities that were not denominated in the functional currency.

Over the long term, the simplest way to ensure that transactions are stated in the functional currency is to initially record them in the accounting system as such; this may call for the conversion of the accounting system to a new one as of a convenient date, such as the first day of the next fiscal year. Doing so results in a complete set of fiscal year financial statements that are already in the designated functional currency.

**Translation of Financial Statements**

When translating the financial statements of an entity for consolidation purposes into the reporting currency of a business, translate the financial statements using the following rules:

- *Assets and liabilities.* Translate using the current exchange rate at the balance sheet date for assets and liabilities.
- *Income statement items.* Translate revenues, expenses, gains, and losses using the exchange rate as of the dates when those items were originally recognized. To reduce the associated workload, average exchange rates can be employed. See the later Use of Average Exchange Rates sub-section for more information.
- *Allocations.* Translate all cost and revenue allocations using the exchange rates in effect when those allocations are recorded. Examples of allocations are depreciation and the amortization of deferred revenues.
- *Different balance sheet date.* If the foreign entity being consolidated has a different balance sheet date than that of the reporting entity, use the exchange rate in effect as of the foreign entity's balance sheet date.
- *Profit eliminations.* If there are intra-entity profits to be eliminated as part of the consolidation, apply the exchange rate in effect on the dates when the underlying transactions took place. Average exchange rates or other approximations can be used.

If the process of converting the financial statements of a foreign entity into the reporting currency of the parent company results in a translation adjustment, report the related profit or loss in other comprehensive income (see the next sub-section).

## EXAMPLE

A subsidiary of Armadillo Industries is located in Argentina, and its functional currency is the Argentine peso. The relevant peso exchange rates are:

- 0.20 to the dollar at the beginning of the year
- 0.24 to the dollar at the end of the year
- 0.22 to the dollar for the full-year weighted average rate

The subsidiary had no retained earnings at the beginning of the year. Based on this information, the financial statement conversion is as follows:

| (000s) | Argentine Pesos | Exchange Rate | U.S. Dollars |
|---|---|---|---|
| **Assets** | | | |
| Cash | 89,000 | 0.24 | 21,360 |
| Accounts receivable | 267,000 | 0.24 | 64,080 |
| Inventory | 412,000 | 0.24 | 98,880 |
| Fixed assets, net | 608,000 | 0.24 | 145,920 |
| Total assets | 1,376,000 | | 330,240 |
| | | | |
| **Liabilities and Equity** | | | |
| Accounts payable | 320,000 | 0.24 | 76,800 |
| Notes payable | 500,000 | 0.24 | 120,000 |
| Common stock | 10,000 | 0.20 | 2,400 |
| Additional paid-in capital | 545,000 | 0.20 | 130,800 |
| Retained earnings | 1,000 | (*) | 220 |
| Translation adjustments | 0 | -- | 20 |
| Total liabilities and equity | 1,376,000 | | 330,240 |

* Reference from the following income statement

| (000s) | Argentine Pesos | Exchange Rate | U.S. Dollars |
|---|---|---|---|
| Revenue | 1,500,000 | 0.22 | 330,000 |
| Expenses | 1,499,000 | 0.22 | 329,780 |
| Net income | 1,000 | | 220 |
| | | | |
| Beginning retained earnings | 0 | | 0 |
| Add: Net income | 1,000 | 0.22 | 220 |
| Ending retained earnings | 1,000 | | 220 |

## Reporting in Other Comprehensive Income

Other comprehensive income (OCI) is a separate reporting block that can appear after the income statement or in an entirely separate statement. Gains and losses recorded in OCI are related to changes in the valuation of different assets and liabilities that have not yet been realized. The amount recorded in OCI accumulates in equity, in the accumulated other comprehensive income (AOCI) account.

Once the designated gains and losses are realized, these gains and losses are shifted into the main body of the income statement from AOCI. A sample statement of OCI appears in the following exhibit.

### Sample Presentation of Other Comprehensive Income

Armadillo Industries
Statement of Other Comprehensive Income
For the Year Ended December 31, 20X2

| | | |
|---|---|---|
| Net income | | $45,000 |
| | | |
| Other comprehensive income, net of tax | | |
| **Foreign currency translation adjustments** | | **2,000** |
| Unrealized holding gains arising during period | | 11,000 |
| Defined benefit pension plans: | | |
| Prior period service cost arising during period | -$4,000 | |
| Net loss arising during period | -1,000 | -5,000 |
| Other comprehensive income | | 8,000 |
| | | |
| Comprehensive income, net of tax | | $53,000 |

In the sample, we noted in bold the presence of foreign currency translation adjustments. These adjustments relate to transactions that have not yet been completed, and so are unrealized. Once the underlying transactions have been completed, the gains or losses will have been realized, and these adjustments will be shifted to the income statement.

Line items relating to foreign currency transactions that can appear in this statement are as follows:

- Foreign currency translation adjustments
- Gains and losses on intra-company foreign currency transactions where settlement is not planned in the foreseeable future
- Gains and losses on foreign currency translation adjustments that are net investment hedges in a foreign entity
- Changes in the fair value of available-for-sale debt securities that are denominated in a foreign currency

To see where AOCI is located, the following sample equity section of a balance sheet shows the line item. The AOCI line is stated separately from common stock, additional paid-in capital, and retained earnings.

---

**EXAMPLE**

Armadillo Industries reports accumulated other comprehensive income within the equity section of its balance sheet as follows:

| | |
|---|---:|
| Equity: | |
| Common stock | $1,000,000 |
| Paid-in capital | 850,000 |
| Retained earnings | 4,200,000 |
| **Accumulated other comprehensive income** | **270,000** |
| Total equity | $6,320,000 |

---

## Impact on the Statement of Cash Flows

In the statement of cash flows, state all foreign currency cash flows at their reporting currency equivalent using the exchange rates in effect when the cash flows occurred. A weighted average exchange rate may be used for this calculation if the result would be substantially the same as if the cash flow-specific rates had been used. In addition, report in the statement of cash flows the effect of exchange rate changes on cash balances held in foreign currencies. This reporting should be noted within the reconciliation of the change in cash and cash equivalents during the reporting period. A sample of this presentation follows, where the applicable line item is noted in bold.

### Sample Reconciliation of Net Income to Net Cash Provided by Operating Activities

| | | |
|---|---:|---:|
| Net income | | $1,000,000 |
| Adjustments to reconcile net income to net cash provided by operating activities: | | |
| Depreciation and amortization | $125,000 | |
| Loss on sale of equipment | 20,000 | |
| **Exchange gain** | **-65,000** | |
| Provision for deferred taxes | 32,000 | |
| Increase in trade receivables | -250,000 | |
| Decrease in inventories | 125,000 | |
| Decrease in trade payables | -50,000 | |
| | | -63,000 |
| Net cash provided by operating activities | | $937,000 |

## Special Translation Situations

There can be situations in which a business records the historical cost of an asset, using in its books of record a currency different from its functional currency. The value of this currency may change in relation to the functional currency of the entity between the date when the asset was acquired and the balance sheet date. This disparity can give rise to asset valuation changes, as noted next.

### Inventory Translation

A special situation can arise when inventory is being carried on the books of a subsidiary in a currency that is not the functional currency of the subsidiary. If so, and as noted earlier in the Translation of Financial Statements sub-section, the inventory must first be remeasured into the designated functional currency, using historical exchange rates. These historical costs are then compared with the market prices of the inventory as stated in the functional currency. This step can result in application of the lower of cost or market (LCM) rule, where an inventory write-down is required in the functional currency, even though no such write-down is called for in the books of the subsidiary (which use an alternative currency).

The reverse situation can also arise. A business might have recognized an LCM write-down in its books of record, using a currency that is not the designated functional currency. Once the currency has been converted to the functional currency, it is possible that the market price now exceeds the adjusted historical cost, in which case the LCM write-down can be reversed.

The LCM rule essentially states that a business must record the cost of inventory at whichever cost is lower – the original cost or its current market price (hence the name of the rule). More specifically, the rule mandates that the recognized cost of an inventory item should be reduced to a level that does not exceed its replacement cost as derived in an open market. This replacement cost is subject to the following two conditions:

- The recognized cost cannot be greater than the likely selling price minus costs of disposal (known as net realizable value).
- The recognized cost cannot be lower than the net realizable value minus a normal profit percentage.

This situation typically arises when inventory has deteriorated, or has become obsolete, or market prices have declined.

---

**EXAMPLE**

Monique Ponto produces high-end women's watches. The company has a subsidiary that operates in the independent republic of Ralston, located in the Caribbean. The subsidiary maintains its books of record in Ralston Pounds. However, the parent company has designated the functional currency of the subsidiary to be U.S. dollars. The exchange rate between the two currencies was 2 RP = 1 USD when the subsidiary bought a gold watch casing for 1,000 RP. Or, as measured in the functional currency, the watch casing cost 500 USD. As of the balance sheet date of the subsidiary, the exchange rate had changed to 2.2 RP = 1 USD.

Scenario 1: The current replacement cost of the watch casing is 1,050 RP, which is higher than its original cost of 1,000 RP. However, when translated into USD at the current exchange rate of 2.2 RP to 1 USD, the current replacement cost in USD has declined to $477 from its original cost of $500. This calls for an inventory write-down of $23 in the functional currency financial statements.

Scenario 2: The current replacement cost of the watch casing is 1,200 RP, which is higher than its original cost of 1,000 RP. When translated into USD at the current exchange rate of 2.2 RP to 1 USD, the current replacement cost in USD has increased to $545 from its original cost of $500. No inventory write-down is required, since the market price now exceeds historical cost.

---

Other Asset Translation

The LCM adjustment just noted for inventory could also apply to other assets. As was the case with inventory, the situation should only occur when the conversion from a different currency to the functional currency results in the market price of an asset being below its cost. The reversal of a previous write-down can also occur under the same circumstances.

**Noncontrolling Interests**

There may be noncontrolling interests in a foreign entity, which are also known as minority interests. If so, allocate any accumulated translation adjustments attributable to the noncontrolling interests to the noncontrolling interests line item in the consolidated financial statements of the parent entity.

## Use of Average Exchange Rates

We have noted that the remeasurement of financial statements may require the use of historical exchange rate information. It can be burdensome to keep track of these exchange rates and the dates on which the rates are to be applied. To reduce the work involved, GAAP allows the use of an average exchange rate, or other labor-saving methods that reasonably approximate the exchange rates that were more frequently applied. If an average exchange rate is used, derive a weighted average based on the volume of currency transactions in the period. For example, a reasonably accurate result might be achieved by developing an average rate for each month of the year, to be applied to those transactions occurring within each month. The translated amounts for each month are then aggregated for inclusion in the annual financial statements.

> **Best Practice:** The derivation of average exchange rates should be carefully documented, since the auditors will need to review this information as part of their year-end audit procedures.

## No Applicable Period-end Exchange Rate

There may be no foreign exchange rate available at the end of a reporting period for use in translating the financial statements. For example, foreign exchange trading may have been temporarily suspended. If so, use the first exchange rate that is available on the next date on which foreign exchange transactions can be made. The following example illustrates the point.

### EXAMPLE

Icelandic Cod (despite its name) is based in the United States, and its reporting currency is the U.S. dollar. It owns a subsidiary on the tiny principality of Heard Island, which uses the Heard Dollar (HD). Icelandic Cod closes its fiscal year on December 31. The following dates and exchange rates apply to the situation:

| Date | Exchange Rate | Commentary |
| --- | --- | --- |
| 12/30/X1 | 3 HD : 1 USD | Currency markets are open and operating normally |
| 12/31/X1 | -- | Official devaluation of the HD is announced by the Heard government; currency trading is suspended until the devaluation has been completed |
| 1/1/X2 | -- | Banks and currency exchanges are closed for the holidays |
| 1/2/X2 | 4 HD : 1 USD | New exchange rate is set by the Heard government; this rate is also effective for all unsettled transactions |

There was no valid market exchange rate at year-end, so the exchange rate to be used for year-end consolidation purposes is the 4:1 exchange rate established on January 2 of the following year.

## Hyperinflationary Effects

An entity may find itself operating in an environment that has cumulative inflation of 100% or more. If this level of inflation continues over a three-year period, a country is considered to have a highly inflationary economy. The same outcome still applies if the cumulative inflation is less than 100%, but the trend of inflation, combined with other economic factors, suggests that the economy is highly inflationary.

**EXAMPLE**

The government of Mirandela, a small country located high in the Andes mountain range, has been printing money to pay for its social programs. The result is the following annual inflation rate:

|  | Year 1 | Year 2 | Year 3 | Year 4 | Year 5 | Year 6 |
|---|---|---|---|---|---|---|
| Annual inflation rate | 4% | 7% | 21% | 34% | 42% | 39% |
| Cumulative 3-year rate* | -- | -- | 35% | 73% | 130% | 164% |

* Calculated as a compounded 3-year inflation rate

Mirandela's economy for Years 5 and 6 is classified as highly inflationary, since the cumulative 3-year rate exceeds 100%. The slight decline in the inflation rate in Year 6 does not overcome the cumulative 3-year rate.

**EXAMPLE**

The adjacent country of Evora also suffers from a high rate of inflation, as noted in the following table. In this case, the government has been slowly reducing its expenditures, but the inflation rate continues to be high.

|  | Year 1 | Year 2 | Year 3 | Year 4 | Year 5 | Year 6 |
|---|---|---|---|---|---|---|
| Annual inflation rate | 23% | 27% | 32% | 24% | 22% | 21% |
| Cumulative 3-year rate* | -- | -- | 106% | 108% | 100% | 83% |

* Calculated as a compounded three-year inflation rate

In this case, the cumulative 3-year rate has dropped below the 100% threshold in Year 6. Nonetheless, the trend of inflation remains high, so it would be appropriate to continue to classify the economy as being highly inflationary.

**EXAMPLE**

The third of this group of countries is Pombal, whose government has clamped down harder on inflation, yielding the results shown in the following table:

|  | Year 1 | Year 2 | Year 3 | Year 4 | Year 5 | Year 6 |
|---|---|---|---|---|---|---|
| Annual inflation rate | 3% | 7% | 49% | 27% | 11% | 4% |
| Cumulative 3-year rate* | -- | -- | 64% | 102% | 110% | 47% |

* Calculated as a compounded three-year inflation rate

In this case, the economy should no longer be considered highly inflationary, for two reasons. First, the cumulative 3-year inflation rate has dropped sharply. And second, there is no evidence that the economy continues to be inflationary. Instead, the information in the table indicates that the country suffered from a brief inflationary spike that is now over.

When the determination is made that an economy is highly inflationary, remeasure the financial statements of the entity operating in that environment as though the functional currency were the reporting currency.

If the economy is no longer considered to be hyperinflationary, restate the financial statements of the relevant entity so that the local currency is now the functional currency. This means translating the reporting currency amounts into the local currency amounts at the current exchange rate on the date of change; these translated amounts then become the new functional currency for the nonmonetary assets and liabilities of the entity.

**EXAMPLE**

A subsidiary of Armadillo Industries is operating in a highly inflationary economy. On March 31 of 20X3, it bought a machine for 50,000 units of the local currency. The exchange rate at that time was five units of the local currency to one U.S. dollar, so the equivalent cost of the machine in U.S. dollars was $10,000. Five years later, on March 31, 20X8, the machine's net book value on the subsidiary's books has declined to 25,000 units of the local currency, due to ongoing depreciation. On March 31 of 20X8, hyperinflation has altered the exchange rate to 25 to one U.S. dollar. During this time, the parent company has been using the historical exchange rate to account for the machine, so the recorded amount has declined to $5,000, based on the depreciation incurred during the intervening years.

On April 1 of 20X8, Armadillo's management no longer considers the local economy of the subsidiary to be highly inflationary, so it establishes a new cost basis for the equipment by translating the current $5,000 cost of the machine back into the local currency at the current exchange rate of 25:1. This means the functional accounting basis for the machine on April 1 of 20X8 would be 125,000 units of the local currency.

## Derecognition of a Foreign Entity Investment

When a company sells or liquidates its investment in a foreign entity, complete the following steps to account for the situation:

- Remove the translation adjustment recorded in equity for the investment
- Report a gain or loss in the period in which the sale or liquidation occurs

If a company only sells a portion of its investment in a foreign entity, recognize only a pro rata portion of the accumulated translation adjustment recorded in equity.

A sale or liquidation is considered to have occurred when a controlling financial interest in the foreign entity has been lost.

## Summary

The translation of financial statements is a highly regimented process that requires great attention to the exchange rates used. It is also necessary to maintain exactly the same conversion template for all periods and all entities, to ensure that financial information is being rolled forward correctly from the subsidiaries. This is a much easier process when a company uses a company-wide financial reporting system, but if that is not the case, financial statement translation can represent a major bottleneck in the process of closing the books.

## Review Questions

1. Financial statement translation involves the following steps, except for:
   a. Determining the functional currency of the foreign entity
   b. Recording gains and losses on currency translation
   c. Remeasuring the functional currency of the foreign entity into its legal currency
   d. Remeasuring the financial statements of the foreign entity into the reporting currency of the parent

2. When translating the financial statements of an entity into the reporting currency of a business, translate assets:
   a. At the weighted-average exchange rate
   b. At the current exchange rate at the balance sheet date
   c. At the exchange rate as of the dates when those items were originally recognized
   d. At the exchange rate in effect at the beginning of the reporting period

3. When the financing of a foreign operation is provided by the parent company, its functional currency is more likely to be:
   a. The reporting currency of the parent company
   b. Its legal currency
   c. Its operating currency
   d. The reporting currency of the ultimate lender

4. The key issue that shifts a transaction from other comprehensive income to earnings is:
   a. The cost principle
   b. When the business entity changes
   c. When costs match revenues under the matching concept
   d. Realization

5. When an entity is operating in a hyperinflationary economy:
   a. Exclude its financial statements from further consolidation
   b. Remeasure its financial statements using the next most applicable foreign currency
   c. Remeasure its financial statements as though its functional currency were the reporting currency
   d. Remeasure its financial statements using the local currency

# Chapter 18
# Accounting for Interest

## Introduction

The interest topic addresses two items, which are the capitalization of interest into fixed assets and the derivation of a different interest rate when the rate associated with a borrowing arrangement diverges from the market rate. The capitalization of interest is not a common issue to be concerned about, unless a business is spending multiple months constructing a fixed asset, and has incurred debt to build the asset. In all other cases, interest capitalization can be ignored. The use of imputed interest is somewhat more common, particularly in regard to situations where a note is issued at a below-market interest rate, or at no interest rate at all.

In this chapter, we describe the mechanics of interest capitalization and imputed interest, as well as the relevant accounting associated with both topics.

## Overview of Capitalized Interest

When a fixed asset is recorded, part of the cost that can be included is the costs incurred to bring it to the condition and location of its intended use. If these activities require some time to complete, capitalize the cost of the interest incurred during that period that relate to the asset. This chapter describes the assets for which interest capitalization is allowable (or not), how to determine the capitalization period and the capitalization rate, and how to calculate the amount of interest cost to be capitalized.

Interest is a cost of doing business, and if a company incurs an interest cost that is directly related to a fixed asset, it is reasonable to capitalize this cost, since it provides a truer picture of the total investment in the asset. Since a business would not otherwise have incurred the interest if it had not acquired the asset, the interest is essentially a direct cost of owning the asset.

Conversely, if this interest cost was not capitalized and it was instead charged to expense, the accountant would be unreasonably reducing the amount of reported earnings during the period when the company incurred the expense and increasing earnings during later periods, when the entity would otherwise have been charging the capitalized interest to expense through depreciation.

> **Best Practice:** If the amount of interest that may be applied to a fixed asset is minor, try to avoid capitalizing it. Otherwise, too much time will be spent documenting the capitalization, and the auditors will spend time investigating it – which may translate into higher audit fees.

The value of the information provided by capitalizing interest may not be worth the effort of the incremental accounting cost associated with it. Here are some issues to consider when deciding whether to capitalize interest:

- How many assets would be subject to interest capitalization?
- How easy is it to separately identify those assets that would be subject to interest capitalization?
- How significant would be the effect of interest capitalization on the company's reported resources and earnings?

Thus, only capitalize interest when the informational benefit derived from doing so exceeds the cost of accounting for it. The positive impact of doing so is greatest for construction projects, where:

- Costs are separately compiled
- Construction covers a long period of time
- Expenditures are large
- Interest costs are considerable

GAAP specifically does *not* allow for the capitalization of interest for inventory items that are routinely manufactured in large quantities on a repetitive basis.

## Assets on Which to Capitalize Interest

Capitalize interest that is related to the following types of fixed assets:

- Assets that are constructed for the company's own use. This includes assets built for the company by suppliers, where the company makes progress payments or deposits.
- Assets that are constructed for sale or lease, and which are constructed as discrete projects.

**EXAMPLE**

Milford Sound builds a new corporate headquarters. The company hires a contractor to perform the work, and makes regular progress payments to the contractor. Milford should capitalize the interest expense related to this project.

Milford Sound creates a subsidiary, Milford Public Sound, which builds custom-designed outdoor sound staging for concerts and theatre activities. These projects require many months to complete, and are accounted for as discrete projects. Milford should capitalize the interest cost related to each of these projects.

If a company is undertaking activities to develop land for a specific use, capitalize interest related to the associated expenditures for as long as the development activities are in progress.

## Assets on Which Interest is not Capitalized

Do not capitalize interest that is related to the following types of fixed assets:

- Assets that are already in use or ready for their intended use
- Assets not being used, and which are not being prepared for use
- Assets not included in the company's balance sheet
- Inventories that are routinely manufactured

## The Interest Capitalization Period

Capitalize interest over the period when there are ongoing activities to prepare a fixed asset for its intended use, but only if expenditures are actually being made during that time, and interest costs are being incurred.

---

**EXAMPLE**

Milford Public Sound is constructing an in-house sound stage in which to test its products. It spent the first two months designing the stage, and then paid a contractor $30,000 per month for the next four months to build the stage. Milford incurred interest costs during the entire time period.

Since Milford was not making any expenditures related to the stage during the first two months, it cannot capitalize any interest cost for those two months. However, since it was making expenditures during the next four months, it can capitalize interest cost for those months.

---

If a company stops essentially all construction on a project, stop capitalizing interest during that period. However, continue to capitalize interest under any of the following circumstances:

- Brief construction interruptions
- Interruptions imposed by an outside entity
- Delays that are an inherent part of the asset acquisition process

---

**EXAMPLE**

Milford Public Sound is constructing a concert arena that it plans to lease to a local municipality upon completion. Midway through the project, the municipality orders a halt to all construction, when construction reveals that the arena is being built on an Indian burial ground. Two months later, after the burial site has been relocated, the municipality allows construction to begin again.

Since this interruption was imposed by an outside entity, Milford can capitalize interest during the two-month stoppage period.

---

A company should terminate interest capitalization as soon as an asset is substantially complete and ready for its intended use. Here are several scenarios showing when interest capitalization should be terminated:

- *Unit-level completion.* Parts of a project may be completed and usable before the entire project is complete. Stop capitalizing interest on each of these parts as soon as they are substantially complete and ready for use.
- *Entire-unit completion.* All aspects of an asset may need to be completed before any part of it can be used. Continue capitalizing interest on such assets until the entire project is substantially complete and ready for use.
- *Dependent completion.* An asset may not be usable until a separate project has also been completed. Continue capitalizing interest on such assets until not only the specific asset, but also the separate project is substantially complete and ready for use.

**EXAMPLE**

Milford Public Sound is building three arenas, all under different circumstances. They are:

1. *Arena A*. This is an entertainment complex, including a stage area, movie theatre, and restaurants. Milford should stop capitalizing interest on each component of the project as soon as it is substantially complete and ready for use, since each part of the complex can operate without the other parts being complete.
2. *Arena B*. This is a single outdoor stage with integrated multi-level parking garage. Even though the garage is completed first, Milford should continue to capitalize interest for it, since the garage is only intended to service patrons of the arena, and so will not be operational until the arena is complete.
3. *Arena C*. This an entertainment complex for which Milford is also constructing a highway off-ramp and road that leads to the complex. Since the complex is unusable until patrons can reach the complex, Milford should continue to capitalize interest expenses until the off-ramp and road are complete.

Do not continue to capitalize interest when completion is being deliberately delayed, since the cost of interest then changes from an asset acquisition cost to an asset holding cost.

**EXAMPLE**

The CEO of Milford Sound wants to report increased net income for the upcoming quarter, so he orders the delay of construction on an arena facility that would otherwise have been completed, so that the interest cost related to the project will be capitalized. He is in error, since this is now treated as a holding cost – the related interest expense should be recognized in the period incurred, rather than capitalized.

## The Capitalization Rate

The amount of interest cost to capitalize for a fixed asset is that amount of interest that would have been avoided if the asset had not been acquired. To calculate the amount of interest cost to capitalize, multiply the capitalization rate by the average amount of expenditures that accumulate during the construction period.

The basis for the capitalization rate is the interest rates that are applicable to the company's borrowings that are outstanding during the construction period. If a specific borrowing is incurred in order to construct a specific asset, use the interest rate on that borrowing as the capitalization rate. If the amount of a specific borrowing that is incurred to construct a specific asset is less than the expenditures made for the asset, use a weighted average of the rates applicable to other company borrowings for any excess expenditures over the amount of the project-specific borrowing.

**EXAMPLE**

Milford Public Sound incurs an average expenditure over the construction period of an outdoor arena complex of $15,000,000. It has taken out a short-term loan of $12,000,000 at 9% interest specifically to cover the cost of this project. Milford can capitalize the interest cost of the entire amount of the $12,000,000 loan at 9% interest, but it still has $3,000,000 of average expenditures that exceed the amount of this project-specific loan.

Milford has two bonds outstanding at the time of the project, in the following amounts:

| Bond Description | Principal Outstanding | Interest |
|---|---|---|
| 8% Bond | $18,000,000 | $1,440,000 |
| 10% Bond | 12,000,000 | 1,200,000 |
| Totals | $30,000,000 | $2,640,000 |

The weighted-average interest rate on these two bond issuances is 8.8% ($2,640,000 interest ÷ $30,000,000 principal), which is the interest rate that Milford should use when capitalizing the remaining $3,000,000 of average expenditures.

These rules regarding the formulation of the capitalization rate are subject to some interpretation. The key guideline is to arrive at a *reasonable* measure of the cost of financing the acquisition of a fixed asset, particularly in regard to the interest cost that could have been avoided if the acquisition had not been made. Thus, it is possible to use a selection of outstanding borrowings as the basis for a weighted average calculation. This may result in the inclusion or exclusion of borrowings at the corporate level, or just at the level of the subsidiary where the asset is located.

**EXAMPLE**

Milford Public Sound (MPS) has issued several bonds and notes, totaling $50,000,000, that are used to fund both general corporate activities and construction projects. It also has access to a low-cost 4% internal line of credit that is extended to it by its corporate parent, Milford Sound. MPS regularly uses this line of credit for short-term activities, and typically draws the balance down to zero at least once a year. The average amount of this line that is outstanding is approximately $10,000,000 at any given time.

Since the corporate line of credit comprises a significant amount of MPS's ongoing borrowings, and there is no restriction that prevents these funds from being used for construction projects, it would be reasonable to include the interest cost of this line of credit in the calculation of the weighted-average cost of borrowings that is used to derive MPS's capitalization rate.

## Calculating Interest Capitalization

Follow these steps to calculate the amount of interest to be capitalized for a specific project:

1. Construct a table itemizing the amounts of expenditures made and the dates on which the expenditures were made.
2. Determine the date on which interest capitalization ends.
3. Calculate the capitalization period for each expenditure, which is the number of days between the specific expenditure and the end of the interest capitalization period.
4. Divide each capitalization period by the total number of days elapsed between the date of the first expenditure and the end of the interest capitalization period to arrive at the capitalization multiplier for each line item.

5. Multiply each expenditure amount by its capitalization multiplier to arrive at the average expenditure for each line item over the capitalization measurement period.
6. Add up the average expenditures at the line item level to arrive at a grand total average expenditure.
7. If there is project-specific debt, multiply the grand total of the average expenditures by the interest rate on that debt to arrive at the capitalized interest related to that debt.
8. If the grand total of the average expenditures exceeds the amount of the project-specific debt, multiply the excess expenditure amount by the weighted average of the company's other outstanding debt to arrive at the remaining amount of interest to be capitalized.
9. Add together both capitalized interest calculations. If the combined total is more than the total interest cost incurred by the company during the calculation period, reduce the amount of interest to be capitalized to the total interest cost incurred by the company during the calculation period.
10. Record the interest capitalization with a debit to the project's fixed asset account and a credit to the interest expense account.

## EXAMPLE

Milford Public Sound is building a concert arena. Milford makes payments related to the project of $10,000,000 and $14,000,000 to a contractor on January 1 and July 1, respectively. The arena is completed on December 31.

For the 12-month period of construction, Milford can capitalize all of the interest on the $10,000,000 payment, since it was outstanding during the full period of construction. Milford can capitalize the interest on the $14,000,000 payment for half of the construction period, since it was outstanding during only the second half of the construction period. The average expenditure for which the interest cost can be capitalized is calculated in the following table:

| Date of Payment | Expenditure Amount | Capitalization Period* | Capitalization Multiplier | Average Expenditure |
|---|---|---|---|---|
| January 1 | $10,000,000 | 12 months | 12/12 months = 100% | $10,000,000 |
| July 1 | 14,000,000 | 6 months | 6/12 months = 50% | 7,000,000 |
| | | | | $17,000,000 |

* In the table, the capitalization period is defined as the number of months that elapse between the expenditure payment date and the end of the interest capitalization period.

The only debt that Milford has outstanding during this period is a line of credit, on which the interest rate is 8%. The maximum amount of interest that Milford can capitalize into the cost of this arena project is $1,360,000, which is calculated as:

$$8\% \text{ Interest rate} \times \$17,000,000 \text{ Average expenditure} = \$1,360,000$$

Milford records the following journal entry:

| | Debit | Credit |
|---|---|---|
| Fixed assets – Arena | 1,360,000 | |
| Interest expense | | 1,360,000 |

**Best Practice:** There may be an inordinate number of expenditures related to a larger project, which could result in a large and unwieldy calculation of average expenditures. To reduce the workload, consider aggregating these expenses by month, and then assume that each expenditure was made in the middle of the month, thereby reducing all of the expenditures for each month to a single line item.

It is not allowable to capitalize more interest cost in an accounting period than the total amount of interest cost incurred by the business in that period. If there is a corporate parent, this rule means that the amount capitalized cannot exceed the total amount of interest cost incurred by the business on a consolidated basis.

## Overview of Imputed Interest

When two parties enter into a business transaction that involves payment with a note, the default assumption is that the interest rate associated with the note will be close to the market rate of interest. However, there are times when no interest rate is stated, or when the stated rate departs significantly from the market rate.

If the stated and market interest rates are substantially different, it is necessary to record the transaction using an interest rate that more closely accords with the market rate. The rate that should be used is one that approximates the rate that would have been used if an independent borrower and lender had entered into a similar arrangement under comparable terms and conditions. This guidance does not apply to the following situations:

- Receivables and payables using customary trade terms that do not exceed one year
- Advances, deposits, and security deposits
- Customer cash lending activities of a financial institution
- When interest rates are affected by a governmental agency (such as a tax-exempt bond)
- Transactions between commonly-owned entities (such as between subsidiaries)

If available, the preferred option for deriving imputed interest is to locate the established exchange price of the goods or services involved in the transaction, and use that as the basis for calculating the interest rate. The exchange price is presumed to be the price paid in a cash purchase. In essence, this means that goods or services shall be recorded at their fair value. Any difference between the present value of the note and the fair value of the goods or services shall then be accounted for as a change in interest expense (i.e., as a note discount or premium) over the life of the note.

If it is not possible to determine the established exchange price, an applicable interest rate must be derived at the time the note is issued. The rate selected should be the prevailing rate for similar borrowers with similar credit ratings, which may be further adjusted for the following factors:

- The credit standing of the borrower
- Restrictive covenants on the note
- Collateral on the note
- Tax consequences to the buyer and seller
- The rate at which the borrower can obtain similar financing from other sources

Any subsequent changes in the market interest rate shall be ignored for the purposes of this transaction.

Once the correct interest rate has been selected, use it to amortize the difference between the imputed interest rate and the rate on the note over the life of the note, with the difference being charged to the interest expense account. This is called the *interest method*. The following example illustrates the concept.

**EXAMPLE**

Armadillo Industries issues a $5,000,000 bond at a stated rate of 5% interest, where similar issuances are being purchased by investors at 8% interest. The bonds pay interest annually, and are to be redeemed in six years.

In order to earn the market rate of 8% interest, investors purchase the Armadillo bonds at a discount. The following calculation is used to derive the discount on the bond, which is comprised of the present values of a stream of interest payments and the present value of $5,000,000 payable in six years, with both calculations based on the 8% interest rate:

| | | |
|---|---|---|
| Present value of 6 payments of $250,000 | = $250,000 × 4.62288 | $1,155,720 |
| Present value of $5,000,000 | = $5,000,000 × 0.63017 | 3,150,850 |
| | | |
| | Total of present values | $4,306,570 |
| | Less: Stated bond price | $5,000,000 |
| | Bond discount | $693,430 |

The initial entry to record the sale of bonds is:

| | Debit | Credit |
|---|---|---|
| Cash | 4,306,570 | |
| Discount on bonds payable | 693,430 | |
| Bonds payable | | 5,000,000 |

The controller of Armadillo creates the following table, which shows the derivation of how much of the discount should be charged to interest expense in each of the following years. In essence, the annual amortization of the discount is added back to the present value of the bond, so that the bond's present value matches its $5,000,000 stated value by the date when the bonds are scheduled for redemption from the bond holders.

| Year | Beginning Present Value of Bond | Unamortized Discount | Interest Expense* | Cash Payment** | Discount Reduction*** |
|---|---|---|---|---|---|
| 1 | $4,306,570 | $693,430 | $344,526 | $250,000 | $94,526 |
| 2 | 4,401,096 | 598,904 | 352,088 | 250,000 | 102,088 |
| 3 | 4,503,184 | 496,816 | 360,255 | 250,000 | 110,255 |
| 4 | 4,613,439 | 386,561 | 369,075 | 250,000 | 119,075 |
| 5 | 4,732,514 | 267,486 | 378,601 | 250,000 | 128,601 |
| 6 | 4,861,115 | 138,885 | 388,885 | 250,000 | 138,885 |
| 7 | $5,000,000 | $0 | | | |

* Bond present value at the beginning of the period, multiplied by the 8% market rate
** Scheduled annual interest payment for the bond
*** Interest expense, less the cash payment

As an example of the entries that the controller would derive from this table, the entry for the first annual interest payment would be:

|  | Debit | Credit |
|---|---|---|
| Interest expense | 344,526 |  |
| Discount on bonds payable |  | 94,526 |
| Cash |  | 250,000 |

The reasoning behind the entry is that Armadillo is only obligated to make a cash payment of $250,000 per year, despite the higher 8% implicit interest rate that its investors are earning on the issued bonds. The difference between the actual interest of $344,526 and the cash payment represents an increase in the amount of the bond that the company must eventually pay back to its investors. Thus, by the end of the first year, the present value of Armadillo's obligation to pay back the bond has increased from $4,306,570 to $4,401,096. By the end of the six-year period, the present value of the amount to be paid back will have increased to $5,000,000.

> **Tip:** GAAP requires that the interest method be used to amortize any discount or premium associated with a note. However, other methods can be used if the results do not differ materially from those of the interest method. Accordingly, we suggest using the simpler straight-line method if the results do not differ materially from those of the interest

## Summary

The key issue with interest capitalization is whether to use it at all. It requires a certain amount of administrative effort to compile, and so is not recommended for lower-value fixed assets. Instead, reserve its use for larger projects where including the cost of interest in an asset will improve the quality of the financial information reported by the entity. It should *not* be used merely to delay the recognition of interest expense. If the choice is made to use interest capitalization, adopt a procedure for determining the amount to be capitalized and closely adhere to it, with appropriate documentation of the results. This will result in a standardized calculation methodology that auditors can more easily review.

If a situation arises where imputed interest must be used, the accounting staff must subsequently account for any associated discount or premium. To avoid this additional accounting, consider advising senior management to avoid notes that include unusual interest rates, or no interest rate at all.

## Review Questions

1.  We capitalize interest in order to:
    a.  Decrease short-term profits
    b.  Reduce the recordation work of the accounting staff
    c.  Provide a truer picture of the total investment in an asset
    d.  Hide the total interest expense from readers of the financial statements

2.  Interest capitalization should be used when:
    a.  Expenditure levels are small
    b.  Construction covers a long period of time
    c.  Interest costs are small
    d.  The cost of accounting for it is greater than the value of the informational benefit derived from doing so

3.  You should not continue to capitalize interest if:
    a.  Interest costs are not being incurred
    b.  Construction interruptions have been imposed by an outside entity
    c.  There is a brief construction interruption
    d.  There are delays that are an inherent part of the asset acquisition process

4.  Under a dependent completion scenario, you should only terminate interest capitalization when:
    a.  A discrete part of a project has been completed
    b.  A separate but related project has also been completed
    c.  No additional interest cost is being incurred
    d.  An entire unit has been completed

5.  You should not impute an interest rate for:
    a.  Security deposits
    b.  Bonds
    c.  Short-term notes
    d.  Long-term notes

## Introduction

This chapter addresses the core concepts surrounding the accounting for leases by all parties entering into these arrangements. There are several fundamental leasing issues that we will cover in the following pages, including the following:

- *Types of leases.* There are several possible designations that can be applied to a lease, depending upon the facts and circumstances associated with it. Each of these designations triggers a different set of accounting rules.
- *Elections.* There are several lease-related elections that an entity can take, which are generally designed to simplify the accounting for leases.

## The Nature of a Lease

A lease is an arrangement under which a lessor agrees to allow a lessee to control the use of identified property, plant, and equipment for a stated period of time in exchange for one or more payments. A lease arrangement is quite a useful opportunity, for the following reasons:

- The lessee reduces its exposure to asset ownership
- The lessee obtains financing from the lessor in order to pay for the asset
- The lessee now has access to the leased asset

An arrangement is considered to give control over the use of an asset when both of these conditions are present:

- The lessee obtains the right to substantially all of the economic benefits from using an asset; and
- The lessee obtains the right to direct the uses to which an asset is put.

---

**EXAMPLE**

Blitz Communications obtains the rights to the entire output of an undersea cable for the next ten years, in order to benefit from an expected increase in traffic from new data centers in Sweden to users in the United States. Since Blitz has the right to substantially all of the economic benefits from using the cable, the underlying contract is considered a lease. If the arrangement had instead been for only a certain proportion of the total capacity of the cable, where the cable operator could choose which fibers within the cable would carry Blitz's data, the arrangement would not be considered a lease.

**EXAMPLE**

The Cupertino Beanery enters into a contract to operate a store from retail space. Part of the contract states that Cupertino must pay 10% of its revenues to the landlord. Cupertino still obtains the right to substantially all of the economic benefits from using the retail space – subsequent to obtaining the revenues, the company then pays 10% to the landlord. This contract clause does not prevent the contract from being designated as a lease.

**EXAMPLE**

Teton Helicopter Rescue leases a helicopter for use in its personnel rescue operations. As part of the lease agreement, Teton is only allowed to operate the helicopter during daylight hours. This restriction is designed to reduce the risk of damage to the craft. This protective right limits the scope of Teton's usage of the helicopter, but does not actually prevent it from having the right to use the asset. Thus, the restriction does not prevent the contract from being designated as a lease.

The following additional points all apply to whether a lease exists:

- *Partial period.* If a leasing arrangement only lasts for a portion of the period spanned by a contract, a lease is still presumed to exist for the partial period specified within the contract.
- *Right of substitution.* If a contract allows the supplier to substitute an identified asset with another asset throughout the usage period, there is no lease. This situation only applies when the supplier has the practical ability to substitute alternative assets, and the supplier obtains a positive economic benefit from doing so. The evaluation of the ability to substitute assets does not include assets that are unlikely to occur.

**EXAMPLE**

Nautilus Tours leases several submarines from Underwater Assets, for use in shallow-water tourist visits to nearby reefs. The lease agreement states that Underwater Assets can substitute a submarine for repairs or maintenance in the event that a submarine is not operating properly. This contract language still allows Nautilus Tours to have the right to an identified asset, so the existence of the lease is not called into question.

**EXAMPLE**

Nova Corporation operates a deep field scanning telescope for sky survey work, which it leases from Alpha Centauri Leasing. If the contract language is interpreted in a certain way, it appears possible that Alpha could substitute the telescope at a later date. However, the telescope is located at Nova's observatory, and would be difficult to dismount and replace. The cost of substitution is therefore likely to be higher than any benefits that Alpha might gain from the substitution. In this case, it appears likely that there is a lease.

**EXAMPLE**

Grissom Granaries stores corn and wheat along the Mississippi River. It enters into an agreement with a local transport firm to transport crops up and down the river. The volume of transport services indicated in the contract translates into the ongoing use of 10 barges. The transport firm has several hundred barges that it can use to fulfill the contract. When not in use, the barges are stored at one of the transport firm's riverside facilities. No specific barges are described in the contract. Given these conditions, it is apparent that Grissom does not direct the use of the barges, nor does it have the right to obtain substantially all of the economic benefits from use of the barges. Consequently, this arrangement is not a lease.

**EXAMPLE**

The Hegemony Toy Company enters into a contract with an international shipping company to deliver a shipload of goods from Singapore to Los Angeles. The specific freighter to be used is named in the contract, and only Hegemony's board games will be shipped. However, the shipping company will operate the freighter during the voyage. This arrangement is not a lease, since Hegemony cannot direct the uses to which the freighter is put.

Since the accounting for a lease only applies to property, plant, and equipment, it does not apply to the following types of assets that may also be leased:

- Assets under construction
- Biological assets (such as orchards)
- Exploration assets (such as oil and gas exploration rights)
- Intangible assets
- Inventory

## Lease Components (Lessee)

Once it has been established that a contract contains a lease, it is necessary to separate the lease into its components (if any). This can result in a business tracking several different leases within one contract. A separate lease component exists when both of the following conditions are present:

- The lessee can benefit from the right of use of a single asset, or together with other readily available resources; and
- The right of use is separate from the rights to use other assets in the contract. This is not the case when the rights of use of the different assets significantly affect each other.

The right to use land is always considered a separate lease component, unless doing so would have an insignificant effect.

**EXAMPLE**

Treetops Telecommunications leases a cell phone tower, along with the land on which it is positioned and the building within which it is located. The building was designed specifically to house the cell phone tower and related equipment. In this case, the rights of use of the different assets significantly affect each other, so one lease arrangement encompasses all of the assets. The inclusion of the land component in the same lease is considered to have an insignificant effect.

There may also be non-lease components to a contract. These components will not meet the criteria just stated for a lease component, but will transfer a good or service to the lessee. There may also be other activities that do not qualify as non-lease components, since there is no transfer of goods or services; for example, the reimbursement of lessor costs falls into this category.

A common charge associated with a lease is common area maintenance. The lessor typically performs maintenance and cleaning services for all common areas in a building, and then charges a portion of these costs through to the building tenants. The lessee would otherwise have to perform these services itself or pay a third party to do so. Common area maintenance costs are considered a non-lease component.

The classifications of lease components are not reassessed after the commencement date of the lease, unless the contract is subsequently modified and the change is not treated as a separate contract. Lease classifications can also be revisited if the lease term changes or there is a change in the probability that an option will be exercised to purchase an underlying asset.

Once all lease and non-lease components have been identified, allocate the consideration in the contract to them. This allocation is derived as follows:

1. Determine the standalone price of each separate lease and non-lease component. This should be based on the observable standalone price. If this price is not available, it can be estimated.
2. Allocate the consideration in proportion to the standalone prices of the various components.
3. If there are any initial direct costs associated with the contract, allocate these costs on the same basis as the lease payments.

**EXAMPLE**

Micron Metallic leases a stamping machine and a CNC (computer numerical control) machine for its washing machine production facility, along with periodic maintenance and repair services. The total consideration that Micron will pay over the five-year term of the lease is $800,000.

Micron's controller concludes that there are two separate leases, since the stamping and CNC machines are to be used separately, in different parts of the factory. The controller also decides to account for the maintenance and repair services as non-lease components of the contract. Further, these services are considered to be distinct for each machine, and so are separate non-lease performance obligations.

The controller needs to allocate the $800,000 of consideration to the various lease and non-lease components. She notes that there are a number of local suppliers that provide similar maintenance and repair services for each of the machines, and that standalone prices can be found to separately lease the two machines. These standalone prices are noted in the following table:

|  | Lease | Maintenance | Totals |
| --- | --- | --- | --- |
| Stamping machine | $200,000 | $30,000 | $230,000 |
| CNC machine | 570,000 | 100,000 | 670,000 |
| Totals | $770,000 | $130,000 | $900,000 |

The controller allocates the $800,000 consideration in the contract to the lease and non-lease components on a relative basis, employing their standalone prices. This results in the following allocation:

|  | Lease | Maintenance | Totals |
| --- | --- | --- | --- |
| Stamping machine | $177,778 | $26,667 | $204,445 |
| CNC machine | 506,667 | 88,888 | 595,555 |
| Totals | $684,445 | $115,555 | $800,000 |

The consideration in a lease should be remeasured and reallocated when either of the following events occurs:

- The lease liability is remeasured. This could be triggered by a change in the term of the lease, or a revision to the assessment of whether a lease option will be exercised.
- There is a contract modification that is not being accounted for as a separate contract.

## Lease Components (Lessor)

In general, a lessor allocates consideration to lease components in the same manner as the lessee. In addition, the lessor allocates any capitalized costs to the lease and non-lease components to which those costs relate. An example of a capitalized cost is the initial direct costs incurred to create a contract. Initial direct costs are discussed in the next section.

If a lessor receives a variable payment amount that relates to a lease component, it should recognize the payment as income in the same period as the one on which the variable payment was based.

---

**EXAMPLE**

Prickly Corporation leases space from Capital Inc., which it uses as a retail store to sell cacti and other thorny plants. Following the end of each month, Prickly is required to pay 2% of its revenue to Capital; this is the variable portion of the lease payment for the retail space. In early March, Prickly sends a payment of $540 to Capital, which is the variable portion of the payment, and which relates to its February sales. Capital should recognize this payment as income in its February income statement.

Prickly discloses in its financial statements the fixed amount of its operating lease cost, while separately disclosing the $540 as a variable lease cost.

---

## Initial Direct Costs

Initial direct costs are those costs that are only incurred if a lease agreement occurs. This usually includes broker commissions and payments made to existing tenants to obtain a lease, because these costs are only incurred if a lease agreement is signed. Legal fees are usually not included, since the parties must pay their attorneys even if a lease arrangement falls through. Also, staff time spent working on a lease arrangement will be incurred irrespective of the lease agreement, and so is not considered part of initial direct costs.

Initial direct costs are capitalized at the inception of a lease, and are then amortized ratably over the term of the lease. Throughout the term of a lease, any unamortized initial direct costs are included in the measurement of the right-of-use asset (which is discussed later).

## Lease Consideration

Consideration is defined as something of value that induces the parties to a contract to exchange mutual performances. The consideration in a leasing arrangement is most obviously the periodic fixed lease payments made by the lessee. Consideration can also include monthly service charges, as well as variable payments that are defined by an index or a rate. For example, a lease payment may be adjusted each year, based on changes in the consumer price index.

## The Lease Term

One of the key components of a lease is the lease term. This is considered to be the noncancelable period of a lease, as well as the following additional periods that may apply:

- Lease extension options if it is reasonably certain that the lessee will exercise these options
- Lease termination options if it is reasonably certain that the lessee will not exercise these options
- Lease extension options where the lessor controls the options

An entity makes a judgment call as of the lease commencement date regarding which of the preceding factors will apply to the derivation of an estimated lease term. This judgment is based on those factors that create an economic incentive for the lessee. Examples of economic incentives are reduced lease payments in the optional period, the significance of any leasehold improvements, and the importance of the underlying asset to the lessee's operations.

---

**EXAMPLE**

Subatomic Research operates a laboratory in leased facilities. The laboratory has been designated as an airborne infection isolation room by the federal government, which is quite a difficult certification to obtain. The lease has an option for Subatomic to extend the lease term by five years. It is highly likely that Subatomic will renew the lease, given the high cost of moving elsewhere and then applying for recertification.

**EXAMPLE**

Newton Enterprises offers free science classes to high school students. These endeavors require Newton to lease training facilities. Its most recent lease is for 10 years, with a termination option after seven years. Annual lease payments are $100,000. If Newton terminates the lease, it must pay a $30,000 termination penalty. The managers of Newton conclude that it is not reasonably certain that Newton will need the facilities after seven years of use, especially considering the relatively small size of the termination penalty when compared to the amount of the annual lease payments. Consequently, Newton elects to measure the lease term as being seven years.

---

If the lessor provides a period of free rent, the lease term is considered to begin at the commencement date and to include all rent-free periods.

A lease term should not extend past the period when it is enforceable. A lease is no longer enforceable when both the lessee and the lessor can terminate the lease without permission from the other party, and by paying no more than an insignificant penalty.

A government entity that leases space may require that a fiscal funding clause be inserted into the lease. This clause allows the government to cancel a lease if it does not have sufficient funding. When this clause is present, the lease term should only include those periods for which there is a reasonable certainty of funding.

## Initial Measurement of Lease Payments

There are a number of possible payments by a lessee that can be associated with a lease component. All of the following payments relate to the use of the underlying asset in a lease:

- Fixed payments, minus any lease incentives payable to the lessee
- Variable lease payments that depend on an index or a rate (such as the consumer price index)
- The exercise price of an option to purchase the underlying asset, if it is reasonably certain that the lessee will exercise the option
- Penalty payments associated with an assumed exercise of an option to terminate the lease
- Fees paid to the owners of a special-purpose entity for creating the transaction
- Residual value guarantees, if it is probable that these amounts will be owed. Note that a lease provision requiring the lessee to pay for any deficiency in residual value that is caused by damage or excessive usage is not considered a guarantee of the residual value.

At the commencement of a lease, a number of direct costs may also have been incurred. Examples of these costs are commissions and payments made to incentivize a tenant to terminate a lease. Costs that would have been incurred even in the absence of a lease (such as general overhead and salaries) are not direct costs.

A lessor might pay a third party for a guarantee of the residual value of an underlying asset. This payment is considered an executory cost of the contract; it is not considered part of the lease payments.

If there is a requirement in a lease agreement that the lessee dismantle and remove an underlying asset following the end of a lease, this cost is considered a lease payment.

## Subsequent Measurement of Lease Payments

It is only necessary to reassess a lessee's option to purchase an underlying asset or the length of the lease term when one of the following events occurs subsequent to the initial measurement of a lease:

- *Contractual requirement.* An event occurs that was addressed in the contract, requiring the lessee to exercise (or not exercise) an option or terminate the lease.
- *No option exercise.* The lessee does not exercise an option despite a previous determination that it was reasonably certain for the lessee to do so.
- *Option exercise.* The lessee exercises an option despite a previous determination that it was reasonably certain that the lessee would not do so.
- *Significant event.* A significant event has occurred that is within the control of the lessee, and which directly affects the lessee's decision to exercise or not exercise an option, or to purchase the underlying asset. Examples of significant events are the construction of significant leasehold improvements that will be of value to the lessee during the option period, and making significant modifications to the underlying asset.

It is only necessary to remeasure the lease payments associated with a lease when one of the following events occurs:

- *Lease modification.* The initial lease is modified, and the modification is not accounted for as a separate contract.
- *Resolved contingency.* A contingency that had resulted in variable lease payments has now been resolved, so that the payments become fixed for the remainder of the lease term.
- *Other changes.* There is a change in the lease term, a change in the assessment of whether an option will be exercised, or a change in the probable amount that will be owed by the lessee under a residual value guarantee.

## Types of Leases

There are several types of lease designations, which differ if an entity is the lessee or the lessor. It is critical to determine the type of a lease, since the accounting varies by lease type. The choices for a **lessee** are that a lease can be designated as either a finance lease or an operating lease. In essence, a *finance lease* designation implies that the lessee has purchased the underlying asset (even though this may not actually be the case), while an *operating lease* designation implies that the lessee has obtained the use of the underlying asset for only a period of time. A lessee should classify a lease as a finance lease when <u>any</u> of the following criteria are met:

- *Ownership transfer.* Ownership of the underlying asset is shifted to the lessee by the end of the lease term.
- *Ownership option.* The lessee has a purchase option to buy the leased asset, and is reasonably certain to use it.
- *Lease term.* The lease term covers the major part of the underlying asset's remaining economic life. This is considered to be 75% or more of the remaining economic life of the underlying asset. This criterion is not valid if the lease commencement date is near the end of the asset's economic life, which is considered to be a date that falls within the last 25% of the underlying asset's total economic life.
- *Present value.* The present value of the sum of all lease payments and any lessee-guaranteed residual value matches or exceeds the fair value of the underlying asset. The present value is based on the interest rate implicit in the lease.
- *Specialization.* The asset is so specialized that it has no alternative use for the lessor following the lease term. In this situation, there are essentially no remaining benefits that revert to the lessor.

When none of the preceding criteria are met, the lessee must classify a lease as an operating lease.

When the lessor is a government entity, the underlying asset may be a more substantial facility, such as an airport, where it is impossible to determine an economic life or the fair value of the asset. For these reasons, such leases should be considered operating leases. All of the following conditions should apply before a lease from a government entity is considered an operating lease:

- *Ownership*. The underlying asset is owned by a government entity, and ownership cannot be transferred to the lessee.
- *Nature of the asset*. The underlying asset is part of a larger facility, such as an airport, and is a permanent structure that cannot be moved.
- *Termination right*. The lessor has the right to terminate the lease at any time.

The choices for a **lessor** are that a lease can be designated as a *sales-type lease, direct finance lease*, or *operating lease*. If all of the preceding conditions just noted for a lessee's finance lease are met by a lease, then the lessor designates it as a sales-type lease (in effect, an asset is being sold to the lessee). If this is not the case, then the lessor has a choice of designating a lease as either a direct financing lease (in effect, the lessor earns interest income from its leasing activities) or an operating lease.

The lessor should designate any remaining lease as a direct financing lease when both of the following criteria are met:

- *Present value*. The present value of the lease payments and any residual asset value that is guaranteed by the lessee or any other party matches or exceeds substantially all of the fair value of the underlying asset. In this context, "substantially" means 90% or more of the fair value of the underlying asset. The present value is based on the rate implicit in the lease.
- *Collection probability*. The lessor will probably collect the lease payments, as well as any additional amount needed to satisfy the residual value guarantee.

When none of these additional criteria are met, the lessor classifies a lease as an operating lease.

## Asset and Liability Recognition (Lessee)

A central concept of the accounting for leases is that the lessee should recognize the assets and liabilities that underlie each leasing arrangement. This concept results in the following recognition in the balance sheet of the lessee as of the lease commencement date:

- Recognize a liability to make lease payments to the lessor
- Recognize a right-of-use asset that represents the right of the lessee to use the leased asset during the lease term

There are a number of sub-topics related to asset and liability recognition, which are stated in the following sub-sections.

### Initial Measurement

As of the commencement date of a lease, the lessee measures the liability and the right-of-use asset associated with the lease. These measurements are derived as follows:

- *Lease liability*. The present value of the lease payments, discounted at the discount rate for the lease. This rate is the rate implicit in the lease when that rate is readily determinable. If not, the lessee instead uses its incremental borrowing rate.
- *Right-of-use asset*. The initial amount of the lease liability, plus any lease payments made to the lessor before the lease commencement date, plus any initial direct costs incurred, minus any lease incentives received.

---

**EXAMPLE**

Inscrutable Corporation enters into a five-year lease, where the lease payments are $35,000 per year, payable at the end of each year. Inscrutable incurs initial direct costs of $8,000. The rate implicit in the lease is 8%.

At the commencement of the lease, the lease liability is $139,745, which is calculated as $35,000 multiplied by the 3.9927 rate for the five-period present value of an ordinary annuity. The right-of-use asset is calculated as the lease liability plus the amount of the initial direct costs, for a total of $147,745.

---

## Short-Term Leases

When a lease has a term of 12 months or less, the lessee can elect not to recognize lease-related assets and liabilities in the balance sheet. This election is made by class of asset. When a lessee makes this election, it should usually recognize the expense related to a lease on a straight-line basis over the term of the lease.

If the lease term changes so that the remaining term now extends more than 12 months beyond the end of the previously determined lease term or the lessee will likely purchase the underlying asset, the arrangement is no longer considered a short-term lease. In this situation, account for the lease as a longer-term lease as of the date when there was a change in circumstances.

## Finance Leases

When a lessee has designated a lease as a finance lease, it should recognize the following over the term of the lease:

- The ongoing amortization of the right-of-use asset
- The ongoing amortization of the interest on the lease liability
- Any variable lease payments that are not included in the lease liability
- Any impairment of the right-of-use asset

The amortization period for the right-of-use asset is from the lease commencement date to the earlier of the end of the lease term or the end of the useful life of the asset. An exception is when it is reasonably certain that the lessee will exercise an option to purchase the asset, in which case the amortization period is through the end of the asset's useful life.

After the commencement date, the lessee increases the carrying amount of the lease liability to include the interest expense on the lease liability, while reducing the carrying amount by the amount of all lease payments made during the period. The interest on the lease liability is the amount that generates a constant periodic discount rate on the remaining liability balance.

After the commencement date, the lessee reduces the right-of-use asset by the amount of accumulated amortization and accumulated impairment (if any).

---

**EXAMPLE**

Giro Cabinetry agrees to a five-year lease of equipment that requires an annual $20,000 payment, due at the end of each year. At the end of the lease period, Giro has the option to buy the equipment for $1,000. Since the expected residual value of the equipment at that time is expected to be $25,000, the large discount makes it reasonably certain that the purchase option will be exercised. At the commencement date of the lease, the fair value of the equipment is $120,000, with an economic life of eight years. The discount rate for the lease is 6%.

Giro classifies the lease as a finance lease, since it is reasonably certain to exercise the purchase option.

The lease liability at the commencement date is $84,995, which is calculated as the present value of five payments of $20,000, plus the present value of the $1,000 purchase option payment, discounted at 6%. Giro recognizes the right-of-use asset as the same amount, since there are no initial direct costs, lease incentives, or other types of payments made by Giro, either at or before the commencement date.

Giro amortizes the right-of-use asset over the eight-year expected useful life of the equipment, under the assumption that it will exercise the purchase option and therefore keep the equipment for the eight-year period.

As an example of the subsequent accounting for the lease, Giro recognizes a first-year interest expense of $5,100 (calculated as 6% × $84,995 lease liability), and recognizes the amortization of the right-of-use asset in the amount of $10,624 (calculated as $84,995 ÷ 8 years). This results in a lease liability at the end of Year 1 that has been reduced to $70,095 (calculated as $84,995 + $5,100 interest - $20,000 lease payment) and a right-of-use asset that has been reduced to $74,371 (calculated as $84,995 - $10,624 amortization).

By the end of Year 5, which is when the lease terminates, the lease liability has been reduced to $1,000, which is the amount of the purchase option. Giro exercises the option, which settles the remaining liability. At that time, the carrying amount of the right-of-use asset has declined to $31,875 (reflecting five years of amortization at $10,624 per year). Giro shifts this amount into a fixed asset account, and depreciates it over the remaining three years of its useful life.

---

## Operating Leases

When a lessee has designated a lease as an operating lease, the lessee should recognize the following over the term of the lease:

- A lease cost in each period, where the total cost of the lease is allocated over the lease term on a straight-line basis. This can be altered if there is another systematic and rational basis of allocation that more closely follows the benefit usage pattern to be derived from the underlying asset.
- Any variable lease payments that are not included in the lease liability
- Any impairment of the right-of-use asset

---

**EXAMPLE**

Nuance Corporation enters into an operating lease in which the lease payment is $25,000 per year for the first five years and $30,000 per year for the next five years. These payments sum to $275,000 over ten years. Nuance will therefore recognize a lease expense of $27,500 per year for all of the years in the lease term.

---

At any point in the life of an operating lease, the remaining cost of the lease is considered to be the total lease payments, plus all initial direct costs associated with the lease, minus the lease cost already recognized in previous periods.

After the commencement date, the lessee measures the lease liability at the present value of the lease payments that have not yet been made, using the same discount rate that was established at the commencement date.

After the commencement date, the lessee measures the right-of-use asset at the amount of the lease liability, adjusted for the following items:

- Any impairment of the asset
- Prepaid or accrued lease payments
- Any remaining balance of lease incentives received
- Any unamortized initial direct costs

---

**EXAMPLE**

Hubble Corporation enters into a 10-year operating lease for its corporate offices. The annual lease payment is $40,000 to be paid at the end of each year. The company incurs initial direct costs of $8,000, and receives $15,000 from the lessor as a lease incentive. Hubble's incremental borrowing rate is 6%. The initial direct costs and lease incentive will be amortized over the 10 years of the lease term.

Hubble measures the lease liability as the present value of the 10 lease payments at a 6% discount rate, which is $294,404. The right-of-use asset is measured at $287,404, which is the initial $294,404 measurement, plus the initial direct costs of $8,000, minus the lease incentive of $15,000.

After one year, the carrying amount of the lease liability is $272,068, which is the present value of the remaining nine lease payments at a 6% discount rate. The carrying amount of the right-of-use asset is $265,768, which is the amount of the liability, plus the unamortized initial direct costs of $7,200, minus the remaining balance of the lease incentive of $13,500.

---

## Optional Lease Payments

When there is an optional payment in a lease agreement that can be made by the lessee to purchase a leased asset, this optional payment is only included in the recognition of assets and liabilities if it is reasonably certain that the lessee will exercise the purchase option.

## Right-of-Use Asset Impairment

If a right-of-use asset is determined to be impaired, the impairment is immediately recorded, thereby reducing the carrying amount of the asset. Its subsequent measurement is calculated as the carrying amount immediately after the impairment transaction, minus any subsequent accumulated amortization.

---

**EXAMPLE**

Horton Corporation enters into a five-year equipment lease that is classified as an operating lease. At the end of Year 2, when the carrying amount of the lease liability and the right-of-use asset are both $100,000, the controller determines that the asset is impaired, and recognizes an impairment loss of $70,000. This reduces the carrying amount of the asset to $30,000.

Beginning in Year 3 and continuing through the remainder of the lease term, Horton amortizes the right-of-use asset at a rate of $10,000 per year, which will bring the carrying amount of the asset to zero by the end of the lease term.

---

## Leasehold Improvement Amortization

A leasehold improvement is a customization of rented property, such as the addition of carpeting, cabinetry, lighting, and walls. This asset should be amortized over the shorter of the remaining lease term and its useful life. The one exception is when it is reasonably certain that the lessee will take possession of the underlying asset at the end of the lease, in which case the amortization period is through the end of the asset's useful life.

## Subleases

A sublease occurs when a lessee leases the underlying asset to a third party. A sublease agreement typically arises when the original tenant no longer needs to use leased space or can no longer afford to make the lease payments. This situation is most common for commercial properties, but can arise for residential properties as well. The following accounting can apply to this situation:

- *Operating lease.* If a lease is classified as an operating lease, the original lessee continues to account for it in the same manner that it did before the commencement of the sublease.
- *Conversion from finance lease.* If the original lease was classified as a finance lease and the sublease is classified as either a sales-type or direct financing lease, then the original lessee must derecognize the right-of-use asset on its books. The accounting for the original lease liability remains the same.
- *Conversion from operating lease.* If the original lease was classified as an operating lease and the sublease is classified as either a sales-type lease or a direct financing lease, then the original lessee must derecognize the right-of-use asset on its books, and account for the original lease liability as of the sublease commencement date as though it were a finance lease (see the preceding Finance Leases sub-section).

## Maintenance Deposits

A lessee may be required to pay the lessor a maintenance deposit, which the lessor retains if the lessee damages the property during the lease term. If it is probable that the lessor will retain this deposit at the end of the lease, the lessee should recognize the payment as a variable lease expense.

## Derecognition

At the termination of a lease, the right-of-use asset and associated lease liability are removed from the books. The difference between the two amounts is accounted for as a profit or loss at that time. If the lessee purchases the underlying asset at the termination of a lease, then any difference between the purchase price and the lease liability is recorded as an adjustment to the asset's carrying amount.

If a lessee subleases an underlying asset and the terms of the original agreement then relieve the lessee of the primary lease obligation, this is considered a termination of the original lease.

# Lease Recognition Topics (Lessor)

The accounting for leases by lessors varies in several respects from the accounting by lessees. In particular, there are more classifications of leases for a lessor; there are sales-type leases, direct financing leases, and operating leases. The accounting for these leases is addressed in the following sub-sections.

## Sales-Type Leases

In a sales-type lease, the lessor is assumed to actually be selling a product to the lessee, which calls for the recognition of a profit or loss on the sale. Consequently, this results in the following accounting at the commencement date of the lease:

- *Derecognize asset.* The lessor derecognizes the underlying asset, since it is assumed to have been sold to the lessee.
- *Recognize net investment.* The lessor recognizes a net investment in the lease. This investment includes the following:
    - o The present value of lease payments not yet received

- The present value of the guaranteed amount of the underlying asset's residual value at the end of the lease term
- The present value of the unguaranteed amount of the underlying asset's residual value at the end of the lease term

- *Recognize profit or loss.* The lessor recognizes any selling profit or loss caused by the lease.
- *Recognize initial direct costs.* The lessor recognizes any initial direct costs as an expense, if there is a difference between the carrying amount of the underlying asset and its fair value. If the fair value of the underlying asset is instead equal to its carrying amount, then defer the initial direct costs and include them in the measurement of the lessor's investment in the lease.

In addition, the lessor must account for the following items subsequent to the commencement date of the lease:

- *Interest income.* The ongoing amount of interest earned on the net investment in the lease.
- *Variable lease payments.* If there are any variable lease payments that were not included in the net investment in the lease, record them in profit or loss in the same reporting period as the events that triggered the payments.
- *Impairment.* Recognize any impairment of the net investment in the lease.
- *Net investment.* Adjust the balance of the net investment in the lease by adding interest income and subtracting any lease payments collected during the period.

However, if the collectability of the lease payments and payments related to a residual value guarantee are not probable as of the commencement date, the lessor should not derecognize the underlying asset. Instead, the lessor recognizes lease payments (including variable lease payments) as a deposit liability as they are received. This treatment continues until the earlier of either of these events:

- *Probable collectability.* It becomes probable that lease payments and payments related to a residual value guarantee will be collectible.
- *Contract termination.* Either of the following occurs:
    - The contract has been terminated *and* the lease payments received to date are not refundable; or
    - The lessor has repossessed the underlying asset, *and* has no further obligation to the lessee, *and* the lease payments received to date are not refundable.

When the collectability of payments from a lessee was initially considered to not be probable, but this assessment was later changed, the lessor should take the following steps as of the latter event:

- *Derecognize asset.* Derecognize the carrying amount of the underlying asset.
- *Derecognize liability.* If there is a deposit liability, derecognize it.
- *Recognize net investment.* Recognize a net investment in the lease. This amount is derived from the remaining lease payments, the remaining lease term, and the rate implicit in the lease at the commencement date.
- *Recognize profit or loss.* Recognize any selling profit or loss, which is calculated as the lease receivable plus the carrying amount of the deposit liability, minus the carrying amount of the underlying asset, net of the unguaranteed residual asset.

If this type of lease is terminated before the end of its lease term, the lessor must test the net investment in the lease for impairment and recognize an impairment loss if necessary. Then reclassify the net investment in the lease to the most appropriate fixed asset category. The reclassified asset is recorded at the sum of the carrying amounts of the lease receivable and the residual asset.

At the end of the lease term, the lessor reclassifies its net investment in the lease to the most appropriate fixed asset account.

---

**EXAMPLE**

Capital Inc. enters into an eight-year lease of equipment with a lessee. Under the terms of the agreement, Capital will receive an annual lease payment of $10,000, payable at the end of each year. The lessee also provides Capital with a residual value guarantee of $15,000. Upon reviewing the credit rating of the lessee, Capital's controller concludes that it is probable that Capital will collect the lease payments and any additional funding necessary to satisfy the lessee's residual value guarantee. Additional pertinent facts are:

- The equipment has a 10-year estimated economic life
- The equipment has a carrying amount of $60,000
- The equipment has a fair value of $71,509 at the commencement date
- The expected residual value of the equipment is $18,000 at the end of the lease term
- There is no transfer of equipment ownership to the lessee, nor is there a purchase option
- The rate implicit in the lease is 6%

The controller classifies the lease as a sales-type lease, because the combined present value of the lease payments and the residual value guaranteed by the lessee is $71,509, which is substantially all of the fair value of the underlying asset.

The controller measures the net investment in the lease at $73,391 at the commencement date of the lease; this equals the fair value of the equipment. This net investment consists of the following:

| | |
|---|---|
| Present value of eight lease payments of $10,000 each | $62,098 |
| Present value of $15,000 residual value guarantee | 9,411 |
| Present value of the $3,000 unguaranteed residual value | 1,882 |
| Net investment in the lease | $73,391 |

The selling profit on the lease is $13,391, which is the difference between the lease receivable (the present values of the lease payments and the guaranteed residual value) and the carrying amount of the equipment net of the unguaranteed residual asset. The calculation is:

| | |
|---|---|
| Lease receivable (present values of lease payments and guaranteed residual value) | $71,509 |
| - Carrying amount of the equipment net of the present value of the unguaranteed residual asset | 58,118 |
| Selling profit | $13,391 |

At the lease commencement date, the controller derecognizes the $60,000 carrying amount of the equipment, recognizes the net investment in the lease of $73,391, and recognizes the selling profit of $13,391.

At the end of the first year of the lease, Capital receives and recognizes the annual $10,000 lease payment. Capital also recognizes interest on the net investment in the lease, which is $4,403 (calculated as $73,391 net investment in the lease × 6% rate implicit in the lease). This results in a reduced balance of $67,794 in the net investment in the lease, which is calculated as the $73,391 beginning balance, plus the $4,403 interest income, minus the $10,000 lease payment.

---

## Direct Financing Leases

In a direct financing lease, the lessor acquires assets and leases them to its customers, with the intent of generating revenue from the resulting interest payments. At the commencement date of a direct financing lease, the lessor engages in the following activities:

- Recognize the net investment in the lease. This includes the selling profit and any initial direct costs for which recognition is deferred.
- Recognize a selling loss caused by the lease arrangement, if this has occurred
- Derecognize the underlying asset

In addition, the lessor must account for the following items subsequent to the commencement date of the lease:

- *Interest income.* Record the ongoing amount of interest earned on the net investment in the lease.
- *Variable lease payments.* If there are any variable lease payments that were not included in the net investment in the lease, record them in profit or loss in the same reporting period as the events that triggered the payments.
- *Impairment.* Record any impairment of the net investment in the lease.
- *Net investment.* Adjust the balance of the net investment in the lease by adding interest income and subtracting any lease payments collected during the period.

If this type of lease is terminated before the end of its lease term, the lessor must test the net investment in the lease for impairment and recognize an impairment loss if necessary. Then reclassify the net investment in the lease to the most appropriate fixed asset category. The reclassified asset is recorded at the sum of the carrying amounts of the lease receivable and the residual asset.

At the end of the lease term, the lessor reclassifies its net investment in the lease to the most appropriate fixed asset account.

## Operating Leases

An operating lease is any lease other than a sales-type lease or a direct financing lease. At the commencement date of an operating lease, the lessor shall defer all initial direct costs. In addition, the lessor must account for the following items subsequent to the commencement date of the lease:

- *Lease payments.* Lease payments are recognized in profit or loss over the term of the lease on a straight-line basis, unless another systematic and rational basis more clearly represents the benefit that the lessee is deriving from the underlying asset. Profits cannot be recognized at the beginning of an operating lease, since control of the underlying asset has not been transferred to the lessee.
- *Variable lease payments.* If there are any variable lease payments, record them in profit or loss in the same reporting period as the events that triggered the payments.
- *Initial direct costs.* Recognize initial direct costs as an expense over the term of the lease, using the same recognition basis that was used for the recognition of lease income.

If the collectability of the lease payments and payments related to a residual value guarantee are not probable as of the commencement date, the lessor limits the recognition of lease income to the lesser of the payments described in the immediately preceding bullet points or the actual lease payments (including variable lease payments) that have been received. If this assessment later changes, any difference between the income that should have been recognized and which had been recognized is recognized in the current period.

---

**EXAMPLE**

Scottish Colonial Leasing enters into a five-year lease where the annual lease payments begin at $5,000 and escalate by $500 for each of the next four years. There are initial direct costs of $2,000. The collectability of lease payments is not probable, so Scottish classifies the lease as an operating lease.

Since the lease is classified as an operating lease, Scottish continues to measure the underlying asset as a fixed asset. Due to the risk of nonpayment, Scottish only recognizes lease income when payments are received from the lessee, and in the amount of those payments. Thus, when the first year payment of $5,000 is received, Scottish recognizes lease income of $5,000.

Scottish recognizes 20% of the initial direct costs in each year, which is a $400 expense recognition per year.

---

There can be some confusion about the treatment of operating leases from the perspectives of the lessor and the lessee. The lessor does *not* capitalize an operating lease (only the underlying asset), while a lessee (with some exceptions) capitalizes the related right-of-use asset.

## Variable Lease Payments

Most variable lease payments should be excluded from the recognition of lease assets and liabilities. However, lease payments that depend on an index or a rate should be included in this recognition.

Any variable charges to a lessee that are essentially a reimbursement of the lessor's costs are not considered part of a lease. For example, a lessor may require a lessee to pay the real estate taxes on a leased property, or the associated building insurance. Neither variable payment is for the right to use the underlying asset and does not depend on an index or a rate, and so is not a component of the contract.

In addition, a payment that is called a variable payment, but which is in reality a fixed payment should be included in the recognition of a leased asset or liability.

## Lease Modifications

When a contract is modified, the change is accounted for as a separate contract, but only when both of the following conditions are present:

- *Additional right of use*. The lessee is granted an additional right of use as part of the modification.
- *Incremental price*. There is an incremental increase in the lease price that is commensurate with the standalone price of the additional right of use that is being granted, adjusted for the contract-specific circumstances.

**EXAMPLE**

Grunge Motor Sports needs additional warehouse space for the storage of its dirt bike products. The lessor of its current warehouse has adjacent warehouse space, which is added onto the current lease. The lease price for this additional space is less than the current market rate in the area, because the lessor did not have to incur several additional charges that it normally would have paid for an entirely new client. It will be accounted for as a separate contract.

**EXAMPLE**

Monk Books currently leases 30,000 square feet of space for its scriptorium, and is in the 6th year of a 10-year lease. Given the increased demand for hand-illuminated books, Monk enters into a lease modification with the lessor, which adds 15,000 more square feet to the scriptorium as of the beginning of the 7th year at the then-current market rate.

Monk's controller accounts for the modification as a new contract, since Monk is being granted an additional right of use in excess of the original contract. The new contract only includes the incremental change noted in the lease modification.

---

If these two conditions are not present, then the existing lease classification is re-assessed as of the date of the contract modification. This reassessment encompasses the modified terms and conditions, as well as the facts and circumstances of the situation as of that date. For example, the fair value of the underlying asset might have changed between the initial contract date and the modification date.

## Lessee Impact

When there is a contract modification, the lessee should reallocate the consideration remaining in the contract to the lease components, and also remeasure the lease liability with a discount rate for the lease that is derived as of the effective date of the contract modification. These changes should only be made when a contract modification causes any of the following to occur:

- An additional right of use is granted to the lessee. This adjusts the amount of the right-of-use asset.
- Alters the term of the lease. This adjusts the amount of the right-of-use asset.
- Either fully or partially terminates the existing lease. This decreases the carrying amount of the right-of-use asset proportionally, based on the amount of lease termination. If this causes a difference between the revised lease liability and the right-of-use asset, the difference is recognized as a gain or loss as of the effective date of the modification.
- Alters the amount of the consideration in the contract. This adjusts the amount of the right-of-use asset.

---

**EXAMPLE**

Lethal Sushi and its landlord agree to extend the existing 5-year lease on a restaurant location to 8 years, thereby adding three years to the existing lease. The modified lease also increases the amount of the lease payments for the three years that have been added. This change is not considered a new contract, since no additional right of use has been granted. The only accounting issue is to remeasure the amount of the remaining lease liability, given the presence of the additional (and larger) payments. The increased amount of the lease liability is also recorded as an adjustment to the right-of-use asset.

**EXAMPLE**

For another restaurant location, Lethal Sushi also agrees to modify an existing lease. However, in this case Lethal obtains the use of a nearby building, so an additional right of use has been granted. The lease modification incorporates a substantial discount for the nearby building, at a rate that is 40% below the current market rate for similar properties. Because the price stated in the modification is not commensurate with the standalone price of the additional right of use, this modification cannot be treated as a separate contract. Instead, the company's controller allocates the lease payments in the modified contract to the two lease components on a relative standalone price basis, based on the remaining lease terms associated with each component. This remaining lease cost will be recognized over the respective lease terms of each lease component on a straight-line basis.

**EXAMPLE**

Country Fresh Produce enters into a 5-year lease for 20,000 square feet of office space. The lease payments are fixed at $100,000 per year. The original discount rate for the lease was 8%. The lease is classified as an operating lease. At the beginning of Year 3, Country Fresh and the lessor agree to modify the original lease for the remaining three years by reducing the lease payments by $10,000 per year. Since only the lease payments are being modified, this alteration cannot be accounted for as a separate contract, nor does the lease classification change.

These changes call for a remeasurement of the lease liability, based on the following information:

- Remaining lease term is three years
- Payments of $90,000 in each year, from Year 3 through Year 5
- Country Fresh's incremental borrowing rate is 6% as of the effective date of the modification

The remeasured lease liability is $240,570, which is $17,140 less than the $257,710 pre-modification lease liability. Country Fresh treats the $17,140 as a reduction in the right-of-use asset.

As of the date of the modification, the remaining lease cost for Country Fresh is $270,000, which is the sum of the remaining three payments of $90,000 each. The lease liability on Country Fresh's balance sheet in the following years will be as indicated in the following table:

| Beginning of | Lease Liability | Derivation |
|---|---|---|
| Year 3 | $240,570 | [Ordinary annuity factor for 3 years] 2.6730 × $90,000 |
| Year 4 | 165,006 | [Ordinary annuity factor for 2 years] 1.8334 × $90,000 |
| Year 5 | 84,906 | [Ordinary annuity factor for 1 year] 0.9434 × $90,000 |

## Lessor Impact

When there is a contract modification and it is not accounted for as a separate contract, the lessor accounts for the change as though the original lease was cancelled and replaced by a new lease as of the effective date of the modification. Those changes are as follows:

- *Operating lease treatment.* If a lease has been classified as an operating lease, any prepaid or accrued lease rentals associated with the original lease are now considered to be part of the payments associated with the modified lease.
- *Direct financing or sales-type lease.* If a lease has been classified as a direct financing or sales-type lease, derecognize the accrued rent asset or deferred rent liability; then adjust the selling profit or loss to match the amount of the derecognition.

## EXAMPLE

Capital Inc. enters into a 5-year operating lease as the lessor. The lease is for 5,000 square feet of prime office space, for which the annual lease payment is $100,000. This amount increases by 5% in each subsequent year, which results in the following schedule of lease payments:

| Year | Lease Payment |
|---|---|
| 1 | $100,000 |
| 2 | 105,000 |
| 3 | 110,250 |
| 4 | 115,763 |
| 5 | 121,551 |
| Total | $552,564 |
| Average | $110,513 |

At the beginning of Year 3, both parties agree to modify the lease for the remaining three years to include an additional 2,000 square feet of office space, which results in a new annual lease payment of $130,000, and which then increases by 5% in each subsequent year. The incremental increase in the lease payment represents a substantial reduction from the market rate for this type of property. Because the pricing of the modification is not commensurate with the standalone price, the modification is not treated as an entirely new lease. Instead, Capital Inc. accounts for the modified lease on a go-forward basis with the following inputs:

- Total lease payments yet to be made of $409,825 (calculated as $130,000 + $136,500 + $143,325)
- At the beginning of Year 3, Capital Inc. has an accrued lease rental asset of $16,026 (calculated as $110,513 annual average lease income × 2 years, minus lease payments of $100,000 and $105,000).

Capital Inc. subtracts the accrued lease rental asset of $16,026 from the $409,825 total lease payments yet to be made to arrive at $393,799 of lease income to be recognized over the remaining three years of the lease. This is recognized on a straight-line basis, at $131,266 per year.

---

If a modified lease was originally classified as a direct financing lease, and the modification is not accounted for as a separate contract, the modified lease is accounted for by the lessor as follows:

- *Continues as direct financing lease.* If the classification of the lease continues to be as a direct financing lease, the discount rate for the lease is adjusted in order to have the initial net investment in the modified lease equal the carrying amount of the net investment in the original lease just before the effective date of the lease modification. The same accounting applies if a sales-type lease is modified to be a direct financing lease.

**EXAMPLE**

Capital Inc. is the lessor in an existing leasing arrangement, which is about to be modified. The lease is classified as a direct financing lease, and will continue to be classified in that manner after the modification has been completed. The carrying amount of Capital's net investment in the lease is $62,000 just before the effective date of the lease modification. The modification will shorten the term of the lease, which increases the residual value of the underlying asset to $40,000. In order to have the $62,000 carrying amount of the investment equal its $40,000 residual value by the end of the lease period, Capital must calculate the interest rate that will generate interest income on the net investment over the remaining four-year term of the lease. Using a derived interest rate of 10.3775%, that calculation is:

| Year | Beginning Balance | Interest Income | Ending Balance |
|---|---|---|---|
| 1 | $62,000 | $6,434 | $55,566 |
| 2 | 55,566 | 5,766 | 49,800 |
| 3 | 49,800 | 5,168 | 44,632 |
| 4 | 44,632 | 4,632 | 40,000 |

- *Reclassified as sales-type lease.* If the classification of the lease is altered to be a sales-type lease, it is subsequently accounted for as a sales-type lease. To calculate the selling profit or loss associated with the lease, the fair value of the underlying asset is derived as of the effective date of the lease modification, and the carrying amount of the net investment in the original lease is that value just prior to the effective date of the modification.

**EXAMPLE**

Capital Inc. is the lessor in a leasing arrangement that was originally classified as a direct financing lease, because the lease covered only a reduced portion of the economic life of the underlying asset. The lease is then modified to extend the lease term, which now encompasses such a large proportion of the economic life of the asset that the lease is reclassified as a sales-type lease. In effect, Capital is now assumed to be selling the asset to the lessee.

At the effective date of the modification, Capital derecognizes the carrying amount of the net investment in the original direct financing lease, which is $71,500. Capital then recognizes a net investment in the sales-type lease of $75,000, which is the fair value of the underlying asset on the effective date of the modification. The $3,500 difference between these two values is the selling profit earned by Capital on the modified lease.

- *Reclassified as operating lease.* If the classification of the lease is altered to an operating lease, the carrying amount of the underlying asset is the same as the net investment in the original lease just prior to the effective date of the modification. The same accounting applies if a sales-type lease is modified to be an operating lease.

**EXAMPLE**

Capital Inc. is the lessor in a leasing arrangement that had originally been classified as a direct financing lease. The lease is then modified, resulting in a reclassification to an operating lease. Just prior to the effective date of the modification, Capital's net investment in the lease is $132,000. Capital derecognizes this net investment, and recognizes the underlying asset as a fixed asset in the same amount. The lease payments are $20,000 annually for the next five years. Capital recognizes these payments on a straight-line basis over the remaining years of the lease. Capital also depreciates the underlying asset during those five years.

## Elections

There are several elections that an organization can use to simplify the accounting for leases. One option is to use a risk-free discount rate for present value calculations, rather than having to justify some other rate. Another election is to include non-leasing components in a leasing arrangement, thereby reducing the number of elements within a contract to which costs may be assigned. These two options are explained within this section. In addition, a lessee can elect not to recognize lease-related assets and liabilities in the balance sheet when a lease has a term of 12 months or less. This option was explained earlier in the Asset and Liability Recognition section.

### Discount Rate

A business that is not publicly-held can elect to use a risk-free discount rate when deriving the present value of a lease. If so, this discount rate should be determined using a period comparable to that of the lease term. This election will apply to all of the entity's leases; it is not available for just a single lease or class of asset.

### Separation of Non-Lease Components

A leasing arrangement may contain non-leasing components. For example, a lease contract might include a maintenance contract under which the lessor provides ongoing servicing of the leased asset. In this case, the consideration stated in the contract is to be allocated by the lessee to these separate parts based on their relative standalone prices. The accounting for non-leasing contract components will vary depending on their nature; it is not covered by the leasing standard.

A lessee can choose to not separate non-lease components from lease components. Instead, it can account for a lease component and any non-lease components associated with that lease component as a single lease component. This election must be made by class of asset; it is not available for just a single lease.

---

**EXHIBIT**

The Slot Master Casino leases two slot machines from Winner Manufacturing, along with maintenance services, for a total of $80,000. The two slot machines are of different types, and so will be accounted for as separate leases. Slot Master has made an accounting policy election to combine non-lease and lease components for its slot machines. This means that there are only two lease components in the contract, with no non-lease components.

The controller of Slot Master can easily find standalone prices for combinations of slot machines and maintenance services. These amounts are noted in the following table, along with the allocation of the $80,000 total contract price that is based on their standalone prices:

|  | Standalone Price | Allocated Price |
|---|---|---|
| Video slot machine lease & maintenance | $40,000 | $36,364 |
| Mechanical slot machine lease & maintenance | 48,000 | 43,636 |
| Totals | $88,000 | $80,000 |

---

This option is also available to lessors, who can choose to not separate non-lease components from lease components. Instead, lessors can account for a lease component and any non-lease components associated with that lease component as a single lease component. This option is only available to the lessor if the timing and pattern of transfer of the non-lease component is the same as that of the lease component, and if the lease component would be classified as an operating lease.

**Definition of Fair Value**

If a lessor is not a manufacturer or a dealer, the fair value of the underlying asset at the commencement of a lease is considered to be its cost, where the cost used reflects any volume or trade discounts that may apply. However, if there has been a significant lapse of time between the purchase of the underlying asset and the commencement of the lease, then the normal definition of fair value shall apply.

## Sale and Leaseback Transactions

A sale and leaseback transaction occurs when the seller transfers an asset to the buyer, and then leases the asset from the buyer. This arrangement most commonly occurs when the seller needs the funds associated with the asset being sold, despite still needing to occupy the space.

When such a transaction occurs, the first accounting step is to determine whether the transaction was at fair value. This can be judged from either of the following comparisons:

- Compare the difference between the sale price of the asset and its fair value.
- Compare the present value of the lease payments and the present value of market rental payments. This can include an estimation of any variable lease payments reasonably expected to be made.

If this comparison results in the determination that a sale and leaseback transaction is not at fair value, the entity must adjust the sale price on the same basis just used to determine whether the transaction was at fair value. This can result in the following adjustments:

- Any increase to the asset's sale price is accounted for as a rent prepayment
- Any reduction of the asset's sale price is accounted for as additional financing provided to the seller-lessee by the buyer-lessor. The seller-lessee should adjust the interest rate on this liability to ensure that:
  - Interest on the liability is not greater than the principal payments over the shorter of the lease term and the financing term; and
  - The carrying amount of the asset is not greater than the carrying amount of the liability at the earlier of the termination date of the lease or the date when asset control switches to the buyer-lessor.

In this arrangement, the consideration paid for the asset is accounted for as a financing transaction by both parties. However, if there is a repurchase option under which the seller can later buy back the asset, then the initial transaction cannot be considered a sale. The only exceptions are when:

- There are alternative assets readily available in the marketplace, and
- The price at which the option can be exercised is the fair value of the asset on the option exercise date.

If a sale and leaseback transaction is not considered a sale, then the seller-lessee cannot derecognize the asset, and accounts for any amounts received as a liability. Also, the buyer-lessor does not recognize the transferred asset, and accounts for any amount paid as a receivable.

**EXAMPLE**

Epic Rest Hotels sells one of its hotel properties to Capital Inc. The sale price is a cash payment of $7 million. At the same time as the sale, Epic Rest enters into a contract with Capital for the right to use the hotel for the next 10 years, in exchange for annual payments of $800,000, payable in arrears. Additional facts are:

- Immediately prior to the transaction, the hotel had a carrying amount on Epic's books of $6 million
- The fair value of the hotel is $7 million
- Capital obtains legal title to the property
- Capital has significant risks and rewards of ownership, such as the risk of loss if the property value declines
- The transaction is classified as an operating lease

As of the transaction commencement date, Epic Rest derecognizes the $6 million carrying amount of the hotel property, recognizes the $7 million cash receipt, and recognizes a $1 million gain on sale of the hotel. Also as of this date, Capital recognizes the hotel at a cost of $7 million.

## Summary

The key elements of the accounting for leases by the lessee are as follows:

- An organization must recognize assets and liabilities for the rights and obligations created by leases that have terms of more than 12 months.
- Leases are classified as either finance leases or operating leases, both of which are capitalized by the lessee.
- The lessee can choose not to capitalize a lease with a term of 12 months or less.
- The lease term is the non-cancellable part of the lease agreement, plus any periods for options to extend the lease when it is reasonably certain that the lessee will exercise the option.
- The expense associated with an operating lease is recorded on a straight-line basis and presented as a single line item on the income statement, which combines interest and amortization.
- The interest and amortization expense associated with a finance lease is recorded on an accelerated basis and is presented as two line items on the income statement, where interest expense and amortization expense are separated.

The key elements of the accounting for leases by the lessor are as follows:

- The lessor can recognize a lease as either a sales-type lease, a direct financing lease, or an operating lease.
- The sales-type lease classification is used when the lessee is expected to use a major part of the economic benefits of the asset; this is likely to be the classification used for most non-property assets. For this lease, the lessor derecognizes the asset, recognizes any profit at the lease commencement date, and records a lease receivable and a residual asset, as well as interest income over the course of the lease.
- The direct financing lease classification is used when a lease is not a sales-type lease, the present value of the lease payments is 90% or more of the fair value of the asset, and the lessor will probably collect the lease payments. For this lease, the lessor defers the selling profit and defers recognition of any initial direct costs.
- The operating lease classification is used when a lease does not qualify as either a sales-type or direct financing lease. For this lease, the lessor retains the asset on its balance sheet and recognizes lease income over the term of the lease.

## Review Questions

1. An arrangement is considered to give control over the use of an asset when this condition is present:
    a. The lessee obtains at least partial control over the economic benefits from an asset
    b. The lessee is responsible for the maintenance of the asset
    c. The lessee can direct the uses to which an asset is put
    d. The lessee becomes a partial owner of the asset

2. The following are steps in the allocation of consideration to lease and non-lease components, except for:
    a. Allocate the consideration in proportion to the standalone prices of the components
    b. Allocate administrative costs on the same basis as the lease payments
    c. Allocate initial direct costs on the same basis as the lease payments
    d. Determine the standalone price of each separate lease and non-lease component

3. The following is one of the events that can make it necessary to reassess a lessee's option to purchase an underlying asset:
    a. The lessee does not exercise an option, despite a prior determination that the lessee would exercise the option
    b. The lessee makes a variable lease payment
    c. A significant event occurs that is within the control of the lessor, and which would have altered its decision to enter into the lease
    d. The lessee's incremental borrowing rate has changed

4. When a lessee has designated a lease as an operating lease, it should recognize the following over the term of the lease, except for:
    a. Any impairment of the right-of-use asset
    b. Any variable lease payments that are not included in the lease liability
    c. A lease cost in each period
    d. Amortization of leasehold improvements over the longer of the remaining lease term and their useful life

5. When there is a contract modification, the change is accounted for as a separate contract, but only when:
    a. The fair value of the underlying asset has changed
    b. The incremental borrowing rate of the lessee has changed
    c. There is an incremental increase in the lease price
    d. The existing right of use is affirmed

6. A lease arrangement is a useful opportunity for a lessee, because:
    a. It hides assets from investors
    b. The lessee's exposure to the risks of asset ownership is reduced
    c. The lessee can obtain the lowest possible interest rate on the lease
    d. A lease arrangement can always be terminated early

7. When a supplier has the right to substitute an identified asset with another asset:
    a. There is no lease
    b. Asset substitutions will trigger a lease modification
    c. The discount rate is revised as of the substitution date
    d. A separate lease agreement is assumed for the substituted asset

8. The accounting for a lease does not apply to:
   a. Land
   b. Foreign property
   c. Mixed properties that contain different asset classes
   d. Biological assets

9. A separate lease component exists when:
   a. The lessee can benefit from the right of use of a single asset
   b. The fair value of an asset exceeds $10,000
   c. There is an insignificant amount of land
   d. The rights of use of different assets affect each other

10. An example of an initial direct cost is:
    a. Staff time spent working on a leasing arrangement
    b. Lease deposits
    c. Broker commissions
    d. Legal fees

11. The following are considered to be lease payments, except for:
    a. The cost to remove an underlying asset following the end of a lease
    b. A payment to a third party to guarantee the residual value of an underlying asset
    c. Fixed payments
    d. The exercise price of an option to purchase an underlying asset, where it is reasonably certain that the lessee will exercise the option

12. When a lease has a term of 12 months or less, the lessee can elect:
    a. To classify the lease as a long-term liability
    b. Not to recognize lease-related assets and liabilities in the balance sheet
    c. To group the lease with a longer-term lease for classification purposes
    d. To terminate the lease without penalty

13. A unique accounting item that occurs only for a sales-type lease at the lease commencement date is:
    a. The recognition of a selling profit
    b. The recognition of the net investment in the lease
    c. Derecognition of the underlying asset
    d. The recognition of initial direct selling costs over the term of the lease

## Introduction

There are times when a business does not use cash to settle its transactions. Instead, it may enter into an exchange of nonmonetary assets, or use cash for only a portion of the settlement. In this chapter, we review the accounting for several variations on the concept of the nonmonetary transaction.

## Overview of Nonmonetary Transactions

Nearly all transactions between parties involve the exchange of cash for goods or services. However, there are a few situations where primarily nonmonetary assets are exchanged. This latter situation is referred to as (predictably enough) a nonmonetary transaction. There are three possible types of nonmonetary transactions, which are:

- *Nonreciprocal transfers with owners.* This is typically a distribution to stockholders, such as the issuance of shares or tangible goods as a dividend.
- *Nonreciprocal transfers with other than owners.* This is a distribution to a third party, such as the contribution of assets to a charity.
- *Nonmonetary exchanges.* This is an asset exchange with another entity, such as the exchange of one real estate holding for another.

In general, a reciprocal transfer of a nonmonetary asset is considered an exchange only when each party gives up any continuing involvement in the asset that it has transferred to the other party.

The accounting for a nonmonetary transaction is based on the fair values of the assets transferred. This results in the following set of alternatives for determining the recorded cost of a nonmonetary asset acquired in an exchange, in declining order of preference:

1. At the fair value of the asset transferred in exchange for it. Record a gain or loss on the exchange.
2. At the fair value of the asset received, if the fair value of this asset is more evident than the fair value of the asset transferred in exchange for it.
3. At the recorded amount of the surrendered asset, if no fair values are determinable or the transaction has no commercial substance.

If there is a nonreciprocal asset transfer, the accounting by the two parties involved in the transaction is:

- *Recipient.* Record the cost of the asset received at its fair value.
- *Transferor.* Record the asset being surrendered at its fair value, which may result in the recognition of a gain or loss on the disposition.

There are some variations on the accounting for nonmonetary exchanges that may apply in limited circumstances, which are:

- *Reacquired stock.* When making a transfer of assets to shareholders to acquire treasury stock or retire stock, the value of the stock retired may represent the best evidence of the value of the surrendered assets.
- *Cash option.* If a party to a nonmonetary transaction had the option to receive cash instead, the amount of the cash alternative could represent the best evidence of the value of the assets exchanged.

**EXAMPLE**

Nascent Corporation exchanges a color copier with a carrying amount of $18,000 with Declining Company for a print-on-demand publishing station. The color copier had an original cost of $30,000, and had incurred $12,000 of accumulated depreciation as of the transaction date. No cash is transferred as part of the exchange, and Nascent cannot determine the fair value of the color copier. The fair value of the publishing station is $20,000.

Nascent can record a gain of $2,000 on the exchange, which is derived from the fair value of the publishing station that it acquired, less the carrying amount of the color copier that it gave up. Nascent uses the following journal entry to record the transaction:

|  | Debit | Credit |
|---|---|---|
| Publishing equipment | 20,000 |  |
| Accumulated depreciation | 12,000 |  |
|    Copier equipment |  | 30,000 |
|    Gain on asset exchange |  | 2,000 |

**EXAMPLE**

Nascent Corporation and Starlight Inc. swap spectroscopes, since the two devices have different features that the two companies need. The spectroscope given up by Nascent has a carrying amount of $25,000, which is comprised of an original cost of $40,000 and accumulated depreciation of $15,000. Both spectroscopes have identical fair values of $27,000.

Nascent's controller tests for commercial substance in the transaction. She finds that there is no difference in the fair values of the assets exchanged, and that Nascent's cash flows will not change significantly as a result of the swap. Thus, she concludes that the transaction has no commercial value, and so should account for it at book value, which means that Nascent cannot recognize a gain of $2,000 on the transaction, which is the difference between the $27,000 fair value of the spectroscope and the $25,000 carrying amount of the asset given up. Instead, she uses the following journal entry to record the transaction, which does not contain a gain or loss:

|  | Debit | Credit |
|---|---|---|
| Spectroscope (asset received) | 25,000 |  |
| Accumulated depreciation | 15,000 |  |
|    Spectroscope (asset given up) |  | 40,000 |

## Purchases and Sales of Inventory with the Same Counterparty

There are situations where a company may sell inventory to another entity, and also buys inventory from that same entity, with the inventory in both transactions being sold in the same line of business. In many cases, the intent behind these transactions is for each party to procure inventory from the counterparty in the most cost-efficient manner, rather than to record a sale. If there is no commercial substance to each individual sale, the exchanges are instead clustered together and treated as a nonmonetary exchange (even if individual invoices or other sale agreements are documented between the parties).

The following factors are indicators that these purchase and sale transactions are entered into as paired units, rather than individual transactions, and so may not have commercial substance:

- *Certainty of transfer.* It is relatively certain that the counterparty will initiate a reciprocal inventory transfer.
- *Off-market terms.* The transactions incorporate off-market terms. This is especially relevant for exchange-traded commodities.

- *Offset.* There is a right of offset of obligations between the parties. This is especially evident when the different purchase and sale transactions are specifically identified by both parties.
- *Simultaneous transactions.* The purchase and sale transactions are entered into simultaneously.

---

**EXAMPLE**

Exotic Cars Limited routinely has an excess number of Ferraris in its Florida dealership, and is not allocated enough Maserati cars to meet demand. High Speed Auto, located in Texas, finds itself in the reverse situation, given the differing demographics and consumer buying habits where it is located. The dealerships enter into an agreement to sell each other their excess cars at roughly equivalent wholesale prices. Each transaction is separately invoiced and settled in cash.

Despite the form of settlement, this is clearly a reciprocal arrangement, and so should be accounted for as a nonmonetary exchange.

**EXAMPLE**

Armadillo Industries and Texas Armor Plating have done business with each other for many years, and routinely buy components from each other at market prices. Purchase orders are used to initiate each transaction, purchases are made at irregular intervals, and there is no arrangement to predicate one purchase on the presence of an offsetting arrangement. Historically, Texas Armor Plating has sold substantially more inventory to Armadillo. Each transaction is paid separately in cash, with no netting of transactions.

Since there is no correlation between the inventory values being exchanged, nor in the timing of exchanges, this scenario is not treated as a nonmonetary exchange, but instead as an ongoing series of sale and purchase transactions.

---

Nonmonetary exchanges of inventory should be recognized at the carrying amount of the inventory transferred (not their fair values). This means that the exchanges appearing in the following exhibit should be recorded at inventory carrying amounts.

**Examples of Inventory Exchanges**

| Transferred Out | In Exchange For |
|---|---|
| Raw materials or work-in-process inventory | Raw materials, work-in-process, or finished goods |
| Finished goods | Finished goods |

If there is a transfer of finished goods in exchange for raw materials or work-in-process inventory, the transferor of the finished goods should record the transaction at its fair value, if fair value is determinable and the transaction has commercial substance.

**Barter Transactions**

In a barter transaction, a company may enter into a transaction where it exchanges a nonmonetary asset for barter credits which can then be used to acquire a different type of asset. These transactions can be directly between two entities, or through an intermediary that acts as a central exchange for a number of businesses that engage in barter transactions.

It is assumed that the fair value of the nonmonetary asset surrendered is more readily evident than the fair value of the barter credits received, which means that the barter credits received should be recorded at the fair value of the asset surrendered, unless one of the following situations is present:

- The company can convert the credits into cash in the near term
- There are quoted market prices available for items that can be acquired with barter credits

A business may need to recognize an impairment loss on the receipt of barter credits if it later becomes apparent that either of the following conditions exists:

- The fair value of unused barter credits has declined below their carrying amount
- The business will not use some or all of its remaining barter credits

## Exchanges Involving Monetary Consideration

There can be any number of variations on the nonmonetary exchange concept, including ones where some cash is exchanged, along with other nonmonetary assets. If there is a significant amount of monetary consideration paid (known as *boot*), the entire transaction is considered to be a monetary transaction. In GAAP, a significant amount of boot is considered to be 25% of the fair value of an exchange. Conversely, if the amount of boot is less than 25%, the following accounting applies:

- *Payer*. The party paying boot is not allowed to recognize a gain on the transaction (if any).
- *Recipient*. The receiver of the boot recognizes a gain to the extent that the monetary consideration is greater than a proportionate share of the carrying amount of the surrendered asset. This calculation is based on the percentage of monetary consideration received to either:
    - Total consideration received, or
    - The fair value of the nonmonetary asset received (if more clearly evident)

The recipient's gain calculation is:

$$\frac{\text{Boot}}{\text{Boot} + \text{Fair value of asset received}} \times \text{Total gain} = \text{Gain recognized}$$

If the terms of the transaction indicate that a loss has occurred, the entire amount of the loss is to be recognized at once.

---

**EXAMPLE**

Nascent Corporation is contemplating the exchange of one of its heliographs for a catadioptric telescope owned by Aphelion Corporation. The two companies have recorded these assets in their accounting records as follows:

|  | Nascent (Heliograph) | Aphelion (Catadioptric) |
|---|---|---|
| Cost | $82,000 | $97,000 |
| Accumulated depreciation | 22,000 | 27,000 |
| Net book value | $60,000 | $70,000 |
| Fair value | $55,000 | $72,000 |

Under the terms of the proposed asset exchange, Nascent must pay cash (boot) to Aphelion of $17,000. The boot amount is 24 percent of the fair value of the exchange, which is calculated as:

$17,000 Boot ÷ ($55,000 Fair value of heliograph + $17,000 Boot) = 24%

The parties elect to go forward with the exchange. The amount of boot is less than 25 percent of the total fair value of the exchange, so Aphelion should recognize a pro rata portion of the $2,000 gain (calculated as the $72,000 total fair value of the asset received - $70,000 net book value of the asset received) on the exchange using the following calculation:

$$24\% \text{ Portion of boot to total fair value received} \times \$2,000 \text{ Gain} = \$480 \text{ Recognized gain}$$

Nascent uses the following journal entry to record the exchange transaction:

|  | Debit | Credit |
|---|---|---|
| Telescope (asset received) | 72,000 |  |
| Accumulated depreciation | 22,000 |  |
| Loss on asset exchange | 5,000 |  |
|     Cash |  | 17,000 |
|     Heliograph (asset given up) |  | 82,000 |

Nascent's journal entry includes a $5,000 loss; the loss is essentially the difference between the book value and fair value of the heliograph on the transaction date.

Aphelion uses the following journal entry to record the exchange transaction:

|  | Debit | Credit |
|---|---|---|
| Heliograph (asset received) | 53,480 |  |
| Accumulated depreciation | 27,000 |  |
| Cash | 17,000 |  |
|     Gain on asset exchange |  | 480 |
|     Telescope (asset given up) |  | 97,000 |

Aphelion is not allowed to recognize the full value of the heliograph at the acquisition date because of the boot rule for small amounts of cash consideration; this leaves the heliograph undervalued by $1,520 (since its fair value is actually $55,000).

---

The accounting is different if the amount of boot is 25 percent or more of the fair value of the exchange. In this situation, both parties should record the transaction at its fair value.

---

**EXAMPLE**

Nascent Corporation exchanges a wide field CCD camera for a Schmidt-Cassegrain telescope owned by Aphelion Corporation. The two companies have recorded these assets in their accounting records as follows:

|  | Nascent (Camera) | Aphelion (Schmidt-Cassegrain) |
|---|---|---|
| Cost | $50,000 | $93,000 |
| Accumulated depreciation | (30,000) | (40,000) |
| Net book value | $20,000 | $53,000 |
| Fair value | $24,000 | $58,000 |

Under the terms of the agreement, Nascent pays $34,000 cash (boot) to Aphelion. This boot amount is well in excess of the 25 percent boot level, so both parties can now treat the deal as a monetary transaction.

Nascent uses the following journal entry to record the exchange transaction, which measures the telescope acquired at the fair value of the camera and cash surrendered:

|  | Debit | Credit |
|---|---|---|
| Telescope (asset received) | 58,000 |  |
| Accumulated depreciation | 30,000 |  |
| Gain on asset exchange |  | 4,000 |
| Cash |  | 34,000 |
| CCD camera (asset given up) |  | 50,000 |

The gain recorded by Nascent is the difference between the $24,000 fair value of the camera surrendered and its $20,000 book value.

Aphelion uses the following journal entry to record the exchange transaction, which measures the camera acquired at the fair value of the telescope surrendered less cash received:

|  | Debit | Credit |
|---|---|---|
| Camera (asset received) | 24,000 |  |
| Accumulated depreciation | 40,000 |  |
| Cash | 34,000 |  |
| Gain on asset exchange |  | 5,000 |
| Telescope (asset given up) |  | 93,000 |

The gain recorded by Aphelion is the difference between the $58,000 fair value of the telescope surrendered and its $53,000 book value.

---

## Exchanges of a Nonfinancial Asset for a Noncontrolling Ownership Interest

There are certain types of nonmonetary exchanges where a business transfers nonfinancial assets to a second entity in exchange for a noncontrolling interest in the second entity. This requires the recognition of the surrendered assets at their fair value (or the fair value of the ownership interest received, if that figure is more readily determinable), and the recognition of a full or partial gain on the transaction.

If the fair value of the assets surrendered exceeds the amount of their carrying value, recognize a gain under either of the following options:

- *Cost method.* If the transferor accounts for the ownership interest received using the cost method, recognize a gain in the full amount of the difference.
- *Equity method.* If the transferor accounts for the ownership interest received using the equity method, recognize a partial gain. In this case, the gain is reduced by the company's portion of its economic interest in the other entity.

**EXAMPLE**

Armadillo Industries exchanges an asset with a carrying value of $1,000,000 and a fair value of $1,500,000 for a 25% economic interest in Armor International. Armadillo accounts for its interest in Armor using the cost method. Armadillo should recognize a gain of $375,000 on the transaction, which is calculated as follows:

($1,500,000 Fair value - $1,000,000 Carrying amount) × (1 - 25% Economic interest) = $375,000 Gain

If the fair value of the assets surrendered is less than the amount of their carrying value, recognize the full amount of the loss at once.

The result of the transfer of a nonfinancial asset for a noncontrolling ownership interest might be the deconsolidation of the entity surrendering the asset, if the asset is a subsidiary or a group of assets that constitute a business.

## Summary

Of the types of nonmonetary transactions described in this chapter, the most common one by far is exchanges using monetary consideration. These transactions arise when a business trades in old equipment for new equipment, and pays a significant sum for the difference between the fair values of the two assets being exchanged. The accountant may never encounter the other types of nonmonetary transactions noted in this chapter.

## Review Questions

1. The purchase and sale of inventory conducted with the same counterparty does not have commercial substance when:
    a. It is unlikely that the counterparty will initiate a reciprocal inventory transfer
    b. The transactions use market terms
    c. The purchase and sale transactions occur at different times
    d. There is a right of offset of obligations

2. The most preferred way to value an asset acquired in a nonmonetary exchange is:
    a. At the fair value of the asset received
    b. At the fair value of the asset transferred in exchange for it
    c. At the recorded amount of the surrendered asset
    d. At the gross amount of the surrendered asset

3. A loss on barter credits should be recorded when:
    a. The business will not use its remaining credits
    b. The carrying amount is less than their fair value
    c. They can be converted into cash
    d. They can only be used through a barter exchange

4. A significant amount of boot is considered to be:
    a. 25% of the fair value of an exchange
    b. Any amount of cash
    c. 51% of the fair value of an exchange
    d. 51% of the book value of an exchange

# Chapter 21
# Accounting for Software

## Introduction

The accounting standards relating to software are included in two sections of the GAAP codification. Section 350 covers internal-use software and website development costs, while Section 985 covers software that is intended for sale. In this chapter, we cover the accounting for both scenarios, as well as software accessed via a hosting arrangement and software inventory.

**Related Podcast Episode:** Episode 270 of the Accounting Best Practices Podcast discusses the accounting for software as a service. It is available at: **accountingtools.com/podcasts** or **iTunes**

## Internal-Use Software

Companies routinely develop software for internal use, and want to understand how these development costs are to be accounted for. Software is considered to be for internal use when it has been acquired or developed *only* for the internal needs of a business. Examples of situations where software is considered to be developed for internal use are:

- Accounting systems
- Cash management tracking systems
- Customer service software
- Data collection and analysis systems
- Database search tools
- Membership tracking systems
- Production automation systems
- Video production systems

Further, there can be no reasonably possible plan to market the software outside of the company, as would be the case when a marketing channel has been selected that has specifically-identified promotional, delivery, billing, and support activities. A market feasibility study is not considered a reasonably possible marketing plan, nor is an arrangement that provides for the joint development of software for mutual internal use. However, a history of selling software that had initially been developed for internal use creates a reasonable assumption that the latest internal-use product will also be marketed for sale outside of the company.

---

**EXAMPLE**

Harrison Manufacturing develops just-in-time software that it uses internally to monitor the flow of jobs through its production process. The IT manager convinces management to sell the JIT software outside the company, which meets with some success. Subsequently, the firm develops warehouse management software to manage the flow of goods through its own distribution warehouses. Since Harrison has a history of selling its internally-developed software outside of the firm, there is a reasonable assumption that the same action will be taken for the new warehouse management software – which prevents the firm from accounting for it as internal-use software. Instead, it must account for the new software using the requirements for software that is intended for sale.

**EXAMPLE**

Inouye Semiconductor uses highly-complex wafer testing software to determine whether the semiconductor chips it is producing are operational. This is internal-use software, since customers do not acquire the software, nor do they obtain the future right to use it.

---

The accounting for internal-use software varies, depending upon the stage of completion of the project. The relevant accounting is:

- *Stage 1: Preliminary project activities.* All costs incurred during the preliminary stage of a development project should be charged to expense as incurred. This stage is considered to include making decisions about the allocation of resources, determining performance requirements, conducting supplier demonstrations, evaluating technology, and supplier selection.
- *Stage 2: Application development.* Capitalize the costs incurred to develop internal-use software, which may include coding, hardware installation, and testing. Any costs related to data conversion, user training, administration, and overhead should be charged to expense as incurred. Data conversion may include purging or cleansing existing data, reconciling old and new data, and converting old data to the new system. Only the following costs can be capitalized:
    - Materials and services consumed in the development effort, such as third-party development fees, software purchase costs, and travel costs related to development work.
    - Costs to develop or acquire software that allow for access to or conversion of old data by new systems.
    - The payroll and benefit costs of those employees directly associated with software development, to the extent of the time spent directly on the project.
    - The capitalization of interest costs incurred to fund the project. These costs can only be capitalized for the period during which there are activities related to software development.
- *Stage 3. Post-implementation.* Charge all post-implementation costs to expense as incurred. Examples of these costs are training and maintenance costs.

Any allowable capitalization of costs should begin *after* the preliminary stage has been completed, management authorizes and commits to funding the project, it is probable that the project will be completed, and the software will be used for its intended function.

The capitalization of costs should end when all substantial testing has been completed. If it is no longer probable that a project will be completed, stop capitalizing the costs associated with it, and conduct impairment testing on the costs already capitalized. The cost at which the asset should then be carried is the lower of its carrying amount or fair value (less costs to sell). Unless there is evidence to the contrary, the usual assumption is that uncompleted software has no fair value. The following are general indicators that software is no longer expected to be completed and placed in service:

- Expenditures are no longer being budgeted or incurred for the software.
- There are programming difficulties that will not be resolved on a timely basis.
- There have been significant cost overruns.
- The costs that have been or will be incurred significantly exceed the cost of competing third-party software, so management intends to stop development and buy the third-party software.
- New technology in the marketplace is driving management to acquire third-party products, rather than completing the internal development project.
- The business unit to which the software relates is either unprofitable or will be discontinued.

A business may purchase software for internal use. If the purchase price of this software includes other elements, such as training and maintenance fees, only capitalize that portion of the purchase price that relates to the software itself. When this purchase results in the replacement of older software, any remaining unamortized cost of the older software should be charged to expense as soon as the replacement software is ready for its intended use.

In addition, any later upgrades of the software can be capitalized, but only if it is probable that extra system functionality will result from the upgrade. These upgrades typically require the formulation of new software specifications, which may alter some portion of the existing specifications. The costs of maintaining the system should be charged to expense as incurred. If the maintenance is provided by a third party and payment is made in advance for the services of that party, amortize the cost of the maintenance over the service period.

Once costs have been capitalized, amortize them over the expected useful life of the software. This is typically done on a straight-line basis, unless another method more clearly reflects the expected usage pattern of the software. Amortization should begin when a software module is ready for its intended use, which is considered to be when all substantial system testing has been completed. If a software module cannot function unless other modules are also completed, do not begin amortization until the related modules are complete.

It may be necessary to regularly reassess the useful life of the software for amortization purposes, since technological obsolescence tends to shorten it. The reassessment may also involve consideration of new technology, competing products, and other economic factors.

The capitalized cost of internal-use software should be routinely reviewed for impairment. The following are all indicators of the possible presence of asset impairment:

- The software is not expected to be of substantive use
- The manner in which the software was originally intended to be used has now changed
- The software is to be significantly altered
- The development cost of the software significantly exceeded original expectations

Once a business has developed software for internal use, management may decide to market it for external use by third parties. If so, the proceeds from software licensing, net of selling costs, should be applied against the carrying amount of the software asset. For the purposes of this topic, selling costs are considered to include commissions, software reproduction costs, servicing obligations, warranty costs, and installation costs. The business should not recognize a profit on sales of the software until the application of net sales to the carrying amount of the software asset have reduced the carrying amount to zero. The business can recognize all further proceeds as revenue.

## Internal-Use Software Accessed via a Hosting Arrangement

The preceding guidance also applies to internal-use software to which the organization gains access via a hosting arrangement – but only if both of the following criteria are met:

- The company has the contractual right to take possession of the software at any time without incurring a significant penalty; and
- It is feasible to run the software on the company's own hardware, or contract with a third party to host the software.

When the preceding criteria are not met, then the hosting arrangement is considered to be a service contract, and so does not constitute a software purchase.

Under a hosting arrangement, it is relatively common for the price to include several elements, such as the software license, hosting, and employee training. When this is the case, the company should allocate the price paid among these various elements, where the allocation is based on the standalone price of each element in the contract.

If any costs associated with a hosting arrangement are capitalized, they should be amortized over the term of the hosting arrangement. The term of a hosting arrangement is considered to be its fixed non-cancellable term, plus any option extension periods, if the company is reasonably certain to exercise the option. The term of the arrangement should be periodically reassessed, with any changes in the period accounted for as a change in accounting estimate.

The straight-line amortization basis should be used, unless another method is more representative of the benefit level provided by the hosting arrangement. Amortization should begin for each module of a hosting arrangement when the module is ready for its intended use (which has occurred when all substantial testing is completed). If the functionality of the module is dependent on the completion of other modules, then amortization should begin when the other related modules are ready for their intended use.

The accountant should examine the capitalized costs associated with a hosting arrangement for impairment when any of the following conditions are present:

- The arrangement is not expected to provide any substantive service potential to the company.
- A significant change has occurred in the extent to which the hosting arrangement is used.
- A significant change has been made to the hosting arrangement.

## Website Development Costs

A company may allocate funds to the development of a company website in such areas as coding, graphics design, the addition of content, and site operation. The accounting for website development varies, depending upon the stage of completion of the project. The relevant accounting is:

- *Stage 1: Preliminary.* Charge all site planning costs to expense as incurred. This stage is considered to include project planning, the determination of site functionality, hardware identification, technology usability, alternatives analysis, supplier demonstrations, and legal considerations.
- *Stage 2: Application development and infrastructure.* The accounting matches what was just described in the last section for internal-use software. In essence, capitalize these costs. More specifically, capitalize the cost of obtaining and registering an Internet domain, as well as the procurement of software tools, code customization, web page development, related hardware, hypertext link creation, and site testing. Also, if a site upgrade provides new functions or features to the website, capitalize these costs.
- *Stage 3: Graphics development.* For the purposes of this topic, graphics are considered to be software and so are capitalized, unless they are to be marketed externally. Graphics development includes site page design and layout.
- *Stage 4: Content development.* Charge data conversion costs to expense as incurred, as well as the costs to input content into a website. Content may include articles, photos, maps, charts, and so forth.
- *Stage 5: Site operation.* The costs to operate a website are the same as any other operating costs, and so should be charged to expense as incurred. Operating costs relate to training, administration, site updates, site security, and maintenance. The treatment of selected operating costs associated with a website are:
  - Charge website hosting fees to expense over the period benefited by the hosting
  - Charge search engine registration fees to expense as incurred, since they are advertising costs

## Software Intended for Sale

When computer software is to be sold, leased, or otherwise marketed for sale, there are a number of accounting requirements for how the associated costs are to be treated. Examples of software intended for sale are as follows:

- Software that is required to operate a company's products
- Machines that are sold with software incorporated into them that is needed to operate the machines
- Vehicles that are sold with automated driving systems installed in them
- A database that is sold with an integrated software search function
- An operating system that is installed on computers sold to customers

The accounting requirements for software intended for sale are noted in the following sub-sections.

### Initial Cost Recognition

The following requirements apply to the initial recognition of various costs associated with computer software that is intended for sale:

- *Research and development costs.* Any cost incurred to establish the technological feasibility of software is to be charged to expense as incurred. Technological feasibility has been established when the developing entity has completed all planning, designing, coding and testing activities required to determine whether the software can meet its design specifications. Evidence of technological feasibility can be proven by engaging in either of the following activities:

  - *Detail program design option.* If a detail program design was developed for the software, then all three of the following requirements must be met in order to establish technological feasibility:

    1. The needed skills, hardware, and software technology are available to produce the product.
    2. The detail program design is sufficiently complete, based on design documentation and by tracing the design to product specifications.
    3. The detail program design has been examined for high-risk development issues and these concerns have been resolved with coding and testing. Examples of high-risk development issues are unproven functions and features that incorporate technological innovations.

  - *No detail program design.* When there is no detail program design, then technological feasibility can be proven by having a completed product design and a working model of the software, where the completeness of the model and its consistency with the product design have been confirmed with sufficient testing. A working model must be operative, written in the same language as the product to be sold, include all planned major functions, and be ready for initial customer testing.

- *Production costs.* The recognition of production costs is addressed in the following topics:

  - *Production masters.* Once technological feasibility has been established, the cost of producing production masters should be capitalized. These costs may include any coding and testing conducted after technological feasibility was established.
  - *Software production costs.* Software production costs cannot be capitalized until technological feasibility has been established, and all research and development activities for the other components of the product have been completed.

- o *Allocated overhead costs.* Overhead costs can be allocated to production. This allocation may include overhead relating to programmers and their work facilities, but should not include an allocation of general and administrative costs.
  - o *Capitalization stoppage.* The capitalization of production costs must stop when the product is available for general release to customers.
  - o *Maintenance and customer support costs.* The costs of maintenance and customer support should be charged to expense at the earlier of when these costs are incurred or when related revenue is recognized.

- *Purchased software.* When software is purchased in order to be integrated into a product, the acquisition cost should only be capitalized if technological feasibility can be established *and* all research and development activities of the other components of the product have been completed as of the software purchase date. If there is an alternative use for the purchased software, then the purchase cost can be capitalized in accordance with its projected use.

---

**EXAMPLE**

Norrona Software buys software for $50,000 that it can resell for $40,000. Technological feasibility has not yet been established. At this point, $10,000 of the purchase cost should be charged to research and development expense, while the remaining $40,000 is capitalized. The technological feasibility of the software product is then established, so Norrona can include the capitalized $40,000 in the cost of the product.

---

## Subsequent Cost Measurement

Once software costs have been capitalized, they should be amortized on a product-by-product basis, beginning with the date when the product is available for general release to customers. The amount of annual amortization recognized should be the greater of the following two calculation options:

- The ratio of current gross product revenues to the total of both current and expected future gross revenues for that product; or
- The straight-line method over the remaining estimated economic life of the product.

At the end of each reporting period, compare the unamortized capital costs of each software product to its net realizable value, and write off any amount by which the unamortized capital costs exceed the net realizable value. Net realizable value is the estimated future gross revenues for that product, minus the estimated future costs of completing and disposing of it, which includes any maintenance and customer service costs. Any amounts written off shall not be restored in future periods.

## Product Enhancements

Enhancements may be made to a product after it has been initially released for sale. The costs incurred for these enhancements should be charged to research and development expense until such time as the technological feasibility of each enhancement has been established. Technological feasibility tends to be easier to establish for a product enhancement, since it was already established for the baseline product. This is particularly the case when a software product has been ported (adapted) to run on different hardware.

If the original product (prior to the enhanced version), will no longer be sold, then include any unamortized cost of the original version in the cost of the enhancement when applying the net realizable value test. However, if the original product will continue to be sold along with the enhanced version, then allocate the unamortized cost of the original product between the original and enhanced versions.

The capitalized costs of a product enhancement, including any costs allocated to it from the original product, should be amortized over the estimated useful life of the enhanced product.

## Software Inventory

When a software provider incurs costs to duplicate software, documentation, and training materials from product masters, as well as to package these items, the costs should be capitalized as inventory. These capitalized costs are then charged to the cost of goods sold when the revenue associated with the sale of these units is recognized.

## Summary

The accounting rules are significantly different for internal-use software and software intended for sale, so there should be clear internal guidelines for how to identify each situation. Impairment is also a significant concern, since software can be rendered technologically obsolete in short order; this means that the accountant must continually monitor the circumstances to see if an impairment analysis is warranted.

## **Review Questions**

1. The accountant should examine the capitalized costs associated with a hosting arrangement for impairment when any of the following conditions are present, except for:
   a. A significant change has been made to the hosting arrangement
   b. The arrangement is not expected to provide any substantial service potential
   c. When the term of the hosting arrangement is unusually long
   d. A significant change has occurred in the extent to which the arrangement is used

2. The following accounting issue applies to the production costs for software intended for sale:
   a. If a working model is not operative, costs are charged to expense as incurred
   b. If there is an alternative use for purchased software, it can be capitalized in accordance with its projected use
   c. If technological feasibility is not established, costs are charged to expense as incurred
   d. The cost of producing production masters should be capitalized

3. The following is an example of internal-use software:
   a. A membership tracking system
   b. Software that is required to operate a company's products
   c. An operating system that is installed on computers sold to customers
   d. A vehicle that is sold with an automated driving system in it

4. The stage of internal-use software development that can be capitalized is:
   a. Preliminary planning
   b. Application development
   c. Subsequent use
   d. Post-implementation

5. When developing a website, the following cost can be charged to expense (rather than being capitalized):
   a. Graphics development
   b. Internet domain registration
   c. Data conversion costs
   d. Code customization

# Chapter 22
# Partnership Accounting

## Introduction

A partnership is a form of business organization in which owners have unlimited personal liability for the actions of the business, though this problem can be mitigated through the use of a limited liability partnership. The owners of a partnership have invested their own funds and time in the business, and share proportionally in any profits earned by it. There may also be limited partners in the business, who contribute funds but do not take part in day-to-day operations. A limited partner is only liable for the amount of funds he or she invested in the business; once those funds are paid out, the limited partner has no additional liability in relation to the activities of the partnership.

A partnership is typically terminated through a winding up process, where the partnership collects all funds due to it from customers, pays off creditors, terminates any other liabilities, and pays any remaining funds to the partners in the business.

In the following sections, our primary topic is an exploration of the different accounting scenarios that an accountant might face when dealing with partnership transactions.

## Structure of Accounts

Each partner has a separate *capital account*. This is used by partnerships to track the net investment balance of the partners from the perspective of the business. In essence, the capital account contains the transactions noted in the following table.

**Capital Account Transactions**

|   | Beginning balance in the capital account |
|---|---|
| + | Investments made by the partner |
| + | Subsequent profits of the partnership |
| - | Subsequent losses of the partnership |
| - | Subsequent draws paid to the partner |
| = | Ending balance in the capital account |

The balance in a capital account is usually a credit balance, since this is an equity account, and all equity accounts have a natural credit balance. However, the amount of losses and draws can sometimes shift the account balance into debit territory. It is usually only possible for the account to have a debit balance if the partnership has received debt funding to offset the loss of capital.

Distributions to partners may be extracted directly from their capital accounts, or they may first be recorded in a *drawing account*, which is a temporary account whose balance is later shifted into the capital account. Once the drawing account balance is shifted to the capital account, the drawing account contains a zero balance to begin the next fiscal year.

Each partner may also have a *loan account*. This account is used to record loans associated with a partner. The account is used for either of the following loan arrangements:

- Funds borrowed by the partnership from a partner
- Funds borrowed by a partner from the partnership

Capital accounts replace the equity accounts normally found in the chart of accounts of a corporation. Thus, there is no common stock account or additional paid-in capital account in the general ledger of a partnership.

## Timing Issues

Profits and losses are not assigned to partner capital accounts on a continual basis. Instead, up to a year may pass before there is a *break period*, when these assignments are made. There may be more than one break period in a year (such as quarterly). However, each additional break period requires more work by the accountant to allocate profits and losses, so the number should be minimized unless there is a demonstrated benefit associated with more frequent assignments.

A major concern for a partner is the beginning balance in the capital account. Depending on the terms of the partnership agreement, the allocation of profits and losses to partner capital accounts is based on the *beginning* balance. Consequently, if a partner makes an investment in a partnership partway through the fiscal year, the amount of this investment may not be included in the calculation of profit and loss allocations – it depends on the terms of the partnership agreement.

The same issue relates to draws paid to a partner. Ideally, draws should be made after profits and losses have been allocated to partners. Otherwise, the amount of a draw even a few days before a break period might count as a reduction in the beginning balance of the capital account, which reduces the amount of profits or losses allocated to the partner. Again, the nature of this calculation depends on the terms of the partnership agreement.

## Partnership Recordkeeping

A partnership is supposed to maintain its own accounting records. This is called the *business entity concept*, which states that the transactions associated with a business must be separately recorded from those of its owners or other businesses. Doing so requires the use of separate accounting records for the partnership that completely exclude the assets and liabilities of the partners. Otherwise, the records of multiple entities would be intermingled, making it quite difficult to discern the financial results of the partnership. A clean split between the records of the partners and a partnership allows the following to occur:

- The calculation of profits and losses, which can then be allocated to the partners' capital accounts.
- The amounts of payouts that can be issued to the partners in the event of a liquidation of the partnership.
- A set of financial records that can be successfully audited.

An appropriately detailed level of recordkeeping requires the accountant to maintain a separate chart of accounts for the partnership and a general ledger in which all transactions are recorded, and to periodically issue a complete set of financial statements that reveal the financial results, position, and cash flows of the partnership.

## The Essential Accounting for Partnerships

There are several distinct transactions associated with a partnership that are not found in other types of business organizations. These transactions are described in the following sub-sections.

### Contribution of Funds

When a partner invests funds in a partnership, the transaction involves a debit to the cash account and a credit to a separate capital account. A capital account records the balance of the investments from and distributions to a partner. To avoid the commingling of information, it is customary to have a separate capital account for each partner.

### Contribution of Other than Funds

When a partner invests some other asset than cash in a partnership, the transaction involves a debit to whatever asset account most closely reflects the nature of the contribution, and a credit to the partner's capital account. The valuation assigned to this transaction is the market value of the contributed asset. If the contributed asset is a fixed asset, the partnership will begin to depreciate it.

---

**EXAMPLE**

The Aquarius Partnership is formed by Holly Davis and India Ermine. Ms. Davis contributes $90,000 in cash, while Ms. Ermine contributes land with a fair value of $50,000 and a building with a fair value of $120,000. The following journal entry is used to record both contributions to the partnership:

|  | Debit | Credit |
|---|---|---|
| Cash | $90,000 | |
|     Capital account – Davis | | $90,000 |
| Fixed assets - land | 50,000 | |
| Fixed assets - buildings | 120,000 | |
|     Capital account – Ermine | | 170,000 |

If the building contributed to the partnership by Ms. Ermine had also been encumbered by a $60,000 mortgage, then the entry would be somewhat different, with the partnership taking on the mortgage liability. The altered entry for Ms. Ermine's contribution is as follows:

|  | Debit | Credit |
|---|---|---|
| Fixed assets - land | 50,000 | |
| Fixed assets - buildings | 120,000 | |
|     Mortgage liability | | 60,000 |
|     Capital account – Ermine | | 110,000 |

Now that Ms. Ermine has contributed the land and building to the partnership, she has no further *individual* right to these assets, because they now belong to the partnership.

---

## Salaries and Salary Allowances

A partnership agreement may state that the partners are to be paid a salary or salary allowance. There may be substantial differences in the salaries awarded to each partner; this is intended to reflect the time spent by certain partners in running the business. Thus, a general partner might be awarded a salary of $100,000, while a passive investor is awarded no salary at all.

These payments are not accounted for as expenses of the business, but rather as part of the calculation used to split net income among the partners. This usually means that each partner estimates his or her share of year-end net income, and withdraws it as a salary allowance over the course of the year, so that the actual distribution at year-end is minimal.

## Interest on Capital Balances

When some partners have contributed a disproportionate amount of assets to a partnership, they may want to be compensated for this contribution by being paid interest on the opening capital balance. This interest payment typically applies to all of the partners, but because some partners have a larger opening balance, the result is a disproportionate distribution of earnings among the partners.

This interest payment does not typically appear in the financial statements of the partnership. Instead, it is simply an additional means by which profits are allocated to the partners. Therefore, the effect of the arrangement appears in the year-end change in capital account balances.

**EXAMPLE**

Arlene, Henry, and Jessica agree to form a partnership. Arlene and Henry have very little cash to contribute, but agree to provide the bulk of the work to run the partnership. Jessica contributes $100,000 to the arrangement, under the provision that the partnership pays out 10% interest on the opening capital balance. The residual profits are paid out in thirds to the partners. In the first year of operation, the partnership earns $62,000. This results in the following allocation to the various partner capital accounts:

|  | Arlene | Henry | Jessica | Total |
|---|---|---|---|---|
| Beginning capital balance | $5,000 | $5,000 | $100,000 | $110,000 |
| Interest payout | 500 | 500 | 10,000 | 11,000 |
| Residual allocation | 17,000 | 17,000 | 17,000 | 51,000 |
| Total payout | $17,500 | $17,500 | $27,000 | $62,000 |

The interest in the example was based on beginning capital account balances, but that is not a mandatory requirement for the calculation. Interest could instead be calculated based on the ending balances, or a weighted average of the balances through the reporting period.

## Withdrawal of Funds

When a partner extracts funds from a business, it involves a credit to the cash account and a debit to the partner's capital account.

## Withdrawal of Assets

When a partner extracts assets other than cash from a business, it involves a credit to the account in which the asset was recorded, and a debit to the partner's capital account. Withdrawals are allowable up to the level of each partner's capital account balance.

## Allocation of Profit or Loss

When a partnership closes its books for a fiscal year, the net profit or loss for the year is summarized in a temporary equity account called the *income summary* account. This profit or loss is then allocated to the capital accounts of each partner based on their proportional ownership interests in the business (or as specified otherwise in the partnership agreement). For example, if there is a profit in the income summary account, then the allocation is a debit to the income summary account and a credit to each capital account.

**EXAMPLE**

Abby, Becky, and Candace are equal partners in ABC Remodeling. The most recent fiscal year has just been concluded, resulting in $45,000 of profit. Each partner will be allocated $15,000 (calculated as $45,000 ÷ 3 partners). The journal entry that records this profit allocation is:

|  | Debit | Credit |
|---|---|---|
| Income summary | $45,000 |  |
| Capital account – Abby |  | $15,000 |
| Capital account – Becky |  | 15,000 |
| Capital account – Candace |  | 15,000 |

**EXAMPLE**

In a different scenario, the profit split stated in the partnership agreement is 50% for Abby, 30% for Becky, and 20% for Candace. Assume the same profits as in the preceding example. This results in a profit allocation of $22,500 to Abby, $13,500 to Becky, and $9,000 to Candace. The journal entry that records this profit allocation is:

|  | Debit | Credit |
|---|---|---|
| Income summary | $45,000 | |
| Capital account – Abby | | $22,500 |
| Capital account – Becky | | 13,500 |
| Capital account – Candace | | 9,000 |

**EXAMPLE**

In a different scenario, the partnership agreement states that Abby, Becky, and Candace will receive salaries of $18,000, $12,000, and $6,000, respectively, after which all remaining profits will be split equally. Assume the same profits as in the preceding example. This results in the following calculation:

|  | Abby | Becky | Candace | Total |
|---|---|---|---|---|
| Salaries paid | $18,000 | $12,000 | $6,000 | $36,000 |
| Residual allocation | 3,000 | 3,000 | 3,000 | 9,000 |
| Total payout | $21,000 | $15,000 | $9,000 | $45,000 |

The journal entry that records this profit allocation is:

|  | Debit | Credit |
|---|---|---|
| Income summary | $45,000 | |
| Capital account – Abby | | $21,000 |
| Capital account – Becky | | 15,000 |
| Capital account – Candace | | 9,000 |

**EXAMPLE**

In a slight variation on the immediately preceding scenario, ABC Remodeling earns a profit of just $30,000, while the partnership agreement still states that Abby, Becky, and Candace will receive salaries of $18,000, $12,000, and $6,000, respectively, after which all remaining profits will be split equally. This means there will be a loss after salaries are deducted from the profit, so the remaining loss is allocated equally among the partners. This results in the following calculation:

|  | Abby | Becky | Candace | Total |
|---|---|---|---|---|
| Salaries paid | $18,000 | $12,000 | $6,000 | $36,000 |
| Residual allocation | -2,000 | -2,000 | -2,000 | -6,000 |
| Total payout | $16,000 | $10,000 | $4,000 | $30,000 |

The journal entry that records this profit allocation is:

|  | Debit | Credit |
|---|---|---|
| Income summary | $30,000 |  |
| Capital account – Abby |  | $16,000 |
| Capital account – Becky |  | 10,000 |
| Capital account – Candace |  | 4,000 |

Conversely, if there is a loss in the income summary account, then the allocation is a credit to the income summary account and a debit to each capital account.

The allocation of a profit to a partner's capital account does not necessarily mean that the partner is paid that same amount in cash. The cash remains in the partnership until the partner chooses to withdraw it.

### Income Taxes

Each partner pays income taxes on his or her share of the partnership's net income. The amount of these taxes paid is irrespective of the amount of cash they actually withdraw from the business. For example, a partner is allocated $50,000 of profit from a partnership and owes income taxes on the entire amount, despite not taking a cash draw from the partnership. In this case, the partner pays the income tax from her own resources.

### Tax Reporting

In the United States, a partnership must issue a Schedule K-1 to each of its partners at the end of its tax year. This schedule contains the amount of profit or loss allocated to each partner, and which the partners use in their reporting of personal income earned.

## Case Study for Standard Partnership Operations

In this section, we cover a series of transactions relating to a partnership, with the intent of showing how an accountant might deal with a full range of issues.

Three people form the Pantheon Partnership. They are Mr. Beadles, Ms. Carpenter, and Mr. Demario. The initial contributions made to the partnership are:

- Mr. Beadles contributes a $45,000 account receivable, for which the likelihood of collection is considered excellent.
- Ms. Carpenter contributes $54,000 of cash.
- Mr. Demario contributes a building that has a fair market value of $81,000.

There is no partnership agreement, so the presumption is that profits will be distributed based on the relative proportion of assets that each person has contributed to the partnership. That calculation is:

| Partner | Contribution Amount | Proportion of Contribution |
|---|---|---|
| Mr. Beadles | $45,000 | 25% |
| Ms. Carpenter | 54,000 | 30% |
| Mr. Demario | 81,000 | 45% |
| Total | $180,000 | 100% |

The first year of operations proves to be a successful one, with the partnership earning $200,000 on sales of $1,000,000. At the end of the fiscal year, the partnership's accountant clears out the revenue and expense accounts with the following entry, which shifts the profit into the income summary account:

| | Debit | Credit |
|---|---|---|
| Revenue | $1,000,000 | |
| Expenses (several accounts) | | $800,000 |
| Income summary | | 200,000 |

The funds are shifted from the income summary account to the individual capital accounts using the preceding contribution proportions, as noted in the following journal entry:

| | Debit | Credit |
|---|---|---|
| Income summary | $200,000 | |
| Capital account – Beadles | | $50,000 |
| Capital account – Carpenter | | 60,000 |
| Capital account – Demario | | 90,000 |

After some discussion, the partners mutually agree to leave $40,000 of the profit in the company, and remove the remaining amounts as draws from their capital accounts. However, Mr. Demario has a reduced need for cash, so he only draws $65,000, while Mr. Beadles draws $35,000 and Ms. Carpenter draws the full $60,000. This results in the following ending balances in their capital accounts:

**Statement of Partners' Capital**

| | Beadles | Carpenter | Demario | Totals |
|---|---|---|---|---|
| Initial investment | $45,000 | $54,000 | $81,000 | $180,000 |
| + Net income | 50,000 | 60,000 | 90,000 | 200,000 |
| - Draws | 35,000 | 60,000 | 65,000 | 160,000 |
| Ending balance | $60,000 | $54,000 | $106,000 | $220,000 |
| Percent ownership | 27.3% | 24.5% | 48.2% | 100% |

Note that the percentages of ownership have changed by the end of the year. This is because the amount drawn from the partnership by each partner did not necessarily match each person's allocated share of profits. When this is the case, and the partnership agreement does not state how profits shall be divided, then by default the latest ownership percentage will drive the amount of profit allocated to each person in the next fiscal year.

## Admission of a New Partner to the Partnership

A new partner may be admitted to a partnership from time to time. This is most likely to involve an investment by the new partner of additional assets in the business, though it is possible that the partner could be acquiring a portion of the interests of the existing partners. In the latter case, a portion of the capital balance stated in the balance sheet for an existing partner is shifted into a new capital balance line item for the new partner, as described in the following example.

**EXAMPLE**

Aldus Smith and Bixby Jones formed a partnership several years ago. Smith currently has a capital balance of $80,000, while Jones has a balance of $60,000, for a total equity balance of $140,000. Allison Ware wants to join the partnership, and does so by purchasing half the interests of Smith and Jones, paying $40,000 to Smith and $30,000 to Jones. This results in the following revised equity balance for the partnership:

| | |
|---|---|
| Smith capital balance | $40,000 |
| Jones capital balance | 30,000 |
| Ware capital balance | 70,000 |
| Total | $140,000 |

The journal entry used to document this change is:

| | Debit | Credit |
|---|---|---|
| Capital account – Smith | $40,000 | |
| Capital account – Jones | 30,000 | |
| Capital account – Ware | | $70,000 |

Thus, the total capital balance invested in the partnership has not changed; it has instead been redistributed among the partners. The key element in the transaction is the agreement to shift ownership interests, not the amount of money paid.

**EXAMPLE**

The same conditions apply, except that Ms. Ware pays a 20% premium to the two existing partners for half of their ownership interests in the partnership. This has no impact on the preceding table stating the revised capital balances, since the premium was paid directly to the original partners, not to the partnership.

Rather than buying out existing interests, a new partner could invest additional assets in the business. For example, a partner could agree to invest $50,000 in exchange for a 25% interest in a partnership. Further, assume that the capital currently invested in the partnership is $160,000. This means that the total amount invested will be $210,000. However, the new partner will be receiving a 25% interest in the partnership, and $50,000 divided by $210,000 is only a 23.8% share. A 25% share of $210,000 is $52,500, so $2,500 must be reallocated from the existing partner accounts to the account of the new partner. This means that the resulting capital account balances will be:

| | Ending Capital Balance | Proportion |
|---|---|---|
| Existing capital balances | $157,500 | 75% |
| New partner capital balance | 52,500 | 25% |
| Total ending capital balance | $210,000 | 100% |

The journal entry required to record this transaction (assuming just one other capital account) is:

| | Debit | Credit |
|---|---|---|
| Cash | $50,000 | |
| Capital account – Existing partners | 2,500 | |
| Capital account – New partner | | $52,500 |

We can also assume the reverse situation, where the new partner is investing more assets into a partnership than will be reflected in the resulting ownership percentage. For example, assume the partner from the last example is still investing $50,000, but in exchange for just a 20% interest in the partnership. The capital currently invested in the partnership is still $160,000, so the total amount invested is still $210,000. However, with the new partner only receiving a 20% interest in the partnership, a 20% share of $210,000 is only $42,000. We deal with this disparity by allocating $8,000 from the new partner's capital account to the existing partner accounts. This means that the capital account balances will be:

| | Ending Capital Balance | Proportion |
|---|---|---|
| Existing capital balances | $168,000 | 80% |
| New partner capital balance | 42,000 | 20% |
| Total ending capital balance | $210,000 | 100% |

The journal entry to record this transaction is:

| | Debit | Credit |
|---|---|---|
| Cash | $50,000 | |
| Capital account – Existing partners | | $8,000 |
| Capital account – New partner | | 42,000 |

## Retirement of a Partner

When a partner retires, the baseline assumption is that the person is paid the amount of her ending capital balance. For example, if a partner has $100,000 in her ending capital account and retires, the transaction could be a simple payment of $100,000 to the outgoing partner, using the following entry:

|  | Debit | Credit |
|---|---|---|
| Capital account – [name of partner] | $100,000 |  |
| Cash |  | $100,000 |

However, a simple payout is not necessarily what happens. A possible scenario is that the partnership agreement specifies that some larger amount be paid. For example, perhaps someone designated as a senior partner receives 10% more than her ending capital balance. When such an overage is paid out, the excess amount is taken from the other partners' capital accounts in proportion to their profit and loss sharing ratios. The concept is dealt with in the following example.

**EXAMPLE**

Smith, Jones, and Williams are partners. Their ending capital account balances are as follows:

|  | Ending Balance | Proportion |
|---|---|---|
| Smith capital account | $300,000 | 30% |
| Jones capital account | 500,000 | 50% |
| Williams capital account | 200,000 | 20% |
|  | $1,000,000 | 100% |

The partnership agreement states that the designated senior partner (Smith) will receive a 10% premium upon his retirement. The 10% premium is $30,000, and is taken from the capital accounts of Jones and Williams in proportion to their ownership interests. Without Smith, Jones has a 71.4% interest (calculated as $500,000 ÷ $700,000), and Williams has a 28.6% interest (calculated as $200,000 ÷ $700,000). Based on these percentages, the Jones capital account is reduced by $21,420 (calculated as $30,000 × 71.4%) and the Williams account is reduced by $8,580 (calculated as $30,000 × 28.6%).

Smith then retires, taking $330,000 of assets from the business. This results in the following ending post-retirement capital accounts:

|  | Ending Balance | Proportion |
|---|---|---|
| Jones capital account | $478,580 | 71.4% |
| Williams capital account | 191,420 | 28.6% |
|  | $670,000 | 100.0% |

# Liquidation of a Partnership

The partners in a partnership may mutually decide to shut down the business, liquidating all assets, settling obligations, and paying the partners any residual amounts remaining. In partnership accounting, the assumption is that there will be a positive amount remaining after all assets have been liquidated and liabilities settled, so that the central concern is how to pay the partners. There are several variations on the liquidation concept, which are explored in the following sub-sections.

## Basic Liquidation Process

The basic arrangement is that all assets are first sold, the resulting cash is used to pay off all obligations, and the remaining cash is apportioned to the partners based on their profit and loss sharing ratio. The baseline concept appears in the following example.

### EXAMPLE

Able, Baker, and Charlie have been partners for the last 20 years, and decide to close down their business as of the end of the current calendar year. It is now October 31. The following highly summarized balance sheet shows the financial position of the partnership as of October 31:

ABC Partnership
Balance Sheet
as of 10/31/20X1

| **Assets** | | **Liabilities** | |
|---|---|---|---|
| Cash | $10,000 | Liabilities | $20,000 |
| Other assets | 110,000 | | |
| | | **Partners' Equity** | |
| | | Able capital | 20,000 |
| | | Baker capital | 30,000 |
| | | Charlie capital | 50,000 |
| | $120,000 | | $120,000 |

During November and December, the partners sell the other assets, which generate $90,000 in cash and a $20,000 loss (which is allocated to the partners). The total cash balance is then $100,000, which is used to pay off the $20,000 of liabilities, leaving $80,000 for final distribution to the partners. These account balances and activities are summarized in a liquidation schedule, which appears next. The three partners divide all profits and losses using a ratio of 20% for Able, 30% for Baker, and 50% for Charlie.

ABC Partnership
Liquidation Schedule

| | Cash | Assets | Liabilities | Able | Baker | Charlie |
|---|---|---|---|---|---|---|
| Beginning balances | $10,000 | $110,000 | $20,000 | $20,000 | $30,000 | $50,000 |
| Asset sale and loss distribution | +90,000 | -110,000 | -- | -4,000 | -6,000 | -10,000 |
| Payment to clear liabilities | -20,000 | -- | -20,000 | -- | -- | -- |
| Balances | 80,000 | 0 | 0 | 16,000 | 24,000 | 40,000 |
| Final payouts to partners | -80,000 | -- | -- | -16,000 | -24,000 | -40,000 |
| Ending balances | $0 | $0 | $0 | $0 | $0 | $0 |

The preceding discussion has assumed that a liquidation transaction uses the normal profit and loss sharing ratio specified or implied in the partnership agreement. It is also possible that a different liquidation ratio is specified in the partnership agreement. If so, this ratio is used instead of the normal ratio.

## Partner Negative Account Balance

What about a partnership liquidation in which a partner has a negative capital account balance? This is most likely to happen when a capital account has a small positive balance, but then assets are liquidated at a loss, with the loss being allocated to the various partner accounts. The result is a negative balance. The partner has an obligation to pay the partnership the amount of this negative balance in an amount sufficient to bring his account balance back up to zero. Otherwise, the other partners are funding the negative account balance.

When a partnership is being liquidated, the relations between the partners are not always amiable (and may have triggered the liquidation), so convincing a negative-balance partner to put funds back into the partnership could be a difficult chore. If so, the other partners will have to absorb the negative amount in the proportions of their profit and loss allocation ratio. After the liquidation is complete, these other partners have the option of pursuing the errant partner in court to recover their lost funds. The situation is described in the following example.

---

### EXAMPLE

Partners Larry, Curly and Mo are winding up their partnership. All assets have been liquidated and all obligations have been settled, resulting in the following capital account balances and ending cash balance:

|  | Debit | Credit |
|---|---|---|
| Cash | $50,000 | |
| Capital account – Mo | 10,000 | |
| Capital account – Larry | | $30,000 |
| Capital account – Curly | | 30,000 |

Mo refuses to pay his $10,000 negative balance back to the partnership, so Larry and Curly must absorb the balance equally, using the following entry:

|  | Debit | Credit |
|---|---|---|
| Capital account – Larry | $5,000 | |
| Capital account – Curly | 5,000 | |
| Capital account – Mo | | $10,000 |

The final distribution of cash to the partners does not include Mo, since his capital account balance is now zero. Instead, the $50,000 of cash is distributed evenly to Larry and Curly.

---

## Partner Loans

A partner may have issued a loan to a partnership. If so, the loan obligation must be paid off as part of the partnership liquidation process *after* liabilities owed to third parties and *before* the final distribution of cash to the partners.

When a partner's capital account is negative and the partner has loaned money to the partnership, it makes little sense to first have the partner pay funds to the partnership to offset the negative account balance, and then the partnership pays the partner the amount of the outstanding loan. Instead, the loan amount can be offset against the balance in the negative capital account. The concept is expanded upon in the following example.

---

**EXAMPLE**

The partners of XYZ Partnership decide to liquidate the business. The balance sheet of the partnership at the time of the decision is as follows:

XYZ Partnership
Balance Sheet
as of 10/31/20X3

| Assets | | Liabilities | |
|---|---|---|---|
| Cash | $5,000 | Liabilities | $20,000 |
| Other assets | 95,000 | Loan from Xavier | 25,000 |
| | | **Partners' Equity** | |
| | | Xavier capital | 2,000 |
| | | Yarrow capital | 23,000 |
| | | Zildjian capital | 30,000 |
| | $100,000 | | $100,000 |

The partnership agreement states that the three partners share equally in all profits and losses. The agreement also states that all liquidation payouts will be apportioned based on ending capital balances. All non-cash assets are liquidated for $77,000, resulting in an $18,000 loss that is apportioned equally among the three partners. The loss apportionment results in the following capital accounts:

| Xavier capital | -$4,000 |
|---|---|
| Yarrow capital | 17,000 |
| Zildjian capital | 24,000 |
| | $37,000 |

Xavier is unable to pay his $4,000 negative capital account balance back to the partnership. However, he had previously loaned $25,000 to the partnership, as stated earlier in the partnership's balance sheet. The loan amount can be offset against his negative account balance. The result is the following liquidation schedule for the partnership:

XYZ Partnership
Liquidation Schedule

| | Cash | Assets | Liabilities | Loan | Xavier | Yarrow | Zildjian |
|---|---|---|---|---|---|---|---|
| Beginning balances | $5,000 | $95,000 | $20,000 | $25,000 | $2,000 | $23,000 | $30,000 |
| Asset sale and loss distribution | +77,000 | -95,000 | -- | -- | -6,000 | -6,000 | -6,000 |
| Payment to clear liabilities | -20,000 | -- | -20,000 | -- | -- | -- | -- |
| Payment to clear loan | -21,000 | -- | -- | -25,000 | +4,000 | -- | -- |
| Balances | 41,000 | 0 | 0 | 0 | 0 | 17,000 | 24,000 |
| Final payouts to partners | -41,000 | -- | -- | -- | -- | -17,000 | -24,000 |
| Ending balances | $0 | $0 | $0 | $0 | $0 | $0 | $0 |

## Liquidations with Interim Payments

Thus far, we have implied that partners can liquidate a business in short order, selling off assets and settling obligations in a month or two. The reality is somewhat different, typically requiring many more months to completely wrap up the affairs of the organization. When it takes a long time to liquidate, the partners may demand that cash payouts be made to them at reasonable intervals during the liquidation process, as cash becomes available. This is not an issue, as long as the following criteria have been met:

- All obligations have been settled; or
- A sufficient reserve has been set aside to settle the obligations; and
- There is no risk of overpaying a partner.

The last risk is a key one, since it can be quite difficult to persuade a partner to return an overpayment. To meet these criteria, the accountant creates an interim liquidation schedule that generates the amounts that can safely be paid to partners. The key assumptions incorporated into this schedule are:

- That all assets not yet liquidated will not bring in any additional cash; and
- That any capital account with a negative balance will be allocated to those partners with a positive balance.

The prudent accountant will also withhold a certain amount of funds to cover any liabilities that have not yet been uncovered. This withholding (if any) is treated as a loss on the liquidation of assets on the liquidation schedule, and is allocated to the partners.

The process for determining the safe amount of interim payments is described in the following example.

### EXAMPLE

The partners of FGH partnership decide to shut down the business by the end of the calendar year. It is currently September 30, 20X2. The partnership's balance sheet on this date is:

FGH Partnership
Balance Sheet
as of 9/30/20X2

| Assets | | Liabilities | |
|---|---|---|---|
| Cash | $4,000 | Liabilities | $35,000 |
| Other assets | 146,000 | | |
| | | **Partners' Equity** | |
| | | Fallow capital | 25,000 |
| | | Grubb capital | 30,000 |
| | | Hinds capital | 60,000 |
| | $150,000 | | $150,000 |

By the end of October, the partnership has liquidated $100,000 of the other assets, absorbing an $18,000 loss in the process. Thus, $100,000 of assets have been liquidated in exchange for $82,000 of cash. The partners have used $30,000 of the cash to pay down the partnership's obligations, leaving $5,000 still to be paid. The expectation is for no additional funds to be received from the sale of assets (meaning that the total loss on liquidation of the other assets is actually $64,000), and there is no indication that an additional reserve will be needed to pay for unrecognized liabilities.

Therefore, at the end of October, the following liquidation schedule shows the maximum amount of cash that can be paid to the partners:

FGH Partnership
Interim Liquidation Schedule

| | Cash | Assets | Liabilities | Fallow | Grubb | Hinds |
|---|---|---|---|---|---|---|
| Beginning balances | $4,000 | $146,000 | $35,000 | $25,000 | $30,000 | $60,000 |
| Asset sale and loss distribution | +82,000 | -146,000 | -- | -13,913* | -16,696* | -33,391* |
| Payment to clear liabilities | -30,000 | -- | -30,000 | -- | -- | -- |
| Balances | 56,000 | 0 | 5,000 | 11,087 | 13,304 | 26,609 |
| Interim payouts to partners | -51,000 | -- | -- | -11,087 | -13,304 | -26,609 |
| Ending balances | $5,000 | $0 | $5,000 | $0 | $0 | $0 |

* Allocated proportionally, based on preliminary ending capital account balances.

The interim schedule shows that $51,000 of the $56,000 cash balance can be paid out to the partners. The remaining $5,000 is to be used to pay down the remaining liabilities still appearing on the balance sheet.

If any additional cash is realized from the $46,000 of other assets that are still on the books of the partnership, this amount will be paid out to the partners based on their respective capital account balances prior to the interim payout.

## Summary

The accounting for a business that has been organized as a partnership does not really vary that much from the accounting used for any other type of organization. The accounting standards mandated by the relevant accounting framework will not vary, just because a partnership has a different organizational structure.

The key accounting difference between the accounting for a partnership and the more common corporation is in the treatment of equity. A partnership records equity in the form of capital accounts for each partner, along with the contributions, draws, and loans related to each partner. This information is needed when determining how to allocate the profits and losses of the partnership to the individual partners, as well as when deciding how to liquidate the entity and return any residual funds to the partners.

An additional difference between a partnership and a corporation is that compensation paid to the partners is considered a drawdown of their capital balances, and so does not appear as an expense on the income statement of the entity. These payments will appear as expenses in the income statement of a corporation.

## Review Questions

1. When a partnership is being terminated, interim payments can be made to the partners, as long as:
    a. The partnership withholds the appropriate amount of income taxes from the interim payments
    b. Partners are willing to pay back any overpayments made to them
    c. Obligations will be settled at a later date
    d. The calculation assumption is made that all assets not yet liquidated will not bring in any additional cash

2. A capital account is designed to:
    a. Keep track of the stock holdings of each partner
    b. Keep track of the securities held by a partnership
    c. Track the net investment balance of each partner
    d. Track all partnership interests bought back from partners

3. A salary paid to a partner is accounted for as:
    a. Part of the calculation used to split net income among the partners
    b. Taxable expenses of the partnership
    c. A reduction of partnership liabilities
    d. A noncash withdrawal of funds

4. Income taxes on partnership income are paid:
    a. On a delayed basis
    b. By the individual partners
    c. By the partnership, using withholding from partner paychecks
    d. When the Form K-1 is issued to the government

5. When a partner retires, the baseline assumption is that the partner:
    a. Continues to invest in the business
    b. Waits for final liquidation of the business to be paid
    c. Is paid the amount of her ending capital balance
    d. Is loaned the amount of her ending capital balance

6. The liquidation of a partnership involves the following steps, except for:
    a. Payment of all cash proceeds to the court handling the case
    b. Liquidation of all assets
    c. Payment of all remaining obligations
    d. Paying the partners any residual cash amounts remaining

# Chapter 23
# Ethical Frameworks in Accounting

## Introduction

The emphasis in accounting classes is primarily on the recordation of accounting transactions and reporting financial results in accordance with the applicable accounting standards. From an ethical perspective, this approach essentially implies that ethical considerations are baked into the accounting standards, so all the accountant has to do is follow the rules. However, there have been many accounting scandals over the years in which accountants have actively bent the rules in order to report fraudulent financial results. Clearly, the accountant requires separate training in ethical conduct, which can provide guidance in compiling financial results that are sufficiently accurate that the public's trust in the accounting profession will be preserved.

In this chapter, we examine the nature of ethics and how the concept can be applied to the resolution of every-day business scenarios.

## The Nature of Ethics

*Ethics* refers to the moral principles that guide a person's behavior. Ethics act as a benchmark for deciding whether an action or decision is good or bad. Accountants find that they routinely have to make decisions that require ethical judgments, since many of their decisions can potentially harm others.

A person typically takes on ethical positions early in life, due to the influence of family, colleagues, schooling, and religious institutions. These influences tend to be the consensus behavior of the local community. There are many ethical positions that a person can take in varying degrees. For example:

- Everyone is entitled to privacy.
- Everyone should be treated fairly.
- One should be honest in dealings with others.
- One should take a course of action that does the least harm to others.
- One should treat others as one would want to be treated.

The exact mix of positions followed will depend on the individual – we do not all possess exactly the same standards. This also means that people may use different approaches to developing a reasoned judgment for how to deal with an ethically challenging situation.

Whatever the mix of ethical positions may be, a person is more likely to follow it when there are clear advantages to doing so. For example, having a strong code of ethics allows a businessperson to enjoy a higher level of customer and employee loyalty and a stronger public reputation, while also reducing the probability of being targeted by lawsuits.

## Accounting Governance

The accounting profession is largely self-governing. The Financial Accounting Standards Board (FASB) creates accounting standards for use within the Generally Accepted Accounting Principles (GAAP) framework. These accounting standards are recognized by the Securities and Exchange Commission (SEC) as being authoritative, and so must be followed by publicly-held companies that file reports with the SEC. The FASB is structured as a non-profit private entity; it is not an extension of any government. It is overseen by the Financial Accounting Foundation (FAF). The board of trustees of the FAF is comprised of several organizations interested in financial reporting, including the American Accounting Association, the AICPA, and the Securities Industry and Financial Markets Association.

The FAF also oversees and funds the Governmental Accounting Standards Board (GASB), which creates accounting standards that are used by government entities to record accounting transactions and produce financial statements. These standards are considered a sub-set of GAAP. By following these standards, governments are producing reports that provide a consistent view of their financial positions to taxpayers and other citizen groups, the holders of government bonds, and legislators.

## Codes of Professional Conduct

The accountant may be subject to one or more codes of professional conduct. One is promulgated by the American Institute of Certified Public Accountants (AICPA), which represents the interests of Certified Public Accountants within the United States. The AICPA's ethical standards are codified into the AICPA Code of Professional Conduct. This code of conduct applies to any CPA who is a member of the AICPA, irrespective of whether they work as public accountants or in other capacities, such as financial planning, management consulting, or internal auditing. In addition, each individual state within the United States has a board of accountancy that directly regulates all CPAs certified with it; these boards of accountancy have usually adopted the AICPA code of conduct, sometimes with modifications, and mandates that their CPAs follow this code. When ethics breaches occur, the state boards of accountancy can suspend or revoke the licenses of the CPAs within their jurisdictions. Given the broad rate of adoption of the AICPA Code of Professional Conduct, it can reasonably be considered the guiding standard of ethical conduct for all accountants within the United States, even if they are not certified public accountants.

Another code of professional conduct is promulgated by the International Federation of Accountants (IFAC). The IFAC is:

> .".…the global organization for the accountancy profession dedicated to serving the public interest by strengthening the profession and contributing to the development of strong international economies."

The IFAC represents nearly three million accountants through the direct membership of professional accounting societies in 130 countries. The IFAC handed off the job of devising a code of ethics to the International Ethics Standards Board for Accountants (located at www.ethicsboard.org), which describes its task as developing and issuing ethical standards for professional accountants worldwide. The Board also provides implementation support, promotes good ethical practices, and supports international debate on ethical issues.

The content of these two codes of professional conduct are substantially the same, so the typical accountant may consider the contents of either one to apply to him or her.

There are other codes of conduct that may be applicable to a CPA's specific situation. For example, the AICPA Code of Professional Conduct states that a CPA should also consult the following, depending on the circumstances:

- The ethical requirements of the applicable state CPA society and state board of accountancy
- The Securities and Exchange Commission
- The Public Company Accounting Oversight Board
- The Government Accountability Office
- The Department of Labor
- Federal, state and local taxing authorities
- Any other body that regulates a CPA who performs professional services for an organization when the CPA or the organization is subject to the rules and regulations of that regulatory body

## The AICPA Code of Professional Conduct

The AICPA Code of Professional Conduct contains a general principles section, followed by a series of rules, stating how CPAs are supposed to conduct themselves. The general principles section essentially provides a broad structure for the later discussion of more specific topics. The general principles are discussed next.

## Responsibilities

The responsibilities principle is as follows:

> In carrying out their responsibilities as professionals, members shall exercise sensitive professional and moral judgments in all their activities.

This principle points out that CPAs perform an essential role in society, and so are responsible to everyone who uses their services. CPAs should cooperate with each other to enhance the state of the accounting profession, maintain public confidence, and engage in the profession's responsibilities to govern itself.

## The Public Interest

The public interest principle is as follows:

> Members should accept the obligation to act in a way that will serve the public interest, honor the public trust, and demonstrate a commitment to professionalism.

This principle recognizes that the accounting profession must accept its responsibility to the public, which relies on the objectivity and integrity of CPAs to ensure that financial information is correct. CPAs are expected to offer services at a level of quality that demonstrates a high degree of professionalism. The public being served by accountants is substantial, including clients, creditors, lenders, governments, employers, and the investment community. Thus, the public interest is considered to be paramount, over the needs of the individual client. This means that the needs of the *reader* of financial statements are placed higher than the needs of the *issuer* of the statements, even though the issuer is paying the CPA for audit services. The same concept applies to a CPA engaged in tax services, whose primary duty is to the taxing entity, not the client; this concept means that the CPA should not advise clients to take untenable tax positions.

This view of serving the public interest is unusually broad when compared to other professions. For example, the legal profession holds that the attorney must serve the interests of the client above all else.

## Integrity

The integrity principle is as follows:

> To maintain and broaden public confidence, members should perform all professional responsibilities with the highest sense of integrity.

This principle focuses on *integrity*, which is defined as firm adherence to a code of moral values. Stated differently, integrity involves having a moral compass that does not waver. It is an essential character trait for anyone who wants to be recognized as a CPA, since public trust is derived from actions that exhibit a consistently high level of integrity. It is so important that the CPA must constantly compare her actions to alternatives that would be considered to show a higher level of integrity. Several examples of issues involving integrity are as follows:

- Being candid with clients regarding the correct course of action when discussing how to record an accounting transaction.
- Standing up to management pressure to take an action that is contrary to the best interests of the general public, such as issuing misleading financial statements.
- Following the spirit of an accounting standard, rather than supporting an accounting treatment that follows the rules but results in an outcome not intended by the writers of the standard. Thus, searching for loopholes in the accounting standards and tax regulations is not a good display of integrity.

In those cases in which there are no rules regarding the accounting treatment for a specific situation, the CPA should test possible decisions by asking whether a decision reflects what a person of integrity would do.

## Objectivity and Independence

The objectivity and independence principle is as follows:

> A member should maintain objectivity and be free of conflicts of interest in discharging professional responsibilities. A member in public practice should be independent in fact and appearance when providing auditing and other attestation services.

This principle partially focuses on *objectivity*, which is defined as the ability to formulate judgments based on observable phenomena while not being influenced by emotions or personal prejudices. A person with a high level of objectivity should be free of conflicts of interest.

The other element of this principle is *independence*, which is defined as freedom from the control, influence or support of others. Thus, a CPA should not enter into any relationships that might appear to impair his or her objectivity in providing services to clients.

It is not possible for a management accountant to have any independence, since this person has a sole employer, and depends on that entity for his or her livelihood. In this case, the accountant is expected to follow the objectivity and independence principle to the greatest extent possible, but it can be difficult to achieve from a practical perspective. The advice given by the Code of Conduct for people in this situation is:

> Regardless of service or capacity, members should protect the integrity of their work, maintain objectivity, and avoid any subordination of their judgment.

The principle mandates a higher standard for CPAs in public practice. These individuals need to continually assess their relationships with clients, as well as their responsibility to the public. A CPA providing auditing and other attestation services must ensure that she is independent in both fact and appearance. When providing all other services to clients, a CPA should strive to maintain objectivity and avoid any conflicts of interest.

## Due Care

The due care principle is as follows:

> A member should observe the profession's technical and ethical standards, strive continually to improve competence and the quality of services, and discharge professional responsibility to the best of the member's ability.

In essence, the Code mandates that a CPA not accept work unless she has an adequate level of expertise to discharge her professional responsibilities. The requisite amount of expertise can be gained through a combination of education and experience, including mastery of the knowledge needed to become a CPA and ongoing attention to professional improvement throughout one's career. If a CPA does not have an adequate level of expertise to complete an engagement, she should consult with other parties or delegate work to them in order to ensure that the client is properly served.

In addition, the Code requires that a CPA be diligent in discharging her responsibilities to clients and other parties. This means that the CPA should be thorough, observe the relevant technical and ethical standards, and render services in a timely manner. Further, the CPA should provide an adequate level of engagement planning and supervision for any professional activity.

<u>Scope and Nature of Services</u>

The scope and nature of services principle is as follows:

> A member in public practice should observe the Principles of the Code of Professional Conduct in determining the scope and nature of services to be provided.

The CPA must consider the preceding principles when deciding whether to provide services to clients. In some cases, following one of these principles could constrain a CPA from providing certain services to a client. To ensure that one is providing services within the constraints of these principles, one should do the following:

- Work in a CPA firm that has adequate internal quality control procedures;
- Determine whether the scope and nature of the services provided would create a conflict of interest; and
- Assess whether a proposed activity is consistent with one's role as a professional.

## Legal Requirements

Besides codes of professional conduct, the accountant needs to abide by any applicable laws. Laws represent baseline levels of behavior that people are expected to abide by. They are usually enacted only *after* incidents occur that society believes are improper, based on the consensus regarding what constitutes ethical behavior.

Society enforces the minimum standards outlined in its laws with specific penalties, such as five years in jail for engaging in fraud. Conversely, there are no explicit penalties for unethical behavior, other than the belief that something could have been done better.

There can be significant differences between compliance with the law and observing morally correct behavior. For example, there may be no specific law against paying suppliers several months late, but it is not ethical to abuse suppliers in this manner.

## The Universal Nature of Ethical Rules

Are the same ethical principles observed around the world, or are there regional differences? There are two viewpoints on the matter. *Ethical absolutism* holds that ethical rules are the same everywhere. As proof of ethical absolutism, consider that the United Nations unanimously passed the Universal Declaration of Human Rights, from which some of those rights are:

- Everyone has the right to life, liberty, and security of person.
- No one shall be held in slavery or servitude.
- No one shall be subjected to arbitrary arrest, detention, or exile.
- No one shall be arbitrarily deprived of his property.

However, this listing of human rights establishes only general principles, leaving considerable room for regional differences. *Ethical relativism* holds that ethics will change over time, and will vary based on many factors, such as the local religion, culture, and beliefs regarding the correct form of governance.

It is likely that both concepts are correct, where some basic ethical structures are considered to prevail everywhere, but beyond which there are many local differences on particular topics. For example, gender equality is vigorously pursued in the Scandinavian countries, while that is not the case in many other parts of the world. As another example, the right to privacy is a strongly held belief in Germany, where there are strict laws about the use by businesses of one's personal data. Conversely, the United States allows much more use of personal data by marketers. Or, consider a topic much closer to the accounting profession, which is the charging of interest on loaned money. Most countries consider a certain amount of interest to be reasonable, but also have usury laws to impose maximum caps on the amount of interest that can be charged – and those interest rate caps vary by state within the United States. At a more draconian level, many Islamic countries prohibit the charging of interest, no matter what the interest rate may be.

## Kohlberg's Stages of Moral Development

When confronted with a moral dilemma, the accountant may rely upon one of the theories pertaining to ethics. One is the stages of moral development theory, which was devised by Lawrence Kohlberg beginning in 1958 and expanded upon for many years thereafter, basing it on how people tend to justify their actions when confronted with moral dilemmas. His underlying thesis was that people go through six developmental stages in their moral reasoning, with each successive stage being more usable for responding to moral dilemmas. In all stages, the primary basis for a developmental stage is justice. A person advances through the various stages based on their training and life experiences.

Kohlberg devised six stages of moral development, which are grouped into three levels of morality. These levels are pre-conventional, conventional, and post-conventional morality. He held that moral behavior is more responsible, consistent and predictable for people in the higher levels of moral development. Further, once a person achieves a higher stage, it is quite rare for the person to regress, because each stage provides a more comprehensive and differentiated perspective than its predecessors.

### Pre-Conventional Level

The pre-conventional level of moral development is mostly found in children. Here, the judgment of a moral action is primarily based on the direct consequences that will be visited upon the individual – in other words, decisions are solely based on the impact on the person making the decision. The first stage of moral development is obedience and punishment driven, since the focus is on the direct consequences of an action to be taken. Thus, an action is considered to be morally wrong when the person is punished for doing it. For example, a child learns that he should not drink alcohol, because he is grounded for doing so. When the punishment associated with an action is more severe than usual, the action that triggered the punishment is considered to be unusually bad. This line of reasoning would keep a child from engaging in any activity that had direct negative consequences for him in the past.

The second stage of moral development is self-interest driven, where the decisions are based on whatever the person believes to be in his best interest, though without considering the impact on one's reputation or relationships with others. At this point, a person is almost entirely self-centered in making decisions, where concern for others is not a consideration unless doing so will trigger an action that helps the person. For example, a teenager steals lunch money from another student at school. Doing so increases his cash balance, but at the expense of the child who can no longer eat lunch.

When an adult has not passed beyond the pre-conventional level of moral development, workplace rules need to be clearly stated and rigidly enforced in order to ensure their compliance. Also, the high level of self-centering at this stage makes an adult quite unsuitable for a management position.

### Conventional Level

The conventional level of moral development can be found in both children and adults. Here, moral reasoning includes a comparison of actions taken to society's viewpoints on what is right or wrong, even when there are no consequences associated with following or not following those viewpoints. The main decision driver is a desire to please others. The third stage of moral development is driven by interpersonal accord and conformity, where the person is expected to conform to social standards. At this stage, the individual tries to live up to the expectations of others, because he has learned that being regarded as a good person provides him with benefits. A logical outcome is that the person begins to evaluate the consequences of an action in terms of the impact on his relationships with others. For example, a person might refrain from engaging in an illegal activity, because being caught would damage the reputation of his family.

The fourth stage of moral development is driven by maintenance of the social order; this means that the person is more concerned with obeying laws and social conventions, due to their importance in supporting a functioning society. At this stage, the person's concerns expand beyond his immediate circle of friends and family, to encompass a broader group of people. This stage encompasses an additional concept, which is that there is a duty to uphold the law; breaking the law is therefore morally wrong. Most adults remain at this level.

**Post-Conventional Level**

The post-conventional level of moral development focuses on the development of personal principles that may differ from those of society. This viewpoint would allow a person to disobey rules that are consistent with his own principles. At this stage, a person views conventional morality as being useful for maintaining the social order, but which are also subject to change. The fifth stage of moral development is driven by an orientation toward the social contract, where the person understands that the laws reflect the consensus of a majority, but that one can formulate opinions about whether a law should be altered through democratic processes to achieve the greatest good for the greatest number of people.

The sixth stage of moral development focuses on universal ethical principles. At this stage, the person relies on his own moral reasoning, which is based on universal ethical principles, which are examined from the viewpoints of others. The individual considers laws to be valid only to the extent that they are based on justice; therefore, unjust laws should not be obeyed. Reasoning at this level could result in breaking the law, leaving the person subject to legal penalties that may include imprisonment. Given the personal risks associated with this final stage, few people advance their moral reasoning to encompass it. Two examples of people who routinely operated in this area were Mahatma Gandhi and Nelson Mandela.

## The Stages of Moral Development as Applied to Accounting

How can we apply the preceding stages of moral development to the accounting profession? At the earliest stages of an accountant's career, there is a greater propensity to follow the dictates of supervisors in all matters, which roughly corresponds to stages one and two of moral development. At this point, a person is still trying to understand the fundamentals of the profession, and so may be less able to form clear judgments about moral issues. The level of moral reasoning tends to increase as an accountant advances into more senior positions, since these positions are associated with more responsibility, and may involve a large number of decisions for which the associated rules are unclear or subject to interpretation.

A possible concern within the accounting profession is that few people who have reached stages five or six are promoted into the most senior positions. This may be due to the nature of the most advanced levels of moral development, where a person is more likely to question the status quo, which positions him as an outsider. Consequently, those who have gained a reputation for resolutely abiding by the existing rules are most likely to reach the most senior accounting positions.

## How to Make Ethical Decisions

Thus far, we have described general models for what constitutes ethical behavior. How is the accountant supposed to translate these generalities into actual ethical decisions? A decision model that may be of use is the *four-component model*, which was devised by James Rest, a professor at the University of Minnesota. The model involves the following four processes:

1. *Moral sensitivity.* The person must be able to interpret a situation in terms of specific courses of action, determine who could be affected by each action, and understand how the affected party would interpret the effect. The essential element here is being able to see things from the perspective of others, which requires a person to pay full attention in order to hear an ethical problem in what someone says. Ethical listening requires a person to avoid lecturing, giving advice, or correcting comments so that the other party feels free to talk openly and move closer to a resolution. For

example, when a fellow employee pays for a hotel suite, rather than a standard hotel room, the person doing so may feel justified because he will be away from home for a prolonged period of time and wants the extra space, while someone else might consider this to be a moral lapse because it violates the company's travel policy.

2. *Moral judgment.* The person must be able to judge which of the possible actions is right, leading to a decision regarding what to do. This step requires knowledge of concepts, codes of conduct, and ethical principles, thereby allowing one to identify the guidelines that can be used to support a decision. For example, if senior management is actively encouraging employees to stay in the office for long periods of time, their personal use of the company copier might be considered acceptable, because that is the context within which the activity is occurring.

3. *Moral motivation.* The person must be able to formulate the actions to be taken to achieve the desired outcome. Consider these actions in relation to the likely pushback from others, and understand what can realistically be accomplished. For example, a controller who investigates a theft of petty cash discovers that the president's cousin is the perpetrator. Bringing this issue to the attention of the president will stop the loss of cash, but also incur the ire of the president.

4. *Moral character.* The person must possess sufficient courage to follow through on his intentions. Thus, a person is lacking in moral character if he is weak willed or is easily distracted or discouraged. For example, when a chief financial officer is aware that her controller has engaged in fraudulent activities but decides not to fire the controller, she is lacking in moral character.

---

**EXAMPLE**

Ms. Anna Bolivar is a fairly new staff accountant at a large government contractor, tasked with project accounting duties. She notices that several projects have been reopened and additional costs charged to them, after which they are again closed. The person engaging in this activity is the manager of project accounting. She investigates further and finds that the project manager can be awarded a bonus when projects exceed a certain profit percentage. It appears that the manager is shifting excess costs out of current projects in order to falsely generate profits and earn a bonus. What should she do?

Using the steps in the four-component model, Ms. Bolivar reviews the facts and tries to view the situation from the perspective of the manager of project accounting. There does not appear to be any other interpretation of the facts, other than fraudulent manipulation of the accounting records. She must then assess the alternatives. She can confront the manager with her findings, go around the manager and discuss the matter with the controller, forward her findings to the internal audit manager, keep quiet, or resign in protest.

Her next step is to review each of the possible actions that could be taken. Does she have a legal or moral duty to act? If so, who is the most appropriate party to inform? Does the AICPA Code of Conduct provide any guidance on this point? What would happen if she were to continue to remain silent? Should she consult with anyone outside the company regarding this matter, such as a religious advisor or mentor?

Finally, Ms. Bolivar needs to consider the consequences of any action that she decides to take. Could she lose her job or be tagged as a whistleblower and thereby forego any future promotions? Could senior management take such a dim view of the discovery that they fire the entire project accounting department, resulting in other people losing their jobs? If she resigns in protest, she may have a hard time obtaining referrals from her previous employer.

Only after working through the preceding steps should she make a decision about which course of action to pursue.

---

Most people do not engage in such a protracted amount of self-analysis every time they encounter an ethical quandary. Instead, they are more likely to make a rapid decision based on their experiences with similar situations in the past. Doing so preserves their time for more difficult ethical issues that they have *not* encountered before. However, the accountant needs to be careful in applying too rapid a decision to situations that appear to correspond to prior scenarios, but which actually contain one or more aspects that differ, and which therefore present a different ethical profile that may call for a different decision.

## Ethical Frameworks

In the preceding sections, we have made reference to ethical principles. Where do these principles come from? Certainly, they have been promulgated by the accounting profession, but where did these principles originate before then? A variety of ethical frameworks have been developed over the years, some of which were more practical than others. One of these frameworks is *consequentialism*, which teaches that an action is considered to be ethical if it enhances the collective happiness of those impacted by it. Thus, an action could be considered ethical even if it does not follow the law, as long as the marginal benefits to society of the decision exceed its marginal costs. In essence, any action that achieves the greatest good for the largest number of people is considered to be ethical. A side benefit of consequentialism is that it forces the decision maker to quantify the pluses and minuses of each decision made, though quantifying pros and cons is not always easy. However, the concept can be taken too far, since this ethical framework essentially allows that the ends justify the means, even if the means used are troubling.

---

**EXAMPLE**

A city government decides to expand the hours during which a local park will be kept open each day. Doing so harms the privacy of 20 local homeowners, but improves park access for approximately 500 people who would otherwise be unable to access the park during their normal working hours. Under consequentialism, this action is good, because the proportion of people helped by it greatly exceeds the number who are harmed.

**EXAMPLE**

The same city government decides to triple the property tax charged on residences having values greater than $2 million. The city can then use the extra tax revenues gained in this manner to pay for low-income housing. Under the tenets of consequentialism, a small number of taxpayers are being harmed and a larger number of people are benefiting, so this action is considered to be acceptable.

---

Though the second of the preceding examples certainly illustrates how consequentialism works, it also illustrates a problem, which is that the rights of minorities can be sacrificed to increase the benefits experienced by the majority.

Another ethical framework that can be applied to the accountant is *deontology*, which mandates that a person do her duty, based on whether the action taken is itself right or wrong under the applicable laws. In essence, fulfilling one's obligations is ethical, no matter what the impact will be on society.

---

**EXAMPLE**

The company controller is the most senior person on-site at the moment, with all senior staff off-site for a strategic planning session. The controller learns of a weather report that a severe hurricane is headed in the direction of the company's facilities. If she follows company policy, she will require everyone to stay until closing time, which is four hours away, to ensure that customer orders are filled on time. Under the tenets of consequentialism, the controller should probably let the staff go home to prepare for the oncoming storm, since doing so minimizes the unhappiness of the staff. If the controller instead elects to follow the tenets of deontology, she will keep the staff on-site, since they have a fundamental duty to the company to complete their standard work hours.

---

Deontology is comprised of two components, which are the reversibility principle and the universality principle. These two principles are explained as follows:

- *Reversibility principle*. This holds that you should treat others as you would want them to treat you. This rule is quite useful for forcing people to view a potential action from the perspectives of those who will be impacted by it.
- *Universality principle*. This holds that certain duties apply in all situations, including the following:
  - *To not physically harm others*. Thus, one should not engage in the torture of others, even if doing so would extract information that could save many lives.
  - *To respect the privacy of others*. Thus, one should not engage in any intrusive observation, such as the electronic monitoring of employees in the office, even when the intent is to spot instances of employee theft.
  - *To respect the property rights of others*. Thus, one should not attempt to copy or steal intellectual property or other assets, even when the owner of those assets is in a competitive position that could severely impact one's own company.
  - *To respect the right of free association*. Thus, one should not try to prevent people from gathering to engage in a political protest, even when there is a risk that the gathering could trigger a riot.
  - *To tell the truth*. Thus, one must always make accurate financial disclosures, even when doing so could have severe financial repercussions for the reporting entity.
  - *To treat others equally*. Thus, the treatment of multiple parties under the law would be the same, irrespective of their economic circumstances, religion, national origin, and so forth.

---

**EXAMPLE**

The manager of a local payday loan company offers an immigrant an advance on his $400 paycheck. The loan agreement states that interest will accrue at a compounded rate of 20% per day. The manager knows that English is the second language of the immigrant, so he glosses over the compounding rate, merely stating that there is a 20% interest rate.

In this case, the manager has violated the duty to tell the truth by not being clear about the compounding feature. In addition, he has violated the duty to treat others equally, since he is taking advantage of the poor language skills of the immigrant.

---

While the precepts of deontology can provide guidance for how to act in certain situations, it suffers from not providing guidance when some of the duties are in conflict with each other. For example, in a situation where it would be necessary to break into a neighbor's home in order to keep a parent from assaulting his children, the first action breaks the imperative to respect the privacy of others, even though taking this action would prevent injuries to the children.

## Consequentialism vs. Deontology

One of the more interesting concepts in deontology is the imperative to always tell the truth. This imperative is based on the logic that the recipient of information uses it to make informed decisions. Thus, imparting false or misleading information has significant negative downstream effects. A consequentialist would instead take the viewpoint that telling a lie is acceptable, as long as doing so benefits society. For example, a parent dies a painful death from a serious neurological disease. Does the surviving parent tell her children about the pain felt by her husband, which may be painful for the children to hear, or tell them that he passed quietly? Similarly, should a supervisor tell a subordinate that her work performance is atrocious, or focus on areas in which she could improve? A blunt statement of poor performance may lead to the person's abrupt departure from the company, while the latter approach could direct her to engage in various self-improvement activities.

From the perspective of deontology, the art of negotiation is a difficult place, since a successful negotiator routinely withholds the full truth from his counterpart or misrepresents the capabilities or intentions of his company during negotiations. Someone fully accepting of deontology would be more inclined to truthfully lay out the exact circumstances of his company during a negotiation, which would likely lead to a less than beneficial negotiated outcome. Someone more aligned with the consequentialist viewpoint would follow the typical negotiating ploys, since his intent is to achieve an outcome that maximizes the benefit for his company.

The two philosophies are in agreement when the issue is taking property owned by others. There is general backing for the concept that property rights are to be respected, both in terms of physical and intellectual property. However, deontology is not supportive of the right of *eminent domain*, where a government can expropriate private property for public use in exchange for payment. Conversely, a consequentialist would be supportive of the concept, when it is specifically targeted at improving society in general. A limited situation that *does* allow for the usage of intangible property is the *fair use doctrine*, which is the copying of copyrighted material for a limited purpose, such as to comment upon or parody it, without permission from the owner of the copyright. A consequentialist would accept the fair use doctrine, since it could benefit the general public, while someone following deontology would be more disapproving.

In other cases, consequentialism and deontology are in alignment. Both philosophies will generally not allow one to engage in theft. For example, if a company buys one software license but then uses the software on several dozen computers, it is engaging in theft of the software. By doing so, it is withholding revenue from the software provider, who therefore has no incentive to keep selling the software or updating it. Under consequentialism, this theft harms society, since the supplier may stop selling the software. Under deontology, this action violates the principle to respect the property rights of others.

Another way of looking at deontology and consequentialism is how quickly they can be trotted out to make a decision. Deontology is more black-and-white in presenting what to do in specific situations, which makes it easier to render a decision within quite a short period of time. Conversely, consequentialism calls for a careful weighing of the outcomes of a decision, which may require a significantly longer period of time. Consequently, it may be more practical to use deontology for the more run-of-the-mill, day-to-day ethical situations, and reserve consequentialism for weightier and less frequent decisions.

---

**EXAMPLE**

The owners of a retail store have had several experiences in the past in which employees chased after shoplifters who ran off with jackets being sold by the store. Chasing them down puts employees at risk of injury, or of being molested by a shoplifter. Accordingly, management imposes a policy of not pursuing shoplifters. This is the standard company rule and also complies with the principle of not physically harming others. It is an easy rule for employees to follow and leaves little room for ethical gray areas, though it can be hard on the store's profits. In this case, the deontology philosophy is being used.

**EXAMPLE**

An employee approaches the human resources director and asks for some confidential advice regarding his medical insurance. This employee suffers from hemophilia, where blood does not clot normally, resulting in potentially life-threatening bleeding. The medicine required to correct this condition costs $250,000 per year. He currently buys medical insurance through the company. Because his condition is so expensive, the medical cost charged to the company is much higher than would otherwise be the case if he were not on the company's insurance policy. The employee's question is whether he should switch to his wife's insurance policy, which also provides coverage through a different employer. However, the wife's insurance policy only pays for a different drug that is not as effective for the employee's condition.

In this case, the human resources director could advise the employee to switch insurance policies, thereby greatly reducing the company's insurance costs, but also putting the person's health at risk and shifting the insurance cost to another company. This decision requires considerably more thought than the preceding example, including weighing the costs and benefits of the recommendation.

## Distributive Justice

*Distributive justice* examines the socially just allocation of goods, which involves how rewards and costs are shared by the members of a group. When a society abides by the principles of distributive justice, there are minimal inequalities in the distribution of goods between individuals. There are several viewpoints on how to approach distributive justice. Donelson Forsyth broke it down into five different norms, each representing a different way in which rewards and costs can be distributed. They are:

- *Equity*. No matter what amount of inputs a group member generates, all members of a group should receive an equal share of the rewards or costs. This can cause significant disparities between the amount of inputs and outputs. For example, a taxpayer might pay $1 million of income taxes to the government, and yet receive only $150,000 of benefits from the government in exchange.
- *Equality*. The outputs given to the member of a group should be based on his inputs. This approach roughly matches inputs to outputs, so that someone who has paid in a significant amount can expect to receive a significant amount back in return. This norm initially seems fair, but provides no assistance to the poorer members of society, who never receive any support to improve their circumstances.
- *Need*. Anyone with a high level of need is given more resources in order to meet those needs, irrespective of the level of their input into the group. While this approach can greatly enhance the lives of those in need, it provides little incentive for those providing the largest amounts of inputs to continue to do so.
- *Power*. Anyone with more authority or status receives more outputs than those in positions of relatively less authority or status. This approach can greatly concentrate outputs in the upper echelons of a group.
- *Responsibility*. Those members of a group who have the most resources have an obligation to share them with other group members who have fewer resources.

Each of these norms presents a different way to distribute outputs. There is no perfect way to do so; society has to determine for itself which alternative works best.

Another viewpoint on how to approach distributive justice was promulgated by Aristotle. His view was that equals should be treated equally, and that unequals should be treated unequally. For example, the commission structure of a sales department should award a 6% commission to any salesperson who achieves the $1 million quarterly sales target. Conversely, when one salesperson displays considerably superior performance, she should be awarded with a larger commission than her less productive associates. When there are differences in performance, the difference in compensation paid should reflect the proportional difference in performance between the various parties.

---

**EXAMPLE**

The actions taken by the president of a company lead to a doubling of the company's profits, from $500,000 in the prior year to $1,000,000 in the current year. Under Aristotle's view of distributive justice, it would be reasonable to double the president's annual bonus to reflect the doubling of profits, but it would not be acceptable to grant an even larger bonus.

---

Yet another viewpoint was presented by philosopher John Rawls, who presented the following views in his book *A Theory of Justice*:

- That the greatest possible amount of liberty should be given to the members of society, limited only by the concept that the liberty of any one member should not infringe on the liberty of any other member.
- That social and economic inequalities should only be allowed if the worst off will be better off than would have been the case under an equal distribution of outputs. This is known as the *difference principle*, which allows for the payment of greater rewards to some people, as long as doing so also improves the lot of those who are less well off.
- That any inequality should not make it more difficult for someone without resources to occupy a position of power, such as an elected position.

---

**EXAMPLE**

Genius Software develops artificial intelligence software applications. The best programmers are extremely difficult to find, and so command large pay premiums over the base level earned by most other employees in the company. If the company is not willing to pay for these programmers, its product features will suffer, resulting in lower sales.

Under the difference principle, it is reasonable to pay certain programmers much more than other employees, since the overall impact on the company is more profits, which improves the job security of everyone employed there.

---

In essence, Rawls seeks to balance liberty and equality within the basic structure of a well-ordered society. This is not easy, since each person has different advantages and disadvantages, such as differing physical capabilities, educations, ethnicities, and so forth. Further, these advantages and disadvantages tend to trigger differing viewpoints on how society should be ordered. For example, someone who has earned great wealth will be more interested in reduced income taxes, while someone with a physical disability is more likely to support laws that require handicapped access in the workplace. Rawls' way out of this dilemma is to structure the ordering of society as though no one has yet developed an advantage or disadvantage – instead, everyone is operating on a level playing field.

According to Rawls, if no one were able to predict whether he would end up rich or poor, a person would be more likely to opt in favor of a society in which everyone earns roughly the same amount and receives roughly the same benefits – as opposed to living in a society in which some people are very poor and some are very rich.

A useful concept when considering the work of Rawls is marginal benefit. *Marginal benefit* is the incremental increase in the benefit to a consumer that is caused by the consumption of one additional unit of a good or service. As a consumer's consumption level increases, the marginal benefit tends to decrease (which is called diminishing marginal utility). Thus, the marginal benefit experienced by a consumer is highest for the first unit of consumption, and declines thereafter.

---

**EXAMPLE**

A customer is willing to pay $5 for an ice cream, so the marginal benefit of consuming the ice cream is $5. However, the customer may be substantially less willing to purchase additional ice cream at the same price. Instead, only a $2 expenditure will tempt the customer to buy another ice cream. If so, the marginal benefit has declined from $5 to $2 over just one extra unit of ice cream. Thus, the marginal benefit declines as the consumer's level of consumption increases.

---

When considering the relative benefits of living in a world in which there are many poor people, one should consider the situation from the perspective of marginal benefit. If a rich person were to transfer $1 to a poor person, the marginal benefit of doing so is quite large, since the poor person could use the money to ensure that he has an adequate supply of food, which is essential for survival. Conversely, the rich person barely notices the loss of $1, since he would otherwise have spent the money to fuel his private jet.

---

**EXAMPLE**

The owner of a small business subscribes to Rawls' views regarding distributive justice. The owner therefore considers what would be the ideal pay scale for his workforce, so that the least fortunate would be able to achieve a standard of living that is roughly comparable to that of their more fortunate, better-trained counterparts within the company. Pay scales within the company vary from $16 per hour to $35 per hour.

The owner realizes that he cannot reduce the pay of the highest-paid employees, since they will be able to find better-paying work elsewhere. However, he can increase the introductory pay rates substantially, though the increased wages will likely reduce the profits of the business. He elects to raise the minimum pay rate to $20 per hour, thereby reducing the pay disparity within the company.

---

## Virtue Ethics

The concept of *virtue ethics* is entirely different from the preceding concepts of distributive justice. Some-one who subscribes to virtue ethics is interested in the nature of virtues and how they are applied to real world situations. Thus, a virtue ethicist wants to understand how virtues are acquired and how they can be applied to specific real world situations. The underlying concepts of virtue ethics were originally developed by Socrates, and then expanded upon by Plato and Aristotle.

A virtue is defined as a positive character trait that makes a person a good human being. Since a virtue is exhibited over a long period of time, it is different from a single action. Thus, morality is based on the intrinsic virtues of a person. Since morality comes from a person's innate virtues, it logically follows that virtue should be pursued through lifelong education and discussions with others.

The philosophers have debated the nature of the various virtues. Plato described four cardinal virtues, which are wisdom, justice, fortitude, and temperance. Aristotle identified a longer list of virtues that a person needs in order to be a well-rounded human being, which he broke down into moral virtues and intellectual virtues. A moral virtue is the mean between two corresponding vices, one of excess and one of deficiency. An intellectual virtue is a mental skill or habit through which the mind arrives at a truth. These virtues are as follows:

<u>Moral Virtues</u>

1. Courage in the face of fear
2. Temperance in the face of pleasure or pain
3. Liberality with one's wealth and possessions
4. Magnificence with great wealth and possessions
5. Magnanimity with great honors
6. Proper ambition with normal honors
7. Truthfulness with self-expression
8. Wittiness in conversation
9. Friendliness in social conduct
10. Modesty in the face of shame or shamelessness
11. Righteous indignation in the face of injury

<u>Intellectual Virtues</u>

1. Intelligence, which discerns fundamental truths
2. Science, which is skill with inferential reasoning
3. Theoretical wisdom, which enhances reasoning skills

Someone who has developed a strong set of virtues is in an excellent position to discern an ethical problem and deal with it in an effective manner, as illustrated in the following example.

---

**EXAMPLE**

Mavis acquires degrees in philosophy and accounting, and is then hired into a general ledger accountant position with a large local manufacturing firm. During the year-end close, she notices that the controller has rigged the overhead allocation methodology so that an unusually large amount of overhead is being allocated to work-in-process inventory, thereby artificially inflating the ending inventory balance, which in turn inflates reported profits.

Mavis has highly developed virtues that she acquired through her philosophy training that leads her to suspect that this system of overhead allocation is triggering fraudulent financial reporting. Her notions of justice initiate this suspicion, while her courage and truthfulness lead her to bypass the controller and bring the matter to the attention of senior management.

---

## Ethical Egoism

Another philosophy of moral behavior is *ethical egoism*, which holds that one should do what is in one's own self-interest, within the confines of the law. Thus, the pursuit of self-interest may harm the interests and well-being of others, or it may be beneficial to them – these outcomes are not relevant to the decisions being made. This viewpoint also holds that one should orient decision making to the pursuit of long-term interests in order to avoid the fulfillment of short-term desires that may be detrimental to the decision maker.

Ethical egoism is present in some economics thinking, where the participants in a market are assumed to engage in competition with each other in order to maximize their individual profits, even if doing so could put competing firms out of business. This viewpoint is considered reasonable, since it leads to the most effective allocations of resources across an economy, toward those most able to generate a profit and away from those that cannot do so. Thus, capitalism is essentially based on the assumption that everyone will act in their own self-interest, which will create a vibrant economy.

Critics point out that ethical egoism can be taken too far, since there is more to life than the pursuit of profit. Society can also be oriented toward, for example, the quality of life through mandated minimum wages, the prohibition of cancer-causing substances, and proper environmental planning – all of which would likely reduce profits.

---

**EXAMPLE**

The president of a company that produces lawn mowers is reviewing proposals to produce lawn mowers with four-stroke and two-stroke internal combustion engines. A two-stroke engine is more compact and lighter than a four-stroke engine, and is therefore less expensive to build. However, a two-stroke engine also produces more exhaust emissions, because the design allows some unburned fuel vapors to exist in the exhaust stream.

Under the tenets of ethical egoism, the president should favor production of the two-stroke model, because it is less expensive to build, and will therefore be more affordable for a larger number of consumers. The negative impact on the environment is not a concern, since it does not impact the profits of the company.

---

## Corporate Social Responsibility

Most people consider a corporation to be a legal artifice that is designed purely for the conduct of business, with the main goals being to limit the liability of the owners, provide a vehicle for transferring ownership to others and – of course – earn a profit. Corporations have additional legal rights, such as the ability to donate money to political candidates. Offsetting these rights are various responsibilities, which are essentially the requirement to obey the laws that apply to them. However, as we have already discussed, laws are enacted in order to set the *minimum* threshold for behavior. Should a corporation be held to a higher standard? There are two views on the subject, which we explore in the following sub-sections.

### Shareholder Theory

The first viewpoint on corporate performance is *shareholder theory*, which holds that the only duty of a corporation is to maximize the profits accruing to its shareholders. This is the traditional view of the purpose of a corporation, since many people buy shares in a company strictly in order to earn the maximum possible return on their funds. If a company were to do anything *not* associated with earning a profit, the shareholder would either attempt to remove the board of directors or would sell his shares and use the funds to buy shares in some other company that is more committed to earning a profit.

Under shareholder theory, the only reason management is working on behalf of shareholders is to deliver maximum returns to them, either in the form of dividends or an increased share price. Thus, managers have an ethical duty to the owners to generate significant value.

To take this concept one step further, a corporation should not engage in any type of philanthropy, since that is not its purpose. Instead, the corporation can deliver dividends to its shareholders, who then have the option to donate the money for philanthropic purposes, if they choose to do so. The only case in which a corporation should donate money is when the amount of the donation creates a benefit that is approximately equivalent to or greater than the amount of the donation.

When a corporation is owned by just a few shareholders, any attempts by management to engage in significant amounts of philanthropy can cause turmoil among the owners, if they are not all supportive of this alternative use of company earnings.

### Stakeholder Theory

The second viewpoint on corporate performance is *stakeholder theory*, which takes a broader view of the constituencies that a corporation serves. A *stakeholder* is any person or entity that has a significant interest in the success or failure of a business. Stakeholders can have a significant impact on decisions regarding the operations and finances of an organization. Examples of stakeholders are investors, creditors, employees, and even the local community. The various categories of stakeholders are noted in the following bullet points:

- *Shareholders* are a subset of the stakeholder community, since they have invested funds in the business, and so are automatically stakeholders. However, employees and the local community have *not* invested in the business, so they are stakeholders but not shareholders. Shareholders are the most likely to lose all of their money in the event of a business shutdown, since they are last in priority to be paid from any remaining funds.
- *Creditors* lend money to the company, and may or may not have a secured interest in its assets, under which they can be paid back from the sale of those assets. Creditors are ranked in front of stockholders to be paid in the event of a business shutdown. Creditors include suppliers, bond holders, and banks.
- *Employees* are stakeholders, because their continued employment is tied to the continued success of the company. If it fails, they may at most be paid severance, but will lose all other continuing income streams from the company.

- *Suppliers* are stakeholders, because a potentially substantial proportion of their revenues may come from the company. If the company were to alter its purchasing practices, the impact on suppliers could be severe.
- *Governments* are stakeholders, because they rely on the taxes remitted by the business. When a government loses tax revenue from failed businesses, it may have trouble providing services to the rest of the community.
- *Customers* are stakeholders, since they need the company to continue supporting its existing products. If the company were to fail, customers would be forced to replace purchased goods as soon as there are maintenance problems.
- The *local community* is the most indirect set of stakeholders; it stands to lose the company's business if it fails, as well as the business of any employees who would lose their jobs as a result of the business closure.

In short, stakeholders can comprise a substantially larger pool of entities than the more traditional group of shareholders who actually own a business.

Stakeholder theory states that the managers of a business must take into account the needs of *all* stakeholders, not just shareholders. This viewpoint implies that a business must maximize the total well-being of everyone and everything impacted by it, which can be taken to mean that the corporation has an obligation to distribute its profits to any disadvantaged stakeholders.

---

**EXAMPLE**

The managers of Bitter Bay Oil & Gas have always followed the letter of the law, ensuring that its drilling crews will never be found in violation of any drilling regulations. Local regulations allow the firm to leave concrete drilling pads in place once extraction activities have ceased. However, leaving the drilling pads disturbs the ground surface and makes it more difficult for native vegetation to grow back.

If Bitter Bay's management subscribes to the classic shareholder theory, it will continue to leave drilling pads behind, thereby enhancing shareholder profits. However, if management subscribes to stakeholder theory, it will also consider the negative impact of these pads on the environment, and so may elect to pay for their removal.

**EXAMPLE**

The managers of SurviveTec learn that the bonding on its inflatable life rafts may break apart after several days of intense sunlight. Recalling all affected life rafts will cost the company in excess of $10 million, which is roughly half of its annual sales. Instead, management elects to preserve profits and not publicize the flaw, electing to fix the problem on a go-forward basis. Management rates the risk of lawsuits as low, since anyone experiencing the flaw will likely drown, and so could not initiate a lawsuit. This decision follows the tenets of shareholder theory, rather than stakeholder theory.

---

Those not agreeing with stakeholder theory point out that it can be difficult for companies to weigh the differing interests of their stakeholders. Should a business contribute more funds to the local community, or simply pay taxes to the government and then let the government figure out what to do with the funds? Or, if company operations might trigger local environmental issues, is it the duty of the business to proactively deal with the issue, or wait for the local government to impose regulations?

**EXAMPLE**

An oil and gas firm begins to receive complaints from homeowners located a half-mile away from one of the company's drilling platforms, complaining that they can smell gas coming from their faucets. Management decides to give these homeowners gas monitoring systems for free, thereby reducing the risk of any home explosions due to the buildup of gas.

Does management have any additional obligations? If it were to conduct more active gas leak monitoring, the firm would incur an additional $250,000 per year, but would minimize the risk of any home explosions due to gas buildup. Also, should it spend $50,000 per year in lobbying fees to convince the local state legislature *not* to impose any additional gas leak monitoring laws, or simply accept whatever laws are passed?

**EXAMPLE**

A satellite launch firm wants to put several thousand small Internet transmission satellites into orbit, thereby bringing the Internet to many parts of the world that currently have no access. Counterbalancing this benefit is the negative impact of rocket launches on the atmosphere. Soot and alumina are dispersed in the trail of each rocket launched and build up in the stratosphere, triggering depletion of the ozone layer.

If the company concentrates on the needs of its customers, it will put a much heavier emphasis on the benefits of Internet access to its clients. If it instead concentrates on the broad range of stakeholder needs, it will be more inclined to shrink the size of its satellites, so that more of them can be inserted on each rocket, thereby reducing the need for additional launches.

## Corporate Social Responsibility

*Corporate social responsibility* is derived from stakeholder theory. It is the viewpoint that a business should be more aware of its impact on society and the environment. The intent is to deliver positive outcomes to all stakeholders in the business that result in long-term sustainability, not just a positive return for its shareholders. The actions taken should extend beyond the narrow interests of the firm and go beyond the basic requirements of the law. There are many aspects to corporate social responsibility, which include the following:

- A low carbon footprint, perhaps coupled with actions to clean up the environment. These activities could include the use of renewable energy, recycling programs, pollution abatement, and reduced water usage.
- Dealing with employees in the most ethical manner possible. These activities may include above-standard working conditions, flexible work hours, and respect for the differences associated with the religious and cultural backgrounds of employees.
- Initiating employee safety programs that are significantly more comprehensive than what is required by local regulations.
- Engaging in philanthropy, especially in the local areas where a business has facilities. These payouts may encompass the construction of park facilities, educational grants, and cleanup activities.
- Engaging in volunteer events, perhaps by allowing employees to do so on company time. These activities may include employee efforts linked to roadside trash pickup campaigns, low-income housing construction work, and the support of local community events.

Not only does this approach result in an improved environment, it also enhances the image of the organization with its stakeholders, who will then be more likely to support it. Further, people may be more willing to work for such an organization, which enhances the quality of its newest employees.

---

**EXAMPLE**

Tsunami Products develops a high-tech line of shower heads that reduce the amount of water flow associated with taking a shower. Though the company is doing so primarily to earn a profit on these sales, management also understands that this product line will have the effect of reducing water usage, which can be quite beneficial in areas where water supplies are low.

---

How can the accountant become involved in corporate social responsibility? One option is to engage in *triple bottom line* reporting. This concept refers to the financial, social and environmental results of a business. Each of these results focuses on a different activity – generating a financial return for investors, having a positive impact on people, and having a positive impact on the planet. The intent behind this manner of reporting is to make corporate managers more aware of their responsibilities outside of the more traditional focus on returns to investors. A difficulty with this more comprehensive method of reporting is the trouble encountered in quantifying results for the last two areas.

When trying to construct such a report, the accountant might consider using the standards developed by the Sustainability Accounting Standards Board (located at www.sasb.org). The Board has developed a sustainability framework that covers the following five general areas:

- *Environment.* Includes environmental impacts, either involving the use of nonrenewable resources or via harmful releases into the environment. Measurements might include:
  - Air quality
  - Energy management
  - Hazardous materials management
  - Particulate emissions
  - Waste management
  - Wastewater management
  - Water management

- *Social capital.* Includes an expectation that the firm will contribute to society, such as dealing with human rights, offering affordable products, and engaging in responsible business practices. Measurements might include:
  - Community relations
  - Customer privacy
  - Customer welfare
  - Data security
  - Human rights
  - Product access
  - Product affordability
  - Product quality
  - Product safety
  - Selling practices

- *Human capital.* Includes the treatment of employees as key assets, thereby enhancing labor relations, safety issues, and the corporate culture. Measurements might include:
  - Employee diversity
  - Employee health
  - Employee inclusion
  - Employee safety
  - Labor practices

- *Business model and innovation.* Involves the integration of social and environmental issues in the firm's business model, including responsible design and product disposal efforts. Measurements might include:
    - Climate change impact
    - Lifecycle management
    - Materials sourcing
    - Product design
    - Supply chain management

- *Leadership and governance.* Includes the balancing of company issues with the interests of stakeholders, such as risk management, safety, sourcing issues, conflicts of interest, and regulatory compliance. Measurements might include:
    - Business ethics
    - Competitive behavior
    - Risk management

To some extent, the role of the accountant in the area of corporate social responsibility can simply involve laying out all possible effects of a decision, so that management is fully aware of all downstream effects. For example, if management is considering keeping a coal-fired power plant open for an additional three years, the accountant could point out similar cases in which local residents obtained legal judgments against a nearby utility to pay for medical claims associated with the particulate emissions from a power plant. This more comprehensive view of all relevant costs may alter management thinking in favor of a more stakeholder-oriented approach.

It is not always easy for a business to adopt the tenets of corporate social responsibility. The central problem is that doing is more expensive. Consequently, it is more common for more profitable companies, and especially those maintaining high profiles with consumers, to engage in corporate social responsibility initiatives. Thus, one might see a business in the consumer goods market engage in this area, rather than an industrial firm that operates on tight margins and which is little-known to the public.

## Ethical Judgments in Accounting

It might seem quite difficult for an accountant to ever encounter an ethically challenging situation, since it might appear that their work is entirely regimented, following a strictly defined set of procedures. However, there are many decisions to be made that lie beyond the transactional aspects of the job. Consider the following situations:

- The Lethal Sushi restaurant incorrectly prepares a side dish of blowfish, resulting in the death of a patron. The spouse of the deceased patron threatens to sue Lethal for $1 million. It seems quite likely that the spouse will sue, and that she will win the case against the company, so it would seem that the accountant should comply with the accounting standards[7] and accrue a $1 million expense for a legal settlement. However, doing so would crush the firm's earnings for the quarter, which could prevent it from obtaining a bank loan. The accountant might be tempted to delay recognition of the expense until after the bank loan has been obtained. The correct action to take is clear, but there may be significant pressure on the accountant by senior managers to delay recognition of the expense.
- Smidges & Croak is a reputable regional CPA firm. The ownership of a manufacturing client has just switched from its founder, who is infirm, to his son. The son is determined to find a CPA firm that will accept a very low reserve for obsolete inventory, despite strong ratio indicators that much

---

[7] An expense should be accrued when the amount can be reasonably estimated and it is probable that the expense will be incurred.

of the client's inventory is unusable. The partners of Smidges must decide whether to acquiesce to his demands, or to take a firm stance in opposing the requested reporting and see the client shift to a different CPA firm. This is a relatively common scenario, and can be particularly concerning when a difficult client comprises a large proportion of a CPA firm's revenues.

- The controller of a distribution company routinely comes under pressure at the end of each month to keep the books open for an extra day, so that the shipping department can jam a few additional deliveries into the reporting period. The pressure is applied by her fellow managers, who will be paid bonuses if the company reaches certain revenue targets. If she refuses to go along with this scheme, she is unlikely to be promoted and may be drummed out of the company. This situation is usually tied to aggressive sales targets that are difficult to attain by any legal means, and which have substantial bonuses associated with them.

- An internal auditor is friendly with an associate in the accounting department, who has been with the company for 20 years and is considered one of the most reliable and trustworthy people in the company. During his audit work, the auditor discovers that the associate has been routinely over-stating the expenses on his expense reports, but in amounts that would normally evade detection. The auditor knows that forwarding this finding to the internal audit manager will cost the associate his job and ruin any job references that he might otherwise have obtained from the company controller. The discovery of low levels of theft can be particularly difficult for the accountant, in light of the severe consequences involved.

- A collections clerk is dating the accounts payable manager of a customer. The customer is having cash flow problems, and so is paying its suppliers several months late. The payables manager asks the collections clerk if he can wait an extra couple of months for payment. The overdue amount is significant to the cash flow of the collections clerk's employer. If the collections clerk agrees to the delay, he is putting his employer at risk of never being paid, since the customer could go bankrupt in the meantime. While not a common scenario, it is possible for connections with family and friends to sometimes cause problems for accountants.

The preceding scenarios indicate the gravity of ethical decisions. The accountant's choices can have a severe impact on other parties, and so must be pondered carefully.

## Specific Reporting Considerations

There are a number of reporting issues that may arise that could test the ethical resolve of the accountant. In the following bullet points, we note the nature of each one, the related concerns, and how it should be resolved:

- *Temporary shortfall.* The financial statements of a business have some sort of shortfall – perhaps profits are unexpectedly low, or there is a shortfall in the funding for a pension, or perhaps the current ratio is lower than the minimum level required by a lender's loan covenants. Any of these scenarios will cause trouble for the company, perhaps in the form of a decline in its stock price, or a loan being called. The accountant knows that the shortfall can be remedied in the near future, perhaps due to a new customer contract or the launch of a new product line. In this situation, the accountant must act in favor of the public interest, which calls for the proper reporting of the actual situation. Thus, truthful reporting at all times enhances the public trust in the veracity of financial statements, even at the cost of financial trouble for the issuer of the financial statements.

- *Transactions in wrong period.* After financial statements have been issued, the accountant discovers that an accounting transaction was recorded in the wrong reporting period. This scenario usually involves the recognition of either revenue or expense, and so will impact the income statement. The transaction should either have been recognized in an earlier period or deferred until a later period. In either case, the aggregate effect of the change over several reporting periods is zero. If the amount of this transaction is material, the accountant should fix the books and report the transaction in the correct reporting period. By doing so, readers of the financial statements can discern a positive or negative trend line in the reported results that would not have been apparent if the transaction had not been shifted into the correct period.

- *Inadequate knowledge.* The company has just started to engage in extensive foreign sales, and so must account for large volumes of foreign currency transactions. A CPA who was hired as the general ledger accountant is tasked with accounting for these transactions. He has no prior experience or training in this area. Under the due care principle, he has an obligation to obtain the necessary level of expertise. This may involve off-site training, the use of a consultant to assist on-site, or some similar arrangement.

## Ethical Rationalizations

Ethical decisions are entirely the responsibility of the accountant. Nonetheless, accountants repeatedly make claims regarding their ethical failings that shift the blame elsewhere. Here are some of the more common excuses:

- *Everyone does it.* The excuse is that an unethical practice is so widespread that it would be disadvantageous *not* to do it. For example, in an industry where everyone pays their suppliers a month late, a company that pays on time is putting itself at a competitive disadvantage, since it has less cash on hand than the competition.
- *It is not illegal.* The excuse is that, because the action taken was not strictly against the law, it is acceptable. For example, in a state where there is no maximum cap on the fees charged for late payments, a business charges fees that are 100% of the overdue amount. Only when a law is passed that constrains targeted behavior is egregious activity considered to be unethical.
- *It was mandated by management.* The excuse is that management's actions effectively mandated unethical behavior. For example, the senior management team routinely pads its expense reports, sets incredibly difficult profit targets for employees, and fires anyone at once who does not meet their targeted goals. In this environment, management has effectively created a situation in which employees are being encouraged to engage in unethical behavior.

## Summary

Why does an accountant need to engage in ethical behavior? There are several reasons for doing so, which are:

- *Trust.* Customers and suppliers are much more likely to be loyal to a company over the long haul when the company develops a reputation for always dealing with them in the most ethical manner possible. Conversely, a reputation that is lost through unethical behavior may only be regained over a protracted period of time.
- *Accountability.* When a business engages in unethical behavior, it will likely be sued at some point by an outside party or disgruntled employee. The cost to defend these claims, as well as the payment of damages, can be a severe financial drain on a business.

Thus, there are strong arguments in favor of consistently making ethically correct judgments throughout one's career. Some of these judgments can be based on the applicable rules of conduct. However, these rules should be considered only the starting point for the development of a comprehensive system of thought regarding how to make decisions. The ethical frameworks described in this chapter should hopefully be of assistance in doing so.

## Review Questions

1. The general principles contained within the AICPA Code of Professional Conduct include the following, except for:
   a. The integrity principle
   b. The familiarity principle
   c. The public interest principle
   d. The due care principle

2. The stage of self-driven interest is classified within Kohlberg's stages of moral development within the ___ level.
   a. Pre-conventional
   b. Conventional
   c. Extra-conventional
   d. Post-conventional

3. The following are elements of the four-component model, except for:
   a. Moral character
   b. Moral sensitivity
   c. Moral attitude
   d. Moral motivation

4. The following norm represents one of Forsyth's representations of a way in which rewards and costs can be distributed:
   a. Disparity
   b. Equality
   c. Weakness
   d. Authority

5. The following is considered an intellectual virtue:
   a. Courage in the face of fear
   b. Proper ambition with normal honors
   c. Intelligence
   d. Liberality with one's possessions

6. The following measurement may be used within the social capital area of the sustainability framework:
   a. Product quality
   b. Waste management
   c. Supply chain management
   d. Risk management

7. Having a strong sense of ethics reduces the probability of a businessperson being targeted by:
   a. Customers with poor credit
   b. Regulators
   c. Scammers
   d. Lawsuits

8.  Ethical relativism holds that:
    a.  Ethics will vary based on many factors
    b.  Ethical rules are the same everywhere
    c.  Ethical rules can only be altered by one's religious institution
    d.  Ethics can be altered by governing bodies through changes to the law

9.  An essential difference between consequentialism and deontology is that:
    a.  Consequentialism respects the right of free association
    b.  Consequentialism makes it difficult for a person to engage in negotiations
    c.  Consequentialism requires one to always tell the truth
    d.  Deontology follows the reversibility principle

10. Deontology is more useful for or supportive of:
    a.  Day-to-day ethical situations
    b.  The fair use doctrine
    c.  The right of eminent domain
    d.  Determining the socially just allocation of goods

11. The difference principle allows for the payment of greater rewards to some people, as long as:
    a.  The greater rewards are based on positions of greater authority
    b.  The outcome is more tax payments to the government
    c.  Doing so also improves the lot of those who are less well off
    d.  The result makes it easier for someone without resources to occupy a position of power

12. The maximization of profits is associated with the ___ theory.
    a.  Investor
    b.  Shareholder
    c.  Bondholder
    d.  Stakeholder

13. The following is an element of triple bottom line reporting:
    a.  Operating results
    b.  Social results
    c.  Turnover results
    d.  Cash flow results

14. The ___ Board has developed a sustainability framework that can be used for corporate social responsibility reporting.
    a.  Financial Accounting Standards
    b.  Suitability Accounting Standards
    c.  Social Responsibility Standards
    d.  Sustainability Accounting Standards

# Answers to Chapter Questions

## Chapter 2 – Comprehensive Income

1. Accumulated other comprehensive income is listed in the:
    a. Income statement
    b. Balance sheet
    c. Statement of cash flows
    d. Statement of retained earnings

**Accumulated other comprehensive income is listed in the balance sheet, since it represents the sum total of other comprehensive income that has been compiled over time and not converted to income. (b)**

2. The following is specifically excluded from other comprehensive income:
    a. Distributions to owners
    b. Prior service costs associated with pension benefits
    c. Gains and losses on derivatives that are cash flow hedges
    d. Unrealized holding losses on available-for-sale securities

**Distributions to owners are specifically excluded from other comprehensive income. (a)**

3. To avoid double counting of items recorded in other comprehensive income:
    a. Verify all journal entries prior to entry
    b. Never shift items from other comprehensive income to net income
    c. Shift items from other comprehensive income to net income
    d. The accumulated other comprehensive income account should never be used

**To avoid double counting of items recorded in other comprehensive income, shift items from other comprehensive income to net income. (c)**

## Chapter 3 – Accounting Changes and Error Corrections

1. An example of a change in accounting estimate is:
    a. A change in the salvage value of a depreciable asset
    b. A change in expense from period to period
    c. The resetting of a product's price
    d. The revaluation of inventory using a different cost layering method

**A change in salvage value is considered a change in accounting estimate. (a)**

2. You should adjust the financial statements of prior interim periods of the current fiscal year when:
   a. The adjustment is not related to the prior interim periods
   b. The amount of the adjustment cannot be estimated
   c. The effect of the change is material to income from continuing operations
   d. The effect of the change is immaterial to income from continuing operations

**Prior interim periods should be adjusted when the effect of an accounting change is material to the reported amount of income from continuing operations. (c)**

3. The following are all disadvantages of retrospective application, except for:
   a. The application of the change
   b. The comparability of financial statements
   c. The effect on loan covenants
   d. The presence of multiple versions of the financial statements

**With retrospective application, a change is incorporated into all presented financial statements, so that they should be very comparable. (b)**

4. Only change an accounting principle when:
   a. Doing so will impair the comparability of presented reporting periods
   b. The result will yield a larger profit
   c. The change is required by an update to GAAP
   d. The use of an alternative principle is not preferable

**Only change an accounting principle when the change is required by an update to GAAP. (c)**

5. Retrospective application to prior accounting periods is required:
   a. For a change in accounting procedure
   b. For a change in accounting practice
   c. For a change in accounting principle
   d. In no situations

**Retrospective application to prior accounting periods is required for a change in accounting principle. (c)**

6. Retrospective application is not considered possible when:
   a. Estimates are required, which are impossible to provide
   b. The company has not made every reasonable effort to make the change
   c. Assumptions about what management intended can be substantiated
   d. There is a change in accounting principle

**Retrospective application is not considered possible when estimates are required, which are impossible to provide. (a)**

7. The following are examples of accounting errors, except for:
   a. A mathematical miscalculation
   b. The misuse of facts existing when financial statements were prepared
   c. A mistake in the application of GAAP
   d. Changing from an unacceptable principle to GAAP

**Changing from an unacceptable principle to GAAP is not an example of an accounting error. (d)**

8.  A disadvantage of only applying a change in estimate on a prospective basis is that:
    a.  These changes tend to be material
    b.  There is a lack of comparability with prior financial statements
    c.  There can be a noticeable impact on prior contractual agreements
    d.  The auditors will have to revise their work papers

**A disadvantage of only applying a change in estimate on a prospective basis is that there is a lack of comparability with prior financial statements. (b)**


## Chapter 4 – Changing Prices

1.  It is allowable to issue price-level adjusted financial statements:
    a.  Whenever the Consumer Price Index for a period exceeds 10%
    b.  When the statements are for businesses operating in countries with highly inflationary economies
    c.  Only for financial statements whose readers are intended to be foreign
    d.  Only for financial statements denominated in U.S. dollars

**Price-level adjusted financial statements can be issued when the statements are for businesses operating in countries with highly inflationary economies. (b)**

2.  The current cost of inventory is based on:
    a.  The retail method of inventory valuation
    b.  The weighted-average method of inventory valuation
    c.  First in, first out cost layering
    d.  Either the current cost of purchasing the items or the lower recoverable amount

**Either the current cost of purchasing items or their lower recoverable amount can be used to derive the current cost of inventory. (d)**

3.  The current cost of a fixed asset can be derived from:
    a.  Its carrying amount
    b.  Its gross purchase amount
    c.  Its lower recoverable amount
    d.  Its short-notice sale price

**The current cost of a fixed asset can be derived from its lower recoverable amount. (c)**

4.  The current cost of timberlands is derived from:
    a.  The price of the land or underlying lease
    b.  Its current market buying price
    c.  The amount for which it could be exchanged in a land swap
    d.  The historical cost to develop the resource

**The current cost of timberlands is derived from its current market buying price. (b)**

5.  Monetary assets include:
    a.  Inventory
    b.  Accrued income taxes
    c.  Advances from customers
    d.  The cash surrender value of life insurance

**Monetary assets include the cash surrender value of life insurance. (d)**

## Chapter 5 – Earnings per Share

1.  The profit or loss available to shares of common stock is known as:
    a.  Basic earnings per share
    b.  Diluted earnings per share
    c.  Book value per share
    d.  Dividend yield ratio

**The profit or loss available to shares of common stock is called basic earnings per share. (a)**

2.  The following method is used to calculate the dilutive effects of a put option:
    a.  Two-class method
    b.  Treasury stock method
    c.  Equity method
    d.  Reverse treasury stock method

**The reverse treasury stock method is used to calculate the dilutive effects of a put option, where a business is required to buy back its own stock from a shareholder. (d)**

3.  The following item is included in the numerator of the earnings per share calculation that is also included in the numerator for basic earnings per share:
    a.  Profit or loss attributable to common equity holders
    b.  Other changes
    c.  Convertible preferred dividends
    d.  After-tax interest on convertible debt

**The only element of the numerators of the two calculations that is the same is the profit or loss attributable to common equity holders. The basic earnings per share calculation does not include any other item in its numerator. (a)**

4.  The basic earnings per share calculation should be adjusted for:
    a.  All dilutive potential common shares
    b.  After-tax interest on convertible debt
    c.  Convertible preferred dividends
    d.  The weighted average number of shares

**The basic earnings per share calculation should be adjusted for the weighted average number of shares. (d)**

5.  The following is a type of dilutive security:
    a.  Convertible bond
    b.  Preferred stock
    c.  Note payable
    d.  Common stock

**A convertible bond is a type of dilutive security. (a)**

6.  The basic principle underlying the calculation of diluted earnings per share is:
    a.  To merge it with the basic earnings per share figure whenever possible
    b.  To present an earnings figure that is rounded to the nearest dollar
    c.  To properly display the impact of preferred stock on earnings per share
    d.  To establish the worst case scenario to arrive at the smallest possible earnings per share

**The basic principle underlying the calculation of diluted earnings per share is to establish the worst case scenario to arrive at the smallest possible earnings per share. (d)**

## Chapter 6 – Interim Reporting

1.  Expenses not paid for in an interim reporting period should be accrued under the:
    a.  Cash basis of accounting
    b.  Discrete view of interim reporting
    c.  Single entry method
    d.  Integral view of interim reporting

**The integral view mandates the use of expense accruals for expenses not paid in an interim reporting period, as long as expenses were incurred. (d)**

2.  Under the integral view, the proper treatment of contingencies is:
    a.  To accrue them at once
    b.  To accrue them only if the amounts are probable and reasonably estimated
    c.  To not accrue them
    d.  To spread the expense recognition over the remainder of the year

**The proper treatment of contingencies is to accrue them only if the related amounts are probable and reasonably estimated. (b)**

3.  Under the integral view, the assumption is that the results reported in an interim period:
    a.  Are not related to the full-year financial results
    b.  May require different segment reporting
    c.  Can be revised later in the year
    d.  Are an integral part of the full-year financial results

**Under the integral view, the assumption is that the results reported in an interim period are an integral part of the full-year financial results. (d)**

4.  The integral view holds that the accountant should:
    a.  Use the income tax relevant to the results of a specific reporting period
    b.  Use the expected tax rate for the entire year in every reporting period
    c.  Use no tax rate until year-end, and then accrue the tax expense
    d.  Apply the historical average tax rate to each reporting period

**The integral view holds that the accountant should use the expected tax rate for the entire year in every reporting period. (b)**

5.  Under the discrete view of interim reporting:
    a.  We assume that the results reported for a specific interim period are not associated with other periods
    b.  Gains or losses are recognized pro rata across all interim periods in the year
    c.  There are an increased number of accruals
    d.  The average expected tax rate for the full year is used in each individual interim period

**Under the discrete view of interim reporting, we assume that the results reported for a specific interim period are not associated with other periods. (a)**

## Chapter 7 – Segment Reporting

1.  If there is a segment that no longer qualifies, but which did so in the past and should qualify in the future, the accountant should:
    a.  Aggregate its results with those of a reportable segment
    b.  Continue to treat it as a reportable segment
    c.  Remove it from the segment reporting in prior periods
    d.  Ignore it for current period reporting purposes

**Continue to treat such a segment as a reportable segment, since the assumption is that it will become a reportable segment again in the future. (b)**

2.  The segment test for revenue states that:
    a.  All segments with reportable revenue be listed as a segment
    b.  Revenue should be imputed for service centers at the market rate of their services
    c.  The revenue of the segment is at least 10% of the consolidated revenue of the entire business
    d.  Transfer prices be considered in the determination of revenue

**The segment test for revenue states that the revenue of the segment is at least 10% of the consolidated revenue of the entire business. (c)**

3.  If segment tests do not yield a group of segments whose combined revenues are not at least 75% of the business, the accountant should:
    a.  Add more segments until the 75% threshold is surpassed
    b.  Proceed with no further changes to the group of selected segments
    c.  Run the calculations again for the preceding year
    d.  Include all segments in segment reporting

**If segment tests do not yield a group of segments whose combined revenues are not at least 75% of the business, the accountant should add more segments until the 75% threshold is surpassed. (a)**

## Chapter 8 – Goodwill

1. Goodwill impairment exists when:
   a. The gross amount of the goodwill is greater than its fair value
   b. The acquirer pays more for an acquisition than the fair value of the tangible assets of the acquiree
   c. The carrying amount of the goodwill is less than its fair value
   d. The carrying amount of the goodwill is greater than its fair value

   **Goodwill impairment exists when the carrying amount of the goodwill is greater than its fair value. An impairment charge is taken in this situation. (d)**

2. Once goodwill impairment has been recognized:
   a. The impairment can only be reversed if the reversal is for an immaterial amount
   b. The impairment cannot be reversed
   c. The impairment can only be reversed by a publicly-held company
   d. The impairment can be reversed only within the same reporting year

   **Once a goodwill impairment has been recognized, it cannot be reversed under GAAP. (b)**

3. When a reporting unit is disposed of:
   a. Recognize any additional intangible assets associated with the reporting unit
   b. Assume all goodwill associated with it has been impaired
   c. Do not allocate goodwill to that unit
   d. Include the goodwill associated with that unit in determining the gain or loss

   **When a reporting unit is disposed of, include the goodwill associated with that unit in determining the gain or loss. (d)**

4. Impairment testing is to be conducted:
   a. On a quarterly basis
   b. On an annual basis
   c. At random intervals
   d. When a company goes public

   **Impairment testing is to be conducted on an annual basis. (b)**

## Chapter 9 – Asset Retirement and Environmental Obligations

1. An asset retirement obligation certainly should be recorded based on:
   a. A projection of future laws
   b. A company press release
   c. A current legal obligation
   d. A statement by a company officer

   **Record an ARO when there is a current legal obligation associated with the retirement of an asset. (c)**

2. If there is a subsequent increase in an asset retirement obligation:
   a. Charge any changes in the liability caused by the passage of time to interest expense
   b. Recognize a new liability layer at its fair value
   c. Charge the new liability to expense at once
   d. Do not subsequently change the estimate of the liability

**Recognize a new liability layer for an asset retirement obligation at its fair value. (b)**

3. Recognition of an asset retirement obligation should be deferred when:
   a. There is a low likelihood of a performance requirement
   b. There has been a history of non-enforcement
   c. A fair value cannot be obtained for it
   d. An expected present value can be calculated for it

**Recognition of an asset retirement obligation should be deferred when a fair value cannot be obtained for it. (c)**

4. When there are only two possible outcomes for the expected present value of an asset retirement obligation and there is no probability distribution, the accountant should:
   a. Assign a 50% probability to each one
   b. Wait until a third outcome can be derived
   c. Do not proceed until the probability distribution is clarified
   d. Assign a 100% probability to one of the outcomes

**When there are only two possible outcomes for the expected present value of an asset retirement obligation and there is no probability distribution, the accountant should assign a 50% probability to each one. (a)**

## Chapter 10 – Revenue Recognition

1. The following conditions are needed for a contract to exist, except for:
   a. The cash flows of the seller will change
   b. Written approval
   c. The rights of the parties are identified
   d. The amount the customer will pay is stated

**Either written or oral approval is allowable for a contract to exist. This means that a specific type of legal agreement to document a contract is not necessarily required. (b)**

2. Two contracts with the same customer can be considered a single contract for accounting purposes when:
   a. They are approved by the same authorized representative of the customer
   b. The prices paid are segregated by contract
   c. Multiple commercial objectives are involved
   d. There is one performance obligation inherent in the contracts

**When there is one performance obligation inherent in the two contracts, the seller's accounting staff can account for them as a single contract, since the result of the two contracts is as though only one contract exists. (d)**

3. The assessment of a possible reversal of revenue can include the following factor:
   a. The time that must pass before the uncertainty can be resolved is relatively short
   b. The seller has a history of accepting price concessions
   c. The seller has tight control over the amount paid
   d. There are two possible outcomes for the amounts that may be paid

**If the seller has a history of accepting price concessions, it is more likely that the amount of revenue recognized will be less than initially expected. (b)**

4. A standalone selling price may be estimated by using all of the following methods, except for:
   a. Residual approach
   b. Adjusted market assessment
   c. Expected cost plus a margin
   d. Transfer pricing

**Transfer pricing is an accounting method used to assign costs to goods that are transferred between subsidiaries; it is unrelated to the concept of the standalone selling price. (d)**

5. The following is an indicator that a customer has gained control over a good or service delivered by the supplier:
   a. The seller retains title to the asset
   b. The goods are segregated on the seller's premises
   c. The customer cannot pledge the asset
   d. The customer has accepted the asset

**When the customer has accepted the asset, this is a strong indicator that the customer now has control over it; this also indicates that the asset is likely on the customer's premises, which is another indicator of control. (d)**

6. The following is an example of an output method used to measure progress toward the fulfillment of a performance obligation:
   a. Machine hours used
   b. Labor hours expended
   c. Milestones reached
   d. Costs incurred

**When a milestone is reached, this is considered an output method, since it is derived from the value to the customer of goods and services transferred to date. (c)**

7. An entity that has contracted to obtain goods or services:
   a. Is a supplier
   b. Is a customer
   c. Cannot also be a subsidiary
   d. Is collaborating on research and development activities

**An entity that has contracted to obtain goods or services is a customer. (b)**

8. Contract criteria must be re-evaluated:
   a. At the end of each reporting period
   b. At the end of the fiscal year
   c. Only when the seller notes a significant change in the relevant facts and circumstances
   d. If the customer does not send back a confirmation as part of the year-end audit

**Contract criteria must be re-evaluated only when the seller notes a significant change in the relevant facts and circumstances. (c)**

9. A contract does not exist when:
   a. There is no signature on the document
   b. It is being combined with another contract for accounting purposes
   c. Each party has a unilateral right to terminate the agreement and without compensating the other party
   d. There has been no prior legal review of the contract terms

**A contract does not exist when each party has a unilateral right to terminate the agreement and without compensating the other party. (c)**

10. A good or service is considered to be distinct when:
    a. The customer separately pays for the item
    b. Delivery of the item is separately identified within the contract
    c. Functionality of the deliverable is not assured unless this item is delivered
    d. There is a standalone price for the item

**A good or service is considered to be distinct when delivery of the item is separately identified within the contract. (b)**

11. The transaction price includes the following, except for:
    a. Sales tax
    b. Fees for services rendered
    c. Freight charge
    d. Rush charge

**The transaction price includes all indicated items, except for sales tax. (a)**

12. The expected value method is used when:
    a. There are a large number of possible payment amounts
    b. The result must match one of the prices that could be paid
    c. The amount of consideration to be paid is fixed
    d. All performance obligations have been fulfilled

**The expected value method is used when there are a large number of possible payment amounts. (a)**

13. The following factor should be present before including a financing component in a contract:
    a. A short payment interval
    b. There is a significant difference between the contract price and the cash price
    c. The credit rating of the customer
    d. The cash reserves of the seller

**There should be a significant difference between the contract price and the cash price before including a financing component in a contract. (b)**


## Chapter 11 – Accounting for Stock-Based Compensation

1. A stock with a highly volatile price:
    a. Is worth less to an option holder than a stock with less price volatility
    b. Is worth more to an option holder than a stock with less price volatility
    c. Has the same price as a stock with less price volatility
    d. Typically has fewer shares outstanding, and so is more difficult to buy and sell

    **A stock with a highly volatile price is worth more to an option holder, since it is possible to trigger a stock option when the stock price spikes. (b)**

2. A clawback arrangement linked to a stock-based award is designed to:
    a. Encourage employees to stay with the company
    b. Extend the required vesting period
    c. Pay an employee the book value of the underlying shares
    d. Increase the fixed cost of compensation

    **A clawback requires an employee to pay back an award under certain circumstances, such as leaving a company soon after receiving the award. (a)**

3. The fair value of shares to be paid out as part of a stock-based compensation arrangement must be derived using a valuation technique that takes into account the following item:
    a. The job classification of the employee being awarded
    b. The profit margin of the entity
    c. The number of shares to be issued
    d. The volatility of the price of the shares to be issued

    **The level of volatility plays a major role in deriving fair value, since a high level of volatility implies that an option holder will have an opportunity to buy shares at a higher price point. (d)**

4. An employer has set up an employee stock ownership plan (ESOP), and makes a loan to it directly, which is not funded by an outside lender, which is classified as employer loan financing. The correct accounting related to the loan is:
    a. To record an allowance for uncollectible loans
    b. To report cash paid to the ESOP that is used by the ESOP to service the debt
    c. To not report the loan as an asset
    d. To record interest income on the loan

    **In employer loan financing, the employer does not record the loaned funds as an asset. (c)**

5. One of the main rules for equity-based payments to non-employees is that the grantor must:
   a. Recognize the fair value of the equity instruments issued or the fair value of the consideration received
   b. Recognize the book value of the equity instruments issued
   c. Recognize the invoiced amount of the consideration received
   d. Recognize the fair value of the consideration received, net of any applicable early payment discounts

**The essential rule for equity-based payments to non-employees is to recognize the award at fair value, which can be derived from either side of the transaction. (a)**

6. The implicit service period associated with a stock-based award:
   a. Is the number of years worked, including gap years
   b. Is the vesting period stated in a stock-based award agreement
   c. Covers any years following formal retirement when an employee continues to perform services for the company
   d. Is the employee service period implied by the facts and circumstances associated with a stock-based award

**The implicit service period associated with a stock-based award is the employee service period implied by the facts and circumstances associated with a stock-based award. (d)**

7. If some of the service associated with stock-based compensation occurs prior to the grant date, accrue the compensation expense during these earlier periods based on the ___ of the award at each reporting date.
   a. Fair value
   b. Expected fair value
   c. Book value
   d. Valuation based on cash flows

**If some of the service associated with stock-based compensation occurs prior to the grant date, accrue the compensation expense during these earlier periods based on the fair value of the award at each reporting date. (a)**

8. When a stock option expires unused:
   a. It is available to be awarded to someone else
   b. Reverse the related amount of compensation expense
   c. Do not reverse the related amount of compensation expense
   d. Remeasure the award at its fair value

**When a stock option expires unused, do not reverse the related amount of compensation expense. (c)**

9. The fair value of a nonvested share is based on:
   a. Its value as though it were vested immediately
   b. An average of the share value during the vesting period
   c. An average of the share value during the service period
   d. Its value as though it were vested on the grant date

**The fair value of a nonvested share is based on its value as though it were vested on the grant date. (d)**

10. The lattice model for pricing stock options assumes that:
    a.  At least two price movements are possible in each measured time period
    b.  Price volatility is constant through the term of the option
    c.  Dividends are constant through the term of the option
    d.  Interest rates are constant through the term of the option

**The lattice model for pricing stock options assumes that at least two price movements are possible in each measured time period. (a)**

11. The following are reasons why an employee stock ownership plan is used, except for:
    a.  To increase employee ownership of a business
    b.  To ensure a smooth management transition to a new generation of the owner's family
    c.  To ward off hostile takeover attempts
    d.  To replace lost benefits when other retirement plans are terminated

**An employee stock ownership plan is not used to ensure a smooth management transition to a new generation of the owner's family. (b)**

12. An employee share purchase plan is not considered compensatory if:
    a.  Few employees qualify for the plan
    b.  The terms offered are more favorable than those available to investors at large
    c.  It contains a purchase discount of less than five percent
    d.  The plan allows a 90-day notice period to enroll in the plan after the share price has been fixed

**An employee share purchase plan is not considered compensatory if it contains a purchase discount of less than five percent. (c)**

13. An employer can use share-based accounting for employees when dealing with awards to leased employees, but only if (along with other requirements):
    a.  The lessee remits payroll taxes on the compensation paid to the leased employees
    b.  The lessor controls the activities of the leased employees
    c.  The leased person qualifies as a common law employee of the lessee
    d.  The lessor has the exclusive right to derive the economic value of leased persons' services

**An employer can use share-based accounting for employees when dealing with awards to leased employees, but only if (along with other requirements), the leased person qualifies as a common law employee of the lessee. (c)**

## Chapter 12 – Accounting for Retirement Benefits

1.  The projected benefit obligation does not include the __ assumption.
    a.  Employee turnover
    b.  Employee service period
    c.  Current pay level
    d.  Future pay level

**Current pay is not an assumption, since it is already known. Therefore, it is not included in the projected benefit obligation. (c)**

2. The accounting for an element of a defined benefit plan is to recognize the cost as incurred. This element is:
   a. Prior service credits
   b. Amortization of prior service costs
   c. Interest cost
   d. Service cost

**The interest cost associated with the projected benefit obligation is recognized as incurred. (c)**

3. A curtailment gain should be recognized in earnings when:
   a. The underlying plan is formally suspended
   b. The impacted employees have been notified that their employment will be terminated
   c. There is a large loss in accumulated other comprehensive income
   d. The amount can be reasonably estimated

**The formal suspension of the plan triggers the recognition of a curtailment gain. (a)**

4. The following are components of net periodic pension cost, except for:
   a. Amortization of future service costs
   b. Service cost
   c. Actual return on plan assets
   d. Amortization of prior service costs

**All indicated items are components of net periodic pension cost, except for the amortization of future service costs. (a)**

5. The calculation of the actual return on plan assets involves:
   a. Subtracting the ending balance of plan assets
   b. Adding back the beginning balance of plan assets
   c. Adding benefits paid out during the period
   d. Subtracting contributions made during the period

**The calculation of the actual return on plan assets involves adding benefits paid out during the period. (c)**

6. The interest rate used to derive the interest on the projected benefit obligation should have the following characteristic:
   a. Be based on the company's own cost of capital
   b. Be derived from investments that roughly match the timing of anticipated benefit payouts
   c. Be based on the risk-free rate
   d. Be based on the rate at which the employer can settle its debt obligations

**The interest rate used to derive the interest on the projected benefit obligation should be derived from investments that roughly match the timing of anticipated benefit payouts. (b)**

7. Under a defined contribution plan, the employer:
    a. Charges its contributions to expense as incurred
    b. Charges the actuarial present value of cash flows to expense
    c. Charges the service cost and interest cost to expense
    d. Amortizes prior service costs

**Under a defined contribution plan, the employer charges its contributions to expense as incurred. (a)**

# Chapter 13 – Accounting for Income Taxes

1. An excess tax credit can be used as:
    a. A carryback
    b. A deferred tax expense
    c. A tax position
    d. A valuation allowance

**An excess tax credit can be used as a carryback, so the credit is applied against a tax liability in a different period. (a)**

2. A business assesses whether a tax position has been effectively settled after having been examined by a taxing authority. In making this determination, the business should consider all of the following, except for:
    a. There is no intent to appeal the current decision
    b. A change in the tax laws or tax rates
    c. There is a remote probability that the taxing authority will examine any part of the tax position
    d. All reviews and appeals have been completed

**A change in the tax laws or tax rates is a subsequent event that may result in a different outcome for the business, but this has nothing to do with the assessment of whether a tax position has been effectively settled. (b)**

3. A business takes a stance in its tax return that results in the permanent reduction or temporary deferral of income taxes. This stance is known as a:
    a. Legal brief
    b. Tax dispute
    c. Tax position
    d. Penalty basis

**A business takes a stance in its tax return that results in the permanent reduction or temporary deferral of income taxes. This stance is known as a tax position. (c)**

4. The applicable tax rate:
    a. Should incorporate discounting to present value
    b. May be increased by the alternative minimum tax
    c. Should be adjusted for anticipated changes in the tax laws
    d. Should be the minimum tax rate when graduated rates apply

**The applicable tax rate may be increased by the alternative minimum tax. (b)**

5. Apply the ___ tax rate to ordinary income in an interim period.
   a. Applicable graduated
   b. Alternative minimum
   c. Minimum possible
   d. Estimated annual

**Apply the estimated annual tax rate to ordinary income in an interim period. (d)**


## Chapter 14 – Business Combinations and Consolidations

1. The acquisition method involves the following step:
   a. Value the acquiree
   b. Sign a letter of intent
   c. Determine the acquisition date
   d. Settle upon the method of payment

**Determining the acquisition date is required under the acquisition method, and so is part of the accounting for an acquisition transaction. (c)**

2. The calculation of goodwill includes the following components, except for:
   a. Liabilities assumed
   b. Consideration paid
   c. Book value of noncontrolling interest
   d. Assets acquired

**The fair value of the noncontrolling interest is included in the goodwill calculation, rather than the book value. Fair value better represents this element of goodwill. (c)**

3. A step acquisition occurs when:
   a. The acquirer is smaller than the acquiree
   b. The acquirer already owns a minority interest in the acquiree and then buys an additional interest
   c. The acquisition is highly leveraged
   d. Management will be the new owner of the acquired company

**A step acquisition occurs when the acquirer already owns a minority interest in the acquiree and then buys an additional interest. (b)**

4. An example of an intangible asset to which a value can be assigned in an acquisition is:
   a. The potential outcome of a lawsuit
   b. The assembled workforce
   c. Noncompetition agreements
   d. Competitor lists

**An example of an intangible asset to which a value can be assigned in an acquisition is a noncompetition agreement. (c)**

5. A reverse acquisition is commonly used to:
    a.  Convert a "C" corporation into an "S" corporation
    b.  Take a company public by acquiring a public shell company
    c.  Acquire a tax loss to offset a company's taxable profits
    d.  Eliminate a noncontrolling interest

**A reverse acquisition is commonly used to take a company public by acquiring a public shell company. (b)**

6. A consolidation may not be allowed when there is no clear indication of a controlling financial interest. An example is when:
    a.  A subsidiary is engaged in a legal reorganization
    b.  A subsidiary is in the process of changing its legal name
    c.  A subsidiary is incorporated in a different country
    d.  There is a noncontrolling shareholder

**A consolidation may not be allowed when there is no clear indication of a controlling financial interest. An example is when a subsidiary is engaged in a legal reorganization. (a)**

7. The presence of ___ can prevent a reporting entity with a majority voting interest from consolidating with another entity.
    a.  Protective rights
    b.  Shareholder voting rights
    c.  A noncontrolling interest
    d.  Substantive participating rights

**The presence of substantive participating rights can prevent a reporting entity with a majority voting interest from consolidating with another entity. (d)**

## Chapter 15 – Accounting for Derivatives and Hedges

1. The documentation of a hedge must include the following, except for:
    a.  The method used to determine hedge effectiveness
    b.  How the transaction was authorized
    c.  Identification of the hedging instrument
    d.  The nature of the hedging relationship

**From a control perspective, all hedges should certainly be authorized. However, this is not a requirement to be included in hedge documentation. (b)**

2. A cash flow hedge should be terminated in all of the following situations, except for:
    a.  The hedging instrument is terminated
    b.  The hedging transaction is expected to occur one month after the originally-stated time period
    c.  The hedging arrangement is no longer effective
    d.  The organization revokes the hedging designation

**The accounting rules allow for a two-month delay after the originally-stated time period, so a one-month delay will not terminate a hedge. (b)**

3. An element of a financial instrument that has the characteristics of a derivative is called a(n):
   a. Swap
   b. Forward contract
   c. Futures contract
   d. Embedded derivative

   **An embedded derivative, as the name implies, is contained within a financial instrument. Depending on its nature, an embedded derivative may be accounted for separately. (d)**

4. The key issue that shifts a transaction from other comprehensive income to earnings is:
   a. The cost principle
   b. When the business entity changes
   c. When costs match revenues under the matching concept
   d. Realization

   **The key issue that shifts a transaction from other comprehensive income to earnings is realization. (d)**

5. When a party is engaged in speculation, the proper accounting for a derivative is to:
   a. Maintain the original cost unadjusted until the position is closed
   b. Recognize changes in the carrying amount in other comprehensive income
   c. Recognize changes in fair value in earnings
   d. Bill the seller for the gross amount of the change in value of the derivative

   **When a party is engaged in speculation, the proper accounting for a derivative is to recognize changes in fair value in earnings. (c)**

6. The investment intent behind an investment classified as a trading security is to:
   a. Sell it in the short term for a profit
   b. Hold it for dividend income for the long term
   c. Hold a minority interest in another entity
   d. Hold it until its maturity date

   **The investment intent behind an investment classified as a trading security is to sell it in the short term for a profit. (a)**

7. The following are the main types of hedging classifications, except for:
   a. Foreign currency hedge
   b. Fair value hedge
   c. Cash flow hedge
   d. Earnings hedge

   **An earnings hedge is not one of the main types of hedging classifications. (d)**

8. A highly effective hedge is one in which the change in fair value or cash flows of the hedge falls between ___ and ___ of the opposing change in the fair value or cash flows of the financial instrument that is being hedged.
   a. 90% | 110%
   b. 80% | 100%
   c. 80% | 125%
   d. 98% | 102%

   **A highly effective hedge is one in which the change in fair value or cash flows of the hedge falls between 80% and 125% of the opposing change in the fair value or cash flows of the financial instrument that is being hedged. (c)**

9. The net result of a fully effective fair value hedge is:
   a. An increase in earnings
   b. An increase in other comprehensive income
   c. An increase in accumulated other comprehensive income
   d. No change in earnings

   **The net result of a fully effective fair value hedge is no change in earnings. (d)**

## Chapter 16 – Fair Value Accounting

1. The following is a valid reason why the fair value for an asset or liability may vary from the actual price paid:
   a. The market in which the sale is made is the company's principal market for that item
   b. The absence of unusual elements in a comparison transaction
   c. The buyer and seller may be related
   d. The company sells an asset or settles a liability in the normal course of business

   **If the buyer and seller are related parties, they may have reasons for settling upon a price that differs markedly from the price that would normally have been achieved with unrelated parties. (c)**

2. Developing fair values based on the prices associated with actual market transactions is called the:
   a. Cost approach
   b. Market approach
   c. Income approach
   d. Level 1 approach

   **Under the market approach, fair values are based on the prices at which actual market transactions are settled. (b)**

3.  The following are valid alternatives for deriving the fair value of a liability, except for:
    a.  Find an active market in which other parties hold the same item, but as a counterparty
    b.  Estimate the income that a counterparty can be expected to receive from holding the liability as an asset
    c.  Poll the employees to determine the amount they would require to take on the liability
    d.  Find an inactive market in which other entities hold the same item, but as a counterparty

**Polling employees results in a highly subjective estimate of fair value. It also relies on the opinions of individuals who are related parties, and who also may have no knowledge of the liability. (c)**

4.  The fair value election can be made on this date:
    a.  When there is a firm commitment
    b.  When a qualification for specialized accounting treatment begins
    c.  At the beginning of the fiscal year
    d.  On the date of the board meeting when the board authorizes the election

**The fair value election can be made as soon as there is a firm commitment to do so, which can be at any time during the year. (a)**

5. The orderly transaction concept implies that:
    a.  The proper legal forms are used
    b.  There is no undue pressure to sell
    c.  Asset sales are approved by authorized managers
    d.  Quotes are obtained

**The orderly transaction concept implies that there is no undue pressure to sell. (b)**

6. For fair value purposes, the principal market is:
    a.  The one in which the highest price can be obtained
    b.  A market with national distribution
    c.  Whichever one company management chooses to use for fair value pricing purposes
    d.  The market in which a business normally sells the asset or settles the liability in question

**For fair value purposes, the principal market is the market in which a business normally sells the asset or settles the liability in question. (d)**

7. Fair value is determined based on:
    a.  The use in which an asset is currently employed
    b.  The use in which an asset is typically used within the same industry
    c.  The highest and best use concept
    d.  The expected use of an asset

**Fair value is determined based on the highest and best use concept. (c)**

8. In fair value analysis, an observable input is:
   a. Only used for tangible assets
   b. Based on a paper document
   c. Usually an internally-generated cash forecast
   d. Derived from market data

**In fair value analysis, an observable input is derived from market data. (d)**

9. The following are examples of Level 2 inputs, except for:
   a. A quoted price for an identical item in an active market
   b. A price for a similar item in an active market
   c. An identical item in an inactive market
   d. Information derived from a correlation with observable market data

**A quoted price for an identical item in an active market is not an example of a Level 2 input. (a)**

10. The fair value option can be applied to:
   a. A loan commitment
   b. Deposit liabilities of depository institutions
   c. Obligations related to pension plans
   d. Financial assets recognized under lease arrangements

**The fair value option can be applied to a loan commitment. (a)**

## Chapter 17 – Foreign Currency Accounting

1. Financial statement translation involves the following steps, except for:
   a. Determining the functional currency of the foreign entity
   b. Recording gains and losses on currency translation
   c. Remeasuring the functional currency of the foreign entity into its legal currency
   d. Remeasuring the financial statements of the foreign entity into the reporting currency of the parent

**The functional currency of a foreign entity is not remeasured into its legal currency. There is no legal currency concept that applies to the translation task. (c)**

2. When translating the financial statements of an entity into the reporting currency of a business, translate assets:
   a. At the weighted-average exchange rate
   b. At the current exchange rate at the balance sheet date
   c. At the exchange rate as of the dates when those items were originally recognized
   d. At the exchange rate in effect at the beginning of the reporting period

**The current exchange rate is used for the translation of assets on the balance sheet. (b)**

3. When the financing of a foreign operation is provided by the parent company, its functional currency is more likely to be:
   a. The reporting currency of the parent company
   b. Its legal currency
   c. Its operating currency
   d. The reporting currency of the ultimate lender

**When the financing of a foreign operation is provided by the parent company, its functional currency is more likely to be the reporting currency of the parent company. (a)**

4. The key issue that shifts a transaction from other comprehensive income to earnings is:
   a. The cost principle
   b. When the business entity changes
   c. When costs match revenues under the matching concept
   d. Realization

**The key issue that shifts a transaction from other comprehensive income to earnings is realization. (d)**

5. When an entity is operating in a hyperinflationary economy:
   a. Exclude its financial statements from further consolidation
   b. Remeasure its financial statements using the next most applicable foreign currency
   c. Remeasure its financial statements as though its functional currency were the reporting currency
   d. Remeasure its financial statements using the local currency

**When an entity is operating in a hyperinflationary economy, remeasure its financial statements as though its functional currency were the reporting currency. (c)**

## Chapter 18 – Accounting for Interest

1. We capitalize interest in order to:
   a. Decrease short-term profits
   b. Reduce the recordation work of the accounting staff
   c. Provide a truer picture of the total investment in an asset
   d. Hide the total interest expense from readers of the financial statements

**We capitalize interest to provide a truer picture of the total investment in an asset. Otherwise, the cost of an asset does not include related financing costs. (c)**

2. Interest capitalization should be used when:
   a. Expenditure levels are small
   b. Construction covers a long period of time
   c. Interest costs are small
   d. The cost of accounting for it is greater than the value of the informational benefit derived from doing so

**Interest should be capitalized when the construction period for an asset covers a long period of time. In this situation, financing can become a large part of the total asset cost. (b)**

3.  You should not continue to capitalize interest if:
    a.  Interest costs are not being incurred
    b.  Construction interruptions have been imposed by an outside entity
    c.  There is a brief construction interruption
    d.  There are delays that are an inherent part of the asset acquisition process

**You should not continue to capitalize interest if interest costs are not being incurred. (a)**

4.  Under a dependent completion scenario, you should only terminate interest capitalization when:
    a.  A discrete part of a project has been completed
    b.  A separate but related project has also been completed
    c.  No additional interest cost is being incurred
    d.  An entire unit has been completed

**Under a dependent completion scenario, you should only terminate interest capitalization when a separate but related project has also been completed. (b)**

5.  You should not impute an interest rate for:
    a.  Security deposits
    b.  Bonds
    c.  Short-term notes
    d.  Long-term notes

**You should not impute an interest rate for security deposits. (a)**


## Chapter 19 – Accounting for Leases

1.  An arrangement is considered to give control over the use of an asset when this condition is present:
    a.  The lessee obtains at least partial control over the economic benefits from an asset
    b.  The lessee is responsible for the maintenance of the asset
    c.  The lessee can direct the uses to which an asset is put
    d.  The lessee becomes a partial owner of the asset

**Being able to direct the uses to which an asset is put is one of the key indicators that control over an asset has passed to a lessee. (c)**

2.  The following are steps in the allocation of consideration to lease and non-lease components, except for:
    a.  Allocate the consideration in proportion to the standalone prices of the components
    b.  Allocate administrative costs on the same basis as the lease payments
    c.  Allocate initial direct costs on the same basis as the lease payments
    d.  Determine the standalone price of each separate lease and non-lease component

**Administrative charges are charged to expense as incurred; they are not allocated to a lease. (b)**

3. The following is one of the events that can make it necessary to reassess a lessee's option to purchase an underlying asset:
   a. The lessee does not exercise an option, despite a prior determination that the lessee would exercise the option
   b. The lessee makes a variable lease payment
   c. A significant event occurs that is within the control of the lessor, and which would have altered its decision to enter into the lease
   d. The lessee's incremental borrowing rate has changed

**There is a change in one of the key underlying assumptions when an option is not exercised for which there had been a contrary assumption. (a)**

4. When a lessee has designated a lease as an operating lease, it should recognize the following over the term of the lease, except for:
   a. Any impairment of the right-of-use asset
   b. Any variable lease payments that are not included in the lease liability
   c. A lease cost in each period
   d. Amortization of leasehold improvements over the longer of the remaining lease term and their useful life

**Leasehold improvements are amortized over the shorter of the remaining lease term and their useful life. (d)**

5. When there is a contract modification, the change is accounted for as a separate contract, but only when:
   a. The fair value of the underlying asset has changed
   b. The incremental borrowing rate of the lessee has changed
   c. There is an incremental increase in the lease price
   d. The existing right of use is affirmed

**A modification will result in accounting as a separate contract, if there is an incremental increase in the lease price that is commensurate with the standalone price of the additional right of use that is being granted. (c)**

6. A lease arrangement is a useful opportunity for a lessee, because:
   a. It hides assets from investors
   b. The lessee's exposure to the risks of asset ownership is reduced
   c. The lessee can obtain the lowest possible interest rate on the lease
   d. A lease arrangement can always be terminated early

**A lease arrangement is a useful opportunity for a lessee, because the lessee's exposure to the risks of asset ownership is reduced. (b)**

7. When a supplier has the right to substitute an identified asset with another asset:
   a. There is no lease
   b. Asset substitutions will trigger a lease modification
   c. The discount rate is revised as of the substitution date
   d. A separate lease agreement is assumed for the substituted asset

**When a supplier has the right to substitute an identified asset with another asset, there is no lease. (a)**

8. The accounting for a lease does not apply to:
   a. Land
   b. Foreign property
   c. Mixed properties that contain different asset classes
   d. Biological assets

**The accounting for a lease does not apply to biological assets. (d)**

9. A separate lease component exists when:
   a. The lessee can benefit from the right of use of a single asset
   b. The fair value of an asset exceeds $10,000
   c. There is an insignificant amount of land
   d. The rights of use of different assets affect each other

**A separate lease component exists when the lessee can benefit from the right of use of a single asset. (a)**

10. An example of an initial direct cost is:
    a. Staff time spent working on a leasing arrangement
    b. Lease deposits
    c. Broker commissions
    d. Legal fees

**An example of an initial direct cost is broker commissions. (c)**

11. The following are considered to be lease payments, except for:
    a. The cost to remove an underlying asset following the end of a lease
    b. A payment to a third party to guarantee the residual value of an underlying asset
    c. Fixed payments
    d. The exercise price of an option to purchase an underlying asset, where it is reasonably certain that the lessee will exercise the option

**A payment to a third party to guarantee the residual value of an underlying asset is not considered to be a lease payment. (b)**

12. When a lease has a term of 12 months or less, the lessee can elect:
    a. To classify the lease as a long-term liability
    b. Not to recognize lease-related assets and liabilities in the balance sheet
    c. To group the lease with a longer-term lease for classification purposes
    d. To terminate the lease without penalty

**When a lease has a term of 12 months or less, the lessee can elect not to recognize lease-related assets and liabilities in the balance sheet. (b)**

13. A unique accounting item that occurs only for a sales-type lease at the lease commencement date is:
    a. The recognition of a selling profit
    b. The recognition of the net investment in the lease
    c. Derecognition of the underlying asset
    d. The recognition of initial direct selling costs over the term of the lease

**A unique accounting item that occurs only for a sales-type lease at the lease commencement date is the recognition of a selling profit. (a)**

## Chapter 20 – Nonmonetary Transactions

1. The purchase and sale of inventory conducted with the same counterparty does not have commercial substance when:
    a. It is unlikely that the counterparty will initiate a reciprocal inventory transfer
    b. The transactions use market terms
    c. The purchase and sale transactions occur at different times
    d. There is a right of offset of obligations

**If there is a right of transaction offset with another party, the transaction is more likely to have commercial substance. (d)**

2. The most preferred way to value an asset acquired in a nonmonetary exchange is:
    a. At the fair value of the asset received
    b. At the fair value of the asset transferred in exchange for it
    c. At the recorded amount of the surrendered asset
    d. At the gross amount of the surrendered asset

**The most preferred way to value an asset acquired in a nonmonetary exchange is at the fair value of the asset transferred in exchange for it. (b)**

3. A loss on barter credits should be recorded when:
    a. The business will not use its remaining credits
    b. The carrying amount is less than their fair value
    c. They can be converted into cash
    d. They can only be used through a barter exchange

**A loss on barter credits should be recorded when the business will not use its remaining credits. (a)**

4. A significant amount of boot is considered to be:
    a. 25% of the fair value of an exchange
    b. Any amount of cash
    c. 51% of the fair value of an exchange
    d. 51% of the book value of an exchange

**A significant amount of boot is considered to be 25% of the fair value of an exchange. (a)**

## Chapter 21 – Accounting for Software

1.  The accountant should examine the capitalized costs associated with a hosting arrangement for impairment when any of the following conditions are present, except for:
    a.  A significant change has been made to the hosting arrangement
    b.  The arrangement is not expected to provide any substantial service potential
    c.  When the term of the hosting arrangement is unusually long
    d.  A significant change has occurred in the extent to which the arrangement is used

    **There is no reason for a long hosting arrangement to trigger an impairment analysis, since it does not impact the viability of the arrangement. (c)**

2.  The following accounting issue applies to the production costs for software intended for sale:
    a.  If a working model is not operative, costs are charged to expense as incurred
    b.  If there is an alternative use for purchased software, it can be capitalized in accordance with its projected use
    c.  If technological feasibility is not established, costs are charged to expense as incurred
    d.  The cost of producing production masters should be capitalized

    **The cost of producing production masters is part of the production costs related to software, since those masters are used to create software copies. (d)**

3.  The following is an example of internal-use software:
    a.  A membership tracking system
    b.  Software that is required to operate a company's products
    c.  An operating system that is installed on computers sold to customers
    d.  A vehicle that is sold with an automated driving system in it

    **A membership tracking system is an example of internal-use software. (a)**

4.  The stage of internal-use software development that can be capitalized is:
    a.  Preliminary planning
    b.  Application development
    c.  Subsequent use
    d.  Post-implementation

    **The stage of internal-use software development that can be capitalized is application development. (b)**

5.  When developing a website, the following cost can be charged to expense (rather than being capitalized):
    a.  Graphics development
    b.  Internet domain registration
    c.  Data conversion costs
    d.  Code customization

    **When developing a website, data conversion costs can be charged to expense, rather than being capitalized. (c).**

## Chapter 22 – Partnership Accounting

1. When a partnership is being terminated, interim payments can be made to the partners, as long as:
   a. The partnership withholds the appropriate amount of income taxes from the interim payments
   b. Partners are willing to pay back any overpayments made to them
   c. Obligations will be settled at a later date
   d. The calculation assumption is made that all assets not yet liquidated will not bring in any additional cash

   **A key part of the interim calculation is that no additional cash will be realized from the liquidation of any remaining assets; this keeps the accountant from issuing overpayments to partners. (d)**

2. A capital account is designed to:
   a. Keep track of the stock holdings of each partner
   b. Keep track of the securities held by a partnership
   c. Track the net investment balance of each partner
   d. Track all partnership interests bought back from partners

   **A capital account is designed to track the net investment balance of each partner. (c)**

3. A salary paid to a partner is accounted for as:
   a. Part of the calculation used to split net income among the partners
   b. Taxable expenses of the partnership
   c. A reduction of partnership liabilities
   d. A noncash withdrawal of funds

   **A salary paid to a partner is accounted for as part of the calculation used to split net income among the partners. (a)**

4. Income taxes on partnership income are paid:
   a. On a delayed basis
   b. By the individual partners
   c. By the partnership, using withholding from partner paychecks
   d. When the Form K-1 is issued to the government

   **Income taxes on partnership income are paid by the individual partners. (b)**

5. When a partner retires, the baseline assumption is that the partner:
   a. Continues to invest in the business
   b. Waits for final liquidation of the business to be paid
   c. Is paid the amount of her ending capital balance
   d. Is loaned the amount of her ending capital balance

   **When a partner retires, the baseline assumption is that the partner is paid the amount of her ending capital balance. (c)**

6.  The liquidation of a partnership involves the following steps, except for:
    a.  Payment of all cash proceeds to the court handling the case
    b.  Liquidation of all assets
    c.  Payment of all remaining obligations
    d.  Paying the partners any residual cash amounts remaining

**The payment of all cash proceeds to the court handling the case is not one of the steps involved in the liquidation of a partnership. (a)**


## Chapter 23 – Ethical Frameworks in Accounting

1.  The general principles contained within the AICPA Code of Professional Conduct include the following, except for:
    a.  The integrity principle
    b.  The familiarity principle
    c.  The public interest principle
    d.  The due care principle

**There is no familiarity principle; though the name seems to imply that the accountant should be familiar with the business of the client, which is covered by the due care principle. (b)**

2.  The stage of self-driven interest is classified within Kohlberg's stages of moral development within the ___ level.
    a.  Pre-conventional
    b.  Conventional
    c.  Extra-conventional
    d.  Post-conventional

**The stage of self-driven interest is classified within the pre-conventional level, and is usually associated with children. (a)**

3.  The following are elements of the four-component model, except for:
    a.  Moral character
    b.  Moral sensitivity
    c.  Moral attitude
    d.  Moral motivation

**There is no element within the four-component model that is called moral attitude. (c)**

4.  The following norm represents one of Forsyth's representations of a way in which rewards and costs can be distributed:
    a.  Disparity
    b.  Equality
    c.  Weakness
    d.  Authority

**The equality norm states that the outputs given to the member of a group should be based on his inputs. (b)**

5. The following is considered an intellectual virtue:
    a. Courage in the face of fear
    b. Proper ambition with normal honors
    c. Intelligence
    d. Liberality with one's possessions

**Intelligence, which is skill with inferential reasoning, is classified as an intellectual virtue. (c)**

6. The following measurement may be used within the social capital area of the sustainability framework:
    a. Product quality
    b. Waste management
    c. Supply chain management
    d. Risk management

**Product quality is considered a suitable measurement to track the social capital reporting of a business. (a)**

7. Having a strong sense of ethics reduces the probability of a businessperson being targeted by:
    a. Customers with poor credit
    b. Regulators
    c. Scammers
    d. Lawsuits

**Having a strong sense of ethics reduces the probability of a businessperson being targeted by lawsuits. (d)**

8. Ethical relativism holds that:
    a. Ethics will vary based on many factors
    b. Ethical rules are the same everywhere
    c. Ethical rules can only be altered by one's religious institution
    d. Ethics can be altered by governing bodies through changes to the law

**Ethical relativism holds that ethics will vary based on many factors. (a)**

9. An essential difference between consequentialism and deontology is that:
    a. Consequentialism respects the right of free association
    b. Consequentialism makes it difficult for a person to engage in negotiations
    c. Consequentialism requires one to always tell the truth
    d. Deontology follows the reversibility principle

**An essential difference between consequentialism and deontology is that deontology follows the reversibility principle. (d)**

10. Deontology is more useful for or supportive of:
    a. Day-to-day ethical situations
    b. The fair use doctrine
    c. The right of eminent domain
    d. Determining the socially just allocation of goods

**Deontology is more useful for or supportive of day-to-day ethical situations. (a)**

11. The difference principle allows for the payment of greater rewards to some people, as long as:
    a.   The greater rewards are based on positions of greater authority
    b.   The outcome is more tax payments to the government
    c.   Doing so also improves the lot of those who are less well off
    d.   The result makes it easier for someone without resources to occupy a position of power

**The difference principle allows for the payment of greater rewards to some people, as long as doing so also improves the lot of those who are less well off. (c)**

12. The maximization of profits is associated with the ___ theory.
    a.   Investor
    b.   Shareholder
    c.   Bondholder
    d.   Stakeholder

**The maximization of profits is associated with the shareholder theory. (b)**

13. The following is an element of triple bottom line reporting:
    a.   Operating results
    b.   Social results
    c.   Turnover results
    d.   Cash flow results

**Social results are an element of triple bottom line reporting. (b)**

14. The ___ Board has developed a sustainability framework that can be used for corporate social responsibility reporting.
    a.   Financial Accounting Standards
    b.   Suitability Accounting Standards
    c.   Social Responsibility Standards
    d.   Sustainability Accounting Standards

**The Sustainability Accounting Standards Board has developed a sustainability framework that can be used for corporate social responsibility reporting. (d)**

# Glossary

## A

*Accounting change.* A change in accounting principle, estimate, or reporting entity.

*Accounting framework.* A published set of criteria that is used to measure, recognize, present, and disclose the information appearing in an entity's financial statements.

*Accounting principles.* The rules and guidelines that an entity must follow when reporting financial information.

*Accretion expense.* An expense arising from an increase in the carrying amount of the liability associated with an asset retirement obligation.

*Accumulated benefit obligation.* The present value of an employee's pension, based on the employee's accumulated work to date.

*Acquisition.* The purchase of a controlling interest in an acquiree by an acquirer

*Acquisition method.* An accounting method used to record an acquired entity at its fair value.

*Active market.* A market in which transaction volumes are frequent enough to provide ongoing pricing information.

*Actuarial present value.* The present value of payments that an entity expects to pay under a retirement benefit plan to its existing and past employees for services already rendered.

*Alternative minimum tax.* A tax that is derived from an alternative determination of tax liability, as stated in the U.S. Internal Revenue Code.

*Amortization.* The systematic reduction of a recognized liability by recognizing gains, or by recognizing losses related to an asset.

*Antidilution.* When an increase in earnings per share or decrease in loss per share occurs.

*Asset retirement obligation.* A liability associated with the retirement of a fixed asset.

*Available-for-sale securities.* Investments that are not classified as held-to-maturity or trading securities.

## B

*Balance sheet.* A report that summarizes all of an entity's assets, liabilities, and equity accounts as of a given point in time. It is also known as the statement of financial position.

*Bargain purchase.* A business combination in which the fair value received by the acquirer exceeds the consideration paid.

*Basic earnings per share.* The amount of earnings in a reporting period that is available to the common shares outstanding in that period.

*Book value.* An asset's original cost, less any depreciation or impairment that has been subsequently incurred.

*Boot.* The cash paid as part of an exchange of assets between two parties.

*Break period.* A designated period during which capital accounts are updated.

*Brokered market.* A market in which brokers match buyers and sellers, but do not trade on their own behalf.

*Business combination.* A transaction that results in an acquirer gaining control of an acquiree.

*Business entity concept.* The concept that the transactions associated with a business must be separately recorded from those of its owners or other businesses.

**C**

*Call option.* A contract that allows its holder to buy a fixed number of shares at a fixed price within a designated date range.

*Capital account.* An account used to track the net investment balance of each partner.

*Carryback.* A deduction or credit that cannot be employed on the current tax return, but which may be used to reduce taxable income or taxes payable in a prior year.

*Carryforward.* A deduction or credit that cannot be employed on the current tax return, but which may be used to reduce taxable income or taxes payable in a future year.

*Carrying amount.* The recorded amount of an asset, net of any accumulated depreciation or accumulated impairment losses.

*Change in accounting estimate.* An alteration that adjusts or will adjust the carrying amount of assets or liabilities. It is derived from new information.

*Change in accounting principle.* A switch from the use of one generally accepted accounting principle to another, when there is a choice of principle.

*Cliff vesting.* When an employee becomes fully vested as of a specific date, rather than gradually over a period of time.

*Coding.* Detailed instructions in a computer language to enact the requirements stated in the associated detail program design.

*Commencement date.* The date on which an asset is made available for use to a lessee by a lessor.

*Committed to be released shares.* Shares that will be released by a scheduled debt service payment and then allocated to employees for services rendered to the employer during the current accounting period.

*Common stock.* Shares that are subordinate to all other classes of stock of the issuer.

*Compensation.* The consideration paid in exchange for goods or services.

*Comprehensive income.* The change in equity of a business during a reporting period, not including the purchase or sale of stock or the distribution of dividends.

*Consequentialism.* When an action is considered to be ethical if it enhances the collective happiness of those impacted by it.

*Consideration.* Something of monetary value paid to a third party in exchange for goods, services, or other benefits.

*Consolidated financial statements.* Financial statements that present the results of a group of entities as though they were a single entity.

*Contingent consideration.* A payment obligation by the acquirer to the former owners of an acquiree if certain events occur or conditions are met.

*Contingent issuance.* An issuance of shares that may occur if certain conditions are satisfied.

*Contingently issuable shares.* Shares that are issuable if certain conditions are met, and requiring a minimal cash payment.

*Contra equity account.* An account that is paired with and offsets an equity account.

*Contract asset.* The seller's right to consideration in exchange for goods or services.

*Contract liability.* The seller's obligation to transfer goods or services to a customer, which is paying consideration to the seller in exchange.

*Contract modification.* A scope or price alteration of a contract that is approved by both parties to the contract.

*Contract.* An agreement between at least two parties that creates enforceable obligations and rights.

*Conversion rate.* The ratio of common shares to be issued to each unit of a convertible security.

*Convertible security.* A security that can be converted into another security at a defined conversion rate.

*Corporate social responsibility.* The viewpoint that a business should be more aware of its impact on society and the environment.

*Cost approach.* A method for valuing an asset based on deriving the cost to replace it.

*Credit default swap.* A contract that transfers credit exposure between parties.

*Credit rating.* A published score relating to an entity's ability to repay a debt obligation.

*Credit risk.* The risk that a borrower will not pay back a loan, or that the counterparty to a contract will not pay.

*Current cost-constant purchasing power.* Accounting based on measures of either current cost or lower recoverable amount.

*Customer.* An entity that has contracted to obtain goods or services from the seller's ordinary activities in exchange for payment.

**D**

*Dealer market.* A market in which dealers are willing to buy or sell for their own accounts, which improves liquidity.

*Deductible temporary difference.* A temporary difference that will yield amounts that can be deducted in the future when determining taxable profit or loss.

*Deferred tax asset.* Income taxes that are recoverable in a future period.

*Deferred tax liability.* Income taxes payable in a future period.

*Defined benefit plan.* A retirement benefit plan under which payments to former employees are fixed based on a formula.

*Defined contribution plan.* An arrangement under which a business pays a fixed amount into a benefit plan for employees.

*Deontology.* The theory that a person do his duty, based on whether the action taken is itself right or wrong under the applicable laws.

*Derivative financial instrument.* A financial contract whose value depends on the price of an underlying asset or benchmark.

*Detail program design.* The detailed specifications of a computer software product that takes product functions, features, and technical requirements to their most detailed form.

*Difference principle.* The concept that larger payments can be made to some parties, as long as doing so improves the lot of those who are less well off.

*Diluted earnings per share.* The amount of earnings in a reporting period that is available to the common shares outstanding and all shares that would have been outstanding if all dilutive common shares had been issued.

*Direct financing lease.* A financing arrangement in which the lessor acquires assets and leases them to its customers, with the intent of generating revenue from the resulting interest payments. This designation is used by the lessor.

*Direct loan.* A loan made by a third-party lender to an employee stock ownership plan.

*Discount rate.* A rate used to reflect the time value of money, which is used to determine the present value of future cash flows.

*Distributive justice.* A theory of the socially just allocation of goods among the members of a group.

*Drawing account.* A temporary account in which is recorded the draws made by partners from their capital accounts.

**E**

*Earnings per share.* The amount of earnings or losses in a reporting period that can be apportioned to each share of common stock.

*Economic life.* The period over which an asset is expected to be economically usable.

*Eminent domain.* The right of a government to expropriate private property for public use in exchange for payment.

*Employee stock ownership plan.* An employee benefit plan that is designed to invest primarily in the stock of the employer.

*Employee.* An individual over which a grantor has sufficient control to establish an employer-employee relationship, based on local laws.

*Employer loan.* A loan made by an employer to an employee stock ownership plan, which is not funded by an outside loan from a lender to the employer.

*Ethical absolutism.* The concept that ethical rules are the same everywhere.

*Ethical egotism.* The view that one should do what is in one's self-interest, within the confines of the law.

*Ethical relativism.* The concept that ethics will change over time, and will vary based on many factors.

*Ethics.* The moral principles that guide a person's behavior.

*Exchange market.* A market in which closing prices are readily available, and which are representative of asset or liability fair values.

*Exchange.* A reciprocal transfer between two entities of assets and/or liabilities.

*Exercise price.* The amount that the holder of an option or warrant must pay for a share of common stock when the option or warrant is exercised.

*Exchange rate.* The ratio at which a unit of one currency can be exchanged for another currency.

**F**

*Fair use doctrine.* The copying of copyrighted material for a limited purpose.

*Fair value hedge.* A hedge of the exposure to changes in the fair value of an asset or liability that is attributable to a specific risk.

*Fair value.* The amount at which an asset could be bought or sold in a transaction between willing parties.

*Finance lease.* A leasing arrangement in which ownership of the underlying asset effectively passes to the lessee by the end of the lease. This designation is used by the lessee.

*Financial accounting.* The practice of recording and aggregating financial transactions into financial statements.

*Financial instrument.* A document that has monetary value or which establishes an obligation to pay.

*Financial risk.* The risk that changes in the markets will have a negative impact on the profits of a business.

*Financial statements.* A collection of reports about an organization's financial results, financial condition, and cash flows.

*Fiscal year.* The twelve-month period over which an entity reports on the activities that appear in its annual financial statements.

*Forecasted transaction.* A transaction that is expected to occur at a later date, but for which there is no firm commitment.

*Foreign currency.* A currency other than the functional currency being used by an entity.

*Foreign currency transactions.* Any transactions having terms that are denominated in a currency other than the functional currency used by a reporting entity.

*Foreign currency translation.* The process of converting amounts stated in a foreign currency into the reporting currency of the parent entity.

*Foreign entity.* An entity whose financial statements use a currency other than the reporting currency of its parent, and whose results are combined with those of a parent entity.

*Foreign exchange rate.* The price at which one currency can be converted into a different currency.

*Foreign exchange risk.* The risk that the value of an investment will be reduced by changes in the applicable foreign exchange rate.

*Four-component model.* The concepts of moral sensitivity, judgment, motivation, and character in making ethical decisions.

*Functional currency.* The currency that an entity uses in the majority of its business transactions.

*Futures contract.* A standardized agreement to buy or sell a financial instrument at a specific price and on a specific date, which can be traded on an exchange.

**G**

*Generally Accepted Accounting Principles.* A cluster of accounting standards and common industry usage that has been developed to provide guidance for organizing financial information, creating financial statements, and disclosing certain supporting information.

*Goodwill.* An intangible asset that represents the future benefits arising from assets acquired in a business combination that are not otherwise identified.

*Grant date.* The date on which an employer and employee mutually reach agreement regarding the terms of a share-based payment arrangement.

*Grantee.* The recipient of stock-based compensation.

*Grantor.* The issuer of stock-based compensation.

**H**

*Hedge.* An action taken to reduce an existing or expected risk.

*Held-to-maturity security.* A debt security acquired with the intent of holding it to maturity, and where the holder has the ability to do so.

*Highest and best use.* The use of an asset that maximizes its value.

*Historical cost.* Costing based on measures of historical prices, without subsequent restatement.

*Hosting arrangement.* An arrangement in which the end user of software does not take possession of it; instead, the software resides on the supplier's or a third party's hardware, where the customer accesses it.

**I**

*Impairment.* A condition that arises when the carrying amount of an asset exceeds its fair value.

*Imputed interest rate.* The estimated interest rate used instead of the established interest rate associated with a debt.

*Income approach.* A valuation technique that converts future cash flows or income into a discounted current value.

*Income statement.* A financial report that summarizes an entity's revenue, cost of goods sold, gross margin, other expenses, taxes, and net income or loss. The income statement shows an entity's financial results over a specific time period, usually a month, quarter, or year.

*Income tax.* A tax that is based on the income of the party subject to the tax.

*Income taxes.* Taxes that are based on the reported amount of income.

*Incremental borrowing rate.* The rate of interest at which a lessee would have to borrow funds, using collateral and over a period of time that equals a set of lease payments.

*Independence.* Freedom from the control, influence or support of others.

*Indirect loan.* A loan made by an employer to an employee stock ownership plan, which is funded by an outside loan from a lender to the employer.

*Initial direct costs.* A cost that is only incurred if a lease agreement occurs.

*Intangible assets.* Assets that have no physical substance.

*Integrity.* Firm adherence to a code of moral values.

*Intercompany transaction.* A transaction that occurs between different entities within a consolidated entity.

*Interest method.* The determination of a periodic interest cost that equates to a flat effective interest rate on the sum total of the face amount of a debt and any related unamortized discounts and premiums.

*Interim period.* A financial reporting period that is shorter than a full fiscal year.

*Intrinsic value.* The excess amount of the fair value of a share over the exercise price of an underlying stock option.

*Investee.* A business whose equity instruments are owned by an investor.

*Investor.* An entity that owns the voting stock of a business.

**L**

*Lease.* An arrangement under which a lessor agrees to allow a lessee to control the use of identified property, plant, and equipment for a stated period of time in exchange for one or more payments.

*Lease liability.* The obligation by a lessee to make payments arising from a lease, as calculated on a discounted basis.

*Lease modification.* An alteration of the terms and conditions of a contract that triggers a change in the consideration for or scope of a lease.

*Lease receivable.* The right of a lessor to obtain lease payments from either a sales-type lease or a direct financing lease.

*Lease term.* The period of a lease that cannot be cancelled, which can include reasonably certain extension options.

*Lessee.* An entity that obtains the right to use an asset for a defined time period in exchange for consideration.

*Lessor.* An entity that agrees to provide the right to use an asset for a defined time period in exchange for consideration.

*Loan account.* An account in which is recorded loans associated with a partner.

*Local currency.* The legal currency being used within a country.

**M**

*Maintenance.* Those actions taken after a product is available for general release, to correct errors or update the product with more current information.

*Management accounting.* A branch of accounting that focuses on the revenues and expenses of a business, as well as its asset usage.

*Marginal benefit.* The incremental increase in the benefit to a consumer that is caused by the consumption of one additional unit of a good or service.

*Market approach.* A valuation technique that employs pricing information from market transactions.

*Market participants.* Buyers and sellers that are independent of each other, are knowledgeable, and are willing to enter into a purchase or sale transaction.

*Measurement date.* The date on which the prices and other factors used to measure a share-based compensation cost are fixed.

*Monetary assets.* Money or the right to receive money, for which the amount is fixed or determinable.

*Monetary liability.* The obligation to pay money, for which the amount is fixed or determinable.

*Mortality rate.* The number of deaths during a period of time among a group of people.

*Most advantageous market.* That market in which the price of an asset will be maximized or the price of a transferred liability is minimized.

**N**

*Net periodic pension cost.* The cost of a pension plan for a reporting period, as stated in an employer's financial statements.

*Net periodic postretirement benefit cost.* The cost of a postretirement benefit plan, as stated in an employer's financial statements.

*Noncontrolling interest.* That portion of the equity in a subsidiary that is not attributable to the parent entity.

*Notional amount.* The face value of a financial instrument, which is used to make calculations based on that amount.

**O**

*Objectivity.* The ability to formulate judgments based on observable phenomena while not being influenced by emotions or personal prejudices.

*Observable inputs.* Those inputs that are developed from market information, and which reflect the pricing assumptions used by market participants.

*Operating lease.* Any lease other than a finance lease, from the perspective of the lessee. Any lease other than a sales-type lease or a direct financing lease, from the perspective of the lessor.

*Option.* A right that gives its holder the option to purchase shares of common stock at a certain price and within a specific date range.

*Option pricing model.* A formula for mathematically deriving the price of an option contract.

*Orderly transaction.* A transaction in which the participants are not forced to participate.

*Other comprehensive income.* A statement that contains all changes not permitted in the main part of the income statement. These items include unrealized gains and losses on available-for-sale securities, cash flow hedge gains and losses, and foreign currency translation adjustments.

**P**

*Parent.* A business that has a controlling interest in a subsidiary.

*Participating rights.* Rights that allow limited partners to participate in certain decisions regarding the finances and operations of a partnership.

*Participating security.* A security that can receive undistributed earnings along with common stock, of which the most common example is sharing in dividends.

*Partnership.* A form of business organization in which owners have unlimited personal liability for the actions of the business, and share in its profits and losses.

*Penalty.* Any requirement for a lessee to pay cash, incur a liability, perform services, or to otherwise suffer an economic detriment.

*Pension benefit.* A payout from a retirement plan to a retired person.

*Performance commitment.* A commitment under which performance is probable because of large disincentives for nonperformance.

*Performance condition.* A condition that affects the determination of the fair value of an award.

*Performance obligation.* The unit of account for the goods or services contractually promised to a customer.

*Period of use.* The time period during which an asset is employed to fulfill a contract.

*Plan amendment.* A change to the terms of an existing retirement plan.

*Plan assets.* Those assets that have been set aside to provide for pension benefits.

*Plan curtailment.* A triggering event that reduces the expected years of future service of current employees, or eliminates the accrual of benefits for future employee service.

*Potential common stock.* A security or agreement that allows its holder to obtain common stock during or after a reporting period.

*Preferred stock.* An equity security that has preferential rights in comparison to common stock.

*Preliminary project stage.* A stage during the development of software when performance requirements are determined, alternatives are explored, and technology feasibility studies are conducted, along with several related activities.

*Primary beneficiary.* An entity that consolidates its results with those of a variable interest entity.

*Principal market.* That market having the greatest volume and activity level for the sale of certain assets or liabilities.

*Prior service costs.* The cost of benefits retroactively granted in a plan amendment.

*Probable.* When a future event is likely to occur.

*Product design.* The logical representation of all product functions in enough detail to serve as product specifications.

*Product enhancement.* Improvements made to an existing product that are intended to prolong its life or significantly enhance its marketability. Product enhancements usually call for a redesign of all or part of an existing product.

*Product master.* A completed version of a software product that is ready for copying.

*Projected benefit obligation.* The actuarial present value of future benefits attributed to service already rendered by employees.

*Prospective application.* When a change is applied on a go-forward basis. No adjustments are made to prior periods.

*Purchasing power gain or loss.* The net gain or loss derived from restating the beginning and ending balances of monetary assets and liabilities in units of constant purchasing power.

*Put option.* A contract that allows its holder to sell a certain number of shares to the originator of the contract at a fixed price within a designated date range.

## R

*Rate implicit in a lease.* The rate of interest that causes the present value of lease payments and the ending asset value to equal the sum of the fair value of an asset, less any investment tax credit and any deferred lessor initial direct costs.

*Reporting currency.* The currency in which a business prepares its financial statements.

*Reporting entity.* An organization whose financial statements are being referred to.

*Residual value guarantee.* A guarantee made by a lessee to the lessor, that the value of a leased asset will be at least a certain amount at the end of the lease.

*Restatement.* The revision of previous financial statements when they are found to contain a material error.

*Restricted share.* A share that cannot be sold for a certain period of time due to contractual or governmental restrictions.

*Retrospective application.* When a principle must be used as the basis for creating financial statements as though the principle had always been used for all periods presented.

*Revenue.* An asset enhancement or liability settlement caused by the delivery of goods or services that comprise an entity's central operations.

*Reverse acquisition.* A business combination in which the legal acquirer is the acquiree for accounting purposes.

*Reversibility principle.* The view that you should treat others as you would want them to treat you.

*Right-of-use asset.* A lessee's right to use an asset over the term of a lease.

## S

*Sales-type lease.* A leasing arrangement in which the collectability of minimum lease payments is predictable and there are no important uncertainties about the amount of unreimbursable costs yet to be incurred. This designation is used by the lessor.

*Security.* An interest in an entity or an obligation of the issuer that is represented by an instrument that is a medium of investment, and which is divisible into a class of shares or other interests.

*Segment.* A distinct component of a business that produces revenue, and for which the business produces separate financial information that is regularly reviewed internally by a chief operating decision maker.

*Selling profit or loss.* An amount as of the commencement date that equals the fair value of the underlying assct, minus the carrying amount of the underlying asset net of any unguaranteed residual asset, minus any lessor initial direct costs that are deferred.

*Shareholder theory.* The view that the only duty of a corporation is to maximize the profits accruing to its shareholders.

*Short-term lease.* A lease that has a term of 12 months or less as of the commencement date.

*Software.* A set of programs that interact with each other, causing a computer to perform work.

*Stages of moral development.* The concept that people go through several stages of moral development, which can be classified as pre-conventional, conventional, and post-conventional.

*Stakeholder.* Any person or entity that has a significant interest in the success or failure of a business.

*Stakeholder theory.* The view that a business must take into account the needs of all stakeholders, not just shareholders.

*Standalone price.* The price at which a component of a contract would be purchased separately.

*Standalone selling price.* That price at which a good or service can be sold by itself in a separate transaction.

*Stock appreciation right.* A right to receive a bonus related to the appreciation of a company's shares over a period of time.

*Stock.* Ownership shares in a business.

*Stock option.* A contract that gives its holder the right, but not the obligation, to buy shares at a certain price and within a certain date range.

*Sublease.* A transaction in which the primary lease remains in effect, while the lessee re-leases the underlying asset to a third party.

*Subsidiary.* A business in which a parent entity owns a controlling interest.

**T**

*Tandem award.* An award with at least two components, under which the exercise of one award component cancels the other component.

*Tax position.* A position taken in a tax return, which the filer uses to measure current or deferred income tax assets and liabilities. A tax position can yield a permanent reduction or deferral of income taxes payable.

*Taxable income.* A taxpayer's gross income, minus any allowable tax deductions.

*Temporary difference.* The difference between the carrying amount of an asset or liability in the balance sheet and its tax base.

*Testing.* The performance of those steps needed to determine whether software meets the function, feature, and technical performance requirements stated in the product design.

*Trading securities.* Securities acquired with the intent of selling them in the near term to generate a profit.

*Transaction price.* The consideration to be paid by a customer in exchange for its receipt of goods or services.

*Translation adjustments.* Corrections arising from the translation of financial statements from a functional currency to the reporting currency.

*Triple bottom line reporting.* The reporting of the financial, social and environmental results of a business.

**U**

*Underlying.* A variable, such as an interest rate, exchange rate, or commodity price, that is used to determine the settlement of a derivative instrument.

*Underlying asset.* An asset for which the right of use has been shifted to a lessee as part of a lease.

*Unfunded projected benefit obligation.* When a plan's projected benefit obligation is greater than the fair value of plan assets.

*Unguaranteed residual asset.* The amount expected to be derived from an underlying asset after a lease term has been completed, and which is not guaranteed by the lessee or any other party.

*Universality principle.* The view that certain duties apply in all situations.

*Unobservable inputs.* Inputs for which there is no market information available, which instead use the best information available for pricing assets or liabilities.

*Unrealized gain or loss.* The difference between the carrying amount and market price of a financial instrument that has not yet been sold.

*Useful life.* The period over which an asset is expected to directly or indirectly contribute to the cash flows of a business.

**V**

*Valuation allowance.* A reserve that is used to offset the amount of a deferred tax asset.

*Variable lease payments.* Payments made by a lessee to a lessor that vary due to changes in facts or circumstances over the lease term.

*Vesting.* The process of earning rights. For example, the passage of time may allow a person to earn the right to a share award.

*Virtue ethics.* The study of the nature of virtues and how they are applied to real world situations.

*Volatility.* The range over which a price varies over time, or is expected to vary.

**W**

*Warrant.* A security that gives its holder the right to buy a certain number of shares at a fixed price within a designated date range.

*Working model.* An operational version of software that performs all major functions planned for it, and which is ready for initial customer testing.

# Index